Understanding Local Government

By

Sandra M. Stevenson
Professor of Law
Albany Law School
Union University

Library of Congress Cataloging-in-Publication Data
Stevenson, Sandra M.
Understanding local government law / by Sandra M. Stevenson.— 1st ed.
p. cm. — (Understanding series)
Includes index.
ISBN 0-8205-5697-1 (softbound)
1. Local government—Law and legislation—United States. I. Title. II. Series:
Understanding series (New York, N.Y.)
KF5300.S74 2003
342.73'09—dc21
2003051597

LexisNexis, the knowledge burst logo, and Michie are trademarks of Reed Elsevier Properties Inc, used under license. Matthew Bender is a registered trademark of Matthew Bender Properties Inc.

ISBN#: 0820556971

Editorial Offices
744 Broad Street, Newark, NJ 07102 (973) 820-2000
201 Mission St., San Francisco, CA 94105-1831 (415) 908-3200
701 East Water Street, Charlottesville, VA 22902-7587 (804) 972-7600
www.lexis.com

To Jim and Tarley...
AND a Jack Russell named Jack

PREFACE

This book reflects the author's abiding interest in local governments. It began when a newly minted law professor was informed that she would be assigned to teach a course in local government law which none of her senior peers wanted to teach. As it turned out, it is the one course that, after over twenty-eight years of teaching, I never relinquished to a junior professor. It is a subject that has consistently offered fresh challenges to those willing to commit time, energy and resources to understanding it. My enthusiasm for learning about local governments is just as strong today as it was when I began teaching. It is my hope that this book captures some of the great affection I have for the subject matter and perpetuates this enthusiasm in learning about it to those who read it.

Local governments are living entities, constantly adapting in order to meet both old and new challenges. Counties, cities, towns, villages and boroughs have personalities that reflect the collective views of those who serve as local officials, as well as those individuals who choose to live within their boundaries. These government personalities are also shaped by the states which create them and prescribe their powers and responsibilities. The federal government also occasionally contributes to the mix by prescribing duties and offering financial assistance, usually conditioned on compliance with a federal standard.

It is not particularly easy to gain a thorough understanding of local governments. Every state has its own structure, names, and delineation of authority so there are many differences from state to state. There are also basic similarities and many generalities that are consistent among most or all local governments. This book is intended to reflect those and in doing so to make it easier to understand them. It attempts to identify the underpinnings and the concepts that determine how local governments function in fulfilling their purpose of providing both needed and desired services to their residents. It is the kind of book that I wish I had been able to read when I first began teaching the subject.

ACKNOWLEDGMENTS

My gratitude to all those who have helped me understand local governments, from Chester J. Antieau who provided me the opportunity to work on his legacy of research that is now in Antieau on Local Government Law, Second Edition, to other scholars and authors such as Professor Osborne M. Reynolds, Jr., for his valuable Local Government Law. Most especially, a heartfelt thanks to Professors Daniel R. Mandelker, Dawn Clark Netsch, Peter W. Salsich, Jr., and Judith Welch Wegner for their seminal text, State and Local Government in a Federal System. I am indeed honored to join with them for a future sixth edition of their book. On a personal note, thanks to Dan and Judith for encouraging me in this effort in a manner that was subtle, meaningful and memorable. Enormous thanks also to those practitioners of local government law who have shared their expertise so freely with both me and my students over the years. I do not know what I would have done without Bob Batson, Bill Collins, Bob Freeman, Bill Sharp, Arnis Zilgme, and the late and greatly missed John Dugan.

The book would not exist if it were not for the assistance of two people in particular. Donna Parent has been my right arm for many, many years. Her patient and consistent work on the manuscript is matched by her superior knowledge of proper grammar and sentence structure. She always manages to make everything better. I will never forget the moment she told me she liked the book. Robert Emery has long been recognized by all the faculty at Albany Law School as clearly our most valuable asset. He is the quiet, unassuming, Associate Director of the Schaeffer Law Library, without whose help nothing would be as good as it is. Bob has not only provided me with the benefit of his superior research skills, but he has been a constant source of encouragement. To these two individuals go my undying gratitude.

Finally, last but certainly not least, my appreciation must be expressed to the wonderful professionals at LexisNexis Matthew Bender. Initial thanks belong to Nellie Howard, who struggled and labored so hard to help me complete the Second Edition of Antieau on Local Government Law. My continual gratitude goes also to Nancy Dawson, my current editor for the annual updates. Her patience and help has made my job so much easier. The final expression of appreciation is reserved for Christopher Pyles, my editor for this book. I have heard that a book is only as good as its editor. I only hope this one is close to being as good as its editor.

SUMMARY TABLE OF CONTENTS

	Page
Chapter 1 Introduction to Local Government	1
Chapter 2 Local Authority	23
Chapter 3 Regulation by Local Governments	39
Chapter 4 Private and Public Land	67
Chapter 5 Local Contracts	93
Chapter 6 Delivery of Services and Assistance	115
Chapter 7 Public Access to Information and Right to Vote	149
Chapter 8 Local Officers and Employees	165
Chapter 9 Local Government Liability	185
Chapter 10 Local Finances	211
Table of Cases	TC-1
Index	I-1

TABLE OF CONTENTS

Page

Chapter 1 Introduction to Local Government   1

§ 1.1 Introduction and Chapter Overview   1

PART I FORMS AND RELATIONSHIPS OF LOCAL
        GOVERNMENTS   2
§ 1.2 Forms From Colonial Days to Present   2
§ 1.3 Relationship to the Federal Government   5
§ 1.4 Relationship to the State Government   8
§ 1.5 Relationship Between and Among Local Governments . . . 11

PART II GEOGRAPHICAL AND POLITICAL STRUCTURE OF
         LOCAL GOVERNMENTS 13
§ 1.6 Creation and Dissolution 13
§ 1.7 Change in Boundary or Structure 16
§ 1.8 Forms of Government 18

Chapter 2 Local Authority 23

§ 2.1 Introduction and Chapter Overview 23

PART I HOME RULE AND OTHER DELEGATED
        AUTHORITY 24
§ 2.2 Delegation of Home Rule Authority 24
§ 2.3 State Concerns and Local Concerns 26
§ 2.4 Implied Authority and *Dillon's Rule* 28
§ 2.5 State and Federal Preemption 30

PART II EXERCISE OF LOCAL AUTHORITY—LIMITATIONS
         AND REQUIREMENTS 32
§ 2.6 Local Governing Body and Local Enactments 32
§ 2.7 Federal and State Constitutional Requirements 33
§ 2.8 Delegation of Authority to Officers and Administrative
      Agencies 36

Page

Chapter 3 Regulation by Local Governments 39

§ 3.1 Introduction and Chapter Overview 39

PART I GENERAL EXERCISE OF POLICE POWER 40

§ 3.2 Nuisances 40

§ 3.3 Business Regulation 42

§ 3.4 Adult Uses 44

§ 3.5 Alcohol, Tobacco, and Firearms 46

§ 3.6 Speech and Movement of Individuals 49

§ 3.7 Other Health, Safety and Welfare Concerns 51

§ 3.8 Civil and Human Rights 53

PART II LICENSES, PERMITS AND FRANCHISES 54

§ 3.9 Local Licenses and Permits 54

§ 3.10 Franchises 57

§ 3.11 Telecommunications 59

§ 3.12 Challenge to the Grant or Denial of License, Permit or
Franchise 63

Chapter 4 Private and Public Land 67

§ 4.1 Introduction and Chapter Overview 67

PART I REGULATION OF PRIVATE LAND USE 68

§ 4.2 Planning 68

§ 4.3 Zoning 70

§ 4.4 Applicability, Variances, Special Permits and
Exceptions 74

§ 4.5 Regulatory Takings and Moratoriums on Development . . . 77

§ 4.6 Development Approval with Conditions of Exaction, Impact
or Linkage Fees 81

§ 4.7 Enforcement and Appeal from Zoning Requirements and
Decisions 83

PART II PUBLIC PROPERTY 85

§ 4.8 Acquisition and Disposition of Local Government
Property 85

Page

§ 4.9 Public Property Liability 89

§ 4.10 Use of Public Property 90

Chapter 5 Local Contracts **93**

§ 5.1 Introduction and Chapter Overview 93

PART I AUTHORITY, PROCEDURE AND FISCAL
        REQUIREMENTS 94

§ 5.2 Authority to Contract 94

§ 5.3 Procedural and Format Requirements 97

§ 5.4 Fiscal Requirements 98

PART II COMPETITIVE BIDS 99

§ 5.5 Requirement for Competitive Bids and Exceptions 99

§ 5.6 Specifications, Restrictions and Formalities 101

§ 5.7 Local Action on Bids 103

§ 5.8 Judicial Challenge to Competitive Bidding 105

PART III QUASI-CONTRACTS 107

§ 5.9 Local Obligation Without a Contract 107

§ 5.10 Local Obligation With an Invalid Contract 108

PART IV ENFORCEMENT OF CONTRACTS 109

§ 5.11 Contract that is Unauthorized, Executed by Unauthorized
       Agent, or in Unauthorized Form or Procedure 109

§ 5.12 Contract That is Prohibited or Contrary to Public
       Policy 111

§ 5.13 Ratification or Estoppel 113

Chapter 6 Delivery of Services and Assistance **115**

§ 6.1 Introduction and Chapter Overview 115

PART I SPECIAL DISTRICTS, AUTHORITIES, AND
        PRIVATIZATION 116

§ 6.2 Education and School Districts 116

§ 6.3 Special Improvement Districts 123

Page

§ 6.4 Public Authorities   125

§ 6.5 Privatization of Services or Assets   128

PART II PROTECTION, ASSISTANCE AND SERVICES TO
         INDIVIDUALS   131

§ 6.6 Local Liability for Law Enforcement and Fire
      Protection   131

§ 6.7 Public Assistance   134

§ 6.8 Housing   136

§ 6.9 Local Response to Changes and Disasters   140

§ 6.10 Local Courts and Dispute Resolution   142

PART III COMMUNITY AND ECONOMIC
         DEVELOPMENT   144

§ 6.11 Community Development   144

§ 6.12 Economic Development   146

**Chapter 7 Public Access to Information and Right to
Vote** **149**

§ 7.1 Introduction and Chapter Overview   149

PART I   ACCESS TO INFORMATION   150

§ 7.2 Freedom of Information   150

§ 7.3 Open Meetings   152

§ 7.4 Protection of Privacy   154

PART II LOCAL ELECTIONS AND CITIZEN RIGHT TO
         VOTE AND GOVERN   155

§ 7.5 Local Elections and Voter Eligibility   155

§ 7.6 Local Elections and Reapportionment   157

§ 7.7 Equality and the Voting Rights Act   158

§ 7.8 Initiative and Referendum   161

Chapter 8 Local Officers and Employees **165**

§ 8.1 Introduction and Chapter Overview   165

Page

PART I   REQUIREMENTS FOR LOCAL OFFICERS AND
          EMPLOYEES 166

§ 8.2 Eligibility and Ethical Considerations 166

§ 8.3 Regulation of Activities and Conduct 170

§ 8.4 Dismissal and Disciplinary Action 171

PART II   PROTECTION AND LIABILITY FOR LOCAL
          OFFICERS AND EMPLOYEES 174

§ 8.5 Constitutional and Statutory Civil Rights Protections ... 174

§ 8.6 Personal Liability and Qualified Immunity 177

§ 8.7 Civil Service 181

Chapter 9 Local Government Liability **185**

§ 9.1 Introduction and Chapter Overview 185

PART I   TORT CLAIMS 186

§ 9.2 Immunity and Liability for Acts of Officers, Employees and
      Independent Contractors 186

§ 9.3 Negligence 189

§ 9.4 Nuisance, Trespass and Unconstitutional Taking of
      Property 191

PART II   CONSTITUTIONAL, CIVIL RIGHTS AND
          ANTITRUST CLAIMS 193

§ 9.5 Constitutional Claims 193

§ 9.6 Section 1983 Actions 196

§ 9.7 Other Federal Civil Rights Acts 199

§ 9.8 Americans With Disabilities and Age Discrimination in
      Employment Act 203

§ 9.9 Antitrust 205

PART III PROCEDURAL REQUIREMENTS 206

§ 9.10 Notice of Injury and Intent to File a Claim 206

§ 9.11 Time Limitations and Damages 208

Chapter 10 Local Finances **211**

§ 10.1 Introduction and Chapter Overview 211

Page

PART I LOCAL REVENUE 212

§ 10.2 Federal and State Aid 212

§ 10.3 Constitutional and Statutory Limitations on Local
      Taxation 214

§ 10.4 Real Property Tax 217

§ 10.5 Sales and Use Taxes 220

§ 10.6 Income, Gross Receipts, and Personal Property Taxes . . . 222

§ 10.7 Fees and Special Assessments 223

§ 10.8 Other Taxes; Lotteries; and Recoupment of Public Costs
      From Tobacco and Gun Manufacturers 226

PART II LOCAL EXPENDITURES 227

§ 10.9 Public Purpose Requirement 227

§ 10.10 Prohibited or Required Expenditures 229

§ 10.11 Expenditure Process 230

PART III LOCAL INDEBTEDNESS 232

§ 10.12 Limitations on Borrowing 232

§ 10.13 Borrowing for Community Development 237

§ 10.14 Borrowing Procedure 238

Table of Cases TC-1

Index I-1

Chapter 1

Introduction to Local Government

§ 1.1 Introduction and Chapter Overview

Local government is a broad term that applies to that unit of government that is closest to the people. It includes local entities created to exercise either general or special governmental authority. According to the U.S. Advisory Commission on Intergovernmental Relations, there were 86,743 units of local government counted in the 1992 Census of Governments, comprised of cities, counties, towns, townships, boroughs, villages, school districts, and special purpose districts, authorities and commissions.[1]

States vary in their forms of local government. Most have a combination of local entities called counties, towns, cities, villages, or boroughs. There is also variety in the way these entities are created, changed, and organized. Some may be created by the state to exist in certain geographical areas, while others may be created by the voluntary action of local inhabitants.

Whether a county, town, city, village or borough, these units of government are viewed as the level of government most often relied upon to provide needed regulation and services that enable people to go about their daily activities of work and play. These governmental bodies are fascinating creatures that reflect the personalities, hopes and desires of the citizens they represent. Their work is carried out by many elected and appointed individuals with diverse interests who are diligent in attempting to do their best to achieve a goal of providing good public service. The local officers and employees are joined by countless volunteers who contribute their energies and skills while serving on numerous boards and advisory groups. They want to make their communities a better place to live.

In addition to general purpose local governments, there are many units of local governments that have been established to perform specific functions of providing specialized services. School districts, fire districts, special purpose districts and other public entities are created to address specific needs for services or regulation.

All local governments interact in numerous ways with the federal and state governments. These relationships are significant in defining local powers, responsibilities, and the financial ability of the local government to meet the needs of its residents. Just as significantly, local governments must continually interact with other local governments. Most have been given authority to contract or work cooperatively with other local governments in order to provide services in a more efficient or cost-effective

---

[1] U.S. ADVISORY COMMISSION ON INTERGOVERNMENTAL RELATIONS (ACIR) A-127 October 1993, Executive Summary.

1

manner. Most have also had to learn to work together in order to solve jurisdictional disputes.

Local governments are not inflexible, rigid entities. To fulfill their functions, they must constantly change and adapt to the needs and expectations of the people who reside within their boundaries. They must also adapt when there are significant changes in their resources. These are difficult challenges to meet. Those governments that excel are those which have been provided with the needed tools and use them wisely.

PART I FORMS AND RELATIONSHIPS OF LOCAL GOVERNMENTS

§ 1.2   Forms From Colonial Days to Present

It is impossible to say there is any typical form of local government structure since there is such tremendous diversity in titles, powers, duties, geographic size and organizational structures both within and among the various states. This is a reflection of each state's unique history, culture, and needs. Even similarly named local governments will vary from state to state because of the differences in the delegation of powers and characteristics bestowed upon them by the charters, state constitutions, and the statutes that create and define them. Generally, their structure and form is not a result of thoughtful planning, but in many respects is a product of their origins in English law and their historical development.[1] However, recognizing this, there are common patterns.

The label "local government" is a broad term that includes municipal corporations and public quasi-corporations, two basic types of local units of government. The municipal corporation is usually defined as an incorporated entity that has been given general governing authority to provide a broad spectrum of public services, exercise general police powers, and raise revenue by imposing taxes within a defined area. Cities, villages, and sometimes towns and boroughs, are names given to municipalities. Quasi-corporations most often include counties and townships (or towns).[2] The traditional distinction between these and municipal corporations was that they were created by the state to administer state as well as local functions, and were not originally given general governing authority. Counties and townships were viewed as arms of the state, created to assist the state,

---

[1] For a discussion of the English origins of various types of local governments, *see* OSBORNE M. REYNOLDS, JR., LOCAL GOVERNMENT LAW § 4 (2d ed. 2001). As noted by Professors Mandelker, Netsch, Salsich, and Wegner in their book STATE AND LOCAL GOVERNMENT IN A FEDERAL SYSTEM, page 38, the local government pattern is least complex in the south and southwest and in the southern middle Atlantic region where county governments are strong and townships non-existent. Local government patterns are more complicated in the northeast and upper middle Atlantic region.

[2] These are sometimes referred to as quasi-municipal entities. *See* U.S. ADVISORY COMMISSION ON INTERGOVERNMENTAL RELATIONS, STATE AND LOCAL ROLES IN THE FEDERAL SYSTEM 227 (1982).

while municipal corporations were created "voluntarily"[3] to serve the population of a local area. However, in modern times the distinction between the two categories has become less meaningful in many jurisdictions because counties and townships have assumed more responsibilities. In many cases, they have been given general governing authority similar to those of municipalities, including home rule authority.[4] In some jurisdictions, the distinction may still retain some significance, with the quasi-corporations relying on their "arms of the state" status to provide them immunity from tort liability.[5]

One of the earliest forms of government is the county. Almost all states have counties, although they are known as parishes in Louisiana and as boroughs in Alaska.[6] Their territory usually encompasses other forms of local government, which may or may not be considered part of the county, as well as territory that is not part of other local entities. The role of counties varies from state to state. Although many were initially established for the delivery of state services, today the more urbanized ones provide a wide variety of services and are partners in federal programs as well. In some states, counties are the predominant form of local government. In other jurisdictions the towns are the dominant provider of services and counties do not play a significant role in the local government structure. Often, rural counties have remained providers of state services and have experienced little change in their simple forms of governance. Of all units of local government, the counties have experienced the greatest expansion in responsibility during recent times. Because of their ability to provide services over a broader area, they have been the logical entity to undertake larger projects that require an ability to cross smaller boundaries and assess the costs over a greater number of residents. In many cases, they are the natural focus of efforts to regionalize the delivery of public services in order to obtain cost savings. Typical responsibilities for counties include tax assessment and collection, economic development, law enforcement and correctional facilities, roads, courts, maintenance of records, welfare and social services, and public health needs. They are also often responsible for hospitals, airports, libraries and recreational facilities.

---

[3] Again, with many exceptions, most municipal corporations are now created by residents who follow incorporation procedures prescribed in state statutes. Reflecting one of the exceptions, cities can only be created in New York by an act of the legislative body.

[4] *See* City of Durango v. Durango Transp. Inc., 807 P.2d 1152 (Colo. 1991). The determination of whether a local entity is a municipal corporation is made by reference to the state constitution, statutes and case law. State *ex rel.* Milham v. Rickhoff, 633 S.W.2d 733, 735 (Mo. 1982). A county was deemed to be a "municipality" because it recognizes the increasing role of counties in providing local services considered to be "municipal functions."

[5] Champlin Petroleum Co. v. Bd. of County Comm'rs, 526 P.2d 1142 (Ok. 1974); Hale v. Port of Portland, 308 Or. 508, 783 P.2d 506 (1989).

[6] Connecticut and Rhode Island are the only states that have not had functioning counties. In Alaska and New York City the counties are known as boroughs. The five counties, or boroughs, of New York City are part of the city government structure. In Louisiana they are known as parishes.

Boroughs, like counties, existed in England, and today remain important units of local government in New Jersey, Pennsylvania, Alaska and Connecticut. The term is also used to delineate parts of local governments in some areas such as New York City and Illinois.[7]

Townships (also known as towns) are forms of government first created in the New England states. Found in the Northeast and Midwest, they are present in a little less than half the states, and are particularly strong in Washington, the North Central and Middle Atlantic states.[8] Typically, townships will consist of all the territory of a county that is outside of the incorporated areas. The responsibilities and authority vary from state to state, with some exercising general authority similar to incorporated entities. Their responsibilities generally include road development and maintenance, social services, and some provide schools. More rural townships perform limited functions and serve only unincorporated areas, remaining true to part of their origin as a deliverer of state services. The evolution of townships has been uneven, with many declining in responsibility while others have become general providers of a vast array of local services.

The New England towns found in the six New England states are in many respects similar to counties in other jurisdictions. Their duties usually include record maintenance, providing for elections, and many services that are typical of general purpose governments such as education. Although even today, many of the New England towns of Connecticut, New Hampshire, Rhode Island, Massachusetts, parts of Maine and Vermont, still maintain many of their earlier characteristics such as participatory government through the town meeting, others have adopted a representative format.

Cities and villages, as true general purpose units of local government, deliver an increasingly broad and extensive range of services to their residents. From transportation and other public utilities, to social services, hospitals and police and fire protection, municipal governments have experienced increased budgetary demands that have in turn required that they become adept at attracting economic development to provide additional revenues. Although a municipality's denomination as a city most often indicates a concentration of inhabitants greater than a village, it is not always so.[9] The structure of government for both varies but typically includes an executive that consists of a strong or weak mayor, manager or commission with an elected strong or weak legislative body, often called a council. In some smaller entities, an elected council may perform both executive and legislative functions.

---

[7] When two or more municipalities merge, the former entities are referred to as boroughs within the united city. *See* 65 ILL. COMP. STAT. § 5/7-2-5; People *ex rel.* Montgomery v. Lierman, 415 Ill. 32, 112 N.E.2d 149 (1953).

[8] *See* REYNOLDS, *supra* note 1.

[9] In New York there are several villages that are more populous than cities within the state.

There are other special forms of local governments that have an increasingly important role in the delivery of services both within and among local governments. Characteristically, these entities provide a single service or a closely-identified group of services. They may be called special districts, improvement districts, authorities, or public benefit corporations and unlike counties, towns, cities, villages or boroughs, do not have general governing authority. Special units of government may be created by the state or by local action in order to provide services that are within the creating entity's responsibilities. Thus, a state may create a system of school districts to provide education to the people of the state. A local government may create a water district to provide water to people within its jurisdiction. Both state and general local governments, where authorized, may choose to carry out their functions by the creation of these specialized governmental entities. These entities may or may not be closely linked to their creating government in both personnel and financial areas. This is reflected in their characterization as either dependent or independent districts. They are discussed in greater detail in Chapter 6.

§ 1.3   Relationship to the Federal Government

Local governments in some ways more closely resemble the federal government than the states. They are created by the states and are totally dependent upon them for the delegation of all of their authority, just as the federal government must look to the United States Constitution for its state-delegated authority. Only the states possess that vast reservoir of sovereign authority that devolved to them when the country was formed. Just as the Tenth Amendment indicates that the federal government can only exercise such authority as has been delegated to it by the states in the U.S. Constitution, so it is with local governments. The local governments possess no inherent sovereign authority.

A local government may have implied powers in addition to those that are specified in a state constitution or statute. Courts have found implied powers that are necessary for a local government to carry out the responsibilities expressly entrusted to them by the states through statutes or state constitutions. This implication of authority resembles the implication of powers found by the courts at the federal level that enable Congress to carry out its broad delegations of Constitutional authority.

The Eleventh Amendment places limitations upon the ability of Congress to waive a state's immunity to suit in federal or state courts.[1] However, this does not restrict Congress from providing for suits against state government officials for injunctive or declaratory relief when there are continuing violations of federal law, as long as this is not the functional equivalent

---

[1] The Eleventh Amendment provides that the judicial power of the United States shall not be construed to extend to any suit in law or equity against a state if brought by citizens of another state or subjects of any foreign state. This has been interpreted to prevent waiver of suit in state courts as well. Alden v. Maine, 527 U.S. 706, 119 S. Ct. 2240, 144 L. Ed. 2d 636 (1999).

of an action against the state itself. It has also been determined that the Eleventh Amendment does not prevent Congress from providing for such private actions when it is acting pursuant to its Thirteenth, Fourteenth[2] or Fifteenth Amendment powers.[3] These Reconstruction Amendments, adopted after the Civil War, were written for the purpose of changing the balance of power between the federal government and the states. They specifically give Congress the power to enforce those particular amendments by adopting appropriate legislation,[4] which includes authorizing private actions against the states when there is a government violation of the Thirteenth, Fourteenth or Fifteenth Amendments.

However, the Eleventh Amendment's protection of state sovereignty does not apply to local governments.[5] Since a local government is not a state, federal legislation can provide for private judicial actions for money damages, as it has done in § 1983 of the Civil Rights Act.[6]

Unlike states,[7] local governments must obey federal antitrust laws. The Supreme Court held that they may not claim antitrust immunity in their regulatory activity, unless able to claim that they are acting pursuant to state direction.[8]

---

[2] See United States v. Morrison, 529 U.S. 598 (2000) (holding that § 5 enforcement powers enable Congress to act with respect to state action but not private action).

[3] Wilson-Jones v. Cabiness, 107 F.3d 358 (6th Cir. 1997).

[4] However, the Supreme Court has held that Congress, in exercising its remedial powers, must identify conduct that violates the Fourteenth Amendment's substantive provisions. It may then adopt a measure that is responsive to it and designed to prevent the offending conduct. See Florida Prepaid Postsecondary Education Expense Board v. College Savings Bank, 527 U.S. 627 (1999). When Congress abrogated state immunity from patent infringement suits it exceeded its delegated authority under the Fourteenth Amendment since it could not be sustained as legislation adopted to enforce the guarantees of the Due Process Clause. Id. at 643. There must be a proportionality between the injury to be prevented and means adopted to that end. Id. at 637.

[5] See Moor v. Alameda County, 411 U.S. 693, 719 (1973) (stating that the county possessed an independent status relative to the state as evidenced by its power to levy taxes, issue bonds and their liability for judgments rendered against it); Mount Healthy City School Bd. of Educ. v. Doyle, 429 U.S. 274, 280 (1977) (focusing on the local school board's power to issue bonds and levy taxes to verify that it is more akin to a county and, therefore, could not benefit from state immunity under the 11th Amendment); Hess v. Port Authority Trans-Hudson Corp., 513 U.S. 30 (1994) (neither of the creating states would be obligated to pay any judgment obtained); Regents of the Univ. of Calf. v. Doe, 519 U.S. 425, 431 (1997) (stating that it is the entity's potential legal liability that is relevant, and not its ability or inability to require a third party to reimburse it).

[6] See Monell v. Dept. of Soc. Svcs. of the City of N.Y., 436 U.S. 658, 690 (1978) (Congress has not chosen to abrogate state immunity in § 1983 but has included local governments since they have been determined to be "persons" within the meaning of most federal civil rights statutes and are subject to suit under most civil rights laws); Howlett v. Rose, 496 U.S. 356, 376 (1990) (state law sovereign immunity may not be applied to bar a § 1983 action against local entities in state court).

[7] Parker v. Brown, 317 U.S. 341 (1943).

[8] City of Lafayette v. Louisiana Power & Light Co., 435 U.S. 389 (1978). See § 9.9 infra for a discussion of local antitrust liability.

Local governments are similar to states in that they must comply with federal constitutional requirements of due process and equal protection when exercising the authority that has been delegated to them by the state. The Due Process Clause requires that local regulation be reasonable and reasonably related to the public health, safety and welfare. Local governments have to construct their regulations so that they are narrowly and explicitly drawn. There also have to be appropriate procedures accompanying the regulation to insure that citizens are afforded reasonable opportunities to comply with or challenge the regulatory action. If local legislation relates to a matter within the legislative power of the local government, the courts presume that it is both reasonable and constitutional. The burden is upon the challenger to prove otherwise.

Since the Supremacy Clause of the Constitution provides that federal law is the supreme law of the land, local enactments which conflict with the exercise of authority delegated to Congress will be preempted.[9] A local enactment that is in conflict with the federal law, or is an obstacle to its objective, is invalid. In determining whether there is preemption, the courts consider whether there is a Congressional intent to preempt by examining the legislation for an express statement of this intent. Even if there is none, an implied preemption may be found if a regulatory structure is so pervasive that it creates an inference of federal preemption, or the subject matter regulated is one that is deemed to be primarily of federal concern with an implication that no other level of government may act. Sometimes this means that the local government is preempted from acting at all in a given area because there is complete federal preemption. Other times it means that they are only prohibited from acting in a way that interferes with federal regulation.

Local governments must respect individual rights guaranteed in the federal Constitution. Their actions, just like those of the states, may not in any way breach liberties protected by the First, Fifth, Fourteenth, and Fifteenth Amendments or any other constitutional provision. Federal statutes that protect individual liberties are applicable to local action. An example of this is the federal Civil Rights Acts. These statutes have had an enormous influence on local government policy, as well as on the procedures used by individuals to enforce their rights and to seek compensation for any infringement that has occurred.

Courts have held that local governments may not restrict or impede the lawful exercise of federal authority through their regulatory actions. A local government is not permitted to impose a tax on the federal government without its permission. Local land use restrictions are not applicable to federal entities unless they have consented to be bound by them.[10] Zoning and building code regulations must yield, even if based on valid police powers, to the exercise of any power possessed by the federal government.[11]

---

[9] *See* § 2.5 *infra* for a discussion of federal preemption of local government action.

[10] Tim v. City of Long Branch, 53 A.2d 164 (N.J. 1947).

[11] United States v. City of Chester, 144 F.2d 415 (3d Cir. 1944); Harrison v. Schwartz, 572 A.2d 528 (Md. 1990), *cert. denied,* Schwartz v. Harrison, 498 U.S. 851 (1990); United States v. City of Philadelphia, 147 F.2d 291 (3d Cir. 1945), *cert. denied,* 325 U.S. 870 (1944).

There are instances where the federal government has expressly provided for an exception to this general rule and has voluntarily submitted to local regulation. An example is the Coastal Zone Management Act which requires federal activities to be carried out in a manner which is consistent, to the maximum extent practicable, with local plans that have been approved by the state.[12]

While the exercise of its delegated powers by a local government may not generally be used to take federal land or regulate the activity of the federal government, the converse is not true. The federal government may exercise its powers of eminent domain to take state or local property and may regulate the state or local activity if acting within its delegated powers. It may also effect the relationship between the state and its local governments. In the Transportation Equity Act for the 21st Century, Congress requires the states to provide local governments with a greater role in transportation decisions.[13]

The federal government has had an increasingly strong influence on the activities of local governments. Federal funds directed toward many areas, including public health, community development, education, and law enforcement, have benefitted local communities. With the carrot has also come the stick. Conditions attached to these funds have meant that local governments have voluntarily assumed the responsibility of meeting many federal regulatory requirements in order to benefit from the federal program.[14] However, local governments may not delegate their governmental authority to the federal government, nor agree to put federal interests above local interests of their citizens.

§ 1.4 Relationship to the State Government

Local governments are completely beholden to state governments for their existence and authority. Even after their creation, it is generally recognized that they have no inherent right to act even in areas of local concern.[1] It is up to the states to provide for their creation and authority. States may delegate to their local governments certain police powers and other powers of a local nature, enabling them to act in matters of local concern.[2] The only restraint upon the states in their determination of the structure, function and powers of their local governments are provisions contained in the federal constitution and those found in their own state constitution. As stated by the Supreme Court in the seminal case of *Hunter v. City of Pittsburgh,*

---

[12] 16 U.S.C. § 1456(c)(1)(A).

[13] INTERMODAL SURFACE TRANSPORTATION EFFICIENCY ACT OF 1991, 49 U.S.C. § 101 (1996) reauthorized in 1998 as the TRANSPORTATION EQUITY ACT FOR THE 21st CENTURY, PUB. L. NO. 105-178, 112 stat. 164 (1998).

[14] *See* § 10.2 *infra* for more discussion of federal aid and mandates.

[1] *See* Chapter 2 *infra* for a discussion of local authority.

[2] State *ex rel.* City of Charleston v. Coghill, 207 S.E.2d 113 (1973).

> Municipal corporations are political subdivisions of the State, created as convenient agencies for exercising such of the governmental powers of the State as may be entrusted to them. . . . The number, nature and duration of the powers conferred upon these corporations and the territory over which they shall be exercised rests in the absolute discretion of the State. . . . The State, therefore, at its pleasure may modify or withdraw all such powers, may take without compensation such property, hold it itself, or vest it in other agencies, expand or contract the territorial area, unite the whole or a part of it with another municipality, repeal the charter and destroy the corporation. All this may be done, conditionally or unconditionally, with or without the consent of the citizens. . . . In all these respects the State is supreme, and its legislative body. . . may do as it will, unrestrained by any provision of the Constitution of the United States.[3]

This sweeping declaration of the right of a state to do as it will with its local governments, unfettered by the federal constitution, was subsequently qualified in *Gomillion v. Lightfoot.*[4] There the Court indicated that specific federal constitutional provisions may limit a state's right to affect its local governments. In other words, a state may not change a local government's boundaries in such a way that it infringes a citizen's right to vote in violation of the Fifteenth Amendment of the Constitution. However, the more general protections of the Federal Constitution such as the Contract, Privileges and Immunities, Equal Protection, and Due Process Clauses have been held inapplicable to state action that affects local governments.[5]

The various state constitutions often do provide protection to local governments from state actions. In addition to delegating home rule authority (or authority to control local matters) many state constitutions also contain provisions that specifically restrain state governments from interfering with the local governments in the exercise of their delegated authority. Some are specific and may require the state to obtain the consent of the local government before it does things such as grant public utilities the right to use the public right-of-ways; or, constitutions may protect the right of local governments to appoint or elect their own officers. Others are more general. New York's, for example, provides that the state legislature is prohibited from acting by special law if it affects a local government's property, affairs or government unless requested by the local government or the governor.[6] Although there are variations, a special law is usually

---

[3] *Hunter,* 207 U.S. 161 (1907). *See also* Town of Godfrey v. City of Alton, 338 N.E.2d 890 (Ill. Ct. App. 1975).

[4] *Gomillion,* 364 U.S. 339, 344 (1960) (stating that it is conclusively shown "that the Court has never acknowledged that the States have power to do as they will with municipal corporations regardless of consequences").

[5] *See Hunter,* 207 U.S. 161 (1907) (Contract); Williams v. Mayor & City Council of Baltimore, 289 U.S. 36 (1933) (Privileges and Immunities); Newark v. New Jersey, 262 U.S. 192 (1923) (Equal Protection); City of Trenton v. New Jersey, 262 U.S. 182 (1923) (Due Process).

[6] N.Y. CONST. art. IX. § 2(b)(2).

one which by its terms or effects applies to one or more but not all local governments of a particular type, while a general law treats all similar local governments the same. The selection is rational and not arbitrary.

Similar protection from state interference with local matters may be granted in state statutes. Powers delegated to the local governments in statutes can be taken away unless prohibited by the state constitution.[7] The same may be true of restrictions on state legislative action that affects the exercise of local powers.

Unlike individual citizens, local governments do not usually have judicial standing to protest actions taken by the states. Since they are viewed as state creations, dependent upon the state for their existence and powers, the courts generally have held that the notion of a local government questioning state action is inconsistent with their status. Challenges to state infringement of the rights of local governments that are based on the Federal Constitution have not been successful because the character of these claims is inconsistent with the local government's legal nature as creatures of the state.[8] However, there is some indication that a local government may be able to challenge state legislation that violates the U.S. Constitution and may question the legitimacy of a state law by arguing that it has been preempted by federal law.[9] Although it has been clearly stated that local governments have no standing to attack the constitutionality of a statute on the ground that it results in a denial of due process, there is some indication that if property taken by the state was held by the local government in a proprietary capacity as opposed to a governmental capacity, there may be a federal constitutional claim.[10] An exception to the general rule of no standing has also been found by state courts where a local government claims that a state has infringed upon authority it was given in the state constitution.[11]

Interestingly, once local governments are created by the states and given authority to function as independent governments, states do not usually supervise the day-to-day exercise of that authority. There may be systematic review of their finances and state preemption of areas that are of

---

[7] City of Coronado v. San Diego Unified Port Dist., 227 Cal. App. 2d 455 (1964); Enger v. Walker Field, Colo. Pub. Airport Auth., 508 P.2d 1245 (1973).

[8] See Williams, 289 U.S. 36 (1933) ("a municipal corporation, created by a state for the better ordering of government, has no privileges and immunities under the federal constitution which it can raise against its creator"); Hunter, 207 U.S. 161 (1907).

[9] Branson School Dist. RE-82 v. Romer, 161 F.3d 619 (10th Cir. 1998), cert. denied, 526 U.S. 1068 (1999) (holding a political subdivision has standing to bring a constitutional claim against its creating state when the substance of the claim relies on the Supremacy Clause). But see Burbank-Pasadena Airport Auth. v. City of Burbank, 136 F.3d 1360 (9th Cir. 1998).

[10] Hunter, 207 U.S. at 179-180 (1907) (suggesting there is dicta that if property is taken by the state that was held by a local government in a proprietary capacity as opposed to a governmental capacity, there may be a constitutional claim). See also Gomillion, 364 U.S. at 342 (1960) (stating that Hunter intimates that states are not omnipotent in their disposition of locally owned property); San Diego Unified Port Dist. v. Gianturco, 651 F.2d 1306 (9th Cir. 1981); Bd. of Educ. of Cent. Sch. Dist. No. 1 v. Allen, 392 U.S. 236 (1968).

[11] Town of Black Brook v. State, 362 N.E.2d 579 (N.Y. 1977).

concern to the entire state, but generally it is up to the citizens of the local government to review and monitor local government activities. It is felt that the people have the ultimate authority to determine whether the local government acts appropriately by the election of its officers who exercise local government powers.

§ 1.5   Relationship Between and Among Local Governments

While there may be a natural competitiveness between local governments, many engage in cooperative activities that benefit all parties. In fact, intergovernmental cooperation has been hailed as the wave of the future for solving problems that need comprehensive area-wide planning.[1] In most states there are general state constitutional or statutory provisions that both permit and regulate such local activities. Typically, there are also many specific authorizations that enable local governments to agree to work together in a particular area.

In order to enter into a mutually beneficial arrangement, local governments may decide who is going to regulate or provide a public service and enter into a contract. In some states both parties must have been given authority to enter into interlocal agreements and the authority to regulate or provide the service that is the subject of the agreement. In others, it is sufficient if one of the local governments has such authority. Often, local governments may contract with each other for the provision of water or other utilities and miscellaneous services such as the provision of jail facilities. If the local governments enter into a contract and there are no specific provisions regulating the relationship, then usually general contract law is applicable. These arrangements have produced relatively few legal problems if both local governments have authority to contract and each has met and followed its own internal requirements and processes for entering into an agreement.

Operation of major facilities like hospitals and airports are often shared responsibilities assumed by multiple local governments. Some local governments share industrial development activities intended to benefit an entire region. Frequently, local governments agree to create a new public entity, often referred to as an authority or commission, to provide a mutually beneficial service.[2] This often requires a special act by the state legislative body and is not normally within the powers of a local government to undertake without such special authorization. In addition to the advantages of economic efficiency, the separate entity can borrow needed capital up to its authorized debt limit without the obligation being included as debts of the participating local governments. Although an independent entity, the local governments typically appoint those individuals who will lead it. It

---

[1] David R. Berman, *State-Local Relations: Authority, Finances, Cooperation,* 59, MUNICIPAL YEAR BOOK 2002 (2002).

[2] *See* § 6.4 *infra* for a discussion of authorities.

is very rare that a local government will be liable in contract or tort for the agency's actions and they are usually prohibited from pledging their full faith and credit for the agency's outstanding indebtedness.

In addition to providing services, sometimes local governments agree to face regulatory challenges in an interlocal manner. Land use, highway and recreational facility planning is often done on a regional basis. This type of cooperation is specifically authorized in many state statutes.

Authority delegated to a local government may usually be exercised solely within its boundaries. It is unusual that it will be entrusted with extraterritorial authority. However, at times, local governments are permitted by a specific or necessarily-implied delegation of state authority to condemn land or impose regulatory controls outside their territorial boundaries. Such extraterritorial authority has been given in statutes that permit local governments to exercise the power of eminent domain to provide needed utilities or services. The maintenance of reservoirs needed for local water supplies or land needed for the development of solid waste disposal facilities may require such special powers. Some grants of extraterritorial authority also permit the extension of regulations that protect health and welfare of local residents. Permission to exercise regulatory control may at times be given where a local government is going to be adversely impacted by activities relatively close to its geographical boundaries. In a variation of this, some local governments have been authorized to preempt conflicting land use regulations of other local governments or veto extraterritorial changes that may adversely affect their territory. The state has great flexibility to determine which local government will be authorized to exercise any specific local authority, unlimited by local boundaries, provided it is not in conflict with the state constitution.

However, when the state has not expressly addressed the issue, deciding interlocal conflicts presents difficult decisions. The question of whether a local government is impliedly exempt from another local government's land use regulations has been particularly troublesome. The often stated common-law rule has been that when a local government is acting in its governmental capacity it is not subject to the land use regulations of another local government. If it is engaging in a proprietary activity it must abide by the restrictions. When the New York Court reviewed a dispute involving a county, which wanted to expand an airport facility on land within a city, it rejected this rule as unworkable. The Court replaced it with a balancing of public interests test that had already been adopted by many other states.[3] The county was permitted to expand, free of land use oversight from the city.[4]

---

[3] Matter of City of Rochester, 530 N.E.2d 202 (N.Y. 1988). The Court noted the Supreme Court's earlier expression of discontent with the governmental/proprietary function test when it decided cases of state regulatory immunity from federal intrusion.

[4] For a discussion of other tests that have been used to determine interlocal conflicts, see DANIEL R. MANDELKER, DAWN CLARK NETSCH, PETER W. SALSICH, JR. & JUDITH WELCH WEGNER, STATE AND LOCAL GOVERNMENT IN A FEDERAL SYSTEM 182-191 (5th ed. 2002).

A power to regulate the conduct of nonresidents may be used by many local governments. Reasonable conditions may be imposed on external businesses seeking the sale of goods and services within the territory by requiring that they obtain licenses, meet specified standards and submit to inspections of production facilities.[5] Any fees imposed on extraterritorial entities must be reasonably related to the cost of the regulation and not for the purpose of raising revenue for the local government. However, business transactions or activities that take place within the local government may be subject to taxation for revenue purposes to the same extent as those of local residents.[6] Local governments are required to act reasonably in differentiating between local and extraterritorial businesses without imposing undue burdens or limitations that violate the Commerce Clause of the Federal Constitution.[7]

Many times, property owned by a local government is constitutionally or statutorily exempt from taxation by another local government. Sometimes this exemption is applicable only to property used for a public purpose. In other states, local governments are required to pay a sum in lieu of taxes for property owned outside their jurisdiction. States vary in permitting or denying local governments the right to impose special assessments and fees on other local governments for water, sewage, fire protection and other special improvements.

It is quite common to have a local government given the responsibility of levying and collecting taxes for another local entity, such as a school district. This responsibility is imposed by state legislation and most often the process is carefully detailed.

The use of interlocal cooperation is a means of addressing what is in some metropolitan areas a basic and underlying problem of too many separate local governments. Each local government has frequently been given broad authority to address the needs of their own inhabitants. However, it is not efficient or even possible to regulate some activities or provide some services individually. The movement toward regionalization is discussed in § 1.7 *infra*.

PART II GEOGRAPHICAL AND POLITICAL STRUCTURE OF LOCAL GOVERNMENTS

§ 1.6 Creation and Dissolution

Although state legislatures have plenary power to establish local governments, the various state constitutions may impose limitations on the exercise of this power. New York's constitution prohibits its legislature from creating villages, preferring that it be done by local effort pursuant to a

---

[5] State v. Nelson, 68 N.W. 1066 (Mn. 1896).

[6] For further discussion, *see* § 10.5 *infra*.

[7] Dean Milk Co. v. City of Aurora, 88 N.E.2d 827 (Ill. 1949).

general statute that permits residents to follow defined steps to create one. Other states have also recognized the right of the people to form a local government by local initiative. At other times, the exercise of the legislature's plenary power may be limited by a state constitutional requirement that a local government be created by a special act of the state's legislature. In any event, every state legislature may establish or modify a system providing for the creation and dissolution of local governments, and is limited only by provisions that may be found in its state constitution. This may be done with or without the approval of a majority of those residing within its geographical boundaries.[1]

Whether a local government is labeled a county, town, city, borough, parish, or village is not necessarily indicative of its geographical size or degree of governmental authority. There are some villages that are larger than cities or towns and vice versa. Many times, local government boundaries overlap and they share governmental authority over the same territory. It is not uncommon for separate units to remain part of larger governmental units. The most complex forms of local governments are often found in the East, with the adopted structures reflecting their early historical beginnings. In New York, for instance, residents living outside of New York City all reside either in a city and a county or they may reside in a county, town and village simultaneously. In the latter case, all three levels of local government exercise regulatory control and residents pay local taxes to all three.

Typical express or implied requirements and limitations that may be found in incorporation statutes include minimum population standards, geographical limitations of size, contiguity,[2] or presence within an existing local government. In some states, courts have found an implied state constitutional or statutory limitation that the area must have the characteristic of seeming to be a community. This may be established by geographical, sociological or political factors. If the population is centered and reasonably compact, it will meet this requirement.[3] Sometimes there is also an implied requirement that the land included in the proposed local government be suitable for urban development and likely to be benefitted by its creation. Although some statutes may accord special recognition to property owners either in their ability to create or block the establishment of local governments, these provisions are increasingly suspect and may be found unconstitutional.[4]

Where local citizens have the option of creating a local government, there must be substantial compliance with the governing statutes that prescribe the procedural steps to be taken. Often the process is initiated by the filing of a petition signed by a specified number or by a percentage of residents, property owners, or voters. A description of the proposed boundaries is

---

[1] Hunter v. City of Pittsburgh, 207 U.S. 161 (1907).

[2] Larkin v. Bontatibus, 145 A.2d 133 (Ct. 1958).

[3] Scharping v. Johnson, 145 N.W.2d 691 (Wis. 1966).

[4] Curtis v. Bd. of Supervisors, 501 P.2d 537 (Cal. 1972).

typically included in the petition which is ultimately submitted to a designated person or board.

The next step in the process is usually a requirement of giving notice either before or after the filing of the petitions to those affected, along with a date and designated place for a hearing to determine if all required steps have been followed. Some statutes permit the filing of protest petitions against the proposal and may even provide that the process be halted if a specified percentage of people sign them. Whether the creation of a new local government is in the public interest may be a subject for discussion at the hearing, but not always. Often the final step is an election whereby the voters residing within the territory proposed to become a local government finally decide whether the new entity will be created.

Some incorporation procedures delegate to administrative agencies or the judiciary the responsibility for determining whether the requirements have been met. If the legislature has established adequate standards, this will ordinarily be acceptable and not be found to be an unconstitutional delegation of legislative authority. Statutes will also generally provide for judicial review of the actions taken with the courts examining whether there has been compliance with the statutory requirements. Initiators seeking incorporation may resort to such judicial authority during the process if needed to overcome resistance from local officials who have not acted as required by the incorporation laws. This is particularly necessary because quite often existing local governments will not be in favor of the creation of a new entity with whom revenues and the exercise of local authority will be shared.

Some states require the consent of existing local governments as a condition precedent to the creation of new ones. In a few states, the state or its administrative agencies may approve or deny the creation of new local governments. In any event, state legislatures generally can enact validating legislation that recognizes a local government even if there were defects or irregularities in its initial creation, provided there are no state constitutional impediments to such action. Where states have the power to authorize the creation of a local entity, it is often deemed to have the authority to subsequently ratify its creation as well. Courts have also been generous in sometimes finding a "de facto" creation. This occurs when a bona fide attempt has been made to incorporate, with substantial compliance with the required process, and the local government has actually been exercising local powers.

In the absence of a state constitutional prohibition, a local entity can be dissolved by state legislative action or by the local government itself when the state has given it authority to do so. A state board or commission may sometimes be designated to oversee this process. Most often, dissolutions take place pursuant to general statutes that provide for local government or citizen initiation of the dissolution. At times, local governments cease to exist because they are merged or absorbed into other local governments.[5]

---

[5] This is discussed in § 1.7 *infra*.

The state constitution or statutes generally prescribe how the disposition or assumption of assets and debts of a dissolved unit are to be handled.

If a local government has never used its powers or engaged in the election of officers, or has ceased to do so, it is known as a dormant local government. Unless a state constitution or statute provides otherwise, the inactivity does not dissolve the local entity.

§ 1.7 Change in Boundary or Structure

States may freely change the existing boundaries of local governments unless restrained by provisions in the federal constitution or their state constitutions. The Supreme Court in *Gomillion v. Lightfoot*[1] held that a state could not violate a specific Constitutional protection, such as the Fifteenth Amendment's guarantee of the right to vote, by changing a local government's boundaries to exclude minorities. In addition, similar protections of individual rights are found in state constitutions which also may prohibit special legislation aimed at one or more but not all of a particular type of local government. Some states have provided additional protection to residents of local governments by requiring that a change in boundaries by the state necessitates the consent of its inhabitants.[2]

The addition of territory to a local government is referred to as an annexation. The annexation process may often be initiated either by resident petition and or by the local legislative body. Standard requirements are that the property be contiguous to the annexing government and that it be land that is suitable for development with the anticipation that the annexing local government will extend services to it. Some states prohibit the annexation of rural or undeveloped lands.

In most states, there are state constitutional or general laws that authorize and provide a procedure for local governments or residents to change local government boundaries. If it is done by residents, generally it is required that a petition be circulated for the required number of signatures and presented to the affected governing boards. This is usually followed by public notice and the proposal is often subject to protest by others who may oppose the annexation and seek to halt the process. Sometimes an annexation may be done by local legislative action alone.[3] At other times, application to a state,[4] regional, or county board may be required.[5]

States may provide for annexation of land even without the consent of the people who live on or own the property unless resident approval is

---

[1] 364 U.S. 339 (1960) (stating that it is conclusively shown that the Court has never acknowledged that the States have power to do as they will with municipal corporations regardless of consequences).

[2] *See* City of Houston v. City of Magnolia Park, 276 S.W. 685 (Tex. Comm'n App. 1925).

[3] Kansas, Texas, North Carolina, Arizona, Texas, Tennessee. Some other states permit it in limited circumstances such as Idaho and Kansas. Still others permit it if the action is not reversed by a referendum petition such as in Illinois.

[4] Alaska, Minnesota, Michigan, Wisconsin, New Mexico.

[5] Kansas, New Jersey, North Dakota, Washington, Oregon, Ohio.

required by the state constitution.[6] However, other states require approval
of a majority of the voters in both the annexing local government and in
the area to be annexed. The question of responsibility for assets and
liabilities associated with the move of land from one local government to
another is provided for in the governing statute. Once the procedure is
completed, the territory that has become part of the annexing local government immediately becomes subject to its regulatory and taxing authority.

The role of the state courts in annexation varies among the states.
Although a determination of the boundaries of local governments is recognized as a state legislative function, the judicial branch of state government
typically may review the action taken for its consistency with prescribed
procedures.[7] In addition, some states have expanded this responsibility by
having courts determine, as a part of their review, the necessity for the
annexation or whether the change is in the best interests of the affected
local governments. Often courts have applied a "rule of reason"[8] which has
been incorporated by some states in their regulatory statutes. A very small
number of states give courts the job of making the first determination of
whether the proposed action is necessary, expedient or in the best interests
of the people.

Reduction in the size of the geographical structure of local governments
may be made through processes known as de-annexation, detachment, or
severance. General statutes in most states permit the removal of rural or
agricultural lands that are not needed for governmental purposes and
which receive little or no benefit from their presence within the local
government. It is felt that inclusion of land that is not benefitted, and would
appear to have been included for the purpose of providing local tax revenue,
is inequitable. Local governments are not permitted to increase their real
property tax base by unreasonably overextending their boundaries. The
typical procedure to exclude such property requires a petition by its
residents, or property owners, or a written request by the legislative body.
It is submitted to a court or agency to determine its compliance with
statutory requirements and the reasonableness of the request. The question
of continued liability for debts incurred for public improvements that might
have benefitted the property has generally been answered by relieving the
property owners of any continued liability.

Other processes that effectuate change in local governments are either
done by the states themselves or through delegated authority to the local
governments or their inhabitants. These processes are provided by statutes
and follow the similar pattern of initiation either by citizen petition or by
local legislative action. Division is a term that means some local government property is removed from one local government and placed in another.

---

[6] Adams v. City of Colorado Springs, 308 F. Supp. 1397 (D.C. Colo. 1970), aff'd mem, 399
U.S. 901 (1970), reh'g denied, 400 U.S. 855 (1970).

[7] It was held by the Supreme Court in 1897 that the states may delegate this responsibility
to the judiciary.

[8] Mayor, Councilmen & Citizens v. Beard, 613 S.W.2d 642 (Mo. App.), aff'd, 613 S.W.2d 641
(Mo. 1981).

Merger refers to one local government absorbing another, which ceases to exist as a distinct entity. Consolidation is the term used when two or more local governments join together to create a new local government, with their previous identities no longer existing. In many of these processes, the goal is to eliminate wasteful duplication of governmental services and obtain greater efficiencies in the expenditure of local revenues.

Local governments may be dissolved, but usually this does not result from mere failure to exercise local authority. Affirmative action is required and most states have general statutes that prescribe the process of petition and election by the residents. The property and debts are handled according to the statute.

Changes in local governments that have been caused by demographic, social and economic factors have led many to criticize existing structures of local government. With shifts in population and jobs to the suburbs, many cities have encountered significant financial pressures. As the population becomes increasingly composed of those least able to afford the growing costs of providing services, the urban tax base is declining in value. At the same time, the tremendous increase in suburban population has led to the development of many local governments, all with the responsibility of providing regulatory and service functions to their inhabitants. The concentration of many local governments in one metropolitan region has led to jurisdictional concerns and inefficiencies in many single efforts to provide services that are best provided on a regional basis by one government. Some planning experts have viewed the regionalization of local government as one solution to the urban/suburban problem.[9] Some examples of this approach are the merger of Louisville and Jefferson County, Kentucky, the transfer of functions in Los Angeles County, California, and numerous consolidations and restructurings that have occurred in places such as Miami-Dade County, Florida, Minneapolis-St. Paul and Portland, Oregon. Some consolidations have produced a new regional government while others have used a more federated approach, separating functions and oversight responsibilities among the local governments. Many other local governments have chosen not to officially consolidate, merge or restructure. Instead, they have sought individual efficiencies in the delivery of public services by using their authority to transfer functions among themselves.[10]

§ 1.8 Forms of Government

Most local governments, regardless of the form of their political structure, have a tripartite model of government which reflects executive, legislative and judicial functions. The local government's charter or relevant statutes may describe its governing body, as well as its rights, powers, privileges,

---

[9] For an excellent discussion on the problem and solutions, *see* DANIEL R. MANDELKER, DAWN CLARK NETSCH, PETER W. SALSICH, JR. & JUDITH WELCH WEGNER, STATE AND LOCAL GOVERNMENT IN A FEDERAL SYSTEM 191-225 (5th ed. 2002).

[10] *See* § 2.2 *infra.*

and limitations. It often specifies the qualifications of its officers and the procedure for choosing its members. Some charters provide for internal subdivisions of the territory of the local government into wards or districts which then may directly affect the composition of the legislative body. The legislative process to be used in exercising local authority may also be contained in the charter or statutes.

Provision for an executive branch may be found in the charter or statutes that are pertinent to a local government. Whether called a mayor, supervisor, commissioner, or manager, people are elected or appointed to serve their communities by exercising day-to-day supervisory control over local departments and employees. This person, or group of people, will generally be responsible for preparing local budgets and seeing that expenditures remain within local revenues. Just as titles vary, there are large differences in the degree of authority given these executives of local governments. In some local governments, the legislative body serves the dual function of exercising executive authority and there is no single executive as such. Various members of the governing board may be delegated responsibility for overseeing particular day-to-day operations of local government. As local governments grow and the tasks in meeting their citizens' need for services become more complex, the ability of the legislative body to fulfill both legislative and executive roles diminishes.

All local governments have some form of legislative branch which is most often called a council or a board of supervisors, commissioners, or legislators. These elected officials establish policy for the local government by adopting resolutions, ordinances and local laws, just as the state legislature establishes state policy. They may also carry out their responsibilities either by directly assuming administrative functions for the local government or creating other offices and boards to do so. It is their responsibility to establish clear guidelines for the exercise of any delegated authority.

Many local governments have been given authority in their charters or through supplemental legislation to create local courts. In some, state constitutions give local governments this authority and if not prohibited by it, state legislative bodies can create local courts or empower local governments to do so. The jurisdiction of local courts varies from state to state but most have limited jurisdiction and no equity jurisdiction. However, there are exceptions and some have concurrent jurisdiction with state courts. Qualifications for judge or justice are usually prescribed in general statutes or in charters. Likewise, qualifications for juries and the procedure for impaneling them are generally found in the same sources. The judgments of local courts have the same effect and authority of judgments from any state court and generally appeals to a higher court are permitted, often being heard in a trial *de novo*.

The organizational structure of a local government is most often characteristic of its origins as either a "municipality" such as a city or village, or an entity that was created to assist the state in its responsibilities, such as a county or township. Increasingly, there is less difference between the two categories, but significant vestiges of their historical origins remain in their government structures.

Cities generally have either a mayor-council form of government, a council-manager, or a commission format. In the mayor-council structure, the executive position of mayor may be a strong executive position, with authority to administer the day-to-day operations, hire and fire department heads, and prepare and submit to the council a proposed budget. In the alternative, the position of mayor may be classified as a weak mayor-council structure, with the mayor having none of these powers and serving basically as a member of the council and ceremonial figure who represents the local government at public functions. Large cities, such as New York City, are more likely to have a strong mayor, while smaller cities can function under the weak mayor format. The council-manager structure is currently the most popular among all cities. It typically has an elected council that establishes policy through its legislative activities, while relying on an appointed city manager to administer the city's business, and hire and supervise its employees. Often the manager is also given authority to prepare the local budget to be submitted to the council for its approval. Finally, the commission form of city government may be found primarily in smaller cities. Here local commissioners are elected to serve as the policy-making body and administer the day-to-day business of the local government. Typically, the categories of responsibility will be divided among full-time commissioners, with each responsible for discrete areas of service, from police and fire protection to water supply and sewage services. This format becomes increasingly cumbersome and less satisfactory as a local government becomes larger and more diverse in its needs.

In counties and townships, there is tremendous diversity in government structure among the various states. In some, they are increasingly similar to "municipalities" and will have similar government administrative structures. Some counties have followed the pattern of adopting a county-manager form of government.

Unless prohibited by a state constitution, the state may change or revoke a local charter or statute that prescribes a local government political structure. It may also authorize the local government itself to adopt changes as it sees fit. The potential need for local governments to change their governmental structures has been addressed by many states which permit the amendment or adoption of new structures of government and allocation of functions and responsibilities. In some states, the state constitution gives local entities the right to adopt or amend local charters.[1] In others, authorization and the process to be followed may be found in statutes, with some requiring approval of the governor or the state legislature. Many require local voter approval of the adoption or amendment in a referendum of all those qualified to vote in local elections. The Supreme Court has held that a state may require voter approval in different local governments as a condition precedent to a change in local government structure, even

---

[1] N.Y. CONST. art. IX, § 1(h)(1).

though it may result in a minority of the total voting against the adoption of the change blocking a majority who favor it.[2]

---

[2] Town of Lockport v. Citizens for Cmty. Action, 431 U.S. 902 (1977).

Chapter 2

Local Authority

§ 2.1 Introduction and Chapter Overview

Local governments, as creations of the state, have no inherent sovereign authority. They are very much similar to the federal government, in that both are totally dependent on delegated authority from the states. Local sources of authority are found in state constitutions, statutes, and in their own charters. Also, the federal government has at times delegated some of its regulatory authority to local governments. Finding the law is not as difficult as defining it. Courts have been called upon to interpret and reconcile both broad and specific grants of authority. In the process, they have had to balance the role of local governments in a complex and multi-layered system of federal, state and local governments.

Most states have chosen to give a degree of independence to their local governments by recognizing their right to determine the many issues that directly relate to the operation and structure of their government. This is generally done by an official grant of "home-rule authority." This most important state-delegated right to self-governance may be found in a state's constitution, statute or local government charter. Most often it is not a question of whether a local government has been given authority to act but whether a state has been foreclosed from acting. The right to home rule is expressed by both a specific grant of affirmative authority for the local government to act in a defined area and by a limitation on the state government to interfere in the local government's exercise of its delegated authority.

There are numerous limitations on the exercise of local authority. Local governments must not exercise their authority in a manner that violates the federal and state constitutional rights of individuals. This imposes both substantive and procedural requirements on local officials and legislative bodies. In addition, local governments may be prevented from exercising local authority because the state or federal governments have explicitly or impliedly preempted their action.

Local governments exercise their authority through official action taken by their legislative bodies. They implement their governmental choices and decisions through local officers and boards. The process of governing is often prescribed in local charters. The authorization to individuals and boards to carry out the actions taken must be done with sufficient legislative guidance to avoid the possibility of an unconstitutional delegation of their legislative authority.

PART I HOME RULE AND OTHER DELEGATED AUTHORITY

§ 2.2 Delegation of Home Rule Authority

Although local governments are creations of the states and it is generally accepted that they are totally dependent upon delegated power with no inherent sovereignty of their own,[1] a majority of states have recognized some right of their local governments to control their own affairs. This is a continuation of the history of a commitment to the right of self-government by local governments that existed in England before this country was formed.[2] The concept known as "home rule" refers to the right of a local government to determine for itself matters related to its local concerns or sometimes more specifically delineated as its local affairs, property and government. In its simplest expression, it is authority of the local government to act on its own behalf and a corresponding limitation on the state from interfering with solely local concerns. Today, it usually consists of an affirmative delegation of authority to local governments to do such things as adopt local legislation, hold elections for local officers, impose taxes to raise revenue to support its activities, to contract for services and supplies, to manage its property and to acquire property through the use of eminent domain. Although initially given only to cities, it has now been extended to other types of local governments. The states have made a variety of choices. Some have chosen to recognize home-rule authority in cities and villages, but not in all of their local governments. Others have adopted a very broad approach and have even given this authority to counties, thus enabling them to address regional concerns.

Home-rule authority also expressly or impliedly includes protection for the local government against state legislative or administrative action that may interfere with the exercise of its delegated authority to manage its local concerns. This grant of local authority does not limit the state's authority to address issues that are of state concern. The most important question often addresses what is local and what is state concern.[3]

---

[1] *See* § 1.4 *supra.*

[2] The most famous statement regarding this history is found in People *ex rel.* Metropolitan St. R.R. v. State Bd. of Tax Comm'rs, 67 N.E. 69, 70-71 (N.Y. 1903), *aff'd,* 199 U.S. 1 (1905) (The principle of home rule, or the right of self-government as to local affairs, existed before we had a constitution. Even prior to the Magna Charta some cities, boroughs and towns had various customs and liberties, which had been granted by the crown, or had subsisted through long use, and among them was the right to elect certain local officers from their own citizens, and, with some restrictions, to manage their own purely local affairs. These customs and liberties, with other rights, had been trampled upon by the King so often as to arouse deep hatred of centralization of power; and we find among the many grants of the Great Charter that 'the city of London shall have all its ancient liberties and its free customs as well by land as by water. Furthermore, we will and grant that all other cities and burghs and towns. . . shall have all their liberties and free customs.')

[3] For a discussion of this, *see* § 2.3 *infra.*

States vary in their expression and application of home rule to local governments. There are two basic types of constitutional home-rule grants. One, referred to as "imperium in imperio," is a broad provision which gives local governments authority over their local affairs. It is sometimes stated as authority to manage their property, affairs and government. Another form that has been recommended by local government organizations, and is not as widely adopted, is known as legislative home rule. In this form, the grant is broadly stated to be for all powers of self-governance that the legislature is able to delegate to the local government, unless they withdraw it or limit it by statute.

Home-rule authority granted in state constitutions may either be self-executing or require legislative enactments before local governments can claim it. In those states where local governments are deemed to have received authority directly from a state constitution that is self-executing, the power is generally viewed as quite broad and subject to only two limitations. The local exercise of authority must address local concerns and it must not conflict with the lawful exercise of state authority to enact state laws. In a state that has used an imperio delegation of authority to a local government to manage its property, affairs and government, a key question may address how to differentiate between local concerns and state concerns. This question should be less relevant in states that have delegated legislative home rule, since the intent is to give all authority possible to the local government, unless specifically limited by statute. Most often the distinction between local and state concern is important and the answer is left to the courts. Although their decisions vary, most do not find it difficult to justify a state concern. If a state legislative body has determined that legislation is necessary to address a problem, it is not easy for a co-equal branch of government to determine that, in fact, the problem is a local one that should only be dealt with at the local level.[4]

Where there is no self-executing home-rule provision in the state constitution, some states have delegated home-rule authority to their local governments by statute. There is an advantage to a local government in having a delegation of authority in the state constitution. The state legislatures cannot repeal or change this local authority in the normal course of their legislative activities. They must go through the more complicated process of amending their state constitution. However, home-rule authority is granted, in most instances it is usually broad and most local governments have been given sufficient power to manage their local concerns. The greater issue is whether it has been restricted by other state action.

The right to home rule is often reflected in a local government's charter, although some local governments which have been viewed traditionally as "arms of the state," and not considered true municipalities, do not have a charter. In some cases, home rule is appropriated by the local governments through the adoption of a charter, and in others, the legislative grant of

---

[4] The subject of state preemption of local action is discussed further in § 2.5 *infra*.

authority becomes the local charter. The term "charter" has been expansively defined by the courts to mean that document or general statute or body of laws that confers upon a local government the power to organize and function. Since it may initially be the fundamental act by which the local government was established, or one that has been adopted by it after its creation, there is tremendous variety in format and style among the local governments. However it came into existence, the charter is basic as it defines or limits local powers, as well as prescribing the framework of the local government. Even local governments in states that have self-executing home-rule provisions in their state constitutions will frequently have charters. Some home-rule charters are even used to impose limitations on the local government's exercise of power, particularly when state constitutions or statutes specify that the home-rule government will have all powers not prohibited by the charter.

Often, state constitutions or statutes give local governments the authority to adopt new charters or amend old ones for the purpose of addressing changing situations or merely improving their ability to serve their residents. This may be a very effective tool for shaping a government structure to fit a local government that has evolved over a period of time and has different needs than when it was first created. Local governments may also have the authority to adopt a new or amend an existing charter for the purpose of transferring functions and responsibilities between and among other local governments.[5]

Local charter provisions are recognized as law and have all the force and effect of legislative enactments. They are interpreted in almost the same way as statutes, gaining all the beneficial rules of statutory construction. They are presumed constitutional and valid. If there is a contradiction between a charter provision and a general law, the charter provision usually is preferred, under the rationale that it was written to specifically apply to a particular local government. However, if general statutes address an area that is not covered in a charter, then typically those provisions may be used to supplement the specific provisions of the charter, provided that they do not violate the local government's home-rule authority.

There are many additional specific constitutional and statutory grants of authority that local governments have been given. For instance, many local governments have been given the power to acquire utilities and engage in activities similar to private businesses.

§ 2.3 State Concerns and Local Concerns

Since home-rule authority is a delegation of power from the state to a local government to manage, control and provide for its local concerns, and never a delegation of authority to act with respect to state concerns, distinguishing and reconciling the interests at stake is important. This is easier said than done. Clearly, if a subject matter is of solely local concern,

---

[5] *See* N.Y. CONST., art. IX, § 1(h)(1).

the local government may act with respect to it, and most likely the state has been prohibited from acting since most grants of home-rule authority also contain a prohibition against state interference in local matters. Areas that are consistently deemed local and protected from state interference include the choice of form of government: council or commission; strong or weak executive; or a professional manager. The creation of local offices, boards or commissions and how they are to be filled, and how officers and employees are compensated, are generally local concerns. Of particular importance to local governments is their local interest in controlling the use and development of land, although this right is often shared with state requirements as well.

If a subject matter is considered solely of state concern, the local government cannot act because it has only been delegated authority to act with respect to local concerns. Examples of such areas that are usually reserved for state action may include criminal laws, divorce laws, establishment and regulation of the court system, and sometimes the regulation of alcohol and gambling. State concern usually extends to the regulation of local taxation and finances if needed to insure that local governments maintain fiscal integrity and viability. However, local governments have generally been given authority that permits the imposition of taxes and fees to support their activities. When exercising this authority, most jurisdictions view the actions taken as purely local in nature. The same is generally true of the power of eminent domain. Although the right to use this authority to effectuate a local purpose is delegated to the local government, controlling how it is to be exercised may be viewed as a state concern.

There are many areas, arguably belonging to both the state and local governments, that involve the general exercise of police powers to protect the health, welfare, safety and morality of citizens. Unless a specific limitation is in a state constitution, the state always has authority to protect its people by use of its police power. Most often, similar authority has also been delegated in home-rule grants to its local governments. Both the state and local governments may act to protect the health, welfare, safety and morals of its people. As Justice Cardozo recognized in his concurrence in New York's seminal home-rule case of *Adler v. Deegan*,[1] there is an "overlap" area, where there are both state and local concerns. When answering the question of which entity had the superior right to act, he rejected a balancing test whereby state and local concerns would be weighed to see which was the greater. Instead, he held that the question to be answered was whether there was a "substantial" state concern. If so, the state could act and any local action must not conflict or be inconsistent with the state's action. Although other state constitutional and statutory delegations of home-rule authority differ from the New York provisions he was interpreting, most jurisdictions have recognized that state concerns are very broad. What may seem like a "local" problem may very well have an effect on other individuals or areas of the state. If so, the state may be justified in addressing the issue.

---

[1] Adler v. Deegan, 170 N.E. 148 (N.Y. 1929).

State legislation that is directed toward the areas of public health, welfare, education, safety, morality, environmental protection, transportation and communication can usually be justified as areas of statewide concern. Although states differ in their interpretation of what is of state or local concern, or what is of concern to both, most jurisdictions have increasingly broad views of the state's interest in exercising its police powers to protect all people in the state. This category of state concern has generally expanded over time. It is a reflection of increasing public recognition of the interconnection of local problems that should be addressed on a regional or statewide basis. The effects of the health, welfare and safety conditions in one community are seldom limited to that geographical region alone.

If both state and local governments are authorized to act, and their actions are incompatible or in conflict, the question becomes one of state preemption. In this situation, it is not a question of whether a local government is exercising home-rule authority or not. If the state is acting within its authority, the question is whether it has indicated either expressly or impliedly that its intent is to preempt local action in that area. If it has, local governments are prohibited from acting. State preemption is discussed in § 2.5 *infra*.

§ 2.4   Implied Authority and *Dillon's Rule*

The basic source of authority for most local governments may be found in their charters. In addition, various other state statutes and constitutional provisions have increased and strengthened a local government's ability to respond to the needs of its inhabitants. The interpretation and definition of the power actually possessed by a local government has some seemingly contradictory principles. It is often said that powers of local governments are generally to be liberally construed. State constitutional grants of authority sometimes expressly state this[1] and courts have found it to be implied from general grants of home-rule authority. In addition, courts have found that when a local government has been given an express grant of authority, it can be inferred that the legislature desired to grant at the same time whatever incidental powers are reasonably necessary to carry out the permitted tasks.[2] Other expressions of this same view have included statements that local governments have essential or incidental powers that accompany specific grants. The determination of what is necessary or reasonable is subject to interpretation and differs from one court's opinion to another. However, the Supreme Court itself has held that powers can be implied only if they are essential to the objects and purposes of the local

---

[1] N.Y. CONST. art. IX § 3(c) (the rights, powers, privileges and immunities granted to local governments by this article shall be liberally construed).

[2] Penn-Dixie Cement Corp. v. City of Kingsport, 225 S.W.2d 270 (Tenn. 1949); Girves v. Kenai Peninsula Borough, 536 P.2d 1221 (Alaska 1975); New Jersey Good Humor v. Board of Comm'rs of Bradley Beach, 124 N.J.L. 162, 11 A.2d 113 (N.J. 1940); Commonwealth v. Reid, 265 Pa. 328, 108 A. 829 (Pa. 1919).

government.[3] Powers that have been deemed by courts to be essential or incidental are basic ones that include the right to sue and be sued,[4] the right to acquire property[5] and erect buildings,[6] and the right to remove local officers.[7]

On the other hand, there is another approach that may seem contradictory to a generous, broad interpretation of local powers. Many courts have regularly held that local governments have only those powers that have been expressly delegated to them.[8] This perspective has its genesis in an often-cited classic rule of interpretation known as *Dillon's Rule*.[9] It holds that local governments only have those powers which have been expressly given them, those which are necessarily or fairly implied by the expressly granted ones, and essential powers. In its application, courts seem to have resorted to this strict rule of interpretation when they seek to rein in local governments from exercising authority that is felt best left to the state or is of a private enterprise nature as opposed to a traditional governmental function.[10] However, the rule has been inconsistently applied and does not appear to have been a bar to, or to have slowed, the increasing judicial perspective that specific grants of local authority should be liberally interpreted by the courts. In particular, a delegation of police powers to protect the general welfare, health and education has been held to justify local activity aimed at improving the economic health of the community,[11] providing public utilities, providing parks and recreational facilities[12] and sponsoring cultural events.[13] Some states have rejected Dillon's rule by enacting provisions requiring that local powers be given a liberal interpretation.

Although there are other rules of interpretation that have been used to narrowly interpret implied powers of local governments, most court opinions are increasingly generous in their interpretation of local authority. This is consistent with the addition of provisions to state constitutions,[14] charters and statutory law stating that delegations of local authority should be liberally construed. There is recognition that local governments need

---

[3] City of Ottawa v. Carey, 108 U.S. 110 (1883).

[4] Barlow v. Friendship Heights Citizens' Comm., 344 A.2d 415 (Md. 1975); Prout v. Pittsfield Fire Dist., 28 N.E. 679 (Mass. 1891); City of Jonesborough v. McKee, 2 Tenn. (Yer.) 167 (1826); Racine Fire and Police Comm'n v. Stanfield, 234 N.W.2d 307 (Wisc. 1975).

[5] Cramton v. Cramton's Estate, 92 A. 814 (Vt. 1915).

[6] Drexler v. Comm'rs of Bethany Beach, 135 A. 484 (Del. Ch. 1926).

[7] Hawkins v. Common Council of Grand Rapids, 158 N.W. 953 (Mich. 1916); State v. Superior Court of Spokane Co., 279 P. 601 (Wash. 1929).

[8] Leischner v. Knight, 337 P.2d 359 (Mont. 1959).

[9] Dillon, MUNICIPAL CORPORATIONS, 1st Edition, § 55 (1872).

[10] Board of Sup'rs of Fairfax County v. Horne, 215 S.E.2d 453 (Va. 1975).

[11] Powell v. City & County of San Francisco, 144 P.2d 617 (Cal. Dist. Ct. App. 1944).

[12] State v. Village of North Palm Beach, 133 So. 2d 641 (Fla. 1961).

[13] McGuire v. City of Cincinnati, 40 N.E.2d 435 (Ohio Ct. App. 1941).

[14] N.Y. CONST., art. IX § 3(c).

flexibility in their ability to address the changing needs of their residents. Broadly delegated grants of authority serve this purpose.[15]

§ 2.5   State and Federal Preemption

Since the Federal Constitution provides that the exercise of authority delegated to the federal government is to be deemed the supreme law of the land, any local action is subject to federal preemption, just as is any state action. Many cases have decided that local government action has been preempted by federal law.[1] Preemption in such a situation occurs where a local enactment interferes with or is contrary to an authorized exercise of federal authority. The two key issues to consider are whether Congress has been given authority to act and whether Congress expressly or impliedly preempted the local government action.

The question of whether Congress has authority to act is considered in the context of the Tenth Amendment which provides that all powers not delegated in the Federal Constitution are reserved to the states. The Tenth Amendment has been interpreted to mean that the federal government may not exceed its lawfully delegated authority by regulating a local activity that is deemed to be within the province of state regulation. However, the federal authority that is typically in question is the Commerce Clause. Drawing the line between proper congressional use of its power and what is reserved to the states has not been easy and has resulted in many Supreme Court opinions that are decided by five justices in favor and four opposed. These cases demonstrate a sensitive concern to the sovereignty retained by the states in the Tenth Amendment and an often-competing concern that issues many times need a solution that crosses state borders.

The Supreme Court has held that Congress is permitted to regulate activities of state and local governments provided the necessary connection to commerce is met. The Court struck down federal regulation of the possession of firearms near schools, finding that Congress exceeded its Commerce Clause authority.[2] The Court held that in order to regulate an activity, it must "substantially affect" interstate commerce. The possession of a gun in a local school zone is not an economic activity that might, through repetition elsewhere, substantially affect interstate commerce. The Court's

---

[15] State v. Hutchinson, 624 P.2d 1116 (Utah 1980).

[1] *See* Consolidated Rail Corp. v. Smith, 664 F. Supp. 1228 (N.D. Ind. 1987) and City of Covington v. Chesapeake & Ohio Ry., 708 F. Supp. 806, 808 (E.D. Ky. 1989) (holding that the Federal Railroad Safety Act of 1970 preempted the imposition of local limits on the speed of trains); Vango Media, Inc. v. City of New York, 34 F.3d 68, 75 (2d Cir. 1994) (providing that Federal law preempts local requirement that permit holders who display cigarettes also display anti-smoking messages); City of New York v. FCC, 486 U.S. 57, 66–67 (1988) (declaring that it was within the FCC's authority to preempt local technical standards for cable television); Golden State Transit Corp. v. City of Los Angeles, 475 U.S. 608 (1986) (stating that the NLRA prevents local governments from imposing restrictions on certain economic weapons of self-help); Environmental Encapsulating Corp. v. City of New York, 855 F.2d 48 (2d Cir. 1988) (certain training requirements were preempted).

[2] United States v. Lopez, 514 U.S. 549 (1995).

concern was that to require less than a substantial impact would tend to convert Congressional authority to a general police power, thus leading to a conclusion that there can never be a distinction between what is truly national and what is truly local.[3] In contrast, Congressional restriction of the disclosure of drivers' information by the states was found to be within their authority under the Commerce Clause since the information is used in interstate commerce.[4]

Assuming that the federal government has the authority to act, the issue becomes whether or not the federal act does in fact preempt state and local action. If Congress specifically addressed the issue and declares its intent in the statute, as it has in the Federal Telecommunications Act of 1996, the answer is easy. The Supremacy Clause establishes that the federal act takes precedence. However, if there is no mention of preemption in the federal statute, then the question becomes whether or not Congress implied preemption when it adopted the statute. If there is a conflict between the local action and the federal enactment, then clearly there is an implied preemption. If not, the courts look at the federal action and if they find that the comprehensive nature of the regulation leaves no room for state or local action, or the subject matter is one that is more conducive to federal regulation, they may find that there is implied preemption. If so, the state and local governments are precluded from acting with respect to that area of concern.

Unless prohibited by the state constitution, the state may similarly preempt local government action, even though a local government has been given a grant of home-rule authority to act with respect to local concerns. As explained in § 2.3 *supra*, the grant of local authority does not diminish the state's sovereign right to act in areas that are deemed to be of state concern. If a state adopts legislation that addresses such an area, and it is rationally related to its interest in protecting the health, welfare, safety, or morality of its people, it is within its authority to either expressly or impliedly preempt all local action in that field.[5]

---

[3] The Supreme Court reaffirmed its *Lopez* holdings in United States v. Morrison, 529 U.S. 598 (2000), *aff'g* Brzonkala v. Virginia Polytechnic and State Univ., 169 F.3d 820 (4th Cir 1999). (Congress had provided that a person who commits a gender-motivated crime of violence shall be liable to the party injured for compensatory and punitive damages, injunctive and declaratory relief, and such other relief that the court deems appropriate. The Court found that the rationale that the gender-motivated violence affects interstate commerce "by deterring potential victims" from traveling interstate, etc., was unacceptable.) *Id.* at 615. (Reasoning that the "but-for causal chain" can lead to every attenuated effect, and this reasoning would allow Congress to regulate any crime with the same type of impact in other areas of traditional state regulation).

[4] Reno v. Condon, 528 U.S. 141 (2000).

[5] If home rule authority has been delegated to a local government by a state statute, the state may preempt at will. If home rule authority was given by an imperio delegation, the state will only be restrained from preempting the local government if it acts with respect to a solely local concern. In a legislative home rule state, the state may expressly limit its delegation of authority by statute. For a discussion of the different types of state delegation of home rule authority, *see* § 2.2 *supra*.

In the cases where the state expressly indicates its intent to preempt local action, the courts have a relatively easy time finding preemption, but such cases are rare. Most often, the question raised is whether there is an implied preemption. The courts find implied preemption when there is evidence of a legislative intent to preempt. This is present if the legislation is deemed to be so comprehensive that it occupies the entire field, leaving no room for local regulation. Implied preemption may also be found where the subject matter of the legislation is one that needs a uniform system of regulation and any local regulation would interfere with this purpose.

Even if there is no intent to totally preempt all local action, any local action that is inconsistent with the state legislation is void.

PART II EXERCISE OF LOCAL AUTHORITY— LIMITATIONS AND REQUIREMENTS

§ 2.6 Local Governing Body and Local Enactments

Local legislative functions are exercised by local government bodies, whether called boards, councils, juries, or commissions, or directly by vote of the people as in the New England town government. They can use all of the home rule, statutory or charter authority delegated to the local government to meet the needs of their inhabitants, provided it is done in a manner that meets all constitutional and statutory requirements and is consistent with any limitations that have been imposed by federal or state law.

State constitutions, statutes, or charters usually provide the qualifications for membership in legislative bodies. Typically there will be reasonable residency requirements,[1] oath requirements, and possibly the requirement that a bond be posted. Holding multiple public offices is often prohibited, especially if they are deemed incompatible. At times, courts have recognized that one person cannot perform both jobs or the offices are inconsistent for some reason.[2] Compensation for legislators is usually specified in statutes, with increases or decreases in the amount often prohibited during a person's term of office.

The exercise of legislative authority must be done at a lawfully-called meeting of the governing body. Local government business may not be conducted at informal gatherings. Typically, if regular meetings have been specified in statutes or charters, no special notice must be given. However, for special meetings, it is generally required that adequate notice, including the time, place, and agenda must be given to all members. Failure to give such notice may be deemed waived if all members appear and participate. Notice to the public is also generally required, in order to comply with state

---

[1] Daves v. City of Longwood, 423 F. Supp. 503 (M.D. Fla. 1976) (holding that one year was reasonable). *But see* Bd. of Comm'rs. v. Gustafson, 616 So. 2d 1165 (Fla. Dist. Ct. App. 1993) (stating that the two-year requirement violates Equal Protection Clause).

[2] State *ex. rel.* Petka v. Bingle, 445 N.E.2d 941 (Ill. App. Ct. 1983).

open-meeting laws.[3] Unless specified otherwise, a simple majority of the full membership usually constitutes a quorum and action may be taken if a simple majority of those voting register favorable votes. Often state statutes and local charters specify that certain actions require a larger quorum or number of votes. Procedural requirements for the enactment of local legislation may be adopted by the local legislative body, if not specified in state constitutions, statutes or charters.

Local action may take the form of a resolution, motion, order, ordinance, or local law. States vary in their terminology and in what each means. Requirements governing what may be done, and in what manner, are found in state constitutions, statutes, and charters. Generally, resolutions (which are similar to motions) are expressions of the opinion, sense, feelings, or will of the legislative body, adopted by a vote.[4] They are adopted with less formality than other local actions and are generally of a temporal nature. In contrast with resolutions, ordinances (or local laws) are used to establish permanent rules of government, not merely to express the sentiments of the local legislature. They accomplish local purposes such as affecting the future conduct of people or creating new offices. Typically, the greater formality required for an ordinance is reflected in its contents, which may include a title, preamble, ordaining clause and purview (the substance of the local law). Ordinances and local laws are exercises in substantive legislation, whereas resolutions typically relate to administrative or ministerial matters.

§ 2.7   Federal and State Constitutional Requirements

Individuals of all states are protected against intrusive local government action by the Bill of Rights in the Federal Constitution. Those rights, viewed by all as basic liberties, are protected in the same manner as they are against unconstitutional state or federal infringement. When the Fourteenth Amendment made these guarantees of personal liberty applicable to the states,[1] they were applied with equal force to the local governments. For this reason, a local government cannot delegate uncontrolled discretion to a board or official to regulate activities affecting an individual's exercise of a First Amendment right of religion, speech, press, assembly or association.[2] Nor has the Supreme Court readily permitted the imposition of flat fees which are unrelated to the expense of regulation upon those desiring to exercise their First Amendment rights.[3]

---

[3] *See* § 7.3 *infra* for a discussion of Open Meeting Laws.

[4] Shaw v. City of WaKeeney, 356 P.2d 832 (Kan. 1960); Int'l Ass'n of Firefighters v. City of Lawrence, 798 P.2d 960 (Kan. Ct. App. 1990).

[1] U.S. CONST. amend. XIV, § 1 provides: ". . . No State shall make or enforce any law which shall abridge the privileges or immunities of citizens of the United States; nor shall any State deprive any person of life, liberty, or property, without due process of law; nor deny to any person within its jurisdiction the equal protection of the laws."

[2] City of Lakewood v. Plain Dealer Publ'g Co., 486 U.S. 750 (1988).

[3] Murdock v. Pennsylvania, 319 U.S. 105 (1943).

Identical or similar provisions guaranteeing individual freedoms are also found in the various state constitutions.[4] These, even though worded exactly the same, may at times be interpreted by a state court to provide even greater protections than the federal right. Since the highest state court is responsible for interpreting its own state constitution, many have decided that theirs requires a stricter standard of conduct by government officials than is required by the Supreme Court's interpretation of the Federal Constitution. Therefore, an individual may never be given less rights than those afforded in the Federal Constitution, but he or she may have greater protection of individual liberties under the state constitution.

The Due Process Clause of the Fourteenth Amendment requires that the exercise of local police powers be reasonable and reasonably related to the public health, safety, morals or general welfare.[5] Although local governments generally have wide discretion in the regulation of businesses, the authority to prohibit a legitimate business is limited. If it does not tend to injure the public health, safety, morals or welfare, it may not be prohibited or made unlawful by the local government under the exercise of the general police power.

There is a presumption that a local government's exercise of its delegated authority to regulate or legislate is constitutionally sound and that it has acted in a reasonable manner. The burden is on those challenging local action to show that it is not. However, where the action is not applicable to all people of a particular class or involves individual liberties protected by the First and Fourteenth Amendments, there is no presumption of constitutionality. The courts use a higher standard of review, requiring that this kind of regulation be narrowly and explicitly drawn. It also must be shown that it is necessary to further a legitimate government interest.[6]

The Equal Protection Clause of the Fourteenth Amendment prohibits local government action that on its face creates unreasonable classifications of people or groups, or provides for unreasonable disparate treatment. A classification must be rationally related to its public purpose and not discriminate in an unjustified manner. A local requirement which discriminates against one form of activity which has no greater relation to the harm sought to be controlled than do other activities will be found to be unreasonable and unconstitutional. For instance, the New Jersey Court has held that it would be unconstitutional to ban storage garages from a zone while permitting private garages.[7] The California Court held that it was arbitrary

---

[4] Begin v. Inhabitants of Sabattus, 409 A.2d 1269 (Me. 1979) (concluding that a limitation on the number of permits which can be issued per mobile home park is arbitrary and discriminatory and violates the equal protection clauses of the State constitution and Fourteenth Amendment).

[5] Rapid City v. Schmitt, 71 N.W.2d 297, 298 (1955) (providing that a requirement that plumbing installation licenses can only be issued to plumbing contractors has no real and substantial relation to the public health, safety or morality or the general welfare).

[6] People v. Glaze, 614 P.2d 291 (Cal. 1980).

[7] Roselle v. Wright, 122 A.2d 506 (N.J. 1956).

discrimination against private schools to forbid their presence in a zone where public schools were permitted.[8] Where there are good reasons for distinguishing between entities or individuals, equal protection is not violated.[9] Motels may be excluded from a residential zone even though boarding and rooming houses were permitted.[10] A requirement that licenses be obtained for electrical contractors in general but exempting those working for utilities and manufacturing concerns is reasonable.[11] The Equal Protection Clause also protects against the enforcement of a government regulation that may be reasonable on its face but is applied in a discriminatory and unreasonable manner. In one case, a court granted relief to plaintiffs who alleged that the local government had treated them adversely compared to others because of an "illegitimate animus."[12]

The Due Process Clauses of the federal and state constitutions impose requirements of clarity in drafting local enactments, rules and regulations.[13] It is often held that local enactments must meet a standard of certainty and definiteness. The person of average intelligence and understanding who reads them must be able to know that conduct which is acceptable and that which is not. Such local restrictions and requirements must be explicit as to whom they apply and what obligations are imposed.[14] They must contain adequate standards, thus not leaving to the whim of local officials the decision of who is denied or permitted the opportunity to engage in regulated activities.[15]

In addition to protecting individual liberties by restraining unlawful government conduct, the Fourteenth Amendment of the Federal Constitution also gives Congress the authority to take remedial action to assure that all people are given due process and equal protection rights.[16] This is the source of power for many federal statutes used to protect basic civil rights such as the right to be free from unlawful discrimination[17] and the right to vote.[18] These statutes, lawfully enacted pursuant to Congress' authority, are applicable to actions taken by the state and local governments. Although Congress is prohibited by the Eleventh Amendment[19] from

---

[8] Roman Catholic Welfare Corp. v. City of Piedmont, 289 P.2d 438 (Cal. 1955).

[9] State *ex rel.* Namer Inv. Corp. v. Williams, 435 P.2d 975 (Wash. 1968).

[10] Pierro v. Baxendale, 118 A.2d 401 (N.J. 1955).

[11] Hughes v. Bd. of Comm'rs of Chattanooga, 319 S.W.2d 481 (Tenn. 1958).

[12] Olech v. Village of Willowbrook, 160 F.3d 386 (7th Cir. 1998). *See also* 528 U.S. 562 (2000). The Supreme Court affirmed Olech, holding that the Equal Protection Clause may provide a remedy for a "class of one" where there are no other members of a class or group.

[13] Barker Bros. v. City of Los Angeles, 76 P.2d 97 (Cal. 1938).

[14] *Id.* at 99.

[15] Hague v. Committee for Indus. Org., 307 U.S. 496 (1939).

[16] U.S. CONST., art. XIV, § 5: "The Congress shall have power to enforce, by appropriate legislation, the provisions of this article."

[17] *See* § 3.8 *infra.*

[18] *See* § 7.06 *infra.*

[19] This amendment provides that the judicial power of the United States shall not be construed to extend to any suit in law or equity against a State if brought by citizens of another State or subjects of any foreign State. This was interpreted to include a limitation on Congress to provide for private law suits against States in both federal and state courts.

providing a judicial remedy to an individual who wants compensation for the infringement of civil liberties by a state,[20] it may provide such a remedy against a local government. The Civil Rights Acts, and specifically Section 1983, have been used by many individuals to obtain compensation from local governments for civil rights violations.[21] Chapter 9 discusses constitutional and civil rights claims.

§ 2.8   Delegation of Authority to Officers and Administrative Agencies

Since a local government acts through its officers and employees, at times it is necessary to delegate authority to various individuals, boards or commissions. However, not all authority may be delegated. Often, the state constitution, statute or charter establishing the local government may expressly or impliedly prohibit the delegation of some responsibilities, such as the right to tax. Local officers may participate in the process but the actual tax levy must be imposed by the local governing board.

No government, whether federal, state or local, may delegate its authority to legislate and establish public policy. However, governments may delegate the responsibility of carrying through on the implementation of established policy to officers, boards, and commissions. It is critical that the legislative body provide sufficient and clear guidance to the administrative body so that it does not engage in any form of legislating. There have been many delegations of functions from local governing boards to administrators or administrative boards that have been declared unconstitutional by the courts because there were inadequate standards or guidelines to direct the local administrators.[1] Some jurisdictions have distinguished between what is and what is not appropriately delegated by explaining that ministerial functions may be assigned to local officers and boards but discretionary functions are the sole responsibility of the local legislators.[2] For instance, a local enactment conditioning permits upon a conclusion by a city official that an applicant was "fit and responsible" was held to be an improper delegation of authority.[3] It vested too much discretion in the local officer.

If there are reasonably adequate standards to guide and circumscribe the exercise of its discretion, then a great deal of flexibility in administering the tasks may rest with the local officer or agency. They have been permitted to develop rules and regulations binding upon the citizenry, ascertain facts, and determine whether to issue or withhold variances, permits and certificates. For instance, local boards or commissions may be

---

[20] *See* Alden v. Maine, 527 U.S. 706 (1999).

[21] *See* § 9.6 *infra.*

[1] Gaudiya Vaishnava Society v. City of San Francisco, 952 F.2d 1059 (9th Cir. 1990), *cert. denied,* 504 U.S. 914 (1992).

[2] Brookpark Entertainment, Inc. v. Taft, 951 F.2d 710 (6th Cir. 1991).

[3] Hoyt Bros. v. City of Grand Rapids, 245 N.W. 509 (Mich. 1932).

charged with investigation of the character or skills of an applicant for a license and with reporting this to the governing body.[4]

Any person appearing before a local government body is entitled to an impartial process. Members of local government boards, commissions or committees must not have an interest in any way, direct or indirect, in the outcome. Members with a personal or pecuniary interest are generally expected or required to recuse themselves from any decision-making process. It is not necessary to establish that the member actually exercised bias, since the mere appearance of unfairness is a sufficient basis upon which to challenge the ultimate determination. However, where there is only indirect, remote or minimal interest, some courts have upheld the administrative action.

The nature of the action being performed by the local administrative body may be viewed as either quasi-legislative or adjudicatory. This determination often affects the due process requirements that attach to it. Although courts have disagreed on whether due process requires that a public hearing be held before final administrative action is taken, it is often required by statute, charter or local legislation. Due process does require that if they are to be held, adequate notice be given before hearings take place. There may be other Constitutional requirements, depending on the type of action that is being taken. For instance, the Supreme Court has required that a local license that implicates First Amendment rights must be issued within a reasonable time.[5]

In adjudicatory proceedings, it has been held that due process requires that there be an opportunity for the parties involved to produce evidence, have an opportunity to learn the facts, to cross-examine witnesses and to offer rebuttal evidence.[6] For instance, the Supreme Court has determined that a welfare board may not terminate benefits without procedural due process which includes notice, hearing and representation by counsel.[7] It has been held by some courts that local administrative bodies must develop findings of facts and conclusions of law, with written explanation for their decision.[8] This is necessary so reviewing courts can determine if the reasons given were supported by the evidence, and thus that the decision reached is one that is justified. In contrast, quasi-legislative proceedings, where a board or committee may be developing rules and regulations, may require less procedural due process safeguards.

Often it is not easy to classify the type of administrative process that is being performed. For example, zoning decisions may be difficult to characterize.

---

[4] Hughes v. City of Detroit, 187 N.W. 530 (Mich. 1922).

[5] FW/PBS, Inc. v. City of Dallas, 493 U.S. 215 (1990).

[6] County of Fairfax v. Southern Iron Works, Inc., 410 S.E.2d 674 (Va. 1991).

[7] Goldberg v. Kelly, 397 U.S. 254 (1970).

[8] Parkridge v. City of Seattle, 573 P.2d 359 (Wash. 1978).

Chapter 3

Regulation by Local Governments

§ 3.1   Introduction and Chapter Overview

Most states have delegated broad authority to local governments to exercise the police power to protect the health, welfare and safety of their residents. In addition to basic concerns that both levels of government share, local governments are able to use this authority to specifically address local needs. The state may have chosen not to act in a given area, or it may not have regulated to the extent thought necessary by the local government. Some concerns are of a local nature and do not rise to the level of state concern.

The sources for the delegation of general police power authority include state constitutions, statutes and local charters. These provisions often contain limitations which expressly or impliedly permit state preemption. The converse is also true. Some provisions limit the ability of the state or the form in which it can preempt the local exercise of police power authority. For instance, the state may be permitted to preempt by the adoption of a general law which applies to all local governments of a particular type, as opposed to a special law which applies to fewer than all of a particular type.

A local government exercises its regulatory power by adopting local legislation or rules and regulations that govern the conduct of those who live or engage in business within the community. Exercise of regulatory power is valid if the local government has been given authority to act and the method chosen meets federal and state constitutional requirements. Areas that many local governments have chosen to regulate include businesses that may affect people adversely, including those which involve adult-use activities, the use of alcohol, tobacco or firearms, and the speech and movement of individuals as it affects others within the community. This chapter examines some of the areas that local governments seek to regulate.

When the local government exercises its police power, the enactment has a presumption of constitutionality. Anyone challenging it has the burden of rebutting this presumption. The courts presume that there is a rational basis for the local regulation and it must be shown that there is none. An exception to this general rule is when the local enactment impinges upon basic personal freedoms protected by the federal constitution.

The federal and state constitutions require that when a local government drafts a regulation it must be clear and unambiguous. Many local enactments have been found void under federal and state constitutions because they are vague. Due process requires that the basis for a local regulation be the protection of the health, welfare and safety of the people within the community. It also demands that any regulation be narrowly drawn to accomplish its legitimate purpose. Local enactments that are broader than necessary will be void. If a regulation deprives an individual of any property interest, procedural safeguards are also required.

Local governments generally have authority to require local licenses and permits in their exercise of delegated police power authority. They are generally not permitted to prohibit a business or occupation that does not injure the public health or welfare.[1] Nor can they impose conditions or requirements that constitute regulatory takings of property. In such a case, the local government may be restrained from imposing the restriction or required to pay just compensation.[2] A fee may be imposed for the license or permit, provided that it is reasonably related to the cost of licensing, inspecting and regulating. A local government cannot use fees as a means of raising revenue.

PART I GENERAL EXERCISE OF POLICE POWER

§ 3.2 Nuisances

The right to ban and ultimately abate a public nuisance is one of the most basic, longstanding exercises of local police power. This governmental remedy is a pillar of home-rule authority, providing to local governments the right to act in a manner designed to protect a community's health, safety and welfare from a multitude of harms. A public nuisance, recognized in the earliest of common law, is broadly defined as something that adversely affects rights that are enjoyed by citizens as members of the public.[1] It is to be distinguished from a private nuisance which is something that affects a single individual or a small number of persons in the enjoyment of private rights not common to the public.[2] The authority to ban and abate a public nuisance is often specifically delegated to local governments in a state constitution,[3] statute or charter provision.[4]

There are two types of public nuisances. A *nuisance per se* is something which is always undesirable. Examples are piles of rotting garbage, unsafe buildings in danger of collapsing, and decaying dead animals. Each of these threaten the health, welfare and safety of citizens in the community. A *nuisance in fact* is something that is not always a nuisance, but has become one because of its location.[5] A pig farm is not a nuisance per se, but if it

---

[1] Delight Wholesale Co. v. City of Prairie Village, 491 P.2d 910 (Kan. 1971).

[2] Regulatory takings are discussed in § 4.5 *infra*.

[1] Spur Industries, Inc. v. Del E. Webb Development Co., 494 P.2d 700 (Ariz. 1972).

[2] *Id.*

[3] OHIO CONST. art. XVIII, § 3 provides "Municipalities shall have authority to exercise all powers of local self-government and to adopt and enforce within their limits such local police, sanitary and other similar regulations, as are not in conflict with general laws."

[4] California: CAL. CIV. CODE § 3479 (1997); Georgia: GA. CODE ANN. § 41-1-1 (2002); Arizona: ARIZ. REV. STAT. § 36-601(A)(1).

[5] Armory Park Neighborhood Ass'n. v. Episcopal Com. Servs., 712 P.2d 914 (Ariz. 1985).

is located in a residential setting, it may become a nuisance in fact. It does not matter that a structure or activity was erected or begun in compliance with all statutes and local enactments in effect at the time.[6] Nor does it matter that others, for the time being, are permitted to continue equally dangerous or obnoxious activities.[7] One of the greatest strengths of this remedy is its flexibility. It has been applied to many varied situations.

Local governments are typically found to have delegated authority to address nuisances within their boundaries. Occasionally, one may be given authority to prohibit and abate public nuisances outside its boundaries but near enough to cause harm.[8] Local governments have been given a great deal of latitude to determine what activity, condition or structure may be a public nuisance within their community.[9] They may declare and regulate both nuisances *per se* or *in fact* and have been given substantial judicial deference to their determination. However, courts require that there be a real and substantial relationship between the declared public nuisance and the public health, safety and general welfare. Any unreasonable or arbitrary classification or regulation of something as a public nuisance will not be permitted.[10]

Local governments may abate public nuisances in order to protect the public health, welfare and safety. This includes the destruction of structures that are fire hazards.[11] If there are proceedings specified for local government abatement, these must be strictly followed. If there are no specified procedures, due process usually requires that when there is no emergency, an owner must be given reasonable notice and a reasonable opportunity to repair the property. There is no state or constitutional violation if after notice and hearing a local government demolishes an unrepaired nuisance.[12] The authority to abate public nuisances is usually limited to the least drastic means. This power must be used in a reasonable manner, avoiding unnecessary property damage.[13] The abatement does not entitle the owner of the property to compensation and he or she can be compelled to pay for the cost of the abatement.[14] In some cases, the local government may claim a lien for the costs it incurred.[15]

If a local government destroys property that is not a nuisance, it must pay the owner damages for the unlawful destruction. The local government may also be liable for damages if it disregards statutory procedures or denies the due process rights of the owner before the destruction. For these

[6] Knapp v. City of Newport Beach, 186 Cal. App. 2d 669 (1960).
[7] Midwest Inv. Co. v. City of Chariton, 80 N.W.2d 906 (Iowa 1957).
[8] *See* V.T.C.A. LOCAL GOVERNMENT CODE § 217.042.
[9] City of Corsicana v. Wilson, 249 S.W.2d 290 (Tex. Civ. App. 1952).
[10] City of Nokomis v. Sullivan, 153 N.E.2d 48 (Ill. 1958).
[11] Eno v. City of Burlington, 209 A.2d 499 (Vt. 1965).
[12] Traylor v. City of Amarillo, 492 F.2d 1156 (5th Cir. 1974).
[13] Welton v. City of Los Angeles, 556 P.2d 1119 (Cal. 1976).
[14] Lane v. City of Mount Vernon, 342 N.E.2d 571 (N.Y. 1976).
[15] *Id.* at 574.

reasons, local governments are usually authorized to appeal to the courts. They may seek a declaration that a particular building is a nuisance and an order for demolition. An equitable action to enjoin the continuation of a public nuisance is another remedy that may be sought.

It should also be noted that local governments themselves may be liable for the creation or maintenance of a nuisance.[16]

§ 3.3 Business Regulation

Although state regulation preempts a good deal of business regulation in most states, there is still room for local governments to exercise their police powers in this field. Most often, the delegated authority used to justify local regulation is the broad grant of police power given to local governments so that they can regulate to protect the public health, safety, morals and welfare of the community.

Local governments have used this authority to impose numerous regulations and permit or license requirements on many different kinds of business activities. They have sought to protect their citizens from fraudulent behavior by regulating pawnbrokers and used car dealerships, and from health problems by regulating restaurants and food vendors. They have imposed rent controls, required fences to block out unpleasant views of junkyards, and required that peddlers obtain licenses. The spectrum of local business regulation is vast.

When local governments regulate, the courts require that the local authority must be used reasonably, with a direct connection between the regulation and its public purpose. In addition, the regulation must meet any due process or equal protection requirement of the federal or state constitution. This means that those who are subject to the regulation must be afforded their due process rights, both substantively and procedurally. Their property may not be taken without just compensation and they must be afforded all procedural due process rights. Equal protection rights demand that any classifications created by the local regulation must be reasonable and supported by a rational basis. A discussion of local authority to require a license or a permit for business activities is found in § 3.9 and the regulation of adult use businesses is discussed in § 3.4 *infra*.

Protection of public health has justified local regulation of many different kinds of businesses, often including restaurants, food stores, vendors, and dairy facilities. The kinds of regulatory efforts have varied from licensing, requiring inspections of kitchens, to specifying the kind of room in which food may be manufactured.[1] Assuming that there has been a broad delegation of police power and the regulation is not preempted by federal or state law, the local government has a large field of possibilities, provided it acts reasonably and meets all constitutional requirements.

---

[16] *See* § 9.4 *infra.*

[1] S.H. Kress & Co. v. Dept of Health, City of New York, 27 N.E.2d 431 (N.Y. 1940).

Local requirements that businesses close on Sunday have been sustained as reasonably related to public health and welfare.[2] If the stated purpose is to provide a uniform day of rest, the mere fact that it is Sunday does not implicate the Establishment Clause of the First Amendment. As noted by the Supreme Court, the Clause does not ban regulation of conduct whose reason or effect merely happens to coincide with the tenets of some religions.[3] However, if some activities are permitted while others are restricted, classifications must be reasonable and reasonably related to the purpose sought to be achieved. Targeting some types of businesses, and not others, has led to invalidation on equal protection grounds because the classifications are not supported by a rational basis.[4] Local regulation of business hours has been troublesome to the courts. Often the presence of exceptions for some groups or particular businesses has led to invalidation.[5] However, if a local enactment is justified with a legitimate local purpose, such as noise control or crime prevention, and is reasonable and nondiscriminatory, it will probably be sustained.

Quite frequently, local governments will adopt regulations that are aimed at protecting local consumers. Regulation of used car dealers has been upheld by the courts, which have found that there is a real and substantial difference between used and new car dealers.[6] Gas stations may be regulated by local governments, justified by the dangerous nature of gasoline. Realtors, if their regulation is not preempted by state action, may also be regulated under a local government's police powers. Local enactments regulating peddlers, where they are narrowly drawn to achieve a defined public purpose, have been sustained by the courts. Attempts to regulate vendors on public streets has met with mixed success. The more successful regulations are those that limit vendors to specified times and places. They are sustained if based on legitimate concerns of public safety and convenience, such as preventing the obstruction of a public way or preventing the creation of a nuisance that may harm the public. Local regulation of solicitors and canvassers has been sustained under the usual test of reasonableness and can include registration and licensing requirements if the standards are clearly stated. If a reasonable fee is imposed, it must not discriminate against or unduly burden interstate commerce.[7] The Supreme Court has reaffirmed the right of local governments to enforce reasonable regulation of door-to-door solicitations to protect citizens from crime and undue annoyance, provided the regulation is narrowly drawn and does not give local officials the undefined power to control the messages

---

[2] Home Depot, Inc. v. Guste, 773 F.2d 616 (5th Cir. 1985).

[3] McGowan v. Maryland, 366 U.S. 420 (1961); Braunfeld v. Brown, 366 U.S. 599 (1961), *reh. denied,* 368 U.S. 869.

[4] People v. Abrahams, 353 N.E.2d 574 (N.Y. 1976).

[5] *Ex parte* Harrell, 79 So. 166 (Fla. 1918).

[6] Aero Motors, Inc. v. Motor Vehicles Admin., 337 A.2d 685 (Md. 1975).

[7] Real Silk Hosiery v. City of Portland, 268 U.S. 325 (1925); Village of Bel-Nor v. Barnett, 358 S.W.2d 832 (Mont. 1962).

residents will hear.[8] The issue of access to public areas and First Amendment Speech concerns is discussed in § 3.6 *infra*.

Local governments have been successful in attempts to regulate amusement arcades, and in particular their use by minors. Courts have sustained such enactments when shown to have an appropriate purpose of protecting the general welfare of minors and the safety of the general public.[9] However, a local enactment, designed to protect minors from the harmful effects of graphic violence in video games by restricting the display and operation of coin-operated amusement machines that include either "strong sexual content" or "graphic violence," was not allowed because of a failure to show a compelling basis for thinking that it would cause harm.[10]

Local regulation of gambling or games of chance is very intertwined with state preemption issues. However, many times a local enactment providing for greater restrictions related to the local welfare is acceptable. Whatever local action is desired, it must be based on local authority to act and the absence of state preemption, and must not conflict with legitimate state action. Some local governments have been sustained in banning some forms of gambling provided they were not specifically permitted by state law.

§ 3.4 Adult Uses

Local regulation of various forms of activity involving adult uses has perhaps been one of the most challenging areas for local governments. It presents questions of First Amendment speech protections as applied to various business activities such as bookstores, theaters for film performances, and venues for live performances. Adding to the difficulty in balancing free-speech concerns with community concerns is the lack of precision in defining what constitutes obscenity and indecent or lewd behavior. The Supreme Court has said that in order to regulate, an offense must be limited to works which, taken as a whole, appeal to the prurient interest in sex; which portray sexual conduct in a patently offensive way; and which, taken as a whole, do not have serious literary, artistic, political or scientific value.[1] The measuring stick is to be the prevailing standards of the local adult community. Local governments can prohibit the possession for sale and sale of obscene publications, if done in a constitutionally acceptable manner.

---

[8] Haynes v. Mayor and Council of Borough of Oradell, 425 U.S. 610 (1976).

[9] Aladdin's Castle, Inc. v. Village of N. Riverside, 383 N.E.2d 1316 (Ill. App. Ct. 1978) (holding that a local enactment, banning the use of coin-operated amusements by minors, was a legitimate use of police power to promote the general welfare of minors and the safety of the public by reducing juvenile delinquency). *See also* People v. Walker, 354 N.W.2d 312 (Mich. Ct. App. 1984) (upholding local prohibition of video games to minors based on evidence of juvenile crime associated with coin-operated games).

[10] American Amusement Machine Ass'n v. Kendrick, 244 F.3d 572 (7th Cir. 2001).

[1] Miller v. California, 413 U.S. 15 (1973), *reh'g denied,* 414 U.S. 881 (1973); Roth v. United States, 354 U.S. 476 (1957), *reh'g denied,* 355 U.S. 852 (1957).

The question of what is obscene for minors may vary from the adult standard. In determining what is obscene for minors, the Supreme Court indicates that the trier of fact is to consider the manner in which the publication is exploited and sold.[2] A publication will be obscene when it has a predominant appeal to the prurient interests of minors and is patently offensive to prevailing standards of the local adult community view of what is suitable material for minors, and when it is utterly without redeeming social importance to minors.[3] In any event, the Court has also determined that a local government cannot keep books or films unsuitable for youth from adults.[4] The Supreme Court has also held that pornography involving children[5] may be regulated since it is not protected by the First Amendment.

Local governments that have sought to impose reasonable time, place, and manner restrictions on adult activities have received support from the courts. It has been held that although such restrictions are not content neutral, because they regulate speech based on the ideas or messages expressed, government has more freedom to regulate this kind of speech. In other words, sexually explicit materials that border on the obscene are entitled to less First Amendment protection than non-sexually explicit material.[6] Local enactments limiting the operation of adult entertainment businesses have been similarly upheld.[7]

Some local governments have sought to impose licensing requirements on adult businesses. In cases challenging this, the Supreme Court has required clarity in the local enactments, finding that vagueness is particularly unacceptable where expression is subjected to licensing. It also has not permitted the delegation to officers or agencies of local government unbridled discretion in the decision-making process.[8] Additionally, there must be adequate procedural safeguards such as reasonable time limits for the local decision to be made and a means of prompt judicial review of denials.[9]

Local governments have been particularly concerned about the regulation of live adult entertainment. The Supreme Court has said that the First Amendment does not prevent the adoption and enforcement of public

---

[2] Splawn v. California, 431 U.S. 595 (1977).

[3] Ginsberg v. New York, 390 U.S. 629 (1968), *reh'g denied,* 391 U.S. 971 (1968).

[4] Butler v. Michigan, 352 U.S. 380 (1957).

[5] Defined as descriptions or depiction of sexual conduct involving live performance, or photographic or other visual reproduction of live performances.

[6] DiMa Corp. v. Town of Hallie, 185 F.3d 823 (7th Cir. 1999).

[7] Schultz v. City of Cumberland, 228 F.3d 831 (7th Cir. 2000).

[8] Bantam Books, Inc. v. Sullivan, 372 U.S. 58 (1963).

[9] FW/PBS, Inc. v. City of Dallas, 493 U.S. 215 (1990). *See also* Baby Tam & Co., Inc. v. City of Las Vegas, 154 F.3d 1097 (9th Cir. 1998); Baby Tam & Co., Inc. v. City of Las Vegas, 199 F.3d 1111 (9th Cir. 2000); Boss Capital, Inc. v. City of Casselberry, 187 F.3d 1251 (11th Cir. 1999) (holding that prompt access to judicial review is required, not prompt judicial determination).

indecency regulations that prevent totally nude dancing.[10] Recognizing that nude dancing may be expressive conduct, the Court said that it falls within ". . .the outer ambit of the First Amendment's protection." If the local government regulates nudity for a purpose unrelated to the suppression of expression, then it need only satisfy the *O'Brien*[11] test for evaluating restrictions on symbolic speech. This requires that the local government be authorized to regulate; the regulation furthers a substantial governmental interest; the regulation is not related to the suppression of free expression; and the restriction is no greater than those essential to further the governmental purpose.[12]

Although local governments may not totally prohibit adult entertainment, they have been successful in limiting adult entertainment facilities to certain locations within the community.[13] Zoning requirements that restrict the location of a sexually oriented business by prohibiting it from locating close to residential areas, churches, schools and parks have been sustained as valid if there are alternative sites. The local government justifies its regulations by seeking to prevent adverse secondary impacts to those excluded areas and seeking to control the activity itself.[14] The secondary impacts are typically described as "further blighting of business and residential communities and to protect property values."[15] These regulations are viewed as content neutral. The burden of establishing that alternative business sites are available is the responsibility of local government.[16] The First Amendment is violated and the restriction is invalid if the local regulation unreasonably limits the areas where such activities can lawfully exist.[17]

§ 3.5 Alcohol, Tobacco, and Firearms

Local governments usually have broad authority to regulate the sale and use of alcohol, tobacco and firearms for the protection of the health, safety and welfare of their residents. It must be done in a manner that does not conflict or is not preempted by federal and state regulation. In some home

---

[10] Barnes v. Glen Theatre, Inc., 501 U.S. 560 (1991).

[11] United States v. O'Brien, 391 U.S. 367 (1968).

[12] The Supreme Court upheld a local enactment that prohibited anyone from knowingly or intentionally appearing in public in a "state of nudity" in City of Erie v. Pap's A.M., 529 U.S. 277 (2000). However, the Seventh Circuit Court of Appeals found a local enactment that prohibited the performance of a variety of sexually explicit dance movements and gestures unconstitutionally burdened protected expression. See Schultz v. City of Cumberland, 228 F.3d 831 (7th Cir. 2000).

[13] City of Renton v. Playtime Theaters, Inc., 475 U.S. 41 (1986), *reh'g denied,* 475 U.S. 1132 (1986). See also Buzzetti v. City of New York, 140 F.3d 134 (2d Cir. 1998), *cert. denied,* 525 U.S. 816 (1998). It has been approved by state courts as well. See Stringfellow's of New York, Ltd. v. City of New York, 694 N.E.2d 407 (N.Y. 1998).

[14] D.H.L. Associates, Inc. v. O'Gorman, 199 F.3d 50 (1st Cir. 1999).

[15] Lydo Entertainments, Inc. v. City of Las Vegas, 745 F.2d 1211 (9th Cir. 1984).

[16] Lim v. Long Beach, 217 F.3d 1050 (9th Cir. 2000).

[17] Basiardanes v. City of Galveston, 682 F.2d 1203 (5th Cir. 1982).

rule states, local governments are permitted to impose licensing and other additional requirements which do not conflict with the state regulation.

Numerous local enactments have been sustained regulating patrons and employees of establishments that serve alcoholic beverages. Many relate to age and lawful identification for verifying age.[1] Also, hours of operation have been sustained as appropriate for local regulation.[2]

Many local governments regulate entertainment in establishments serving alcoholic beverages. Topless dancing has been proscribed in establishments serving alcohol and the Supreme Court has upheld a local enactment prohibiting nudity in an establishment licensed to serve liquor. The Court relied on the broad power of a state to regulate the sale of intoxicating beverages under the Twenty-First Amendment and the presumption of validity that this requires.[3] As noted by the Eleventh Circuit Court of Appeals, such a prohibition of nude dancing is content-neutral because the activity is not banned totally, just in places that serve alcoholic beverages.[4]

Even though a state has exercised its authority to license and regulate the sale of alcohol, a locality may still be able to adopt zoning regulations that specify the location of vendors.[5] Placing a reasonable limitation on the number of vendors in a community has been upheld,[6] as has a local regulation prohibiting the possession of opened containers in cars or parks.[7]

Local governments with delegated police powers may regulate the sale and use of cigarettes if not preempted by state law and if done in a reasonable manner. The Federal Cigarette Labeling and Advertising Act[8] (FCLAA) has preempted the state and local governments in requirements for warnings in advertising or promotions regarding the potential harmful effects of smoking. In other words, state and local governments are preempted from regulating the content of cigarette advertisements.

Many state and local governments have also attempted to regulate the location of advertisements, by banning them from certain locations. However, the Supreme Court has determined that just as the FCLAA has preempted the regulation of the content of cigarette advertising, it has also preempted regulations which target outdoor and point-of-sale cigarette

---

[1] State v. Greco, 207 A.2d 363 (N.J. Super. Ct. App. Div. 1965).

[2] Hardage v. City of Jacksonville Beach, 399 So.2d 1077 (Fla. Dist. Ct. App. 1981); State ex rel. Floyd v. Noel, 169 So. 549 (Fla. 1936).

[3] City of Newport v. Iacobucci, 479 U.S. 92 (1986).

[4] Sammy's of Mobile, Ltd. v. City of Mobile, 140 F.3d 993 (11th Cir. 1998).

[5] City of Norfolk v. Tiny House, Inc., 281 S.E.2d 836 (Va. 1981); Barnes v. City of Dayton, 392 S.W.2d 813 (Tenn. 1965).

[6] Triangle Oil, Inc. v. North Salt Lake Corp, 609 P.2d 1338 (Utah 1980); Pence v. Village of Rantoul, 298 N.E.2d 775 (Ill. App. Ct. 1973).

[7] City of Lyons v. Suttle, 498 P.2d 9 (Kan. 1972). But see People v. Lee, 448 N.E.2d 1328 (N.Y. 1983) (holding that an enactment prohibiting the possession of an open container was unconstitutional unless there was a requirement of proof of intent to consume).

[8] 15 U.S.C. §§ 1331-1340 (1965), amended by PUB. L. NO. 91-222 § 2, 84 Stat. 87 (1970).

advertising.[9] The Court refused to distinguish between the preemption of content and location of advertisements. It said that the states remain free to adopt generally applicable zoning regulations with respect to advertisements of products which include cigarettes. This means that restrictions on the location and size of advertisements in general that apply to cigarettes and other products equally, are not preempted by the federal statute. For instance, local governments may regulate the size and location of billboards in general. However, the cigarette advertisements may not be singled out for restrictions.

The Supreme Court has held that regulation of conduct with respect to cigarette use and sales is not preempted by the FCLAA.[10] Local enactments prohibiting the sale of cigarettes to minors or banning vending machines have been upheld.[11] Local bans on smoking in food-service establishments, lounges, and bars are becoming increasingly prevalent and it appears that, if they are reasonable and applied on a rational and nondiscriminatory basis, they will not be found to be preempted by the FCLAA.[12] They may be preempted by state regulation.

It is firmly established that the police power includes the right to impose reasonable regulations upon the possession and use of guns.[13] This includes the right to prohibit the discharge of a firearm within the jurisdiction;[14] carrying one in any public place;[15] and requiring that a firearm be registered with the local government within a reasonable time after acquisition.[16] Local police power to regulate firearms has even been said to include a local enactment prohibiting the sale or possession of a toy or imitation pistol.[17] On the other hand, the Supreme Court struck down federal regulation of the possession of firearms near schools, finding that Congress exceeded its Commerce Clause authority.[18] The Court held that in order for Congress to regulate an activity, it must "substantially affect" interstate commerce. The possession of a gun in a local school zone is not an economic activity that might, through repetition elsewhere, substantially affect interstate commerce.

---

[9] Lorillard Tobacco Co. v. Reilly, 533 U.S. 525 (2001).

[10] *Id.*

[11] State v. Crabtree Co., 15 N.W.2d 98 (Minn. 1944); Illinois Cigarette Serv. Co. v. City of Chicago, 89 F.2d 610 (7th Cir. 1937). *But see* Coast Cigarette Sales, Inc. v. Mayor of Long Branch, 297 A.2d 599 (N.J. Super. Ct. App. Div. 1972) (holding that state had preempted local regulation of cigarette sales and vending machines).

[12] Tri-Nel Management, Inc. v. Bd. of Health of Barnstable, 741 N.E.2d 37 (Mass. 2001).

[13] Quilici v. Village of Morton Grove, 695 F.2d 261 (7th Cir. 1982), *cert. denied,* 464 U.S. 863 (1983).

[14] State v. Horn, 250 N.W.2d 912 (Neb. 1977).

[15] City of St. Paul v. Kekedakis, 199 N.W.2d 151 (Minn. 1972).

[16] Brown v. City of Chicago, 250 N.E.2d 129 (Ill. 1969).

[17] People v. Judiz, 344 N.E.2d 399 (N.Y. 1976).

[18] United States v. Lopez, 514 U.S. 549 (1995). *See* § 2.5 *supra.*

§ 3.6 Speech and Movement of Individuals

Local governments have a heavy burden of justification when they seek to control speech within their jurisdictions.[1] Although obscene language and fighting words have long been viewed as beyond First Amendment protection,[2] courts have increasingly narrowed the characterization of this exception. In 1971, the Supreme Court held that a state could not punish someone who wore a jacket with an obscene phrase on the back.[3] In 1972, they held that the "fighting words" exception to freedom of speech does not permit a local government to punish "opprobrious words or abusive language, tending to cause a breach of the peace."[4] The Court also held that a local enactment, prohibiting the placement on public or private property of a symbol, object, appellation, characterization or graffiti (including a burning cross or swastika), ". . .if one knows or has reason to know it arouses anger, alarm or resentment in others on the basis of race, color, creed, religion or gender," was unconstitutional.[5] It was clearly stated that a government may not regulate speech based on hostility, or favoritism toward the content of the speech. Even though the Supreme Court has held that a local government may stop speeches in public when the speakers genuinely "incite to riot,"[6] they have also held that merely stirring people to anger, inviting public dispute or unrest, is not enough.[7]

Any regulation of speech must be narrowly drawn and clear. The Supreme Court has struck down many local enactments for failure to meet these standards. One local enactment making it unlawful to ". . .assault, strike or in any manner oppose, molest, abuse or interrupt any policeman in the execution of his duty" was held to give the police unconstitutional discretion in enforcement and ruled, therefore, unconstitutional.[8] Another one that prohibited ". . .indecent, vile, profane or blasphemous language on or near the streets, alleys, sidewalks, or other places of public resort" suffered from overbreadth and vagueness.[9]

Local governments cannot base denial of the right to participate in its government programs on the viewpoint of an individual or organization. When a local government wanted to deny the right to participate in its Adopt-a-Highway program to the Ku Klux Klan, it was found to be a violation of the First Amendment.[10] A government may not deny any of

---

[1] Local authority to license conduct which involves the exercise of First Amendment rights is discussed in § 3.9 *infra*.

[2] Chaplinsky v. New Hampshire, 315 U.S. 568 (1942).

[3] Cohen v. California, 403 U.S. 15 (1971).

[4] Gooding v. Wilson, 405 U.S. 518 (1972).

[5] R.A.V. v. City of St. Paul, 505 U.S. 377 (1992).

[6] Feiner v. New York, 340 U.S. 315 (1951).

[7] Henry v. City of Rock Hill, 376 U.S. 776 (1964). *See also* Cox v. Louisiana, 379 U.S. 536 (1965).

[8] City of Houston v. Hill, 482 U.S. 451 (1987).

[9] City of Baton Rouge v. Ewing, 308 So.2d 776 (La. 1975).

[10] Cuffley v. Mickes, 208 F.3d 702 (8th Cir. 2000).

its benefits on the basis of disapproval of someone's exercise of a First Amendment right of expression.[11]

Often, local governments have sought to limit the distribution of printed materials. The Supreme Court has addressed the government regulation of commercial speech in several cases. In *Central Hudson Gas & Electric Corp. v. Public Service Commission of N.Y.*,[12] it established a test to determine whether commercial speech is protected by the First Amendment. The Court considers whether the printed material concerns a lawful activity and whether or not it is misleading. Next, the Court considers whether the governmental interest in regulating the distribution is substantial. If the answer to both is affirmative, then the court proceeds to consider whether the proposed regulation directly advances the governmental interest and whether it is more extensive than is necessary to serve that interest. Although the Supreme Court subsequently acknowledged that this test has been criticized, it has not chosen to replace it.[13] Early cases held that local governments could generally impose reasonable controls upon the distribution of printed materials. Some local enactments have also been sustained,[14] prohibiting distribution to homes, without the consent of the residents, of advertising matter in order to curb potential crime,[15] or prohibiting the scattering or depositing of handbills or circulars in yards, on automobiles, in mailboxes, or on porches. However, increasingly, courts have refused to permit local enactments that either prohibit or severely restrict distribution of printed materials. One case found a local enactment that prohibited the distribution of material in yards, driveways, or porches unconstitutional under both the federal and state constitutions. The regulation, intended to control letters, exempted paid subscriptions, material delivered by mail, and those distributed by using doorknobs or "mailbox hanging devices."[16]

The key tenets of clarity, reasonableness and a strong connection to protecting the health, safety and welfare of citizens, are also required for local enactments regulating the movement of individuals. Whether for riot control, curfews, or peaceful protest, local governments must carefully draft their regulations in order to have them sustained when challenged on First Amendment grounds.

Curfews are most often directed toward minors and have been upheld.[17]

---

[11] This was established in Perry v. Sindermann, 408 U.S. 593 (1972).

[12] 447 U.S. 557 (1980).

[13] Greater New Orleans Broadcasting Ass'n, Inc. v. U.S., 527 U.S. 173 (1999).

[14] Buxbom v. City of Riverside, 29 F. Supp. 3 (S.D. Cal. 1939); Sieroty v. City of Huntington Park, 295 P. 564 (Cal. Dist. Ct. App. 1931); Goldblatt Bros. Corp. v. City of E. Chicago, 6 N.E.2d 331 (Ind. 1937).

[15] Allen v. McGovern, 169 A. 345 (N.J. Sup. Ct. 1933).

[16] Statesboro Pub. Co., Inc. v. City of Sylvania, 516 S.E.2d 296 (Ga. 1999).

[17] Schleifer v. City of Charlottesville, 159 F.3d 843 (4th Cir. 1998). A regulation that prohibits minors under the age of 17 from any public place, motor vehicle, or establishment from midnight until 5 a.m., with some exceptions, is not unconstitutionally vague and does not violate the First or Fourteenth Amendments.

So have curfews banning people from parks after dark.[18] Other local restrictions, ostensibly for the same purposes, have been invalidated, primarily because of overbreadth and vagueness.[19]

Loitering and vagrancy regulations have also been sustained, provided that they are narrowly and clearly drawn, and reasonably related to the protection of the community health, safety and welfare. Constitutionally acceptable reasons for the regulation have included the prevention of solicitation for prostitution[20] and the prevention of obstruction of ingress into and egress out of buildings.[21] A city's regulation against begging within a five-mile strip of beach and two sidewalks was found to be narrowly drawn, content-neutral and designed to serve a significant government interest. The Court found that it left open ample alternative channels for communication.[22] Many attempts to regulate against loitering and vagrancy have been found unconstitutional, primarily for vagueness and overbreadth. The Supreme Court has said that such a regulation may be challenged as facially void if its overbreadth inhibits the exercise of First Amendment rights or if it does not have standards for those who enforce it that are sufficient to protect people from the arbitrary deprivation of their liberty.[23] In this case, the Court agreed with the Supreme Court of Illinois in finding that a local enactment failed to establish sufficient guidelines to govern law enforcement and covered a great deal of harmless behavior.

§ 3.7 Other Health, Safety and Welfare Concerns

Concerns about public health issues clearly form a longstanding and well recognized area, justifying the exercise of local police power. As noted in earlier sections, regulation may target individual or business behavior that poses a threat to the public health, welfare and safety of local residents. There are numerous areas where this broad power has been used, from control of pests to quarantining persons afflicted with contagious diseases. In addition, some local governments have used their delegated authority to regulate health-related activities, such as hospitals, nursing homes and homes for the aged. Safety and welfare concerns also give local governments broad discretion in identifying a legitimate basis for the promulgation of a local regulation. Local regulations have been used to justify imposing

---

[18] Peters v. Breier, 322 F. Supp. 1171 (E.D. Wis. 1971).

[19] Johnson v. City of Opelousas, 658 F.2d 1065 (5th Cir. 1981) (finding that the enactment is unconstitutionally overbroad, but if a curfew ordinance is narrowly drawn to protect society's valid interest, it would be upheld). *See also In re* Doe, 513 P.2d 1385 (Haw. 1973) (holding that a local enactment imposing a curfew on those under the age of 18 suffers from vagueness and overbreadth).

[20] City of Milwaukee v. Wilson, 291 N.W.2d 452 (Wis. 1980).

[21] Cameron v. Johnson, 390 U.S. 611 (1968).

[22] Smith v. City of Fort Lauderdale, 177 F.3d 954 (11th Cir. 1999).

[23] City of Chicago v. Morales, 527 U.S. 41 (1999), *citing* Kolender v. Lawson, 461 U.S. 352 (1983).

limitations on individual speech and movement[1] and the control of the development of land.[2]

Environmental concerns are of increasing interest to local governments. Although federal and state governments have preempted and imposed controls on many activities that produce harmful environmental effects, often local governments are explicitly or impliedly permitted to impose even stricter standards. They may also be able to tailor existing requirements to address unique local concerns. Where the federal or state government has not already acted, local governments are generally free to use their delegated police power to regulate for the public health, welfare and safety. Even if the federal or state government has addressed a particular problem, the local governments may still exercise their authority to impose additional requirements, provided they act in a manner that is consistent with the other acts and their act has not been preempted. Often they can also impose charges that reflect the government's cost in mitigating the potentially harmful effects of such things as discharging waste into public sewer and water treatment facilities. Activities that contribute to air pollution may be addressed, if not preempted, by such local government remedies as public nuisance.

The disposal and management of solid waste is a major focus of most local governments. Reasonable regulations may be adopted which do not impose an undue burden on interstate commerce. An outright prohibition or imposing additional costs on the garbage from other areas is generally not permitted.[3] Some local governments have used their authority to build and operate disposal facilities which are open to all of their residents. Nondiscriminatory fees may be charged, provided they are reasonable with a rational basis for any price differentials.

Local governments have sought to control noise and have been supported in their efforts by the Supreme Court, which upheld their right to restrict the amplification of sound with reasonable restrictions that limit intensity, time and location.[4] Many have also imposed controls on the hours of operation of industrial equipment that produces substantial noise.

Programs and facilities devoted to the cultural, recreational and educational welfare of local residents are becoming ever more popular with local government as people increasingly expect their local government to be a facilitator or provider of these resources. Public parks and libraries have been created and maintained by local governments for many years. Sports stadiums and performance venues are increasingly favorite local projects.

---

[1] See § 3.6 supra.

[2] See §§ 4.2–4.6 infra.

[3] City of Philadelphia v. New Jersey, 437 U.S. 617 (1978) (holding that a total ban on importation of waste originating out of state is not permitted). See also Fort Gratiot Sanitary Landfill, Inc. v. Michigan Dep't of Natural Resources, 504 U.S. 353 (1992) (deciding that it is a violation of the Commerce Clause to prohibit private landfills from accepting solid waste originating outside locality).

[4] Kovacs v. Cooper, 336 U.S. 77 (1949), reh'g denied, 336 U.S. 921 (1949).

These are justified as serving a public purpose and, provided a local government has been delegated sufficient authority and complies with all state requirements, should become increasingly popular as local governments strive to improve the quality of life they can provide their citizens.[5]

§ 3.8 Civil and Human Rights

Unless preempted by federal or state law, local governments are able to exercise their police powers to provide protection for civil and human rights.[1] Various forms of discrimination have been prohibited through these local enactments. Even privacy concerns have been addressed. As is true of all exercises of police power, these local enactments will only be upheld if the local government has been delegated authority and the regulation meets the constitutional requirements of clarity, is not overly broad, and has a reasonable relationship to a legitimate local government purpose.

Many local governments have chosen to regulate public accommodations and restaurants by prohibiting discrimination based on race, gender, religion, ancestry, or national origin. These have been sustained by state[2] and federal courts. The Supreme Court upheld a local enactment that prohibited discrimination against women and minorities in private clubs that were determined to be sufficiently public in nature.[3]

Fair housing regulations that prohibit discrimination have also been adopted by many local governments. These have most commonly regulated sales and rentals of property. Courts have consistently upheld these regulations when they address racial discrimination.[4] However, a regulation prohibiting discrimination against renters based on marital status may face greater challenge. It has been held unacceptable when a regulation burdens the religious rights of the landlord without furthering compelling state interests.[5] The Supreme Court has determined that fair housing regulation may overcome Free Exercise challenges by establishing a rational basis, but where there are additional constitutional issues, the regulation may be subject to strict scrutiny.[6]

Local enactments containing "blockbusting" prohibitions have also been upheld. This unscrupulous practice involves an attempt to induce owners of property to sell because of the actual or rumored entrance into the

[5] For a discussion of local expenditures of public funds, see § 10.9 infra.

[1] For a discussion regarding the obligation of local governments to abide by federally imposed requirements for the protection of employees, see Chap. 8 infra. For a discussion of voting rights, see §§ 7.5–7.7 infra.

[2] Marshall v. Kansas City, 355 S.W.2d 877 (Mo. 1962); Commonwealth v. Beasy, 386 S.W.2d 444 (Ky. 1965).

[3] New York State Club Ass'n. v. City of New York, 487 U.S. 1 (1988).

[4] Porter v. City of Oberlin, 205 N.E.2d 363 (Ohio 1965).

[5] Thomas v. Anchorage Equal Rights Comm'n, 165 F.3d 692 (9th Cir. 1999).

[6] Employment Div., Dept of Human Resources of Oregon v. Smith, 494 U.S. 872 (1990).

neighborhood of a member of a racial, religious or ethnic group.[7] Several efforts to address this problem have been sustained.[8]

Local enactments that prohibit discrimination in employment have also been sustained.[9] The creation of local commissions to oversee the enforcement of human rights enactments has been found valid, provided the delegation of local authority contains sufficient guidelines so that the commission is not exercising its own discretion but merely carrying out established policy.[10]

Some local governments have adopted regulations to protect individual privacy by prohibiting the disclosure of information. This must not conflict with state freedom of information or state privacy requirements. A reviewing court will determine whether the stated purpose is advanced by the regulation and whether there are exceptions inconsistent with the purpose. It has been held by the Supreme Court that permitting law enforcement agencies to release information for a "scholarly, journalistic, political, or governmental" purpose, but prohibiting its release for a commercial use, violates the First Amendment.[11]

PART II LICENSES, PERMITS AND FRANCHISES

§ 3.9   Local Licenses and Permits

As noted in § 3.1 *supra*, local authority to regulate activity usually includes authority to require local licenses and permits. It may be implied from the delegation of expressly granted powers when it is reasonably necessary to effectuate their use.[1] This regulatory mechanism assists the local government in its implementation of standards and requirements on targeted activity. The authority to require a license or a permit does not necessarily indicate authority to prohibit the activity altogether. Local governments must always be able to justify the extent of the regulation because of its interest in protecting the health, safety or general welfare of the people.

If the federal or state government has preempted the issuance of licenses or permits in a particular area, the local government may not impose such a requirement. However, the local authority is not automatically preempted

---

[7] Sumner v. Teaneck Township, 251 A.2d 761 (N.J. 1969); Howe v. City of St. Louis, 512 S.W.2d 127 (Mo. 1974).

[8] Clayton v. Village of Oak Park, 453 N.E.2d 937 (Ill. App. Ct. 1983). The local government created an equity assurance program whereby a village reimbursed participants eighty percent of the difference between the appraised value of their homes upon initial certification and the appraised value upon sale. *Id.* at 940-941.

[9] National Asphalt Pavement Ass'n v. Prince George's County, 437 A.2d 651 (Md. 1981).

[10] Human Rights Comm'n of Worcester v. Assad, 349 N.E.2d 341 (Mass. 1976); Allstate Ins. Co. v. Municipality of Anchorage, 599 P.2d 140 (Alaska 1979).

[11] Houchins v. KQED, Inc., 438 U.S. 1 (1978).

[1] Tamiami Trail Tours, Inc. v. City of Orlando, 120 So.2d 170 (Fla. 1960); Father Basil's Lodge v. City of Chicago, 65 N.E.2d 805 (Ill. 1946).

just because the applicant is regulated by another level of government, even if a state or federal permit is required. Preemption depends upon the express or implied intent of those regulations. Clearly, the local government cannot permit or license an activity that is prohibited or denied by federal or state law. However, it may not be preempted from imposing additional requirements or even prohibiting something that is permitted by the other governments. It depends on whether there is an intention indicated in the federal or state regulation to foreclose the local government from imposing additional requirements. Sometimes this is determined by examining the goal of the other regulation. If the purpose is to generate revenue for the state or federal government, the local government is not usually preempted from imposing additional requirements.[2] If the goal is to protect citizens' health and welfare, then the court looks for either an expression of preemption or an implication based on either the comprehensiveness of the regulatory action or the nature of the subject being regulated.

All local regulation requiring a license or permit must be reasonable and have a reasonable relationship to the public health, safety or general welfare. It must further a legitimate concern of the local government in a reasonable manner or it will be found unconstitutional under the federal and state due process clauses.[3] Due process also requires that the local regulation for a license or permit clearly specify who must have one and what must be done in order to obtain it.[4] Proceedings before local licensing authorities must be fair. There must be clear standards set by the local governing board, leaving little or no discretion to local administrative officers or boards.[5] License fees may be imposed, provided they are reasonably related to the cost of licensing, inspecting and regulating. A local government cannot use license or permit fees as a means of raising revenue.

License and permit requirements must not unfairly, unreasonably, invidiously or arbitrarily discriminate against a particular person or class of persons or they will be found to violate state and federal equal protection clauses.[6] Singling out one form of activity for licensing, which has no greater relation to the harm sought to be controlled than another, may be found impermissible.[7] Reasonable classifications where differing treatment is based upon distinctions that relate to a legitimate purpose for licensing will be upheld.[8] Unreasonable quotas have also been invalidated by the courts.[9] One local regulation was declared void when it limited the number

---

[2] City of Owensboro v. Smith, 383 S.W.2d 902 (Ky. 1964).

[3] City of St. Paul v. Dalsin, 71 N.W.2d 855 (Minn. 1955); City of Guthrie v. Pike & Long, 243 P.2d 697 (Okla. 1952).

[4] Barker Bros. v. City of Los Angeles, 76 P.2d 97 (Cal. 1938).

[5] Hague v. Committee for Indus. Org., 307 U.S. 496 (1939); Junglen v. El Paso Co., 518 P.2d 826 (Colo. 1974).

[6] Lewis v. City of Grand Rapids, 356 F.2d 276 (6th Cir. 1966), cert. denied, 385 U.S. 838, (1966).

[7] Frecker v. City of Dayton, 90 N.E.2d 851 (Ohio 1950).

[8] State ex rel. Namer Inv. Corp. v. Williams, 435 P.2d 975 (Wash. 1968).

[9] Kipperman v. City of Markham, 265 N.E.2d 166 (Ill. 1970).

of permits which could be granted per mobile home park per year. The court found that it violated the equal protection clauses of both the state and federal constitutions.[10]

If a local government requires a license or permit for the exercise of a First Amendment freedom of religion, speech, press, assembly or association, it will be carefully scrutinized. Licenses and permits may be required for First Amendment activities but must not permit censorship or impose a prohibitory fee. The only justification for denial is the protection of the health, safety and welfare of others.[11] Any time, place and manner restrictions must be reasonable and manifest a neutral viewpoint. The local government cannot delegate unbridled discretion or flexibility for arbitrary decision-making to those administering the regulation.[12] Local licensing and permitting has been sustained for religious processions,[13] solicitation of funds for religions or charity,[14] distribution of literature,[15] and for the operation of a church's homeless shelter.[16] The Supreme Court held that a local government's enactment declaring door-to-door canvassing without first registering and obtaining a permit (which must be made available for public inspection) a misdemeanor, violated the First Amendment when applied to religious proselytizing, anonymous political speech and the distribution of handbills.[16.1]

Local governments have been permitted to use licensing to censor films or theatrical productions that are obscene. The local government must establish neutral criteria to protect against decision-making based on the content or viewpoint of the speech being reviewed.[17] Whenever the licensing involves a prior restraint of a First Amendment right, the decision on the application for the license must be made within a specified brief period with the status quo preserved pending a final judicial determination; the licensing procedure must assure a prompt final judicial decision; and if the decision requires a public official to pass judgment on the content of speech, the burden of instituting judicial proceedings and establishing that the expression is unprotected must be on the local government rather than the applicant.[18] The Supreme Court is not favorably disposed toward flat permit or license fees where First Amendment rights are involved, but has

---

[10] Begin v. Inhabitants of Sabattus, 409 A.2d 1269 (Me. 1979).

[11] Cox v. New Hampshire, 312 U.S. 569 (1941).

[12] City of Lakewood v. Plain Dealer Publ'g Co., 486 U.S. 750 (1988); Saia v. New York, 334 U.S. 558 (1948).

[13] Cox v. New Hampshire, 312 U.S. 569 (1941).

[14] Pa. Alliance for Jobs & Energy v. Council of Borough of Munhall, 743 F.2d 182 (3d Cir. 1984).

[15] City of Manchester v. Leiby, 117 F.2d 661 (1st Cir. 1941), *cert. denied,* 313 U.S. 562 (1941).

[16] First Assembly of God v. Collier County, 20 F.3d 419 (11th Cir. 1994).

[16.1] Watchtower Bible and Tract Soc. v. Village of Stratton, 536 U.S. 150 (2002).

[17] City of Lakewood v. Plain Dealer Publ'g. Co., 486 U.S. 750 (1988).

[18] FW/PBS, Inc. v. City of Dallas, 493 U.S. 215 (1990); Freedman v. Maryland, 380 U.S. 51 (1965).

indicated its approval of a charge to defray the expenses of regulating the activities involved.[19]

The regulatory structure cannot unconstitutionally discriminate against persons engaged in interstate commerce or products entering interstate commerce.[20] Local governments cannot unreasonably burden interstate commerce either by the regulation itself or by the fees imposed.[21]

§ 3.10   Franchises

Generally, local governments have been authorized through state constitution, statutes or charters, to grant franchises to private utilities for the use of public right-of-ways within their boundaries. Such franchises typically involve the installation of pipes, wires or towers for the delivery of water, electricity, gas, or telecommunications services. This authority is, of course, subject to federal or state preemption. However, many state constitutions prohibit the state from granting a franchise for the use of local streets without local permission, with some limiting the prohibition solely to rail transportation. Without this restriction, the state may possibly use its state concern to justify its grant of permission for public utilities to use local streets. With increasing federal and state interest in regulating the provision of public services, there is significant local government interaction with state and federal statutes and regulatory agencies.

Some delegated authority to local governments may require that the local entity obtain citizen approval before granting a franchise or that the process itself must be initiated by local residents. Other procedural requirements may be imposed, such as a requirement that the local government publicly advertise for bids and award the franchise to the highest responsible bidder. Requirements contained in the grants of authority must be strictly followed.

If the local government has followed the prescribed procedure, the courts generally uphold the local decisions. In the absence of clear proof of fraud or an obvious abuse of discretion, the decision of the local government is respected and affirmed.[1] Courts will not usually explore the motives of local government bodies in granting or denying franchises.

Typically, local governments are permitted to impose reasonable conditions on the grants of a franchise. This authority has been used to effect the rates charged consumers by the utility, the fees owed the local government, and a requirement that there be provision of service for use by the local government itself. However, most often, rates and operating rules are guided or set by the state. The right to establish rates may not be delegated to the local government or it may be subject to state or federal preemption.

---

[19] Murdock v. Pennsylvania, 319 U.S. 105 (1943); Cox v. New Hampshire, 312 U.S. 569 (1941).

[20] For further discussion, *see* § 2.7 *supra*.

[21] South Central Bell Telephone Co. v. Alabama, 526 U.S. 160 (1999).

[1] Hatcher v. Kentucky & W. Va. Power Co., 133 S.W.2d 910 (Ky. 1939); Morristown Emergency and Rescue Squad, Inc. v. Volunteer Dev. Co., 793 S.W.2d 262 (Tenn. Ct. App. 1990).

Franchise grants are treated like local contracts. As such, the contract is protected by the Contract Clause of the Federal Constitution[2] which prohibits impairment by the state or local government.[3] The local governments may not take away what they have given in the franchise agreement.[4] The most frequent problem has been local government unilaterally attempting to change rate and fare provisions. The Supreme Court has found this to be an impairment of the obligation of contracts and unconstitutional.[5] This does not mean that the local government may not exercise its police power in a way that impacts the franchisee. The Supreme Court interprets the Contract Clause to allow state and local governments to affect franchise rights by subsequent legislation that is reasonably necessary to protect the public health, safety or welfare.[6] Many courts have held that a franchisee accepts a local franchise with the condition that the privilege is accepted subject to the power of the government to exercise its police power to protect the health, safety and welfare of its citizens.[7]

The franchisee is bound by the obligations contained in the franchise.[8] State and local enactments existing at the time of the grant are considered part of the franchise.[9] Courts narrowly construe franchise agreements and any ambiguity will be construed in favor of the local government.[10] If it is not specified, a franchise will not be construed to give exclusive privileges[11] and there is no implied contract that the local government will not grant similar franchises to others or that it will not itself compete with the franchisee.[12] Similarly, there is no implied exemption from taxes.[13] However, typically there is an implied term that local utilities will relocate their facilities at their own expense when necessary for governmental improvements.

Local authority to regulate utilities may be found in constitutions, statutes and charters. However, where states have established public utility commissions with general authority, local governments may regulate only

---

[2] U.S. CONST. art. I, § 10, cl. 1. No state shall pass any law impairing the obligation of contracts.

[3] Boise Artesian Hot & Cold Water Co. v. Boise City, 230 U.S. 84 (1913).

[4] Grand Trunk W. Ry. v. City of South Bend, 227 U.S. 544 (1913).

[5] City of Minneapolis v. Minneapolis St. Ry. Co., 215 U.S. 417 (1910).

[6] Home Bldg. & Loan Ass'n v. Blaisdell, 290 U.S. 398 (1934).

[7] City of New Haven v. New Haven Water Co., 45 A.2d 831 (Conn. 1946); Peoples Gas Co. of Kentucky v. City of Barbourville, 165 S.W.2d 567 (Ky. 1942); Delony v. Rucker, 302 S.W.2d 287 (Ark. 1957).

[8] St. Cloud Pub. Serv. Co. v. City of St. Cloud, 265 U.S. 352 (1924); Southern Utils. Co. v. City of Palatka, 268 U.S. 232 (1925).

[9] Boyce v. City of Gastonia, 41 S.E.2d 355 (N.C. 1947).

[10] Delmarva Power & Light Co. v. City of Seaford, 575 A.2d 1089 (Del. 1990).

[11] James Cable Partners, L.P. v. City of Jamestown, 818 S.W.2d 338 (Tenn. Ct. App. 1991).

[12] City of Joplin v. Southwest Missouri Light Co., 191 U.S. 150 (1903).

[13] Minneapolis St. Ry. v. City of Minneapolis, 40 N.W.2d 353 (Minn. 1949), *appeal dismissed,* 339 U.S. 907 (1950).

to the extent that is consistent with principles of state preemption. Although zoning powers may not be used to prohibit the presence of a utility that has received state permission to locate within the local government, some land-use controls may be acceptable.

Some local governments reserve the right to terminate the franchise in the grant. Otherwise, it can be revoked if the franchisee fails to abide by the specified terms. Courts have also held that local governments can terminate it for misuse or failure to utilize the franchise and provide services.[14] A franchisee may surrender its franchise to the local government. If it is operating at a loss and is reasonably certain that it will continue to do so, the franchisee may terminate it if there is no contract provision obligating it to continue under those circumstances. Compelling the franchise to continue to operate at a loss, when it has not agreed to do so, would deprive it of property without due process of law.[15]

Local governments can refuse to renew a utility's franchise and require that it remove its property from the public right-of-way. However, whatever local action is taken, it must be consistent with the constitutional and statutory rights of the franchisee. The Supreme Court found that a local government improperly conditioned renewal of a taxi franchise on the settlement of a pending labor dispute between the company and a union. The local government was held liable for compensatory damages in a federal civil rights action.[16]

Some localities have chosen to own and operate public utilities, either building them or acquiring existing ones by purchase or using their powers of eminent domain. Utilities owned by local governments may be subject to state regulation but most often their operation and rates for services within their own geographical territory are not controlled by the state. They are generally entitled to set rates that insure them a reasonable rate of return on their investment, provided they are reasonable and not discriminatory.

§ 3.11　Telecommunications

Local governments play a special role in the developing field of telecommunications. Unlike other areas involving the grant of a local franchise which often have a great deal of state regulation, telecommunications is primarily regulated by the federal government. It is federal law that first defines the role local government is to take in exercising its police powers to protect the benefit its citizens receive from the proliferation of cable or satellite television and wired or cellular telephonic services.

The Cable Television Consumer Protection and Competition Act of 1992[1]

---

[14] New York Elec. Lines Co. v. Empire City Subway Co., 235 U.S. 179 (1914); City of St. Louis v. Melhar Corp., 650 S.W.2d 633 (Mo. Ct. App. 1983).

[15] Georgia Power Co. v. City of Decatur, 281 U.S. 505 (1930).

[16] Golden State Transit Corp. v. City of Los Angeles, 493 U.S. 103 (1989).

[1] 47 U.S.C. § 521 (2001).

and the Telecommunications Reform Act of 1996[2] define the role of state and local governments. Courts have differed on whether the federal law preempts states from preventing local governments from providing telecommunications services or facilities.[3] The federal law preserves the authority of a state or local government to manage the public right-of-ways or to require fair and reasonable compensation from telecommunications providers on a competitively neutral and nondiscriminatory basis. However, the compensation charged must be publicly disclosed.

On the other hand, there is broad preemption of state and local authority to regulate in this field. Congress has indicated a clear intent to encourage the development and dissemination of multimedia technology. The law provides that there can be no state or local regulation that prohibits or has the effect of prohibiting any company's ability to provide telecommunication services, unless the regulations fall within the "safe harbor" provisions that permit management of public right-of-ways and a local requirement of fair and reasonable compensation. The courts are still in the process of determining how much local government authority is preserved. One early case has applied a two-step analysis. First, do the local government's regulations prohibit or have the effect of prohibiting the applicant from providing telecommunications services? If the answer is yes, then the relevant inquiry is whether they are imposed on a competitively neutral and nondiscriminatory basis. They must also be based on authority reserved to the local government to either regulate the public right-of-ways or to charge fair and reasonable compensation.[4]

Local issues differ, depending on the type of technology the local government is regulating. Federal law is very extensive in controlling local action in the field of cable television. The power to control the use of its streets has traditionally given local governments power to require a franchise grant before installing cable television equipment. Initially, local governments were permitted to grant an exclusive franchise for a cable television provider. This was changed in the 1992 Act which provides that local governments may not grant exclusive franchises and may not unreasonably refuse to award an additional competitive franchise.[5] Local governments are now preempted from regulating rates of the cable system unless the Federal Communication Commission (FCC) finds that a cable system is not subject to effective competition. If the FCC finds insufficient competition, then the local government may regulate the rates for basic cable service.[6]

---

[2] PUB. L. NO. 104-104, 110 Stat. 56 codified at 47 U.S.C. §§ 251-260.

[3] City of Abilene v. FCC, 164 F.3d 49 (D.C. Cir. 1999). States may still preempt local action if not prohibited by state law. *But see* Missouri Mun. League v. FCC, 299 F.3d 949 (8th Cir. 2002). The 1996 Telecommunications Act preempts states from preventing local governments from providing telecommunications services or facilities. The statute contains a "plain statement" that "no State or local statute or regulation . . . may prohibit or have the effect or prohibiting the ability of any entity to provide any interstate or intrastate telecommunications service." A local government is an "entity."

[4] TCG New York, Inc. v. City of White Plains, 125 F. Supp. 2d 81 (S.D.N.Y. 2000).

[5] 47 U.S.C. § 541 (2001).

[6] 47 U.S.C. § 543 (2001).

The Act also limits the franchise fees imposed by local governments to no more than 5% of the company's gross revenue.[7]

Many questions have surrounded the regulation of cable televison. A seemingly basic determination of what is a cable system has resulted in court challenges. Since it is regulated by the federal act, as opposed to a utility that is subject to state or local control, it is a critical question. The issue was raised by a satellite master antenna television system (SMATV) which provided service to several large apartment buildings by using cables owned by a common carrier. The FCC's decision that SMATV operators are not "cable operators" and therefore not subject to the federal law has so far been sustained.[8]

Another federal statute, the Pole Attachments Act,[9] has been particularly important to utilities which have existing franchises to use local right-of-ways. This law provides that a utility which owns such a franchise must provide a cable television system or any telecommunications carrier with nondiscriminatory access to any pole, duct, conduit, or right-of-way owned or controlled by it. Challenged on Fifth Amendment grounds, it has been held that such a requirement is not an unconstitutional taking because the statute provides an acceptable process for the utility to obtain just compensation.[10] If the parties do not agree on an amount for compensation, the FCC is to decide what is just and reasonable. Questions have also been raised about whether the FCC, under the Pole Attachments Act, has authority to regulate the placement of wireless communications equipment and attachments for Internet service on existing utility poles. Settling the dispute, the Supreme Court held that this Act grants access to attachments that provide both cable television and high-speed Internet service, and to attachments by wireless telecommunications providers. The FCC may regulate the rent to be paid for both of these types of attachments should the parties be unable to agree on compensation.[11]

The Supreme Court has held that state and local governments may not regulate the technical standards governing the quality of cable television signals. A concern has been voiced by some local governments that the telecommunications equipment might interfere with other electronic devices used in emergency situations and hinder local assistance. However, the courts have held that there can be no local regulation because of federal preemption.[12] Pursuant to this same authority, the FCC has preempted all zoning enactments that harm an individual's right to satellite reception.

---

[7] 47 U.S.C. § 622(b).

[8] Chicago v. FCC, 199 F.3d 424 (7th Cir. 1999). *See also* City of Austin v. Southwestern Bell Video Svs., Inc., 193 F.3d 309 (5th Cir. 1999), *cert. denied,* 529 U.S. 1082 (2000).

[9] 47 U.S.C. § 224(f)(1) (2001).

[10] Gulf Power Co. v. FCC, 187 F.3d 1324 (11th Cir. 1999).

[11] Nat'l Cable & Telecommunications Assoc., Inc. v. Gulf Power Co., 534 U.S. 327 (2002).

[12] Freeman v. Burlington Broadcasters Inc., 204 F.3d 311 (2d Cir. 2000), *cert. denied,* 531 U.S. 917 (2000); Southwestern Bell Wireless Inc. v. Johnson County Bd. of County Commissioners, 199 F.3d 1185 (10th Cir. 1999), *cert. denied,* 530 U.S. 1204 (2000).

However, it appears that there may be local regulation with reasonable requirements for the installation and use of reception equipment.[13]

First Amendment speech concerns have been raised in the review of local regulations of cable television. A local government was not permitted to limit access to a portion of the community to only one cable provider. The court said that it might be acceptable if the government limited the installation of equipment to one and had other cable providers share it.[14]

Numerous other local issues have arisen. A court held that New York City could not place a private company's programs on a government access channel. This reflected "content-based favoritism."[15] The Supreme Court held that a federal statute violated the First Amendment when it required cable television operators to fully scramble or otherwise block sexually oriented programming (or limit it to hours when children are unlikely to be viewing). The Court said that it was not shown to be the least restrictive means for preventing the harm that was the basis for the regulation.[16] The Court of Appeals for the District of Columbia Circuit upheld federal limits on the number of subscribers cable operators may reach and on the number of channels a cable system may devote to programming in which it has a financial interest.[17] However, the same Court subsequently determined that the FCC rules promulgated pursuant to this authority violated the First Amendment and, in part, exceeded statutory authority.[18]

The federal Telecommunications Act preserves the right of state and local governments to regulate the siting of telecommunications towers under its authority to manage the development of the public right-of-ways. However, it cannot be done in a manner that prevents service from developing in the community or unreasonably discriminates among providers of functionally equivalent services. Disapproval of a particular site by a local government does not mean that the local government has unlawfully prohibited the development of service. Examples of prohibited local conduct include a local policy banning any siting; general hostility toward siting; repeated denials of individual applications; and a permit denial for the only site feasible.[19]

In regulating wireless telecommunication facilities, the Telecommunications Act requires that local denial of permits for wireless facilities be in a written format that indicates the substantial evidence supporting the decision. Cases are beginning to explain what this requires. It has been held that immediate notification to an applicant by writing "Disposition

---

[13] Abbott v. City of Cape Canaveral, 840 F. Supp. 880 (M.D. Fla.), aff'd, 41 F.3d 669 (11th Cir. 1994).

[14] Preferred Communications, Inc. v. City of Los Angeles, 13 F.3d 1327 (9th Cir. 1994).

[15] Time Warner Cable v. City of New York, 943 F. Supp. 1357 (S.D.N.Y. 1996).

[16] U.S. v. Playboy Entertainment Group, Inc., 529 U.S. 803 (2000).

[17] Time Warner Entertainment Co. v. U.S., 211 F.3d 1313 (D.C. Cir. 2000).

[18] Time Warner Entertainment Co. L.P. v. FCC, 240 F.3d 1126 (D.C. Cir. 2001).

[19] 360 Degrees Communications Co. of Charlottesville v. Bd. of Supervisors of Albemarle County, 211 F.3d 79 (4th Cir. 2000), citing AT&T Wireless PCS, Inc. v. City Council of Virginia Beach, 155 F.3d 423 (4th Cir. 1998).

Denied" on the first page of the application, followed three months later by a written decision, was sufficient to meet the "writing" requirement.[20]

If a local government violates federal law in its regulations of telecommunications companies, declaratory or injunctive remedies may be sought.[21]

§ 3.12   Challenge to the Grant or Denial of License, Permit or Franchise

Applicants who have been denied a license, permit or franchise have standing to challenge the denial after they have exhausted their administrative remedies. If, however, the challenge is based on an argument that the local process is unlawful or that no proper relief may be obtained, an unsuccessful applicant may proceed to a judicial remedy. If a non-applicant wants to challenge the award or denial of a license, permit or franchise to someone else, the challenger must be able to show a direct injury to himself or herself in order to meet standing requirements. Some states have adopted legislation that permits taxpayers to sue local officials to prevent unlawful grants of franchises.

In general, for a court to reverse a local action, it must be found that the determination of the local government was arbitrary, capricious, unreasonable or unlawful. The burden of proving this is upon the one challenging the denial or grant of a permit or license. A local government cannot engage in invidious and unreasonable discriminations in denying or granting licenses or permits.[1]

In some states, taxpayers have been given statutory authority to sue local officials to prevent the unlawful grant of a franchise. They are also permitted to seek injunctive, declaratory or mandatory decrees against unlawful acts of officials or boards that will result in a loss of taxpayer revenue. Without the loss, there may or may not be standing to challenge the grant of a franchise. Other jurisdictions have held that a taxpayer action, seeking injunctive, declaratory or mandatory decrees based on the unlawful actions of local officials with possible loss to taxpayers, may be brought even without specific statutory authorization.[2]

There are mixed opinions about local governments themselves challenging a franchise they have granted. Some courts find estoppel,[3] while others do not.[4] Yet others have "disregarded technical defects" where a utility has

---

[20] AT&T Wireless PCS, Inc. v. Winston-Salem Zoning Bd. of Adjustment, 172 F.3d 307 (4th Cir. 1999).

[21] AT&T Wireless PCS, Inc. v. City of Atlanta, 210 F.3d 1322 (11th Cir. 2000).

[1] Rutland Cable T.V. Inc. v. City of Rutland, 166 A.2d 191 (Vt. 1960).

[2] Johnson v. City of Alma, 149 S.E.2d 661 (Ga. 1966); Sermon v. City of Duluth, 97 N.W.2d 464 (Minn. 1959). Some cases have permitted taxpayer suit to enjoin unlawful acts even without allegations of loss. See Green v. Shaw, 319 A.2d 284 (N.H. 1974).

[3] City of Sikeston v. Missouri Utils. Co., 53 S.W.2d 394 (Mo. 1932); City of Summerville v. Georgia Power Co., 55 S.E.2d 540 (Ga. 1949); City of Sheridan v. Montana-Dakota Utils. Co., 157 F. Supp. 664 (D. Wyo. 1958).

[4] Mississippi Power & Light Co. v. Town of Coldwater, 168 F. Supp. 463 (N.D. Miss. 1958).

operated for years under authority of a flawed grant.[5] Other courts have held that regardless of payments of franchise taxes or the expenditure of large sums by the utility or service over a long period of time, the local government is not estopped from preventing or attacking the validity of a franchise.[6] Of course in these cases, the franchisee will be permitted a reasonable amount of time to remove its equipment or gain a lawful franchise. Franchises are presumed to be valid and the person challenging the grant has the burden of proving its invalidity.[7] Local governments usually have statutory power to suspend licenses and permits and arguably have implied power to do so.[8]

An action in mandamus may be brought when an applicant can show that he or she has fully complied with all requirements and has a right to a license or permit. If the local government officials have acted arbitrarily or capriciously or unreasonably in withholding it, the court will issue a writ of mandamus, compelling the issuance of the permit or license.[9] It will not be granted where there is discretion and judgment committed to local officials or boards,[10] unless it is shown that the exercise of discretion has been arbitrary and capricious.[11] It has also been deemed an appropriate remedy when a denial is void on its face, or has no reasonable relationship to the public health, safety or welfare.[12]

If a regulation is alleged to be unconstitutional on its face, and a person does not seek a license or permit and is penalized for actions taken without one, judicial review will be granted. The Supreme Court has held that failure to apply for a permit or license does not preclude review.[13] It will require, however, that relief (including mandamus) be sought first in state courts since a local interpretation might save its constitutionality, if there is an easy, expeditious and inexpensive appeal available from the unlawful denial.[14]

---

[5] Incorp. Town of Mapleton v. Iowa Light, Heat & Power Co., 216 N.W. 683 (Iowa 1927).

[6] Cumberland Telephone & Telegraph Co. v. City of Calhoun, 151 S.W. 659 (Ky. 1912); Continental Illinois Nat'l Bank & Trust Co. v. City of Middlesboro, 109 F.2d 960 (6th Cir. 1940); City of Princeton v. Princeton Elec., Light & Power Co., 166 Ky 730 179 S.W. 1074 (Ky. 1915).

[7] Continental Oil Co. v. City of Twin Falls, 286 P. 353 (Idaho 1930).

[8] Thompson v. Town of E. Greenbush, 512 A.2d 837 (R.I. 1986).

[9] Hernandez v. Bd. of Comm'rs, 247 S.E.2d 870 (Ga. 1978).

[10] Gopher Sales Co. v. City of Austin, 75 N.W.2d 780 (Minn. 1956); Larkin Co. v. Schwab, 151 N.E. 637 (N.Y. 1926).

[11] State ex rel. Craven v. City of Tacoma, 385 P.2d 372 (Wash. 1963).

[12] Kurpinski v. Vreeland, 82 N.W.2d 435 (Mich. 1957); City of Miami Beach v. State ex rel. Fontainebleau Hotel Corp., 108 So.2d 614; State ex rel. Ohio Oil Co. v. City of Defiance, 133 N.E.2d 392 (Ohio App. 1955).

[13] Staub v. City of Baxley, 355 U.S. 313 (1958).

[14] Poulos v. New Hampshire, 345 U.S. 395 (1953). See also Shuttlesworth v. City of Birmingham, 394 U.S. 147 (1969).

In seeking mandamus, it is not enough to show that someone similarly situated has a permit or license. Also, the remedy is generally denied where issuance would violate a statute or local enactment.[15]

Another remedy that may be available is an equitable injunction. This has been successful when the licensing or permitting enactment is clearly unlawful and there is no adequate remedy at law, and irreparable injury will occur if the regulation is enforced.[16] A declaratory judgment action may also be available to attack the license and permit requirement or to have permits that are possessed declared valid.[17] Some jurisdictions limit review of local government denials or grants to certiorari, with courts reviewing whether there is evidence to support the determination or whether the local officer or board has exceeded the delegated authority.[18]

---

[15] Illusions on Peachtree Street, Inc. v. Young, 356 S.E.2d 510 (Ga. 1987). *But see* Goldrush II v. City of Marietta, 482 S.E.2d 347 (Ga. 1997).

[16] Oklahoma City v. Poor, 298 P.2d 459 (Okla. 1956).

[17] Willis v. Town of Woodruff, 20 S.E.2d 699 (S.C. 1942).

[18] City of Melbourne v. Hess Realty Corp. 575 So.2d 774 (Fla. Dist. Ct. App. 1991); Fink v. Bureau of Licenses, 158 A.2d 820 (R.I. 1960); Kovacs v. Bd. of Adjustment of Ross Tp., 95 A.2d 350 (Pa. Super. Ct. 1953).

Chapter 4

Private and Public Land

§ 4.1 Introduction and Chapter Overview

The role of local government in the planning, development and use of land is one of the most fundamental and highly valued exercises of local authority. The right to use this authority is also one of the strongest motivations for the voluntary creation of a new local government. People who dislike the way their community is regulated or unregulated often at least think of the possibility of forming their own local government, with local authority to regulate the development of property in a manner that will reflect their view of a good community.

The right to engage in the control of land is dependent on the delegation of state authority through the state constitution, statutes or charters. The particular authority delegated, and by which means, varies from state to state. Unless prohibited in the state constitution, the local authority may be preempted by the state, and is always subject to federal preemption if Congress acts pursuant to its constitutionally delegated powers.

When a local government engages in planning, zoning, and the management of public land, it must always comply with basic constitutional requirements. The actions taken must respect the protections afforded individual liberties in both federal and state constitutions. All government regulations and actions must meet First and Fourteenth Amendment guarantees of freedom of speech, religion, equal protection and due process. Although local government can regulate private property in order to benefit all members of the community, it cannot expect private owners to unreasonably bear public burdens. The local government must pay compensation if the regulation imposed on property is so severe it results in an unconstitutional taking of private property.

Many local governments are required by their states to plan for the future growth of their community. This is usually done through the development of a comprehensive plan that establishes the goals of, and provides guidance on, the orderly future development of the community. Some states require that local zoning be consistent with this plan. This requirement becomes particularly important when a community addresses the many issues that arise as diverse people reconcile their differences and live together in harmony.

PART I REGULATION OF PRIVATE LAND USE

§ 4.2 Planning

Planning at the local level presents the opportunity for a local government to consider what it is presently and what it will become. It requires an honest assessment of its residents' current needs, and the anticipation of what those needs will be in the future. It provides an opportunity to establish goals. The purpose of the comprehensive plan is to plot the harmonious growth of the community as it seeks to develop effective and efficient ways of achieving the goals established. The adoption of a plan is not an end, but rather a beginning. Planning must be an ongoing process that requires flexibility since demographics, information, expectations, and resources are constantly changing.

Some, but not all, states require local governments to engage in comprehensive planning. Sometimes, those that do specify that it is a precondition to the exercise of local zoning authority. In these jurisdictions, it may also be required that zoning regulations be consistent with the local comprehensive plan. In other jurisdictions, development of a plan may follow the adoption of zoning regulations.

The task of creating a comprehensive plan for a local government is generally assigned to a local board or commission. The board is totally dependent upon delegated authority, whether in a statute, charter or local enactment, since it has no inherent authority to act. Members of local planning boards are usually volunteers who serve without financial remuneration. They may be appointed by the chief executive of the local government (sometimes with the approval of the legislative body) or elected by members of the community. It is not unusual for local government officials to also serve on the board.[1]

In developing a comprehensive plan, the planning board will usually work with experts to forecast future business and residential growth patterns, along with demands for new public services such as schools, libraries, water and sewerage, fire protection, streets, transportation facilities, and recreational areas. The plan will discuss current uses and contain recommendations for redevelopment of some existing uses. It will most likely have an accompanying statement of objectives, policies and goals. Maps and technical reports are also typically included. The sole purpose of the plan is to direct the private and public development of the land in a manner that will best address the health, safety and welfare of those living within the community. Many local planning boards have concluded that a temporary moratorium on residential development should be imposed either while the planning process is taking place or until needed public infrastructure and services can be provided. Often this will be included as a part of the plan.[2]

---

[1] Burgess v. City of Concord, 391 A.2d 896 (N.H. 1978).

[2] The constitutionality of this action is discussed in § 4.5 *infra*.

After the plan has been developed, the planning board submits it to the local governing body for its adoption. Generally, statutes, local laws, or charters will require that local residents be given notice and an opportunity to be heard before any action is taken by the local governing board on the proposed plan.

A local plan adopted by the governing body serves many purposes. Since local governments are not generally permitted to act in a manner that is inconsistent with its comprehensive plan, the existence of a plan often limits local government action in acquiring, developing or disposing of public property.[3] Some states require that local governments not only develop comprehensive plans but that local zoning be consistent with a plan.[4] This has not always been interpreted to require a formally adopted plan. Whether the plan is solely advisory or necessary as a precondition to the exercise of zoning authority, it is valuable because it serves to focus public attention on both the decision-making authority of local officials and the ways in which their choices will affect the character of the community in the future.

Since planning is an ongoing process, the planning board usually continues to function. The courts have been generous in permitting wide delegation of authority to these boards. The board, however, must be given standards to guide them in carrying out their responsibilities.[5] It also must abide by procedural requirements that govern its actions.[6] Planning boards often will be given responsibility for reviewing zoning proposals for the purpose of making recommendations to the legislative body. In addition, many local governments require that all proposals for new public buildings, subdivisions or developments requiring site-plan approval be submitted to the planning board for its determination as to whether the proposals are consistent with the comprehensive plan.[7] Courts have sustained the delegation of these responsibilities to the planning board, provided there are clear standards established for the exercise of this authority.[8] The planning board may also be authorized to impose conditions on its subdivision approvals by requiring that an applicant meet requirements lawfully adopted by the local governing board. It has been held that delegating plan approval or authority to place conditions on the exercise of local zoning authority is not an unconstitutional delegation of legislative authority.[9] Of

---

[3] Ash Grove Cement Co. v. Jefferson, 943 P.2d 85 (Mont. 1997).

[4] See CAL. GOV'T CODE ANN. § 65300 et seq.; FLA. STAT. ANN. §§ 163.3161–163.3211; OR. REV. STAT. ch. 197. See also SANDRA M. STEVENSON, ANTIEAU ON LOCAL GOVERNMENT LAW § 55.09[3] (2d ed. 2001).

[5] Beach v. Planning & Zoning Comm'n. of Milford, 141 Conn. 79, 103 A.2d 814 (Conn. 1954); Borough of Oakland v. Roth, 100 A.2d 698 (N.J. Super. Ct. App. Div. 1953).

[6] Boulder Corp. v. Vann, 345 So. 2d 272 (Ala. 1977) (holding that the failure to meet a requirement that a formal approval or disapproval be given within 30 days constitutes grounds for consent of the plat plan).

[7] City of Chicago v. Central Nat'l Bank, 125 N.E.2d 94 (Ill. 1955).

[8] Id.; Gore v. Hicks, 115 N.Y.S.2d 187 (Sup. Ct. 1952); Beach v. Planning and Zoning Comm'n of Town of Milford, 103 A.2d 814 (Conn. 1954).

[9] Fine v. Galloway Township Comm., 463 A.2d 990 (N.J. Super. Ct. Law Div. 1983); City of Chicago v. Central Nat'l Bank, 125 N.E.2d 94 (Ill. 1955).

course the board may not deny approval of plans that meet regulatory standards.[10]

Local governments are increasingly included in regional or area planning that goes beyond their local boundaries. This may be accomplished through interlocal cooperation, or by a delegation of authority to larger units of local government or by the state. Occasionally, local governments are authorized to engage in planning for areas surrounding their geographical boundaries. This extraterritorial planning is done to minimize adverse impacts that may occur by uncontrolled development within a short distance of the local government boundaries. More often there may be a joint planning agreement between or among contiguous or overlapping local governments to enable consideration of mutual concerns about the impact of future development on the region. Such regional planning is authorized in a number of states.[11] Most regional planning agencies have advisory powers only, but a few do have authority to implement their plans.[12]

Unless provided otherwise in the state constitution or statute, state actions are not restricted by a local government's comprehensive plan.[13]

§ 4.3   Zoning

In 1926, the Supreme Court, in the landmark case of *Village of Euclid v. Ambler Realty Co.,*[1] recognized the right of local government to use its delegated police powers to regulate the use and development of land by engaging in the legislative act of zoning. It held that the imposition of reasonable regulations that are reasonably related to the protection of the health, safety, morality or welfare of residents is a legitimate exercise of the police power.

In today's world, zoning is considered one of the most fundamental and important exercises of local police power. All states have delegated this authority to at least some of their local governments. Although most often the authority is given in state constitutions or statutes as part of a grant of home rule authority, it may be delegated in a local charter.[2] Unless prohibited by state law, the states may limit or withdraw this authority.[3] In addition, the zoning authority of local governments is always subject to federal[4] and state preemption.[5] Consistent with this, federal and state

---

[10] Dewitt Apparel, Inc. v. Four Seasons of Romar Beach Condominium Owner's Assoc., 678 So. 2d 740 (Ala. 1996).

[11] CAL. GOV'T CODE § 65060 *et seq.*; OHIO REV. CODE ANN. § 713.21; CONN. GEN. STAT. ANN. § 8-31a; 55 ILL. COMP. STAT. 5/5-14001 *et seq.*; MASS. GEN. LAWS ANN. ch. 23A, §§ 1, 3, 4 and ch. 40B, §§ 1-29; N.Y. GEN. MUN. § 239-b.

[12] N.J. STAT. ANN. § 13:18A-8 *et seq.*

[13] Kunimoto v. Kawakami, 56 Haw. 582, 545 P.2d 684 (Haw. 1976).

[1] Village of Euclid v. Ambler Realty Corp., 272 U.S. 365 (1926).

[2] City of Colorado Springs v. Smartt, 620 P.2d 1060 (Colo. 1980).

[3] Wilmington Medical Center v. Bradford, 382 A.2d 1338 (Del. 1978); N.J. State League of Municipalities v. Dep't. of Community Affairs, 729 A.2d 21 (N.J. 1999).

[4] Lng v. Loqa, 79 F. Supp. 2d 49 (D.R.I. 2000).

governments are not subject to local zoning restrictions unless a federal or state law specifically provides otherwise.[6]

A local government zones by dividing its land into districts and then defining the uses and restrictions that will apply to each. In zoning, the local government typically classifies its division of land by use, with the more basic types being residential, commercial, and industrial. Often, it may also subdivide the zones into various subcategories, such as single-family use or multiple-family use. The local government may then develop further restrictions that are applicable within each subcategory, such as building location on lots, and area and height restrictions.

Since zoning is deemed a legislative function, states have not been permitted to delegate the authority to zone to courts.[7] In addition, courts which have held local zoning invalid may not usurp the legislative function by determining the correct zoning classification.[8] The characterization of zoning enactments as either legislative or administrative has been used by courts to determine whether the use of initiative and referendum procedures are appropriate.

Local governments must adhere strictly to state statutes prescribing their use of this authority.[9] Often there are procedural and format requirements. Sometimes there are requirements that maps showing the boundaries adopted in the zoning regulations be filed. In addition, states may impose a requirement that zoning must be consistent with a local comprehensive plan. Prior submission to other governmental bodies for their approval or review may also be required.[10] Since zoning is viewed as legislative action, a majority of courts have held that due process does not require notice and a public hearing prior to the adoption of zoning requirements,[11] but it is often required by statute. Some courts have held that due process requires notice and a hearing for property owners affected by the zoning.[12]

The exercise of this broad authority to zone land is not unlimited. Each and every restriction on the use and development of land must be both reasonable and reasonably related to the local government's purpose to

---

[5] Soaring Vista Properties, Inc. v. Bd. of County Comm'rs of Queen Anne's Co., 741 A.2d 1110 (Md. 1999); Sheffield v. Rowland, 716 N.E.2d 1121 (Ohio 1999).

[6] U.S. v. City of Chester, 144 F.2d 415 (3d Cir. 1944); Evans v. Just Open Gov't, 251 S.E.2d 546 (Ga. 1979); City of Evanston v. Regional Transp. Auth., 559 N.E.2d 899 (Ill. App. Ct. 1990).

[7] Tampa v. Consolidated Box Co., 110 So. 2d 446 (Fla. App. 1959); Copple v. City of Lincoln, 315 N.W.2d 628 (Neb. 1982); Munch v. City of Mott, 311 N.W.2d 17 (N.D. 1981); Coe v. Albuquerque, 418 P.2d 545 (N.M. 1966).

[8] Schwartz v. City of Flint, 395 N.W.2d 678 (Mich. 1986); City of Naples Airport Auth. v. Collier Dev. Corp., 513 So. 2d 247 (Fla. App. 1987); Skillken & Co., v. Toledo, 528 F.2d 867 (6th Cir. 1975).

[9] Bowling Green-Warren County Airport Bd. v. Long, 364 S.W.2d 167 (Ky. 1963).

[10] Manning v. Reilly, 408 P.2d 414 (Ariz. Ct. App. 1965); Village of McGrew v. Steidley, 305 N.W.2d 627 (Neb. 1981); Davis v. Imlay Township, 151 N.W.2d 370 (Mich. Ct. App. 1967).

[11] Culver v. Dagg, 20 Or. App. 647 (Or. Ct. App. 1975); First Assembly of God v. Collier County, 20 F.3d 419 (11th Cir. 1994).

[12] Masters v. Pruce, 274 So. 2d 33 (Ala. 1973).

contribute to the health, safety and welfare of its people. In performing their judicial role of examining restrictions to determine whether they meet this test, the courts have actively participated in the development of zoning regulation. In deciding what are legitimate local purposes to support zoning, the courts have held that zoning may be used to encourage the orderly development of land in a manner that both maintains its value and permits the adequate provision of public services. Zoning has been appropriately used to reduce overcrowding and to assist in adequately meeting housing and commercial needs. Reviewing local government regulations, the Supreme Court has determined that landmark preservation,[13] historic preservation, aesthetics, and preservation of open space[14] are proper goals for the exercise of police power through zoning enactments. Often several goals are used to support the basis for a local government's zoning decision.

Just as with any other exercise of the police power, zoning must not violate federal and state constitutional protections afforded individuals. If zoning restrictions so severely reduce the value of private property, a local government may find that it must pay compensation for taking that property. This is discussed in § 4.5 *infra*. Zoning regulations must meet due process requirements of clarity. Limitations on the use of private property must be clearly expressed and not left to inference.[15] Equal protection prohibits discriminatory zoning and requires that local governments treat similar activities the same. An activity cannot be banned from a particular district if similar activities are permitted.[16] Likewise, so called "spot zoning," which occurs when a small area is unreasonably classified differently from other nearby land, is invalid. Even if a zoning enactment does not facially violate equal protection, it may be found to do so if it is applied in a discriminatory and unreasonable manner.[17] Similarly, local governments must not violate the Commerce Clause in their zoning regulations by discriminating against foreign merchants in favor of local businesses. A local government cannot impose an undue or unreasonable burden upon interstate commerce.

The Supreme Court has also reviewed local zoning restrictions to ensure that they do not violate First Amendment rights when regulating activities involving free speech.[18] These concerns have been raised frequently when local governments have sought to regulate adult uses such as bookstores, theaters and entertainment facilities that market items or performances considered inappropriate in certain locations.[19] The Supreme Court has

---

[13] Penn Central Transp. Co. v. City of New York, 438 U.S. 104 (1978).

[14] Dolan v. City of Tigard, 512 U.S. 374 (1994); San Diego Gas & Elec. Co. v. City of San Diego, 450 U.S. 621 (1981); Agins v. City of Tiburon, 447 U.S. 255 (1980).

[15] Zoning Comm'n of Sachem's Head Ass'n v. Leninski, 376 A.2d 771 (Conn. C.P. 1976).

[16] City of Cleburne v. Cleburne Living Center, 473 U.S. 433 (1985); Roman Catholic Welfare Corp. v. City of Piedmont, 289 P.2d 438 (Cal. 1955).

[17] Cobb County v. Peavy, 286 S.E.2d 732 (Ga. 1982).

[18] City of Renton v. Playtime Theaters, Inc. 475 U.S. 41 (1986); Schad v. Borough of Mt. Ephraim, 452 U.S. 61 (1981); Young v. American Mini Theaters, 427 U.S. 50 (1976).

[19] *See* § 3.4 *supra* for a discussion of regulation of adult uses.

invalidated a zoning regulation that banned all live entertainment, including nude dancing, from commercial districts while permitting regulations that restrict such activities from operating within certain distances of any other adult theater,[20] or within 1,000 feet of any school, residential zone, church or park.[21] In permitting local governments to confine adult activities to certain defined areas, the Supreme Court emphasizes that the restriction must be a reasonable "content-neutral" time, place and manner regulation that is not aimed at the content of the speech but rather at the secondary affects of the activities on the surrounding community. If there is a total ban on the activity, it is unlikely to escape the argument that it is in fact directed at the content of the speech. Local governments generally will be expected to make some accommodation for the speech it wants to control. However, the Supreme Court has sustained a ban on nude dancing in public places. It acknowledged that it is expressive conduct and entitled to some quantum of protection; however, it ". . .falls only within the outer ambit of the First Amendment's protection."[22] The Court concluded that such a restriction was constitutionally sound, since the local regulation was aimed at combating crime and other negative secondary effects caused by the presence of adult entertainment establishments, and not the message conveyed.

Other activities that local governments have sought to control by zoning that arguably affect the right to free speech include rock concerts, amplified sound outside buildings, and the erection of billboards and signs. In reviewing a ban on the posting of signs on public property, the Supreme Court again found that the regulation was not directed at the content of the speech, was impartially administered, and was a reasonable time, place and manner restriction narrowly drawn to foster an important or substantial government interest of preventing visual clutter.[23] Clearly, courts have determined that aesthetics is a substantial governmental goal and local governments may seek to achieve that goal.[24] Time, place and manner restrictions must be imposed in a content-neutral manner, narrowly drawn to serve government's purpose, and leave open ample channels of alternative means of communication.[25]

When zoning regulation impacts religion, First Amendment concerns are present also.[26] Courts have permitted reasonable time, place and manner restrictions on religious activities if imposed in order to protect health, safety and welfare of the community at large. It is necessary to determine

---

[20] *Young*, 427 U.S. 50.

[21] *City of Renton*, 475 U.S. 41.

[22] City of Erie v. Pap's A.M., 529 U.S. 277 (2000).

[23] Members of City Council of City of Los Angeles v. Taxpayers for Vincent, 466 U.S. 789 (1984).

[24] Oregon City v. Hartke, 400 P.2d 255 (Or. 1965); Cromwell v. Ferrier, 225 N.E.2d 749 (N.Y. 1967); Racine County v. Plourde, 157 N.W.2d 591 (Wis. 1968).

[25] City of Ladue v. Gilleo, 512 U.S. 43 (1994).

[26] Heffron v. Int'l Soc'y for Krishna Consciousness, Inc., 452 U.S. 640 (1981).

whether the regulated activity is religious, whether the burden imposed by the zoning is significant, and whether there are reasonable alternatives available for the religious activity. The zoning regulation must be narrowly drawn so its impact is no greater than necessary to further a compelling governmental interest.[27]

§ 4.4 Applicability, Variances, Special Permits and Exceptions

Zoning has become the most prevalent form of land use control in the United States. Along with its increased usage, local governments have developed ways of adding flexibility to make it work. The introduction of variances, floating zones, planned unit development and special permits provides the ability to tailor the regulatory structure to better fit the needs of the community. Extraterritorial zoning is permitted in some states. Local governments are usually limited to a short distance such as one or two miles outside its boundaries, with the justification that activities taking place in the near proximity directly impact the community.[1] Often, states vary in their treatment of territory annexed to a local government. In some, the restrictions in effect prior to annexation continue.[2] In others, the restrictions in the area to which the land has been annexed immediately apply to the newly-annexed territory.

A local government may adopt a zoning regulation for its land, but what if existing land uses are not consistent with the new restrictions? Typically, these nonconforming uses, which are those lawfully in existence prior to the enactment of the zoning regulation, are permitted to continue. If the use was not lawful, was not permitted, or was contrary to existing zoning at the time, it will not gain the protection of being classified as a nonconforming use. It is not a non-conforming use merely because it would have been permitted, or because it was merely contemplated by the owner that it would be used in a nonconforming manner. Nor can one claim a nonconforming use just because a permit to use it in a particular way had been obtained. It has to have been actually used in such a way. Some jurisdictions refer to this as "notorious use," meaning that it was generally known in the neighborhood that the property was used in a particular way.

Most zoning enactments expressly exempt lawful nonconforming uses, recognizing both constitutional and equitable concerns. However, it may be a limited right that is not granted in perpetuity. Some states authorize local governments to adopt amortization provisions requiring the termination of nonconforming uses within a specified period of time. These have been upheld, provided they are based on a substantial public purpose and the time allowed is reasonable.[3] In addition, recognizing nonconforming

---

[27] Keeler v. Mayor & City Council of Cumberland, 951 F. Supp. 83 (D. Md. 1997).

[1] *See* N.D. CENT. CODE § 40-47-01.1 (1982).

[2] *See* SANDRA M. STEVENSON, ANTIEAU ON LOCAL GOVERNMENT LAW § 56.08 (2d ed. 2001).

[3] Harbison v. Buffalo, 152 N.E.2d 42 (N.Y. 1958) (*citing* ANTIEAU ON LOCAL GOVERNMENT LAW); Donrey Communications Co. Inc. v. City of Fayetteville, 660 S.W.2d 900 (Ark. 1983); Village of Valatie v. Smith, 632 N.E.2d 1264 (N.Y. 1994).

uses does not prevent the local government from regulating the use if necessary to protect the health, safety and welfare of the community.[4] Local
governments may also prohibit structural and use changes, including
expansion and extension of uses. Often, zoning enactments will specify that
a discontinuance or abandonment of a nonconforming use bars its resump-
tion. This does not apply to temporary closings for remodeling[5] or absences
that are part of the business,[6] or one resulting from causes beyond the
owner's control. An intent to abandon may be shown by the facts of the
case. If there has been a significant period of nonuse, or a conversion to
a conforming use, intent to abandon may be found. Some zoning regulations
specify a time limit for the discontinuance, signaling when the right to
engage in the nonconforming activity ends.[7] If a nonconforming use is
totally destroyed, local governments are not required to permit the owner
to rebuild.

Local governments often have provisions in their zoning regulations,
enabling statutes or charters that give them a degree of flexibility in
applying the zoning rules they have adopted. Two types of government
action, commonly referred to as "exceptions" and "special or conditional use
permits," can be used to permit certain activities or uses on the property
that would not normally be allowed under the zoning regulations. Neither
of these two options require a variance from the existing rules because they
are part of the zoning regulations.

Zoning statutes often contain provisions that specifically except certain
activities from their prohibitions. These are called "exceptions" and may
require an administrative determination that they are applicable to a
particular landowner.[8] The zoning regulation may also provide that conditions may be imposed on those who claim a right to the exception. The
exception is specified by the legislative body when the zoning is enacted
and is generally contained in the zoning regulation itself. It is a provision
that states that the restriction is applicable except for the listed action.
Even though a property owner is entitled to claim this clearly specified
right, the application and review process insures that those claiming an
exception are in fact entitled to it.

The "special or conditional use permit" is used when a variation to a
zoning regulation would benefit the welfare of the community. Educational
or medical facilities have been able to locate in areas that have been zoned
for other uses by applying for and receiving special use permits. The
potential for their existence has been foreseen and it has been decided that
their presence can be of benefit to the community. This must be authorized

---

[4] Outdoor Sys. Inc. v. City of Mesa, 819 P.2d 44 (Ariz. 1991).

[5] Franklin County v. City of St. Albans, 576 A.2d 135 (Vt. 1990).

[6] Flowerree v. City of Concord, 378 S.E.2d 188 (N.C. Ct. App. 1989) (finding no cessation
from the delay in finding new tenants).

[7] Toys "R" Us v. Silva (N.Y. 1996) (holding that intent is irrelevant where the local enactment
prescribes a limiting grace period for the discontinuance of non-conforming use).

[8] Graves v. Bloomfield Planning Bd., 235 A.2d 51 (N.J. Super. Ct. Law Div. 1967).

by delegated authority from the state to the local government and then to the administrative board responsible for granting or denying the application. It is also necessary that the local legislative body prescribe standards to govern the board's discretionary actions so that the local government is not subject to a claim of unconstitutional delegation of legislative authority.

The reviewing board may be authorized to impose conditions on its grant of both exceptions and special use permits. There may be undesirable traits associated with the activity, such as size, density or noise that are of concern to the local government. By requiring an application and review process, reasonable conditions can be imposed that minimize the negative impacts. Judicial review of the condition is one of determining whether the governmental agency has acted reasonably. If there is no reasonable basis for a condition, it may be overturned.

Local governments also grant variances from zoning restrictions. Unlike an exception or a special use permit, this is a relaxation of a zoning restriction applied to a specific property. In giving a variance, the local government grants relief from the restrictions of a zoning regulation because its enforcement would cause a substantial hardship to the property owner without serving a significant, corresponding benefit to the public.[9] There are two types of variances with very different standards. Both contain rights that apply to the land, so that subsequent owners are usually entitled to the benefits of the variance once it is granted. The first type is an area variance which provides relief from specific restrictions on how the property can be developed. It relates to issues like building height, lot size, and setback requirements.

The second type of variance is a use variance which permits the property to be developed for a particular use that is otherwise prohibited by the zoning restrictions. This type is much more difficult to obtain than an area variance since it is generally held that it should not be granted unless it is found, on the basis of substantial evidence, that the property cannot reasonably be used in a manner consistent with the applicable zoning restrictions.[10]

Many jurisdictions have established that the local board can grant variances to an applicant who establishes a practical difficulty or unnecessary hardship in meeting the existing zoning restrictions.[11] The difficulty or unnecessary hardship must be unique to the property for which the variance is sought. Additional considerations are whether the property can produce a reasonable return if used only for the purpose permitted in that zone and whether the proposed use or change would alter the essential character of the neighborhood. A financial hardship alone is not usually

[9] Arcadia Dev. Corp. v. City of Bloomington, 125 N.W.2d 846 (Minn. 1964).

[10] Worrell v. Del Sesto, 357 A.2d 443 (R.I. 1976); Puritan-Greenfield Improvement Ass'n v. Leo, 153 N.W.2d 162 (Mich. Ct. App. 1967).

[11] Matthew v. Smith, 707 S.W.2d 411 (Mo. 1986); Snyder v. Waukeska Co. Zoning Bd. of Adjustment, 247 N.W.2d 98 (Wis. 1976).

sufficient.[12] It may be a factor to be considered,[13] and if the zoning restriction destroys or greatly decreases the value, it may justify a variance[14] or indicate an unconstitutional taking.[15]

A self-inflicted hardship is one that has been created by the voluntary act of the property owner. An example is where an owner purchases property with zoning limitations present at the time of purchase. Another example is where the owner conveys a portion of the property and the remainder does not meet minimum lot-size standards. States differ in their treatment of self-inflicted hardships. In some jurisdictions it is a bar to obtaining a variance,[16] while in others it is merely a factor to be considered.[17]

A board that is authorized to grant a variance cannot do so in such a way that is, in effect, an amendment of the zoning regulations. It could not, for instance, grant variances to a number of property owners in a wholesale manner. Some states limit the discretion that may be used by requiring that a variance must be consistent with a local government's comprehensive plan,[18] or limiting the granting of variances to specific situations.[19] The burden of proof needed to obtain a variance has been specified in some states by statute[20] and in others by courts.[21]

§ 4.5 Regulatory Takings and Moratoriums on Development

Local decisions in establishing and enforcing zoning, or denying special permits or variances, are subject to claims by property owners that the local government has taken property without paying just compensation. Sometimes such claim is raised in the context of the severity of the restriction. The federal and state constitutions require that compensation be paid when private property is taken by governments for a public purpose. Many state constitutions also require payment when private property is damaged as well. Local governments can take private property through the exercise of eminent domain or by actions that do not comply with such formalities,

---

[12] Bd. of Zoning Adjustment of Mobile v. Williams, 636 So. 2d 413 (Ala. 1994)

[13] Homan v. Lynch, 147 A.2d 650 (Del. 1959); Marino v. City of Baltimore, 137 A.2d 198 (Md. 1957).

[14] Matter of Citizens Savings Bank v. Bd. of Zoning Appeals of Lansing, 638 N.Y.S.2d 179 (3d Dep't 1996); Culinary Institute v. Bd. of Zoning Appeals of New Haven, 121 A.2d 637 (Conn. 1956).

[15] See § 4.5 infra for a discussion of regulatory takings.

[16] M & R Enters., Inc. v. Zoning Bd. of Appeals of Southington, 231 A.2d 272 (Conn. 1967); Elwyn v. City of Miami, 113 So. 2d 849 (Fla. App. 1959).

[17] M & R Enters., Inc.; Bd. of Oklahoma City v. Shanbour, 435 P.2d 569 (Okla. 1967).

[18] Antrim v. Hohlt, 108 N.E.2d 197 (Ind. Ct. App. 1952).

[19] State ex rel. Shaker Square Co. v. Guion, 145 N.E.2d 144 (Ohio Ct. App. 1957).

[20] IND. CODE ANN. § 36-7-4-918(f); N.J. STAT. ANN. § 40:55D 70.

[21] Otto v. Steinhilber, 24 N.E.2d 851 (N.Y. 1939); Frank v. Russell, 70 N.W.2d 306 (Neb. 1955); Moore v. City of Rochester, 427 A.2d 10 (N.H. 1981).

often referred to as inverse condemnation.[1] Actions that have led to this characterization are physical invasions, including permanent flooding of private land during the construction of a dam,[2] and repeated flights over private land by low-flying airplanes.[3] Whether the *physical appropriation* fosters a public purpose or whether it deprives the owner of all economically valuable use of the land is irrelevant to a determination of whether this is an unconstitutional taking that requires compensation. Once it is established that part or all of someone's private property has been *physically taken* by a local government, there is a categorical duty to pay compensation.[4] These appropriations of private property are referred to as categorical takings.

Property can also be taken when a local government uses its regulatory authority in a manner that unconstitutionally deprives the owner of its use.[5] As far back as 1922, when the Supreme Court decided *Pennsylvania Coal Co. v. Mahon*,[6] courts have recognized that government must pay compensation when its regulations diminish the value of land to a sufficiently low enough level. The Supreme Court has not established a set formula for separating acceptable regulation from compensable taking. It has said that courts are to consider the economic effect on the landowner, the extent to which the regulation interferes with investment-backed expectation, and the character of the government action. Government is not to impose public burdens on individuals when they should be borne by the public as a whole, and there is therefore a balancing of public and private interests.[7]

The *regulatory appropriation* presents difficult issues because local governments may adopt reasonable and constitutionally sound regulations of the use of private property. The question to be answered is whether the regulation imposes such a severe restriction on the use of the property that it produces nearly the same result as a direct appropriation. In regulatory takings cases, the courts are often asked to balance public and private interests. The Supreme Court, in *Agins v. City of Tiburon*,[8] held that there is an unconstitutional taking if the regulation does not substantially advance a legitimate state interest or if it denies the owner all economically beneficial or productive use of his or her land. The Court continues to shed light on how the ad hoc factual analysis is to be used in determining whether or not a regulatory taking has occurred. Later, in *Lucas v. South Carolina*

---

[1] For an excellent discussion of inverse condemnation, *see* D. MANDELKER, LAND USE LAW §§ 8.19–8.22, 8.25 (4th ed. 1997).

[2] United States v. Lynah, 188 U.S. 445 (1903).

[3] Griggs v. Allegheny County, 369 U.S. 84 (1962).

[4] Tahoe-Sierra Preservation Council, Inc. v. Tahoe Regional Planning Agency, 535 U.S. 302 (2002).

[5] Pennsylvania Coal Co. v. Mahon, 260 U.S. 393 (1922).

[6] *Id.*

[7] Palazzolo v. Rhode Island, 533 U.S. 606 (2001).

[8] Agins v. City of Tiburon, 477 U.S. 255 (1980).

Coastal Council,[9] it held that when a regulation deprives an owner of *all* economically beneficial use of his land, a taking has occurred and compensation must be paid even though the regulation was adopted to prevent serious public harm. An exception was noted by the Court when it held that compensation would not be required if the regulation was based on existing principles of law. In other words, if the state had the right to effectuate the same result because of an existing nuisance, then implementation of the regulation would not require compensation. In this particular case, plaintiff purchased property that was rendered valueless by a statute that was enacted two years later. The taking was unconditional and permanent and the government was required to pay full compensation. In this type of taking there is no balancing of public or private interests. The exercise of regulatory authority in such a way that it deprives an owner of *all* economically beneficial use of his property is a categorical taking and is to be treated the same as a direct physical appropriation of private property. However, the Court has indicated that it is not enough to show that an owner has been deprived of the *most beneficial* use of his property,[10] and it may not be enough to show that there is a *temporary* denial of all economically beneficial use.[11]

In those cases where a regulation has deprived an owner of some but not all economically beneficial uses, the courts are to consider the facts of each case. In the seminal case of *Penn Central Transportation v. New York City*,[12] the Supreme Court decided that a government decision to deny the owners of Grand Central Terminal the right to construct an office building over the terminal did not constitute a taking. The Constitution does not require that government always compensate private property owners for reductions in the economic value of property. The public and private interests are to be balanced in an effort to decide whether or not the impact *on the whole property*[13] is such that a compensable taking has occurred. During this review, a court must consider the regulation's economic effect on the landowner, the extent to which it interferes with reasonable investment-backed expectation, and the character of the government action.[14] By adopting this approach, the Court seeks to prevent government from imposing public burdens on individuals when such burdens should be imposed on the public as a whole.

The Supreme Court has held that once a taking is established, government is obligated to pay just compensation even if the taking was not permanent. In *First English Evangelical Lutheran Church of Glendale v.*

---

[9] Lucas v. South Carolina Coastal Council, 505 U.S. 1003 (1992).

[10] Goldblatt v. Town of Hempstead, 369 U.S. 590 (1962).

[11] Tahoe-Sierra Preservation Council, Inc. v. Tahoe Regional Planning Agency, 535 U.S. 302 (2002).

[12] Penn Central Transportation v. New York City, 438 U.S. 104 (1978).

[13] *Tahoe-Sierra Preservation Council, Inc.,* 535 U.S. 302 (2002), *referring to* Penn Central Transportation v. New York City, 438 U.S. 104 (1978).

[14] *Id.*; Palazzolo v. Rhode Island, 533 U.S. 606 (2001).

Los Angeles County,[15] a flood destroyed the owner's buildings and the local government adopted an interim ordinance that prohibited construction or reconstruction of its buildings. The Court held that "temporary" regulatory takings of all use of the property, like permanent ones, require compensation.

The issue of temporary moratoriums on the use of land and how they are to be treated was addressed in *Tahoe-Sierra Preservation Council, Inc. v. Tahoe Regional Planning Agency.*[16] In this case, the Supreme Court reviewed a thirty-two month moratorium on development that was imposed on property for the purpose of allowing a land use planning agency to prepare a comprehensive regional plan. The Court held that a temporary denial of the use of property is not to be treated in the same manner as a direct taking or a permanent denial of all use. It is not a categorical taking that automatically entitles an owner to compensation. Acknowledging that any moratorium longer than a year is suspect, the Court held that in order to determine whether a temporary moratorium effects a taking, a fact-specific inquiry is to be undertaken. This requires careful examination and weighing of all relevant factors, including the length of the deprivation of use. The Court rejected an argument that even a *temporary* deprivation of *all* economic use of property should be categorically compensated in order to protect property owners from unfairly bearing a public burden. Noting that there are normal delays in government activities such as obtaining permits or zoning changes, restrictions in the use of property are normal and to be expected while governments engage in their authorized regulatory authority. If there is to be change in this area, the Court expressed the view that it is more appropriately a subject for legislative consideration. The Court's approach to temporary deprivations caused by temporary moratoriums appears to differ from its decision on compensation for temporary deprivations caused by other forms of regulatory takings in *First English Evangelical Lutheran Church of Glendale v. Los Angeles County.*[17]

When a regulation imposes conditions on the use or development of land, the Court has held that there is no taking if it substantially advances legitimate public purposes and at the same time allows an owner an economically viable use of his land.[18] However, it has also held that government cannot impose a requirement that has little or no relationship to the public benefit sought. In other words, there must be a connection between the legitimate state interest that is prompting the government requirement and the permit condition imposed on the landowner. If there is an adequate nexus between the two, then the Court examines the requirement to see if it bears an appropriate relationship to the projected impact of the landowner's proposed action.[19] In a case where government sought a

---

[15] First English Evangelical Lutheran Church of Glendale v. Los Angeles County, 482 U.S. 304 (1987).

[16] *Tahoe-Sierra Preservation Council, Inc.,* 535 U.S. 302 (2002).

[17] *First English Evangelical Lutheran Church of Glendale,* 482 U.S. 304 (1987).

[18] *Agins,* 447 U.S. 255 (1980).

[19] Nollan v. California Coastal Comm'n, 483 U.S. 825 (1987).

dedication of a portion of the applicant's property for flood-control purposes, the Court adopted a "proportionality test" to be used when approval of a permit is conditioned on the dedication of land.[20] There must be a determination that any required dedication of property is related in both nature and extent to the impact of the proposed development. In other words, the exaction must address problems created by the applicant's proposed action.

The Supreme Court has determined that a landowner may challenge a government regulation as an unconstitutional taking even though he or she obtained the property after the regulation was enacted.[21]

§ 4.6 Development Approval with Conditions of Exaction, Impact or Linkage Fees

In addition to single-facility approvals, local governments have been delegated authority to impose controls on the development of a tract of land. Most often, these applications are for subdivided parcels or planned-unit developments which are a mixture of different types of uses. A subdivision is typically a division of one piece of land into lots with eventual separate ownership of each one. The local government often requires approval of a plan (or a plat) by a government body before the developer can proceed. The requirements vary, but typically, the local government wants to see that there are adequate provisions for streets, utilities, parks, access of firefighting apparatus, and other public necessities that contribute toward the orderly development of a residential community. Information will probably be required on lot sizes, location of sewage and water facilities, plans for drainage, and about the impact the development will have on the remainder of the community.

Some states have prescribed mandatory procedures for private development and may require review by the state or another local government before final approval is granted.[1] Time limits for the approval process and a requirement of public hearings have been specified in some states. Others have provided by statute that public hearings are permissible[2] or even that summary approval may be granted if a proposal is in conformity with the subdivision regulations adopted by the local government.[3]

If a local government needs time to insure that adequate planning or infrastructure exists, moratoria on development have been upheld, provided the time is reasonable.[4] This is discussed in § 4.5 *supra*.

---

[20] Dolan v. City of Tigard, 512 U.S. 374 (1994). *See also* City of Monterey v. Del Monte Dunes at Monterey, Ltd., 526 U.S. 687, 702-03 (1999) (holding that the proportionality test is applicable when approval is conditioned on the dedication of lands and is not applicable in denial of permit cases).

[21] Palazzolo v. Rhode Island, 533 U.S. 606 (2001).

[1] CAL. GOV'T CODE § 66455.5 (repealed 1996).

[2] PA. STAT. ANN. tit. 53, § 10508 (West 1997).

[3] Forest Const. Co. v. Planning & Zoning Comm'n of Town of Bethany, 236 A.2d 917 (Conn. 1967).

[4] Collura v. Town of Arlington, 329 N.E.2d 733 (Mass. 1975); Almquist v. Town of Marshan, 245 N.W.2d 819 (Minn. 1976).

After review of a proposed development, local governments often impose conditions upon the approval. Authority to do this may be found in the police power that has been delegated to the local government by state constitution, statute or charter. However, courts have found that some local governments do not have adequate authority.[5] If there are statutes that specify how conditions may be imposed, they must be carefully followed.

Some local governments have imposed a requirement that an applicant pay development or impact fees to help offset the public costs of infrastructure such as roads, sewers, water, and drainage that will be needed as a result of the growth. Other local governments have required that some of the applicant's land be set aside for schools, parks, recreational areas or other public facilities. These conditions requiring land dedications and fee contributions for school sites, parks and other amenities have been upheld as valid conditions for plan approval if statutorily authorized, constitutionally applied, and if they are reasonable.[6] Conditions that do not substantially advance a legitimate public purpose or that deny the property owner an economically viable use of his or her land have been found to violate the Due Process Clause.[7] The Supreme Court has also held that there must be a connection between the public purpose and the permit condition imposed on the landowner. Where land is required to be dedicated to a public purpose, the requirement must also appropriately relate to the landowner's proposed action.[8] In other words, the exaction must address problems created by the applicant's proposed action. This is discussed *supra* in § 4.5, *Regulatory Takings and Moratoriums on Development.*

An impact fee increasingly imposed on developers of commercial property is the "linkage" fee. It is based on the additional public costs that will be incurred by providing public transportation "linking" to the new facility. It has also been used as a means of offsetting the public costs of providing low cost housing for those who will be displaced by the new development.

After projects are approved, developers are often required to post performance bonds or guarantees in the amount estimated to cover the cost of compliance with the conditions established for final approval. Some statutes permit local governments to give a tentative approval of a plan for a subdivision, with final approval given after completion of the homes and required public improvements.[9]

---

[5] Midtown Properties v. Madison Tp., 172 A.2d 40 (N.J. Super. Ct. Law Div. 1961); Coronado Dev. Co. v. McPherson, 368 P.2d 51 (Kan. 1962); Hoepker v. City of Madison Plan Comm'n, 563 N.W.2d 145 (Wis. 1997).

[6] City of Mobile v. Waldon, 429 So. 2d 945 (Ala. 1983); Remmenga v. California Coastal Comm'n, 209 Cal. Rptr. 628 (Cal. App. 2d Dist. 1985); Aunt Hack Ridge Estates, Inc. v. Planning Comm'n, 273 A.2d 880 (Conn. 1970); Pioneer Trust & Sav. Bank v. Village of Mount Prospect, 176 N.E.2d 799 (Ill. 1961); Home Builders Ass'n of Greater Kansas City v. City of Kansas City 555 S.W.2d 832 (Mo. 1977); Golden v. Town of Ramapo, 285 N.E.2d 291 (N.Y. 1972), *appeal dismissed*, 409 U.S. 1003 (1972).

[7] Agins v. City of Tiburon, 447 U.S. 255 (1980).

[8] Nollan v. California Coastal Comm'n, 483 U.S. 825 (1987).

[9] PA. STAT. ANN. tit. 53, § 10509 (West 1997).

§ 4.7   Enforcement and Appeal from Zoning Requirements and Decisions

Local comprehensive plans are merely expressions of policy and generally are not subject to challenge by those property owners who disagree with them. Until implemented by zoning enactments or other land use regulations, the courts hold that they indicate future intent and are nonbinding declarations.[1] Conversely, unless required by state or local law, local governments will not generally be required to abide by their comprehensive plan. Zoning enactments have been upheld even when challenged because they are inconsistent with the local government's comprehensive plan.[2]

The ability of local governments to enforce their zoning regulations varies because of state legislative prescriptions and judicial interpretations of local zoning authority. Generally, local governments are found to have authority to enforce their zoning restrictions against violators and may do so by seeking injunctive relief, issuing cease and desist orders and imposing fines. In extreme cases they may be able to abate a public nuisance. In some jurisdictions, even private individuals are permitted to obtain injunctive relief against continuing violations of zoning restrictions if they can show that they suffer special damages, different from those of the general public. However, most states require that enforcement actions be brought by the local government.

A local government may be estopped on equitable grounds from enforcing a zoning regulation if the government has encouraged or permitted a developer to rely on its representation that an action is in compliance with local regulations and it is subsequently revealed that it is not.[3] This exception to the general rule that estoppel does not apply to local governments is used in particularly egregious situations. It is conditioned on a finding that there has been good-faith reliance on the actions of the local government and that little harm will occur to the general public by the application of equitable estoppel. The doctrine is applied cautiously and used by the courts only when it would be highly inequitable to enforce the zoning restrictions. Other courts disagree and have held that prior tolerance of a violation, even if a permit was issued and some expenditures made, will not stop a local government from enforcing its zoning regulations.[4] If the detrimental reliance was caused by an unauthorized local government officer, courts generally refuse to find equitable estoppel.

---

[1] Cervase v. Kawaida Towers, Inc., 308 A.2d 47 (N.J. Super. Ct. Law Div. 1973), aff'd, 322 A.2d 477 (N.J. Super. A.D. 1974).

[2] Bone v. City of Lewiston, 693 P.2d 1046 (Idaho 1984); State by Rochester Ass'n of Neighborhoods v. City of Rochester, 268 N.W.2d 885 (Minn. 1978).

[3] Hilton Hotels v. District of Columbia Bd. of Zoning Adjustment, 435 A.2d 1026 (D.C. Cir. 1981); City of Auburn v. Desgrosseillers, 578 A.2d 712 (Me. 1990); Dupuis v. Submarine Base Credit Union, 365 A.2d 1093 (Conn. 1976).

[4] Boyd v. Donelon, 193 So. 2d 291 (La. Ct. App. 1966); City of Milwaukee v. Leavitt, 142 N.W.2d 169 (Wis. 1966).

The doctrine of laches does not usually apply to local government actions. It has very limited applicability to zoning regulation. Failure to enforce zoning regulations in the past will not prevent local governments from choosing to do so in the present. Nor will the fact that others are violating the zoning restrictions prevent a local government from enjoining or prosecuting a violator.[5] Courts are not sympathetic to individuals who consciously disregard the law, and they do not look favorably upon laches as a defense against proper enforcement of the law.[6]

A person challenging a zoning enactment can gain judicial relief if it is shown that the restrictions upon his property are arbitrary and unreasonable. The challenger has the burden of proof that it is unreasonable and must overcome any presumption of reasonableness, constitutionality, and validity that may accompany a local legislative action. The court may grant mandamus, an injunction or declaratory relief. If the zoning is found to violate a constitutional or other federally-protected right of an individual, relief may be sought against the local government under Section 1983 of the Civil Rights Act. A typical argument would be that the zoning enactment, or failure to rezone, diminishes the use and value of the property so as to amount to a taking without just compensation or a deprivation of property without due process of law. Attorney fees may also be awarded when such a violation is found.[7]

Before bringing an action challenging the local zoning regulation, it is usually required that the property owner exhaust all administrative remedies. This is particularly true when a zoning regulation is not claimed to be facially invalid but invalid as applied to a particular landowner.[8] A person must use an administrative appeal process before bringing a claim of an unconstitutional taking or the claim may not be ripe for adjudication.[9] This requirement may include an obligation by the claimant to first seek a variance. However, exhaustion of administrative remedies is not required where the argument is that the entire zoning enactment is invalid, not merely as applied. Courts have indicated that constitutional and other legal questions presented by such a challenge are not appropriate for determination by administrative bodies.[10]

When a court reviews the decision to grant or deny applications for relief, it will review the record and decide whether the decision is supported by the evidence and is reasonable. It will not reverse unless there is strong

---

[5] City of Gastonia, 157 S.E.2d 154 (N.C. 1967).

[6] Town of Seabrook v. Vachon Management, Inc., 745 A.2d 1155 (N.H. 2000). Laches may be used in New Hampshire to bar local government action but the Court held that it would not apply where one consciously disregards the law. *Id.* at 1161.

[7] Goss v. City of Little Rock, Ark., 151 F.3d 861 (8th Cir. 1998). *See* CIVIL RIGHTS ACT, 42 U.S.C. § 1988(b) (1994).

[8] City of Glasden v. Entrekin, 387 So. 2d 829 (Ala. 1980).

[9] Hoepker v. City of Madison Plan Comm'n, 563 N.W.2d 145 (Wis. 1997).

[10] City of Rome v. Pilgrim, 271 S.E.2d 189 (Ga. 1980); Steinlage v. City of New Hampshire 567 N.W.2d 438 (Iowa Ct. App. 1997).

proof of an abuse of authority. If there is substantial evidence to support it, the court will uphold it. There is no weighing of benefits and detriments, just a determination of whether the administrative body acted in a supportable manner. There is generally a presumption that the decision is correct and the burden of showing otherwise is on the appellant. Different wording is found among the state court opinions but all express an intent to determine whether the board acted arbitrarily, fairly or abused its discretion. It has often been stated that a court will not reverse a decision unless there is a clear showing of an abuse of discretion.

PART II PUBLIC PROPERTY

§ 4.8   Acquisition and Disposition of Local Government Property

Most local governments have been delegated authority, either expressly or impliedly, in their general grant of home-rule powers or through specific provisions in state constitutions or statutes, to acquire property for public use. Property may be acquired either by purchase, gift, lease or eminent domain. The courts have interpreted this authority expansively, giving local governments a great deal of flexibility to use it to achieve many goals, ranging from redevelopment to economic development.[1]

State statutes may prescribe the factors to be considered and the procedure to be followed when a local government decides to exercise its power of eminent domain, which is also known as taking property by condemnation. This authority must be exercised strictly as prescribed and all constitutional requirements must be met. Federal and state constitutions require that property may only be taken for a public purpose; just compensation must be paid to the property owner; and the local government must adhere to due process of law.

The question of public purpose for the property has been challenged many times in the courts. However, the cases reveal that courts are hesitant to second guess local government decisions, and will only reverse their determination when a challenger can show an abuse of discretion, or that fraud was involved in the local decision.[2] The acquisition of property for industrial, manufacturing or other private economic development purposes has been sustained, with the courts holding that some incidental benefit to private individuals does not change the nature of the action.[3] Local governments have often taken property for urban renewal or redevelopment purposes.[4] If the courts determine that the primary purpose is to benefit

---

[1] Hawaii Housing Auth. v. Midkiff, 467 U.S. 229 (1984).

[2] Poremba v. City of Springfield, 238 N.E.2d 43 (Mass. 1968), *citing* Antieau on Local Government Law, § 20.01.

[3] Waldo's Inc. v. Village of Johnson City, 543 N.E.2d 74 (N.Y. 1989); *In re* Kansas City Ordinance No. 39946, 252 S.W. 404 (Mo. 1923).

[4] Cannata v. City of New York, 182 N.E.2d 395 (N.Y. 1952); Chicago Land Clearance Comm'n v. White, 104 N.E.2d 236 (Ill. 1952), *cert. denied*, 344 U.S. 824 (1952).

the public, incidental benefit to private individuals will not prevent the exercise of eminent domain. On the other hand, if the primary purpose is to benefit individuals and the action will incidentally benefit the public, use of eminent domain will not be sustained.[5]

Assuming that a local government is successful in meeting the challenge of establishing a public purpose, in many states it must also be prepared to show that the particular property is necessary for the project. The courts have been similarly generous in deferring to local discretion. If a local government can show reasonableness and that the determination was not arbitrary or fraudulent, generally the courts will uphold the decision. The same pattern holds true for challenges based on the extent of property necessary for the public purpose, when it is actually needed and when it is taken. Courts do not like to second-guess these governmental decisions. A challenger must have a strong case of arbitrary or fraudulent conduct on the part of the local government in order to succeed.

Local governments can also acquire title to easements by prescription or fee title to land by adverse possession. The statutory requirements that specify how long property must have been used by anyone in order to obtain title is the length of time that local government must have used the property. Local use must be adverse, exclusive, continuous, under claim of right, with the knowledge of the owner and without consent.[6] There is a high burden of proof for local governments since generally all presumptions favor the owner.[7]

Local governments may also acquire property by purchase, gift or lease. The acquisition must be reasonable, done for a public purpose, pursuant to delegated authority, and in accordance with all prescribed procedures. Gifts to local governments are often classified as statutory or common law dedications. At common law, a local government had to show an intention by the owner of land to donate it to the local government for public use and an acceptance by the government.[8] The intent to transfer must be shown by a clear declaration or an act which is evidence of the clearest intention on the part of the landowner to give the land for a public use.[9] Sometimes courts have found an implied intent where an owner has permitted long-term use by the local government.[10] This is particularly true

---

[5] Baycol, Inc. v. Downtown Development Authority, 315 So. 2d 451 (Fla. 1975); Burger v. City of Beatrice, 147 N.W.2d 784 (Neb. 1967).

[6] Kratina v. Bd. of Comm'rs of Shawnee County, 548 P.2d 1232 (Kan. 1976); City of Derby v. Di Yanno, 118 A.2d 308 (Conn. 1955); Packard v. Fuller, 28 So. 2d 207 (Ala. 1946); Koontz v. Town of Superior, 746 P.2d 1264 (Wyo. 1987).

[7] Town of Kaneville v. Meredith, 184 N.E. 883 (Ill. 1933).

[8] Poynter v. Johnston, 338 N.W.2d 484 (Wis. 1983); McKinney v. Ruderman, 121 Cal. Rptr. 262 (1962); Star Island Assocs. v. City of St. Petersburg Beach, 433 So. 2d 998 (Fla. Dist. Ct. App. 1983).

[9] City of Lufkin v. DuPuy, 327 S.W.2d 781 (Tex. Civ. App. 1959); Chicago v. Borden, 60 N.E.915 (Ill. 1901); Tischauser v. Newport Beach, 37 Cal. Rptr. 141 (1964). *But see* Volpe v. Marina Parks, Inc., 220 A.2d 525, 529 (R.I. 1966) (finding that evidence that reasonably tends to demonstrate intent is sufficient).

[10] East v. Wrightsville, 126 S.E.2d 407 (Ga. 1962).

where the property has been used for a long time, improvements were made by the local government and the owner was aware and took no action.[11] Subdividers of property have been found to have manifested sufficient intent when they have filed or recorded plats that indicate streets and alleys.[12] In fact, dedication of streets is frequently required before a plat for a new subdivision is accepted by a local body.

Acceptance by the local government is optional and, until accepted, the local government assumes no rights or liabilities.[13] Since ownership carries an obligation to maintain and potential tort liability for failure to do so, the courts require a clear and unequivocal proof of acceptance by the local government.[14] Formal acceptance is not usually required either by common law or statute, but offers at times are accepted by a resolution of the governing body. Generally, acceptance can be shown by deed or public record, by public acts consistent with acceptance, by long public use, or by express official action. Where an adverse-possession claim existed and the local government was not shown to have accepted the dedication, the private individual was deemed to have acquired title.[15]

It is necessary that a local government have authority to convert property from one public use to another since the rule at common law was that property is held in trust for the public purpose for which it was acquired.[16] Inroads in this doctrine began to surface with cases upholding conversions of a street to a public rest area[17] or to a pedestrian mall.[18] The court said that this was not a change of use in a legal sense. The decision to convert would not be reversed unless there was strong proof of arbitrariness or gross abuse of discretion by the local government. However, if the local government reserves easements, such as walkways, the private purchaser may be limited in its control over the use of that portion of the property.[18.1] Generally, unless encumbered by a limiting condition, property that has been acquired by means other than dedication may now be converted to another public use. Property that has been acquired through dedication

---

[11] Moon v. City of Conyers, 150 S.E.2d 873 (Ga. 1966); Brown v. Bd. of County Comm'rs for Pennington County, 422 N.W.2d 440 (S.D. 1988).

[12] Walton v. Clermont, 109 So. 2d 403 (Fla. Dist. Ct. App. 1959); Kinney v. Brown, 216 S.E.2d 798 (Ga. 1975); Windsor Resort Inc. v. Mayor & City Council of Ocean City, 526 A.2d 102 (Md. Ct. Spec. App. 1987); *Application of Stein*, 99 N.W.2d 204 (Minn. 1959).

[13] Star Island Assocs. v. City of St. Petersburg Beach, 433 So. 2d 998 (Fla. Dist. Ct. App. 1983); Henry Walker Park Ass'n v. Mathews, 91 N.W.2d 703 (Iowa 1958); Hand v. Rhodes, 245 P.2d 292 (Colo. 1952).

[14] Watson v. Albuquerque, 417 P.2d 54 (N.M. 1966).

[15] Windsor Resort Inc. v. Mayor & City Council of Ocean City, 526 A.2d 102 (Md. Ct. Spec. App. 1987).

[16] Edison Illuminating Co. v. Misch, 166 N.W. 944 (Mich. 1918).

[17] Herlitz v. City of Baton Rouge, 298 So. 2d 140 (La. Ct. App. 1974).

[18] G.C. Murphy Co. v. Redevelopment Auth. of City of Erie, 326 A.2d 358 (Pa. 1974).

[18.1] *See* First Unitarian Church of Salt Lake City v. Salt Lake City Corporation, 308 F.3d 1114 (10th Cir. 2002). Private property owner cannot limit Free Speech on public pedestrian easement retained by city.

may often be converted to a similar use but may be enjoined or revert to its original owner if the use is substantially changed.[19]

If a local government decides it no longer needs the property, the general rule has been that it will need authorization to lease or sell it if it is held in its governmental capacity since it is deemed held in trust for the public.[20] There is such statutory authorization in many states. However, even in states without such statutes, courts have permitted the lease or sale, provided it does not adversely affect governmental functions.[21]

Local government property may not usually be taken by adverse possession. The rationale is that the property belongs to the public and, just as it cannot be sold without state authorization, neither can it be taken as a result of the negligence or laches of local officials.[22] The courts have permitted, however, the use of the doctrine of estoppel where it considers inequitable conduct has occurred. If private individuals have been misled by local government officials into believing in good faith, that a piece of land was private property and, in reliance on that, they have made significant improvements, the local government may be prevented from asserting ownership.[23] Although the collection of taxes on the property is not usually sufficient to create estoppel, it is one factor to consider.[24] The use of equitable estoppel prevents the sometimes harsh result that follows from protecting local governments from claims of adverse possession.[25]

Another route to claim public property is through the doctrine of abandonment. It differs from an estoppel argument in that it is necessary to show an intent to abandon by local government. The person claiming the property does not have to establish good faith reliance with substantial improvements, as required in estoppel. The claimant must show actual and notorious abandonment for at least as long as the legal period of prescription and demonstrate that it would be unjust and inequitable to not recognize that the local government had abandoned the property. Generally there must be more than mere nonuse by the local government.[26]

---

[19] McIntyre v. Bd. of Comm'rs of El Paso County, 61 P. 237 (Colo. Ct. App. 1900); Miller v. City of New York, 203 N.E.2d 478 (N.Y. 1964).

[20] Duckworth v. Robertsdale, 28 So. 2d 182 (Ala. 1946).

[21] Center v. City of Benton, 110 N.E.2d 223 (Ill. 1953).

[22] Yates v. Warrenton, 4 S.E. 818 (Va. 1888); Wolfe v. Town of Sullivan, 32 N.E. 1017 (Ind. 1893); Steele v. Fowler, 41 N.E.2d 678 (Ind. Ct. App. 1942).

[23] Sioux City v. Johnson, 165 N.W.2d 762 (Iowa 1969), *cited in* Pearson v. City of Guttenberg, 245 N.W.2d 519 (Iowa 1976); City of Imperial Beach v. Algert, 19 Cal. Rptr. 144 (Cal. App. 1962); Kelroy v. City of Clear Lake, 5 N.W.2d 12 (Iowa 1942); Brewer v. Claypool, 275 N.W. 34 (Iowa 1937).

[24] Lee v. Walker, 68 S.E.2d 664 (N.C. 1952); City of Peoria v. Central Nat'l Bank, 79 N.E. 296 (Ill. 1906); Schooling v. City of Harrisburg, 71 P. 605 (Or. 1903); Page & Crane Lumber Co. v. City of Clear Lake, 225 N.W. 841 (Iowa 1929).

[25] *Windsor Resort, supra* note 15 at 106. *But see* Baltimore v. Chesapeake Marine Ry. Co., 197 A.2d 821 (Md. 1964).

[26] *Pearson, supra* note 23 at 529; Dunlap v. Tift, 71 S.E.2d 237 (Ga. 1952).

§ 4.9   Public Property Liability

Local governments, as property owners, should manage their property in a reasonable manner, but liability for harm may depend on state statutes or charters that waive local sovereign immunity and impose such liability. If there are no such statutes or charters, the common law recognition of local sovereign immunity may apply. In almost all states, local governments have qualified immunity.[1] If the local government was acting in a governmental capacity, sovereign immunity applies, unless modified by state constitution, statute or charter. If it was acting in a proprietary capacity, there is no sovereign immunity and the local government is liable for its tortious conduct. Determining the category of an action is not only difficult but has led to some perplexing results in local property liability. A discussion of sovereign immunity and its application to local governments in general may be found in Chapter 9 *infra*.

Local government liability for negligently maintained property has increased over the years. In its early beginnings, courts were hesitant to impose liability and held that it would exist only when the building was used in a proprietary capacity. There would be none if it were used for a governmental purpose. This confusing distinction led to conclusions of liability that were seemingly inconsistent. Most cases held that local governments were immune from liability for harm occurring at city, town or village halls and courtrooms.[2] However, liability would be found for harm suffered in parts of buildings, such as a restroom.[3] Local operation of arenas and convention centers has been deemed proprietary and liability imposed for negligence.[4] Local government garages have been viewed as proprietary, even if they served the purpose of maintaining vehicles used for governmental purposes. Educational operations are viewed as governmental and common law immunity from tort liability has been found for harm related to school buildings and grounds,[5] libraries and museums.[6] Activities that are clearly classified as proprietary and thus are not protected by sovereign immunity include the operation of public utilities[7] and the construction and maintenance of public ways, including streets and sidewalks.[8]

Many states have addressed the property liability issue in statutes. Generally, these recognize that local government owes a duty of care to

---

[1] *See* OSBORNE, LOCAL GOVERNMENT LAW, Ch. 26, § 173 (2d ed. 2001) (showing that the local governments of South Carolina do not have tort liability under the common law).

[2] Schwalk's Administrator v. City of Louisville, 122 S.W. 860 (Ky. 1909); Griggs v. City of Goddard, 666 P.2d 695 (Kan. 1983).

[3] Pickard v. City & County of Honolulu, 452 P.2d 445 (Haw. 1969).

[4] Steinberg v. City of Atlanta, 444 S.E.2d 873 (Ga. Ct. App. 1994).

[5] Dillon v. York City Sch. Dist., 220 A.2d 896 (Pa. 1966); Lambert v. City of New Haven, 30 A.2d 923 (Conn. 1943).

[6] Paar v. City of Birmingham, 85 So. 2d 888 (Ala. 1956).

[7] City of Troy v. McLendon, 188 So. 2d 281 (Ala. 1966).

[8] City of Paducah v. Konkle, 33 S.W.2d 608 (Ky. 1930); Turner v. City of Tacoma, 435 P.2d 927 (Wash. 1967).

properly maintain local property toward those lawfully upon it.[9] Therefore, often by state law, local governments are liable for their negligence in maintaining public buildings. The question of the degree of duty owed still depends in some states upon the status of the individual who has suffered harm. The categories of invitee, licensee and trespasser, used to define the degree of care owed by landowners in many private landowner cases, have also been applied to local liability. Increasingly, the use of these categories to define the duty of care is being abandoned, giving way to a single requirement that the private or public property owner use reasonable care for the safety of all reasonably anticipated persons on the premises.[10]

Local governments are generally liable for the creation or maintenance of nuisances and for trespass, whether acting in a governmental or propri-etary capacity. Typical nuisance actions against local governments have included claims for the creation or maintenance of nuisances involving sewage ponds or for harm resulting from the operation of sewage plants.[11] Other nuisance cases relate to the diversion of surface water from landfill operations onto private property, which also may be seen as a trespass by the local government. Some courts have created an exception for local liability where a nuisance was not created by its own actions. In other words, a local government will not be liable for its failure to remedy a dangerous condition that it did not create.[12] Some states have also sought to limit responsibility for nuisances by statute.[13]

§ 4.10   Use of Public Property

If local governments own street easements, they may be used for all lawful purposes consistent with every reasonable means of travel, transpor-tation and communication which is suitable and necessary for the good of the public.[1] Typically, acceptable uses include equipment for sanitary sewers and drains; storm sewers, water pipes and mains; subways and trains; and cables and conduits for telecommunications.

Local governments may also permit private parties to use the easements or the property it owns in fee, provided there is no interference with public use and the local decision is not arbitrary or an abuse of discretion. They may not give permanent use to a private entity at the expense of the public use. Although local governments have no inherent right to authorize franchises or licenses for the permanent use of their rights-of-way, states frequently have delegated such authority to them. Federal legislation, like

---

[9] First Nat'l Bank v. City of Aurora, 373 N.E.2d 1326 (Ill. 1978).

[10] *Pickard, supra* note 3 at 446; Latimer v. City of Clovis, 495 P.2d 788 (N.M. 1972).

[11] Hartzler v. Town of Kalona, 218 N.W.2d 608 (Iowa 1974).

[12] Wright v. Brown, 356 A.2d 176 (Conn. 1975).

[13] Osborn v. City of Akron, 171 N.E.2d 492 (Ohio 1960); Bragg v. City of Dallas, 605 S.W.2d 669 (Tex. Civ. App. 1980).

[1] Hall v. Lea County Elec. Co-Op., 438 P.2d 632 (N.M. 1968); Lubelle v. Rochester Gas & Elec. Co., 250 N.Y.S.2d 844 (4th Dep't 1964).

the Telecommunications Reform Act of 1996,[2] can limit the exercise of this power but does not prevent the individual states from choosing what authority will be given to local governments through state constitutions or statutes.

Many public properties are widely open to the public. However, if access is regulated, local governments have to provide access in a constitutionally acceptable manner. If governments require a license or permit for the exercise of First Amendment freedoms of religion, speech, press, assembly or association on public property, they must do so in a reasonable manner. Fundamental rights cannot be restricted except where necessary to protect a substantial public interest, and then it must be done in the less restrictive way. Time, place and manner restrictions must be for a legitimate public purpose and be imposed in a nondiscriminatory, content-neutral basis. The Supreme Court has upheld the right of government to impose reasonable, nondiscriminatory regulations that preserve peace and order.[3] Local governments may also require licenses for expressive conduct but they must first establish neutral criteria to insure that the grant or denial of a license is not based on the content of the expression or the viewpoint of the applicant.[4]

Often, religious organizations will request the use of school or other public facilities. If local governments decide to permit private organizations to use public buildings, they cannot discriminate on the basis of the content of the speech.[5] School districts in particular receive regular requests from community religious organizations for use of their facilities. If the school has decided not to open its buildings to use by any external group, then it is not required to permit use by a religious organization. However, if it has permitted other external groups to use its buildings, the schools may not discriminate on the basis of the subject matter of the speech.[6]

---

[2] Pub. L. No. 104-104, 110 Stat. 56 (1996) (codified at 47 U.S.C. §§ 251-260).

[3] Poulos v. New Hampshire, 345 U.S. 395 (1953).

[4] City of Lakewood v. Plain Dealer Publ'g Co., 486 U.S. 750 (1988).

[5] Lamb's Chapel v. Center Moriches Union Free Sch. Dist., 508 U.S. 384 (1993).

[6] *Id.* at 395-96.

Chapter 5

Local Contracts

§ 5.1 Introduction and Chapter Overview

Local governments have been given authority to enter into contracts through general grants of home rule powers and by statutes that often delegate specific authority. Even where there is arguably no specific delegation of authority, courts have found implied authority to contract for those goods or services necessary for the local government to carry out its governmental responsibilities.[1]

State constitutions, statutes and local charters often provide exactly the way in which the local authority is to be exercised. Many designate the process that must be followed and provide the format to be used. Some require competitive bidding while others require approval by local voters or local government officers. Occasionally, contracts must be published and recorded. Whatever the authority or the procedure, local governments must act within it and carefully follow the requirements imposed. Just as importantly, those who contract with local governments must understand the scope of the authority that has been given the local government and how it is to be exercised. Without an express or implied power to contract, the local contract is void. The courts consistently hold that it is the responsibility of the person contracting with a local government to know whether the local government is authorized to act.

At times, local governments are required to budget the contract costs or appropriate revenue prior to entering into a contract. At other times, state constitutional or statutory mandates require the local government to take steps to provide revenue sources before contracting, whether it be the adoption of a tax or the imposition of a fee. The posting of bonds is often required by those who intend to contract with local governments.

Courts that interpret the terms of local government contracts do so in a manner that is very similar to their interpretation of private contracts. The basic requirements for finding a binding agreement between two private individuals must be present for a contract to exist with a local government. The courts hold that the terms of the contract must be definite or capable of being made certain through ordinary rules of construction[2] and there must be adequate consideration.[3]

---

[1] Carruth v. City of Madera, 43 Cal. Rptr. 855 (Cal. App. 1965).

[2] Wm. Muirhead Constr. Co. v. Housing Auth. of Durham, 160 S.E.2d 542 (N.C. Ct. App. 1968); Stanley Smith & Sons v. Limestone College, 322 S.E.2d 474 (S.C. Ct. App. 1984); City of Reno v. Silver State Flying Service, Inc., 438 P.2d 257 (Nev. 1968).

[3] Burger v. City of Springfield, 323 S.W.2d 777 (Mo. 1959); Spray v. City of Albuquerque, 608 P.2d 511 (N.M. 1980).

In certain instances, the courts use equitable remedies to address irregularities in the formation of the local government contract. For instance, courts may recognize an implied obligation by local governments to pay for goods or services that have been delivered and accepted, based on a theory of unjust enrichment. When a local government has authority to contract but has done it in an unauthorized manner, or through an unauthorized agent, the courts may find that it would be unjust for the local government to not be bound by its terms. In other instances, the court may find a quasi-contract or may conclude that the local government has ratified the contract or is estopped from denying its validity.

PART I AUTHORITY, PROCEDURE AND FISCAL REQUIREMENTS

§ 5.2 Authority to Contract

The authority of a local government to contract is usually found in state constitutions, statutes, and charters. It is typically both broad and narrow, and general and specific. Courts have also found implied authority by noting that such authority is anticipated in the recitation of responsibilities that local governments have been given.[1] A governmental entity could not fulfill its duties unless it has been given some kind of contractual authority.

When a local government enters into a contract that is outside the scope of its delegated authority, the contract is void and unenforceable.[2] The term used to describe it is *ultra vires*, or outside the law. The courts are firm in protecting taxpayers, often at the expense of seemingly innocent contractors who may have provided extremely valuable products or services to the local government.[3] Taxpayers have successfully restrained local governments from entering into or fulfilling the terms of ultra vires contracts.[4] The message is that those who choose to contract with local governments are responsible for determining whether or not the local entity has the authority to enter into the contract. The private contractor is presumed to know the limits of local authority and is required to find out what it does not know or it will be proceeding at its own risk.[5] With few exceptions,[6] the courts will not recognize a quasi-contract or a claim of unjust enrichment against a local government for goods or services received if there was no authority to enter into the contract. Some local governments have

---

[1] Cahn v. Town of Huntington, 278 N.E.2d 908 (N.Y. 1972).

[2] Kane v. City of Marion, 104 N.W.2d 626 (Iowa 1960).

[3] Moody v. Transylvania County, 156 S.E.2d 716 (N.C. 1967).

[4] McKaig v. Mayor and City Council of Cumberland, 116 A.2d 384 (Md. 1955).

[5] Foley v. Consolidated City of Indianapolis, 421 N.E.2d 1160 (Ind. Ct. App. 1981).

[6] State for Use of Russell County v. Fourth Nat'l Bank, 117 So. 2d 145 (Ala. 1959); Haskins v. Clary, 338 So. 2d 166 (La. Ct. App. 1977). *See also* Marrone v. Town of Hampton, 466 A.2d 907 (N.H. 1983) (holding that when payment is sought out of non-taxpayer funds, local governments may be liable).

successfully retrieved funds that they had previously paid on an ultra vires contract.[7]

When a local government enters into a contract that is *within* its authority but is flawed because an unauthorized agent entered into it on behalf of the local government or some requirement was not met, performance by the local government may be required by an unjust enrichment or quasi-contract rationale.[8] Even if there were no attempt to formalize a contract, but circumstances indicated that there was an implied contract, this remedy may be available. The significant factor is that the local government did have authority to contract for the goods or services it has received. For these contracts that are not ultra vires, courts infer a promise to pay if the goods or services have been provided to and accepted by a local officer authorized to accept such goods or services on behalf of the local government. It must also be shown that an expectation of payment was communicated to the local government and that it would be unjust for it not to pay.

It is also possible for a provider of goods or services to recover through ratification on an invalid contract that was within the authority of the local government.[9] This is accomplished when the appropriate local officer or board complies with the requirements that should have been met originally. A contract that is beyond the powers of the local government cannot be ratified. Another option for recovery on an invalid contract is estoppel. A local government may be estopped from denying the legitimacy of a contract that is within its authority. It must be shown that the contracting party justifiably relied upon the local government's actions and delivered goods or services that benefitted the local government.[10]

Some types of local government contracts have been specifically prohibited by state constitutions, statutes or charters. If a local government enters into a prohibited contract, the contract is also void. No claim of unjust enrichment or quasi-contract will be entertained by the courts. The rationale is that to do so would circumvent the law and the intent of the legislature.[11] It has also been held that to pay an invalid charge would be an unconstitutional gift of public funds which would violate many state constitutions.[12]

Local contracts that are viewed as contrary to public policy of the state are also unenforceable. Some transactions included in this category are contracts of local governments that promise to exercise governmental

---

[7] School Dist. No. 9 Fractional of Waterford and Pontiac Tps. v. McLintock, 237 N.W. 539 (Mich. 1931).

[8] Normandy Estates Metro. Recreation Dist. v. Normandy Estates Ltd., 553 P.2d 386 (Colo. 1976).

[9] Day v. City of Beatrice, 101 N.W.2d 481 (Neb. 1960).

[10] Hitchcock v. Galveston, 96 U.S. 341 (1877); Riddlestorffer v. City of Rahway, 197 A.2d 883 (N.J. Super. Ct. Law Div. 1964).

[11] Granada Bldgs., Inc. v. City of Kingston, 444 N.E.2d 1325 (N.Y. 1983).

[12] County of Riverside v. Idyllwild County Water Dist., 148 Cal. Rptr. 650 (Cal. App. 1978).

powers in a predetermined manner,[13] agreements to defend or indemnify local officers in their personal capacities,[14] and agreements with employees to accept less compensation for their work than the amount fixed by law.[15] Local governments are not allowed to contract or surrender away their governmental powers by promising to do such things as enact local legislation, change zoning classifications, close streets for private benefit, or provide free goods or services.[16] These contracts are void and unenforceable.

Generally, local officials are not permitted to enter into a contract for a period of time that extends beyond their term of office. The rationale is that they should not be permitted to restrict subsequent governing boards.[17] This is not an absolute rule but one that depends on many factors. Some long-term contracts are deemed reasonable, and therefore valid, because it was reasonable to contract for an extended period of time. If the terms are fair, entered into in good faith, and the length is necessary or advantageous to the local government, the contract may be upheld. Some courts have distinguished between contracts that relate to proprietary activities as opposed to those that are governmental. They hold void long-term contracts that relate to governmental activities, while permitting those that are of a proprietary nature. Of course, this does not answer the perplexing question of which activities fall into what category.[18]

Most courts agree that a contract is void if a local officer has a personal interest in it. Many jurisdictions have statutes that address this conflict of interest, and such contracts have also been found to be void as a matter of common law.[19] There are some situations where courts have given local governments the option of voiding the contract.[20] In other situations, courts have upheld the contract if the interested officer did not vote or if the vote was not controlling.[21]

---

[13] City of Louisville v. Fiscal Court of Jefferson Co., 623 S.W.2d 219 (Ky. 1981).

[14] Chapman v. City of New York, 61 N.E. 108 (N.Y. 1901); State v. Foote, 186 N.W. 230 (Minn. 1922).

[15] City of Louisville v. Thomas, 78 S.W.2d 767 (Ky. 1935).

[16] Gardner v. City of Dallas, 81 F.2d 425 (5th Cir. 1936), cert. denied, 298 U.S. 668 (1936); Deshore v. Town of Bel Air, 206 A.2d 678 (Md. 1965); Rockingham Square Shopping Ctr., Inc. v. Town of Madison, 262 S.E.2d 705 (N.C. Ct. App. 1980).

[17] Marco Dev. Corp. v. City of Cedar Falls, 473 N.W.2d 41 (Iowa 1991).

[18] Town of Graham v. Karpark Corp., 194 F.2d 616, 619 (4th Cir. 1952) (stating that a contract for the purchase of parking meters is proprietary); New Castle Co. v. Mayor and Council of New Castle, 372 A.2d 188, 190 (Del. 1977) (citing ANTIEAU ON LOCAL GOVERNMENT LAW, for the proposition that an agreement for the rate of compensation for sewer services was proprietary).

[19] Price v. Edmonds, 337 S.W.2d 658 (Ark. 1960); Thomson v. Call, 699 P.2d 316 (Cal. 1985), cert. denied, 474 U.S. 1057 (1986); Schaefer v. Berinstein, 295 P.2d 113 (Cal. Ct. App. 1956).

[20] Polk Township v. Spencer, 259 S.W.2d 804 (Mo. 1953).

[21] Michael v. City of Rochester, 407 A.2d 819 (N.H. 1979).

§ 5.3   Procedural and Format Requirements

Most often the statutes, charters and constitutional grants that delegate contract authority to local governments will prescribe what local governments must do to enter into a contract. If not, then it is up to the local government to establish its own procedures and format. The courts consistently hold that it is the responsibility of both the local government and the person contracting with it to know and comply with these requirements.[1] A contractor must also know whether the local officer with whom he or she is contracting is in fact authorized to enter into a contract on behalf of the local government.

Although the general rule is that, in order to have an enforceable contract, the procedures and format requirements must be met, courts have sometimes recognized some flexibility. They have held that there are two types of requirements; namely, those that are mandatory and those that are directory. A failure to comply with mandatory requirements will result in unenforceable contract rights, while failure to comply with directory requirements may still permit recovery. The classification of requirements has been somewhat inconsistent. A requirement that the local government seek competitive bids before entering into a contract is mandatory and failure to do so will prevent recovery. Competitive bidding requirements are discussed in Part II of this chapter.

Typical procedural requirements include that the contract be in writing,[2] recorded and published. Voter approval of a local contract is seldom required, but, if it is, failure to obtain voter approval will result in a void and unenforceable contract. If state constitutions, statutes or charters require local legislative or state approval, failure to get such approval will result in an unenforceable contract.

Often there are very specific format requirements for local contracts that are found in state constitutions, statutes or charters. Other format requirements have been implied by the courts. Typically, contracts must be in writing so that the terms are definite.[3] Terms may not be left for future determination. This requirement may be met if the writing is in the form of a local enactment, provided that it is signed by the appropriate government official.[4] Courts have differed on whether a contract that is not in writing as required is enforceable, with most finding that it is not.[5]

---

[1] Duncan Parking Meter Corp. v. City of Gurdon, 146 F. Supp. 280 (W.D. Ark. 1956); Moody v. Transylvania County, 156 S.E.2d 716 (N.C. 1967).

[2] Bride v. City of Slater, 263 S.W.2d 22 (Mo. 1953). *See also* Burger v. City of Springfield, 323 S.W.2d 777, 781 (Mo. 1959) (holding that this may be satisfied by a local enactment that is signed by the appropriate official(s)).

[3] Sena Sch. Bus Co. v. Bd. of Educ. of Santa Fe Public Schools, 677 P.2d 639 (N.M. Ct. App. 1984); *Bride, supra* note 2 at 26-27.

[4] *Burger, supra* note 2 at 781.

[5] Cook v. Navy Point, Inc. 88 So. 2d 532 (Fla. 1956); Richard D. Kimball Co. v. City of Medford, 166 N.E.2d 708 (Mass. 1960). *But see* Bd. of Pub. Works of Rolla v. Sho-Me Power Corp., 244 S.W.2d 55 (Mo. 1951); Lathrop Co. v. City of Toledo, 214 N.E.2d 408 (Ohio 1966).

Often there is a requirement that a local appropriation or identification of the source of funding be made before a local government enters into a contract.[6] Other requirements that frequently control the contracting process include that specified officials sign the contract on behalf of the local government; notification be given of the local government's intent to enter into a contract; and security be posted by the person contracting with the local government. Courts differ on the effects of failure to meet these requirements, preferring to make their determination based on the particular circumstances surrounding the contract.

Some jurisdictions require approval of contracts by local officers, local legislative action, or by a referendum of the voters. Where approval has not been obtained, courts have varied in granting or denying equitable remedies to contractors. Some have held that the local government is not estopped from denying the validity of the contract even though it has benefitted. Others deny quasi-contractual relief. Still other courts have disagreed and awarded both types of remedies. Failure to comply with reasonable conditions to assure fiscal stability, such as posting a bond, or deposit, or security, required before engaging in bidding, may result in invalidity of the contract.

Even though there is a deficiency in meeting procedural and format requirements, if there is authority for the kind of contract that has been attempted, it is possible that recovery may be obtained through a claim based on unjust enrichment or quasi-contract, ratification or estoppel.[7]

§ 5.4 Fiscal Requirements

Many local governments have statutory or constitutional debt limitations that must be considered before a local government enters into a contract that will result in a violation of its debt limitation.[1] Beyond this, there are many statutes and charters that require a sufficient appropriation or budget item be adopted by a local government prior to entering into a contract for goods or services. Taxpayers have been found to have standing to seek injunctions against local governments that have not met this precondition.[2] Buyers as well should be concerned, for if this step is omitted, the person contracting with the local government may be unable to collect the amount owed under the terms of the contract.[3] There have been some exceptions where courts have occasionally permitted recovery under an unjust enrichment[4] or estoppel argument. However, there is general

---

[6] This requirement is discussed in § 5.4 *infra*.

[7] These remedies are discussed in § 5.2 *supra*.

[1] For further discussion of debt limitations, *see* § 10.12 *infra*.

[2] Miller v. City of Evansville, 189 N.E.2d 823 (Ind. 1963).

[3] In contracting with local governments, contractors are required to know legal requirements and whether the local official with whom they are contracting has the legal authority to act on behalf of the local government. *See* § 5.2 *supra* for further information.

[4] Home Owners Constr. Co., v. Borough of Glen Rock, 169 A.2d 129 (N.J. 1961), *citing* ANTIEAU ON LOCAL GOVERNMENT LAW.

judicial reluctance to find a quasi-contract or permit a contractor to succeed on an estoppel basis.[5]

In addition to a requirement of an appropriation or budgeted item, some statutes and charters require that a local auditor, comptroller, budget director, or a state entity certify that there are in fact unencumbered funds sufficient to pay the cost that the local government is to assume in the proposed contract. Since the policy behind such requirements is to match current funds with the current assumption of obligations, some courts have found that long-term contracts are not acceptable. Others have disagreed, finding that the requirement of previous appropriation is not violated by a local government's promise to make annual payments as services are received.[6] Other statutes and constitutional provisions require that a local government identify a source of future revenue, such as a tax or fee to be used to meet its fiscal obligation before entering into a contract.

Other precontractual requirements often imposed on local governments include an obligation to seek preliminary cost estimates by its engineers or local officials. Some courts have denied recovery of payment to contractors if a local government has not met this requirement or has failed to require a contractor to post a bond or security that guarantees that the work will be done.

Generally, the requirements that regulate local contracts may be ignored during a time of local emergency.

PART II COMPETITIVE BIDS

§ 5.5   Requirement for Competitive Bids and Exceptions

Local governments with contractual authority are free to contract for goods or services without seeking competitive bids if it is not specifically required. They are not limited to contracting with an entity offering the lowest price. However, statutes, charters, state constitutions and local enactments often require competitive bidding before local governments enter into certain contracts. Usually there will be an additional requirement that a contract be awarded to the lowest responsible bidder. A fundamental purpose of competitive bidding is to limit the exercise of discretion by local officials in awarding contracts. This is done in order to insure that taxpayers receive goods or services at the most reasonable price and most favorable terms, that public resources are preserved, and that potential providers or contractors are treated equitably by eliminating fraud, collusion or favoritism.[1]

---

[5] Chicago Patrolmen's Ass'n v. City of Chicago, 309 N.E.2d 3 (Ill. 1974), *cert. denied*, 419 U.S. 839 (1974); Slurzberg v. City of Bayonne, 148 A.2d 171 (N.J. 1959).

[6] Int'l Assoc. of Firefighters Local 1596 v. City of Lawrence, 798 P.2d 960 (Kan. Ct. App. 1990); Salisbury Water Supply Co. v. Town of Salisbury, 167 N.E.2d 320 (Mass. 1960).

[1] Excelsior v. F.W. Pearce Corp., 226 N.W.2d 316 (Minn. 1975).

The provisions will usually specify that competitive bidding is required for contracts involving in excess of a certain amount of money. This permits rather routine transactions to take place without the formalities of a bidding process. However, courts have not permitted local governments to circumvent bidding requirements by breaking contracts into smaller parts.[2]

At times it is impossible or impracticable to competitively bid for a particular kind of product or service. Exceptions to bidding requirements may be found in statutes, charters or state constitutions, and some have been held by courts to be implied.[3] Competitive bidding may not be required if a local government needs a product, service or property that has some unique attribute and can be provided by only a very limited number of vendors. A contract for a unique piece of real property may involve a location or structure that is particularly important to the local government. The same rationale may apply when local governments contract for professional services of particular attorneys,[4] architects,[5] engineers,[6] or accountants.[7] In these situations, negotiation is the preferred method of concluding a contract on behalf of a local government because there may not be a competitive supply of similar property or service. In some decisions, the lowest possible price may not be the most important factor to the local government and its taxpayers.[8] Many other kinds of contracts have been considered exempt from competitive bidding rules. These include banking, financial and insurance services, as well as contracts for those jobs where the personality of the individual is important.[9]

Competitive bidding has been found inapplicable where the item or service sought could be furnished by only one source.[10] This generally encompasses the supply of a public utility where there is a lawful monopoly.[11] The exception is also applicable to situations where it would be impracticable or even impossible to draw specifications that would permit a competitive bidding process.

Another exception to competitive bidding requirements are true emergencies. Even if statutes, charters or state constitutions do not contain an emergency provision, courts have generally found implied exemptions.[12]

---

[2] Kunkle Water & Elec., Inc. v. City of Prescott, 347 N.W.2d 648 (Iowa 1984) (*citing* ANTIEAU ON LOCAL GOVERNMENT LAW); Secrist v. Diedrich, 6 Ariz. App. 102, 430 P.2d 448 (Ariz. Ct. App. 1967); Menzl v. City of Milwaukee, 145 N.W.2d 198 (Wis. 1966); State v. Kollarik, 126 A.2d 875 (N.J. 1956).

[3] Whelan v. New Jersey Power & Light Co., 212 A.2d 136 (N.J. 1965).

[4] Commonwealth v. Tice, 116 A. 316 (Pa. 1922).

[5] Cobb v. Pasadena City Bd. of Educ., 285 P.2d 41 (Cal. Ct. App. 1955).

[6] Potts v. City of Utica, 86 F.2d 616 (2d Cir. 1936).

[7] Braaten v. Olson, 148 N.W. 829 (N.D. 1914).

[8] Mongiovi v. Doerner, 546 P.2d 1110 (Or. Ct. App. 1976).

[9] Layman's Sec. Co. v. Water Works & Sewer Bd. of Prichard, 547 So. 2d 533 (Ala. 1989).

[10] General Elec. Co. v. City of Mobile, 585 So. 2d 1311 (Ala. 1991).

[11] Young v. Vill. of Glen Ellyn, 458 N.E.2d 1137 (Ill. Ct. App. 1983); Telcom Sys. Inc. v. Lauderdale Co. Bd. of Supervisors, 405 So. 2d 119 (Miss. 1981).

[12] Grimm v. City of Troy, 303 N.Y.S.2d 170 (1969).

Courts generally accept a statement that an emergency exists when made by a local government, although it is not binding upon them. A mere potential for an emergency will not be enough to justify disregarding competitive bidding requirements.[13] If there is a provision in a competitive bidding statute that specifies the procedure to be followed for a waiver in case of an emergency, the local government must strictly comply with it.[14]

If there is unforeseen additional work that is needed on existing projects that were competitively bid, or changes made to the original plan, courts differ on whether competitive bidding is required. Most favor providing some degree of flexibility to the local government and are fairly lenient in permitting insubstantial additions and changes without bidding.[15] If, however, there is any indication of an attempt to evade the requirement in order to favor one contractor by making substantial changes after the contract is awarded, the court will not permit it.[16]

§ 5.6   Specifications, Restrictions and Formalities

It is usual for statutes, charters or state constitutions to require that notice and invitation to bid be given to prospective bidders in a manner that will allow them sufficient time to prepare their bids. This announcement will state the need for materials, construction or services and provide all information that will enable them to compete on an equitable basis. Every prospective bidder has to be given identical information.[1]

The specifications must be clear, definite, precise, and complete. The notices must indicate a common standard so as to permit comparisons of the bids. There can be no uncertainty in the specifications that would permit local officials to show favoritism. Bid specifications may not be substantially changed during the interim period between the time that the notice is given and the award is made.[2]

Local governments that have included suggestions made by possible bidders in their specifications have been sustained by the courts when it is shown that they acted reasonably and in the best interests of the community.[3] However, specifications may not be written by a bidder, nor may local

---

[13] *Appeal of Laskey*, 475 A.2d 966, 969 (Pa. Commw. Ct. 1984) (holding that the local government wrongfully bypassed competitive bidding because there was only the potential for an emergency).

[14] Majestic Radiator Enclosure Co. v. County Comm'rs of Middlesex, 490 N.E.2d 1186 (Mass. 1986).

[15] Sekerez v. Lake County Bd. of Comm'rs, 345 N.E.2d 865 (Ind. Ct. App. 1976); Home Owners Constr. Co. v. Borough of Glen Rock, 169 A.2d 129 (N.J. 1961) (*citing* ANTIEAU ON LOCAL GOVERNMENT LAW); Whelan v. New Jersey Power & Light Co., 212 A.2d 136 (N.J. 1965); Thomsen-Abbott Constr. Co. v. City of Wausau, 100 N.W.2d 921 (Wis. 1960). *But see* Probst v. City of Menasha, 13 N.W.2d 504 (Wis. 1944).

[16] Glatstein v. City of Miami, 399 So. 2d 1005 (Fla. Dist. Ct. App. 1981), *review denied*, 407 So. 2d 1102 (Fla. 1981).

[1] Brewer Environmental Industries, Inc. v. A.A.T. Chem., Inc., 832 P.2d 276 (Haw. 1992).

[2] Metropolitan Express Services, Inc. v. Kansas City, 23 F.3d 1367 (8th Cir. 1994), *appeal after remand*, 71 F.3d 273 (8th Cir. 1995).

[3] Davies v. Village of Madelia, 287 N.W. 1 (Minn. 1939).

governments request that bidders formulate and submit their own plans and specifications with bid prices.[4] This would be a violation of the requirement that all bidders respond to the same specifications. Local governments have often included in their specifications certain requirements regulating the conditions of work, such as minimum wages and maximum hours of work. Courts have differed on whether this is permissible.[5]

Local governments will not be permitted to break a project into parts in order to avoid compliance with a requirement that contracts involving a certain amount of money be subject to competitive bidding.[6] However, if breaking up a project is not done with this intent and the division has a reasonable basis, the courts will accept the judgment of the local government. If there is any substantial and material change from the specifications that is beneficial to the successful bidder, even if there was only one bid,[7] the contract will be void.

Often, local governments require bidders to post a deposit, bond, or security. Sometimes, bidders must provide affidavits or certificates indicating that a surety company will provide a performance bond for the full contract amount, should the bidder win the contract. These conditions are upheld as long as they are reasonable in terms and equitably applied.[8] Failure to comply may be grounds for invalidating a contract.

Local governments have been permitted in some cases to exercise a degree of control over who is permitted to bid and who will be a preferred bidder. Barring individuals or companies with a proven record of dishonesty has been permitted.[9] Certain local preferences for a particular bidder may be permitted. Some local governments have given preference to contractors who had paid state and county taxes or to contractors who use local labor and materials. This practice has been upheld and found not to violate the Equal Protection or Commerce Clauses since it serves a legitimate government interest.[10] However, courts have differed on the inclusion of many

---

[4] Gamewell v. City of Phoenix, 216 F.2d 928 (9th Cir. 1954), amended, 219 F.2d 180 (9th Cir. 1955).

[5] Iowa Elec. Co. v. Town of Cascade, 288 N.W. 633 (Iowa 1939); R.D. Anderson Constr. Co., Inc. v. City of Topeka, 612 P.2d 595 (Kan. 1980). But see Parish Council of East Baton Rouge v. Louisiana Highway & Heavy Branch of Assoc. Gen. Contractors, 131 So. 2d 272 (La. Ct. App. 1961); Philson v. City of Omaha, 93 N.W.2d 13 (Neb. 1958).

[6] Kunkle Water & Elec., Inc. v. City of Prescott, 347 N.W.2d 648 (Iowa 1984) (citing ANTIEAU ON LOCAL GOVERNMENT LAW); Secrist v. Diedrich, 430 P.2d 448 (Ariz. Ct. App. 1967); Bd. of Educ. v. Hall, 353 S.W.2d 194 (Ky. 1962).

[7] Glatstein v. City of Miami, 399 So. 2d 1005 (Fla. Dist. Ct. App. 1981), review denied, 407 So. 2d 1102 (Fla. 1981).

[8] J. Turco Paving Contractor, Inc. v. City Council of City of Orange, 213 A.2d 865 (N.J. Super. Ct. App. Div. 1965); Sutton v. City of St. Paul, 48 N.W.2d 436 (Minn. 1951); F.H. Myers Constr. Co. v. City of New Orleans, 570 So. 2d 84 (La. Ct. App. 1990).

[9] Trap Rock Indus., Inc. v. Kohl, 304 A.2d 193 (N.J. 1973), cert. denied, 414 U.S. 860 (1973); Spielvogel v. Aiello, 432 N.Y.S.2d 228 (2d Dep't 1980).

[10] Smith Setzer & Sons, Inc. v. South Carolina Procurement Review Panel, 20 F.3d 1311 (4th Cir. 1994).

other preferences. The Supreme Court held that preferences involving racial classifications must be shown to serve a compelling governmental interest and be narrowly tailored to further that interest. In addition, it must be based on evidence of past discrimination and it must be a narrowly tailored remedy.[11]

Local governments are permitted to preclude the participation of particular individuals or groups in bidding on contracts. In reviewing these decisions, courts require that it be reasonable to do so. Prohibition is reasonable if the entity has engaged in bribery or other unlawful activity, or is not licensed to do the particular work.[12] However, local governments cannot impose a condition that would require a prospective bidder to waive federal constitutional rights.[13]

Local governments may impose reasonable pre-bid requirements that those who want to submit bids provide information indicating their financial ability and experience before receiving copies of the plans and specifications. This saves local resources because it eliminates from local review those who are clearly not qualified.

All bids submitted for review must comply with format and time requirements, which may be prescribed in statutes, charters, state constitutions or local enactments. Courts have generally interpreted these requirements as mandatory and have held void bids that were not signed, or did not contain a check, or did not have all the drawings and data requested.[14] Some courts have disagreed and held otherwise.[15] There are decisions sustaining bids that have minor irregularities that are immaterial and not tainted by any fraud, bad faith or collusion.[16] Although local officials may not waive the requirements, some have been permitted to allow a bidder to correct the minor irregularity.[17] The fundamental rationale for a court decision is that a level playing field must be created for bidding to be fair. No bidder should be given an advantage by not having to comply with the requirements.

§ 5.7　Local Action on Bids

The required notice of competitive bidding given by the local government is not an offer to contract, but rather a solicitation of an offer. There is no contractual right when a bid is submitted. The local government must

---

[11] Adarand Constructors, Inc. v. Pena, 513 U.S. 200 (1995); City of Richmond v. J.A. Croson Co., 488 U.S. 469 (1989).

[12] *Trap Rock Indus., Inc., supra* note 9 at 194-95; *Spielvogel, supra* note 9 at 228.

[13] Lefkowitz v. Turley, 414 U.S. 70 (1973).

[14] Whitemarsh Township Authority v. Finelli Brothers, 184 A.2d 512 (Pa. 1962).

[15] Eastside Disposal Co. v. City of Mercer Island, 513 P.2d 1047 (Wash. Ct. App. 1973).

[16] Township of River Vale v. R.J. Longo Constr, Co., 316 A.2d 737 (N.J. Super. Ct. Law Div. 1974).

[17] Cedar Bay Constr., Inc. v. City of Fremont, 552 N.E.2d 202 (Ohio 1990); Township of River Vale v. R.J. Longo Constr. Co., 316 A.2d 737 (N.J. Super. Ct. Law Div. 1974).

accept the bid in order for the bidder to have a contractual right. However, it has been held that local governments have a vested contract right when a bid is submitted, and the bid cannot be withdrawn unless it consents. Courts have not hesitated to sustain this rule when the request for withdrawal is motivated by the discovery of a mistake in the bid that is clearly the fault of the bidder.[1] However, in many jurisdictions, such a harsh result has been ameliorated by permitting a bidder to revoke a bid if the mistake is so substantial and material to the contract that it would be unconscionable to enforce it; it did not result from negligence or violation of a legal duty; and the local government was notified promptly and will not be severely harmed (other than losing the benefit of the bargain).[2] Penalties may be attached to the withdrawal.

All bids must conform substantially to the advertised specifications, plans and solicitations to bid. Any submitted bid that materially or substantially varies must be rejected. Something that gives one competitor an advantage over another is always viewed as material and substantial.

Bids must be opened at the time, in the manner, and at the place required by the applicable statute, charter, state constitution or local enactment. The same rules that are used in interpreting contracts are applicable in interpreting bids. If the bid is not definite or it is uncertain, it is invalid and will not be considered by the local government. A bidder usually will not be permitted to amend a bid if, when opened, it is determined that it does not conform to the specifications. Minor changes have been occasionally permitted, but one is not to supply missing information at a later date.

The determination of the lowest responsible bidder, which is the standard used in most statutes requiring bidding, is to be made by the local government. Courts will not supplant their judgment without clear proof that the decision is fraudulent, in bad faith, arbitrary, or an abuse of discretion. In making this determination, local governments will consider many factors in addition to cost. The experience, past history, ability, financial stability, integrity, reputation and record for reliability are relevant factors in choosing the lowest *responsible* bidder. Local governments may also consider the assets that will be necessary to perform the contract. A local government is merely required to make a reasonable decision based on all relevant considerations. Some jurisdictions are required to notify the lowest-cost bidder when he or she is not selected and provide an opportunity to rebut the factors that led the local government to choose another. Ultimately, judicial review may be sought and the courts will determine whether the local government made a reasonable determination that was supported by the information it had at its disposal.

At times, local governments have been permitted by law to reject all bids and the courts have held that the lowest responsible bidder has no vested right to be awarded the contract. However, where it is not expressly provided, some courts have held that if the right was not reserved by the local

---

[1] Nelson, Inc. v. Sewerage Comm'n of City of Milwaukee, 241 N.W.2d 390 (Wis. 1976).

[2] Santucci Const. Co. v. County of Cook, 315 N.E.2d 565 (Ill. Ct. App. 1974).

government, it is obligated to accept the submission of the lowest responsible bidder.[3] In the advertisement soliciting bids, often a local government will expressly reserve the right to reject all bids. A decision to reject will then be upheld, provided it is reasonable and not arbitrary, illegal or an act of collusion or fraud. The mere submission of the lowest bid does not in and of itself create a contract between the bidder and the local government. Bids are not effective until accepted.[4]

If there has been collusion in submitting a bid, a contract that was awarded will be found void, although some have suggested that it should be at the option of the local government to decide its fate. Contractors will not be able to recover even though the government has received benefits.[5]

Some courts have held that it is acceptable for a local government to try to negotiate with the lowest responsible bidder for a lower price before the contract is awarded.

§ 5.8   Judicial Challenge to Competitive Bidding

Bidding requirements are mandatory and local governments must comply with them. Local taxpayers usually have standing to attack the grant of a contract without required competitive bidding as well as the grant of a contract that is not in accordance with the prescribed procedures. The taxpayer can obtain relief if he or she can establish that a local government contract was entered into without the required competitive bidding even if the local government suffered no injury.[1] Unless the omission is justified by one of the few recognized exceptions, failure to comply with the process will result in the contract being declared void.[2] After a contract has been found void, some jurisdictions have permitted the recovery of the reasonable value of the goods or services received by the local government under a theory of quasi-contract, provided there is no fraud or collusion.[3]

Although it is often said that there must be strict compliance with bid requirements, some courts have shown flexibility in accepting reasonable compliance as sufficient. There are decisions sustaining bids that have minor irregularities that are immaterial and not tainted by any fraud, bad faith or collusion.[4] However, anything in the process that defeats the basic purpose of competitive bidding to limit the potential for fraud and abuse will result in the invalidation of a contract, even if no actual fraud is shown.[5]

---

[3] Austin v. Housing Auth. of City of Hartford, 122 A.2d 399 (Conn. 1956).

[4] City of Merrill v. Wenzel Bros., Inc., 277 N.W.2d 799 (Wis. 1979).

[5] Jered Contracting Corp. v. NYC Transit Auth., 292 N.Y.S.2d 98 (N.Y. 1968).

[1] Gerzof v. Sweeney, 211 N.E.2d 826 (N.Y. 1965).

[2] Los Angeles Dredging Co. v. City of Long Beach, 291 P. 839 (Cal. 1930).

[3] Lykes v. City of Texarkana, 265 S.W.2d 539 (Ark. 1954).

[4] Townsend v. McCall, 80 So. 2d 262 (Ala. 1955).

[5] Griswold v. Ramsey Co., 65 N.W.2d 647 (Minn. 1954); 426 Bloomfield Ave. Corp. v. City of Newark, 621 A.2d 59 (N.J. Super. Ct. App. Div. 1993).

Sometimes there are mistakes in the specifications issued by a local government. In order to invalidate an award based on a deficiency in the specifications, it must be shown that it was substantial and affected the fairness of the bidding process. Manipulation of the specifications in order to permit unfair advantage or limit the competition will invalidate the process.[6] Local taxpayers have been found to have standing to challenge specifications, but nontaxpayers may not. Contracts that are awarded after competitive bidding must be substantially in compliance with the terms of the invitation to bid and the specifications.

Since a notice posted by a local government seeking competitive bids is not an offer, but rather a solicitation of offers, there is no binding contractual obligation when a bidder submits a bid. This has led courts to deny bidders any right to challenge a local government decision not to award any contract. However, a bidder who has submitted the lowest bid has standing to challenge the determination to award the contract to another bidder.[7] If it is successfully shown that the local government made an unreasonable, unsupported determination of the lowest responsible bidder, a court may reverse the local government action. The form of relief varies in different jurisdictions. Because they are not inclined to impose costs upon the public, courts will not normally award damages although some have granted compensation for the costs incurred for preparation of the bid[8] and reasonable attorney fees.[9]

The Supreme Court held that if government has created a barrier that makes it more difficult for members of a group to obtain a benefit, a person within the group has standing to challenge the requirement without alleging that he or she would have obtained the benefit but for the barrier.[10] This means that if a person shows that he or she is able and ready to bid and a discriminatory policy prevents it, there is standing to challenge the unlawful government action. A local bidding requirement that violates the constitutional rights of a bidder may be subject to challenge under § 1983 of the federal Civil Rights Act.[11]

---

[6] Metropolitan Express Services, Inc. v. Kansas City, 23 F.3d 1367 (8th Cir. 1994), *appeal after remand*, 71 F.3d 273 (8th Cir. 1995).

[7] Owen of Ga., Inc. v. Shelby Co., 648 F.2d 1084 (6th Cir. 1981).

[8] City of Atlanta v. J.A. Jones Constr. Co., 398 S.E.2d 369 (Ga. 1990), *cert. denied*, 500 U.S. 928 (1991).

[9] Carl Bolander & Sons v. City of Minneapolis, 451 N.W.2d 204 (Minn. 1990).

[10] Northeastern Florida Chapter of the Associated Gen. Contractors of America v. City of Jacksonville, 508 U.S. 656 (1993).

[11] City of Richmond v. J.A. Croson Co., 488 U.S. 469 (1989); Adarand Constructors, Inc. v. Pena, 515 U.S. 200 (1995).

PART III QUASI-CONTRACTS

§ 5.9   Local Obligation Without a Contract

The general rule in most states is that a court may treat local governments just as it does individuals by finding an obligation to pay for the reasonable value of goods or services, even when there is not an express contract.[1] The court may do this by finding a quasi-contract, which is an implied obligation based on a theory of unjust enrichment. The elements that must be present include: delivery of the goods or services; acceptance by the local government; circumstances that reasonably indicate the provider expected to be paid by the local government; and unjust enrichment of the local government if it did not pay.[2]

In finding a quasi-contract, the court is finding an *implied obligation*, not an implied contract. The parties may not have even attempted to enter into an agreement. The obligation arises from the benefit that has been delivered and accepted with the reasonable expectation of payment. Voluntarily giving a local government a gift does not meet this requirement. It is not enough to show that a benefit has been bestowed. The court will look at all the circumstances to see if there was a delivery by the provider with a reasonable expectation of being paid. The local government must have been aware of the delivery and must have accepted the product or service under circumstances that clearly indicate it reasonably understood that payment would be expected. Having decided that these elements are present, the court may conclude that it is unjust for the local government not to pay and it will therefore grant recovery to the provider by finding a quasi-contract.

Before a court will find a quasi-contract, it must be shown that the local government had the authority to enter into such a contract with the provider. A court will not recognize a quasi-contract if the result would be that the local government has engaged in an activity that is outside the scope of its delegated powers. This would result in an unauthorized circumvention of a limitation in its delegated powers and is contrary to public policy.

Quasi-contract has also been found when local governments have wrongfully taken or retained funds belonging to others. It has been used where money has been seized in police raids and not returned to its owner.[3] Courts have granted quasi-contractual relief when a local government refused to return securities or money deposited to guarantee a contractor's performance. Involuntary payments of unlawfully imposed fees or taxes have been found to be unjust enrichment and subject to the court finding that there is a quasi-contract to repay. Courts have used the same approach to require rent to be paid by local governments when they unlawfully use a private

---

[1] R. Zoppo Co. v. City of Manchester, 453 A.2d 1311 (N.H. 1982).

[2] City of Ingleside v. Stewart, 554 S.W.2d 939 (Tex. Civ. App. 1997).

[3] City of El Paso v. Nicholson, 361 S.W.2d 415 (Tex. Civ. App. 1962).

owner's real property.[4] Courts have also used their discretion to find a quasi-contract and require restitution when private property has been wrongfully taken. A duty is imposed on the local government to pay the fair value of the property.

Quasi-contractual relief has also been granted when a local government failed to perform a mandatory duty and a private entity performed it for them.[5] Doctors and hospitals that have taken care of individuals entrusted to local responsibility have recovered for their services under quasi-contract law.[6]

In determining the value of the quasi-contract, a provider must be able to establish the extent of the benefit by showing the actual value of the goods or services. The amount awarded by the court will be measured by the extent of enrichment or the value of the benefits received. Courts have described it as the reasonable value of the goods or services that unjustly enriched the local government or the benefits received by it.

§ 5.10 Local Obligation With an Invalid Contract

Some jurisdictions have used the quasi-contractual remedy to impose liability where local governments attempted to enter into a contract that they were authorized to undertake, but failed to comply with some requirement. Courts do not like to see a local government, after it has accepted goods or services pursuant to a contract that is not properly executed,[1] gain benefits but pay no compensation. At other times courts have refused such equitable relief, even though the local government has received a benefit under the invalid contract, finding it incompatible with statutes, state constitutions or charters.[2] Sometimes, courts have given a local government the choice of either paying for the benefits received or returning the goods accepted.

The distinction between which invalid contract may benefit from a plea for a quasi-contract and which will not often depends on the kind of noncompliance that caused the failure in the attempt to create a binding obligation. Requirements imposed on local governments for the exercise of their authority to enter into contracts have sometimes been classified as either mandatory or directory. If there is noncompliance with a mandatory provision, then quasi-contractual relief will be denied. However, noncompliance with a directory provision will not bar relief. This distinction has not

---

[4] Lytle v. Payette-Oregon Slope Irrigation Dist., 152 P.2d 934 (Or. 1944); Zimring-McKenzie Constr. Co. v. City of Pinellas Park, 237 So. 2d 576 (Fla. Dist. Ct. App. 1970). *But see* City of Ft. Meyers v. Hospital Bd. of Directors of Lee County, 505 So. 2d 590 (Fla. Dist. Ct. App. 1987) (holding that the city was not liable because patients were county prisoners).

[5] Hurdis Realty, Inc. v. Town of N. Providence, 397 A.2d 896 (R.I. 1979); Grand Forks Co. v. City of Grand Forks, 123 N.W.2d 42 (N.D. 1963).

[6] Mt. Carmel Medical Ctr. v. Bd. of County Comm'rs, 566 P.2d 384 (Kan. Ct. App. 1977).

[1] Harris Co. v. Emmite, 554 S.W.2d 203 (Tex. Civ. App. 1977).

[2] Stratton v. City of Detroit, 224 N.W. 649 (Mich. 1929); Missouri International Investigators, Inc. v. City of Pacific, 545 S.W.2d 684 (Mo. Ct. App. 1976).

produced clearly-defined categories and most often courts simply try to interpret the requirements, balancing the equities of the situation as best they can. For instance, if the failure in compliance was competitive bidding, courts generally refuse to imply a contract.[3] On the other hand, failure to comply with the requirement that a contractor post a bond was held not to bar the imposition of a quasi-contract. In that case, the local government had to pay to the provider the reasonable value of the goods and services it had received.[4]

Some courts have consistently denied quasi-contractual relief for invalid contracts because such relief is viewed as a circumvention of state constitutional, statutory or charter prohibitions that extra compensation may not be paid for goods or services.[5] In these jurisdictions, there is concern that recognizing a quasi-contract when there is a failure to meet lawful requirements may be contrary to public policy.[6]

PART IV ENFORCEMENT OF CONTRACTS

§ 5.11   Contract that is Unauthorized, Executed by Unauthorized Agent, or in Unauthorized Form or Procedure

As noted earlier, local governments have been given broad authority to enter into contracts through statutes, state constitutions, and charters. In addition, courts have found implied power to contract where it is necessary for a local government to fulfill its responsibilities.[1] The grant of authority is often accompanied with provisions specifying how local governments are to exercise this authority and which local officers are authorized to enter into contracts on behalf of the local government.

A contract that is ultra vires is one that is "outside the law." Simply stated, the local government has no authority to enter into such a contract. There is no express or implied delegation of authority to the local government to enter into a contract relating to that particular subject matter. The courts consistently hold that if it is found to be ultra vires, the contract is unenforceable either by specific performance or quasi-contract. This is nonnegotiable and there is little or no flexibility in this rule. It is also usually held that an ultra vires contract cannot be subsequently ratified by local government action.[2] In addition, courts have refused to apply estoppel against a local government for an ultra vires contract, even if it has

---

[3] Blumenthal v. Town of Headland, 31 So. 87 (Ala. 1901).

[4] Royal School Labs., Inc. v. Town of Watertown, 358 F.2d 813 (2d Cir. 1966).

[5] Stratton v. City of Detroit, 224 N.W. 649 (Mich. 1929).

[6] Louisville Extension Water Dist. v. Sloss, 236 S.W.2d 265 (Ky. 1951); Zehenni v. City of Akron, 250 N.E.2d 630 (Ohio Com. Pl. 1968).

[1] See § 5.02 supra.

[2] Tuxedo Cheverly Volunteer Fire Co. v. Prince George's County, 385 A.2d 819 (Md. Ct. App. 1978).

received benefits.[3] In fact, nothing done subsequent to entering into the ultra vires contract will prevent the local government from using its invalidity as a defense in an action for payment brought by a contractor who has furnished goods or services. In a very few jurisdictions there are some exceptions.[4] However, the courts are generally quite firm in holding that they will not permit a local government to contract in an unauthorized area by their recognition of a quasi-contract.[5] As a practical matter, this means that the individual who contracts with a local government does so at his or her peril. He or she must understand the authority of the local government, the process for creating a binding contract and who is authorized to enter into it.

Local governments have successfully recovered funds that were paid to a contractor pursuant to an ultra vires contract.[6] Some courts have even denied the recovery of goods that were given to a local government under an ultra vires contract. A claim that a contractor was not aware of the fact that a local government did not have authority to contract is immaterial. The courts hold that it is the duty of everyone who contracts with a local government to know the extent of its authority and the procedural requirements for the lawful exercise of the authority.[7]

The rationale for this seemingly harsh approach is that the courts do not want to permit the expansion of local powers by recognizing ultra vires actions as legitimate. There is also concern for the expansion of the risks and liabilities of local taxpayers. Local taxpayers may seek injunctive relief, restraining a local government from entering into an ultra vires contract or from complying with its terms.[8]

Ordinarily, the local government will not be bound by a contract that was entered into by an unauthorized person who was acting on its behalf.[9] The courts express the view again that it is the responsibility of the contractor to determine that the person or group representing the local government in its negotiations is, in fact, an authorized agent of the local government. However, the ultimate outcome in this situation may not be as rigid or severe as it is for the ultra vires contract. Courts have frequently granted quasi-contractual relief where there was local authority to contract but the transaction was executed by an unauthorized representative of the local government.[10] In addition, almost all jurisdictions hold that a local government can subsequently ratify a contract that was entered into by an

---

[3] Moody v. Transylvania County, 156 S.E.2d 716 (N.C. 1967).

[4] Marrone v. Town of Hampton, 466 A.2d 907 (N.H. 1983).

[5] Rockingham Square Shopping Ctr., Inc. v. Town of Madison, 262 S.E.2d 705 (N.C. Ct. App. 1980).

[6] School Dist. No. 9 v. McLintock, 237 N.W. 539 (Mich. 1931).

[7] City of N. Charleston v. N. Charleston Dist., 346 S.E.2d 712 (S.C. 1986).

[8] McKaig v. Mayor and City Council of Cumberland, 116 A.2d 384 (Md. 1955).

[9] Villa v. City of Chicago, 924 F.2d 629 (7th Cir. 1991).

[10] Central Bitulithic Paving Co. v. City of Mt. Clemens, 106 N.W. 888 (Mich. 1906); Wakely v. St. Louis Co., 240 N.W. 103 (Minn. 1931).

unauthorized agent.[11] In some circumstances, courts have even held that governments may be estopped from denying the authority of their representative.[12]

Local contracts may be held invalid because the prescribed procedures and formats for entering into them have not been followed. Statutory, constitutional and charter prescriptions establishing how a local government is to enter into a contract have often been classified by the reviewing courts as either mandatory or directory. If it is found that a mandatory requirement has not been met, the contract is void and may not be saved by quasi-contract, ratification, or estoppel.[13] However, if the provision is only directory, it may be enforceable under one of these theories.[14] Unfortunately, from the inconsistent interpretations, it is not clear what fits into each category. Courts will sometimes use equitable remedies to do justice where there has been some irregularity in procedure or format. Increasingly, they examine the public purpose of the requirement, the degree of compliance, the intent of the parties and the equities involved. But, some procedures and formats are too closely connected to the grant of authority for a court to uphold a contract that has not complied with them. This is true where bidding is required. Courts will usually find a contract void where local governments have totally bypassed this requirement.

§ 5.12   Contract That is Prohibited or Contrary to Public Policy

Many states have statutes, constitutions or charters that prohibit local governments from entering into specific types of contracts. Statutes prohibit contracts between local governments and local officials because of conflict of interest concerns.[1] Local governments are prohibited from entering into contracts requiring local expenditures that will violate state constitutional, statutory, or charter debt limitations.[2] Any contract that is prohibited by law is void and unenforceable. This means that a local government may raise the defense of illegality and will not be liable on the contract even if it has already received a benefit. The courts will not grant relief by quasi-contract or estoppel because to do so would circumvent the law.[3]

---

[11] School Admin. Dist. No. 3 v. Maine Sch. Dist. Comm'n, 185 A.2d 744 (Me. 1962); M. & O. Disposal Co. v. Township of Middletown, 242 A.2d 841 (N.J. 1968).

[12] *See* § 5.13 *infra* for a discussion of ratification and estoppel.

[13] Utica State Savings Bank v. Vill. of Oak Park, 273 N.W. 271 (Mich. 1937); Scarborough Properties Corp. v. Vill. of Briarcliff Manor, 16 N.E.2d 369 (N.Y. 1938); City of Plattsmouth v. Murphy, 105 N.W. 293 (Neb. 1905); Everds Bros. v. Gillespie, 126 N.W.2d 274 (Iowa 1964).

[14] Webb v. Wakefield Township, 215 N.W. 43 (Mich. 1927); Wilson v. Vill. of Forest View, 217 N.E.2d 398 (Ill. Ct. App 1966); Alford v. City of Gadsden, 349 So. 2d 1132 (Ala. 1977); Hatch v. Maple Valley Township Unit School, 17 N.W.2d 735 (Mich. 1945).

[1] Although held void at common law, many states have specifically prohibited this by statute. Thomson v. Call, 699 P.2d 316 (Cal. 1985), *cert. denied*, 474 U.S. 1057 (1986); Bosworth v. Hagerty, 99 N.W.2d 334 (S.D. 1959).

[2] City of Litchfield v. Ballou, 114 U.S. 190 (1885).

[3] Neisius v. Henry, 5 N.W.2d 291 (Neb. 1942).

If a local government enters into a contract that is contrary to the public policy of the state, it too is unenforceable. Courts will generally not grant recovery under specific performance or any equitable theory of quasi-contract or estoppel. Such contracts may not be ratified by the local government.[4]

Where a contract is for an undue length of time, unfairly and unwisely tying the hands of successor local officials, it may be found void for violating public policy.[5] Such a contract may not be ratified by the local government.[6] If there is no constitutional, statutory, or charter provision limiting the length of a contract, the duration must be reasonable under all the circumstances. Although the general rule is that local officials may not contract for longer than their term of office, the contract may be upheld if it is fair and the length of time is reasonable based on the existing situation and benefit to the community.[7] Sometimes courts have avoided the general rule by finding that a legislative body is a continuing body, regardless of change in membership.[8] Yet another distinction that has been used to uphold contracts with extended duration is to classify it as one that relates to the local government's proprietary activities and not its governmental ones.[9] This has been used particularly in long-term utility contracts where the local government either promises to provide or purchase gas, electricity, water, telephone or other services. Jurisdictions differ in classifying governmental actions as governmental or proprietary.

Courts have consistently found that contracts promising the exercise of governmental powers in predetermined ways violate public policy and are void and unenforceable.[10] Promises to rezone land, to enact legislation for the collection of garbage, to close streets for private benefit and to provide free goods or services, have all been found unenforceable. Promises to not exercise governmental authority are treated similarly. Local governments cannot restrict their own ability to legislate for the public good. They cannot contract to surrender their police powers.[11]

---

[4] Whatcom County Water Dist. No. 4 v. Century Holdings, Ltd., 627 P.2d 1010, *review denied*, 96 Wash.2d 1002 (1981).

[5] Marco Dev. Corp. v. City of Cedar Falls, 473 N.W.2d 41 (Iowa 1991).

[6] Utica State Savings Bank v. Village of Oak Park, 273 N.W. 271 (Mich. 1937).

[7] Denio v. City of Huntington Beach, 140 P.2d 392 (Cal. 1943), *overruled on other grounds*, Fracasse v. Brent, 494 P.2d 9 (Cal. 1972); Bd. of Comm'rs of Edwards Co. v. Simmons, 151 P.2d 960 (Kan. 1944).

[8] Town of Graham v. Karpark Corp., 194 F.2d 616 (4th Cir. 1952); Bd. of Comm'rs of Edwards Co. v. Simmons, 151 P.2d 960 (Kan 1944). *But see* Harrison Central Sch. Dist. v. Nyquist, 400 N.Y.S.2d 218 (3d Dep't 1977), *appeal denied*, 378 N.E.2d 126 (N.Y. 1978).

[9] Southern Airways Co. v. DeKalb County, 118 S.E.2d 234 (Ga. Ct. App. 1960); Schenley Farms Co. v. Allegheny County, 37 A.2d 554 (Pa. 1944).

[10] Gardner v. City of Dallas, 81 F.2d 425 (5th Cir. 1936), *cert. denied*, 298 U.S. 668 (1936); Rockingham Square Shopping Ctr., Inc. v. Town of Madison, 262 S.E.2d 705 (N.C. Ct. App. 1980).

[11] Lamar Bath House Co. v. City of Hot Springs, 315 S.W.2d 884 (Ark. 1958), *appeal dismissed*, 359 U.S. 534 (1959).

Contracts of a local government that benefit a local official violate public policy and are void.[12] There are many state statutes that address this. Such a violation is also prohibited by common-law jurisprudence. It is not necessary to show that the contract is unfair or unreasonable.[13] Employees of local governments have at times been permitted to have an interest in a local contract, but only if the employee cannot influence the award of the contract.[14]

When courts review local contracts, it is not their role to determine the wisdom or providence of the local action.[15] However, if it is shown that the local government has abused its discretion in a grossly unreasonable and inequitable manner, the local action may be found contrary to public policy and void.

§ 5.13   Ratification or Estoppel

Ratification is the adoption by the local government of a contract that was not properly executed. The contract may be flawed because the procedure prescribed for the exercise of local authority to contract was not followed, or because it was not executed by an authorized agent. The local government can adopt the flawed contract by ratification only if it had the delegated authority to enter into the contract if it was properly executed.[1] Usually the process of ratification is accomplished by taking the action or following the procedure that was omitted in the first instance.[2] Through this process, the local government is indicating its intent to perform the contract because it is beneficial to the public welfare. In other words, it does not want to exercise any option that it might have to declare the contract void because of the irregularities.

Local governments have used the ratification process when there has been an omission in following prescribed procedures. As long as these requirements can be accomplished, it is an effective remedy. However, if the omitted step, such as submitting a request for goods or services for competitive bidding, cannot be supplemented to the flawed contract, then ratification is generally held to be an inappropriate remedy.[3] The only way to meet that requirement is to advertise and resubmit the request for competitive bidding.

---

[12] Watson v. City of New Smyrna Beach, 85 So. 2d 548 (Fla. 1956).

[13] *Thompson, supra* note 1 at 325-26.

[14] City of Coral Gables v. Weksler, 164 So. 2d 260 (Fla. Dist. Ct. App.), *aff'd*, 170 So. 2d 844 (Fla. 1964).

[15] Foss v. Spitznagel, 97 N.W.2d 856 (S.D. 1959).

[1] Chemical Bank v. Washington Pub. Power Supply System., 691 P.2d 524 (Wash. 1984), *cert. denied*, 471 U.S. 1065 (1985).

[2] Goin v. Bd. of Educ., 183 S.W.2d 819 (Ky. 1944). *But see* City of Kenai v. Filler, 566 P.2d 670 (Alaska 1977) (holding that the government would not have to comply with all the required formalities).

[3] Seim v. Indep. Dist. of Monroe, 17 N.W.2d 342 (S.D. 1945).

Local governments have also used ratification to legitimatize contracts regarded as defective only because they were entered into by a person who was not authorized to represent the local government.[4] It is generally held that if the contract met all requirements and was entered into by one who indicated he was acting on behalf of the local government, it may be ratified by those who were in fact authorized to do it.

Ratification can only take place if the government body with authority to enter into the contract has full knowledge of all the material facts at the time of its ratifying action. If it is done by a local legislative body, it can take the form of a resolution or local enactment, depending on what is required to enter into the contract. Ratification can also take place by implication. If the governing body evidences an intent to approve the unauthorized transaction, either by its affirmative action or by its inaction, ratification may be implied.[5] For instance, ratification has been found when the local government paid the bills submitted to it pursuant to an unauthorized contract.[6] Ratification has also been implied when the benefits were retained and the local government was silent after learning of the unauthorized nature of the contract.[7] However, there can be no ratification of a contract which is unauthorized, prohibited, or violates public policy.[8]

Sometimes, local governments have been found to be estopped from denying the validity of a contract where there have been procedural omissions, if its actions have led the contracting party to rely on the legitimacy of the contract.[9] If the contractor acted reasonably, in good faith, and in reliance on the appearance created by the local government, the court may find that the local government is estopped from denying the validity of the contract where benefits have been received by it.[10] Courts have similarly held that a local government that accepts goods or services under a contract entered into by an unauthorized agent is estopped from denying the agent's authority if the contractor rightfully relied upon him or her.[11]

Estoppel may not be used to preserve a contract that is void because it is ultra vires, prohibited, or contrary to public policy even if the local government has received benefits from it.[12]

---

[4] Riddlestorffer v. City of Rahway, 196 A.2d 550 (N.J. Super. Ct. Law Div. 1963); Johnson v. Hospital Service Plan of N.J., 135 A.2d 483 (N.J. 1957).

[5] *Id.* at 486–87.

[6] Ridley Township v. Haulaway Trash Removal, Inc., 448 A.2d 654 (Pa. Commw. Ct. 1982).

[7] City of Gainesville v. Edwards, 145 S.E.2d 715 (Ga. Ct. App. 1965);

[8] *See* § 5.12 *supra* for a discussion of these types of contracts.

[9] 405 Monroe Co. v. City of Asbury Park, 193 A.2d 115 (N.J. 1963).

[10] Wiggins v. Barrett & Assocs., Inc., 669 P.2d 1132 (Or. 1983).

[11] Got-It Hardware & Gifts, Inc. v. City of Ashburn, 270 S.E.2d 380 (Ga. Ct. App. 1980). *But see* Chicago Food Management, Inc. v. City of Chicago, 516 N.E.2d 880 (Ill. Ct. App. 1987), *appeal denied*, 522 N.E.2d 1241 (Ill., 1988).

[12] Carter Co. v. City of Elizabethton, 287 S.W.2d 934 (Tenn. Ct. App. 1956); Incorporated City of Humboldt v. Knight, 120 N.W.2d 457 (Iowa 1963).

Chapter 6

Delivery of Services and Assistance

§ 6.1 Introduction and Chapter Overview

The development of local governments in the various states took place because of two strong factors. States were driven to create local government structures because units of government closer to the people were needed through which the states' responsibilities to protect the health and welfare of their populations could be fulfilled. These so-called "arms of the state" enabled the states to implement many of the policies adopted in their exercise of sovereign authority. Whether used to provide state assistance to the needy or to maintain safeguards for public health, local governments have performed a vital role in the delivery of state services.

The second motivating factor occurred when people, living in clusters within the larger local government structure, wanted additional services or government regulation. Many times these needs could best be met through the creation of a governmental structure with authority to assess taxes, develop infrastructure, contract, and regulate conduct. States responded to this by creating some local governments and establishing procedures whereby additional local governments could be created by the initiative of the residents.

Over the years, the responsibilities and powers of all local governments, whether initially created by the state or by local initiative, have come to possess more similarities than differences. Most counties, towns, cities, boroughs, and villages are general-purpose units of government, possessing broad authority to respond to local needs and provide the many services that their residents desire and have come to expect.

Subsequently, another type of local entity was devised that had the effect of slowing the creation of new local governments. The creation of special districts and public benefit corporations (or public authorities) has had an enormous impact on the delivery of services by local governments. The creation of a special improvement district is a way to provide a service to a portion of the local government and assess the costs solely to those within the district. No longer was it advantageous or necessary to create a new general-purpose local government within a larger one, because specific needs could be addressed in a targeted manner. The creation of authorities gives the state and local governments a new means of providing services that do not burden the debt limitations and may be exempt from many restrictions that would apply if the governments themselves directly undertook the project. The authorities do not rely on taxpayer revenues but are designed to be self-supporting. They also give governments the ability to address regional needs and overcome jurisdictional problems.

Privatization of state and local services is an increasingly popular way to provide services as governments search for ways to deliver better services in the least costly manner. There are different ways to use privatization. It may be done through a government contract with a private service provider who agrees to provide a public good or service. It may also be done through the transfer of a public asset in exchange for good consideration, or it can be used as a process to inject competition into a decision of whether the service or product can be most efficiently provided by a private or public source.

The types of services and goods provided by local governments encompass protection, health and medical assistance, education, assistance for the needy, housing, sports and recreation, cultural, and dispute resolution forums. Local governments continually are expected to adapt and meet the evolving needs of their residents. Demographic factors such as age, wealth, and education of a local government's population changes over time. So do people's expectations of the proper role of government. Because of this, local governments have had to involve themselves in new areas to meet new challenges. Economic development in order to attract new jobs or retain existing employers, and the development of new programs addressing an aging population, have become important concerns requiring local attention and action.

PART I SPECIAL DISTRICTS, AUTHORITIES, AND PRIVATIZATION

§ 6.2 Education and School Districts

It is universally recognized by all levels of government that providing public school education is primarily a state responsibility even though there is direct local participation. In addition, there is an increasing federal role that will have a significant effect on public education in the future. This is reflected in the adoption by Congress of the No Child Left Behind Act of 2001[1] (NCLB). This federal law imposes increased levels of accountability for states, school districts, and schools receiving federal education funds. It requires statewide standards in reading and mathematics, annual testing for all students in grades 3-8 and annual statewide progress objectives to ensure that all groups of students reach levels of proficiency within twelve years. Assessment of results must be given by poverty, race, ethnicity, disability, and limited English proficiency to make sure no group is left behind. Failure of schools and districts to make progress toward meeting standards will have consequences, while those that meet or exceed standards, or close achievement gaps, will be eligible for awards. There are also provisions in NCLB for students in poorly performing schools to transfer

---

[1] Pub. L. No. 107–110 (H.R.1). This was part of the re-authorization of the Elementary and Secondary Education Act of 1965.

to a better public school in the district. As an incentive, the states are given greater flexibility in the use of their federal funds.[2]

Although the Supreme Court has determined that education is not a fundamental right under the Federal Constitution, it has noted that it is perhaps the most important function of state and local governments. The Court also held that where it is undertaken, it must be made available to all on an equal basis.[3]

States have expressly recognized their responsibility for providing public education in specific provisions that are included in their state constitutions. The New Jersey provision is an example, providing that "The Legislature shall provide for the maintenance and support of a thorough and efficient system of free public schools for the instruction of all the children in the State."[4] State courts have held that in carrying out their responsibilities under these provisions, states have plenary authority to establish educational policy, create a system of schools, exercise authority over local educational governing boards, and regulate all matters relating to school facilities and curriculum. Although states have chosen various methods of fulfilling their responsibility, there are many essential similarities. Most states have created a structure of shared responsibility with local communities through the creation of local school districts. These school districts have a long, extensive, and continuous history in this country. They differ from other types of special districts[5] because of their independence and ability to raise revenue by imposing a tax.

Most school districts are governed by a board that is independent from the local government. The exception is the dependent school district found in many metropolitan areas where schools are part of the local government structure. There are both independent and dependent school districts in many states. In the independent school districts, local governments may appoint, or citizens may elect, members of local boards of education. In the dependent districts, the geographical boundary is usually coterminous with a local government and the members of the school's governing board are usually appointed by the local government, although they are sometimes elected by its voters. All local school boards exercise varying degrees of control over budgets, facilities, programs, and appointment of educators. At the same time, overall policy and a great deal of the curriculum requirements are usually established by a state agency.

Most school districts have been given authority to raise revenues needed to pay for the schools by imposing a real property tax. The independent districts generally have geographical boundaries that are not coterminous with a local government. They possess independent authority to establish

---

[2] See www.ed.gov/nclb/ for further information (last visited December 26, 2002).

[3] Brown v. Bd. of Educ., 347 U.S. 483 (1954). See also Plyler v. Doe, 457 U.S. 202 (1982). Equal protection prohibits a state from denying a free public education to the children of illegal aliens.

[4] N.J. CONST. art. VIII, § 4, par. 1.

[5] See § 6.3 infra for a discussion of special districts.

budgets and propose capital expenditures which may be subject to voter approval. They can levy taxes and issue bonds to raise the funds needed to meet their operating and capital expenses. Usually, the dependent school district must rely upon the county, township, city, or village for financial support and generally cannot raise funds without the local government's approval. One of the strongest arguments in favor of the independent district is that its governing board will be elected on a nonpartisan basis and function in a manner that is separate from any political considerations of the local governments.

Funding for local schools is usually composed of federal, state and local revenues. Because of this mixture of funding, there have been continuing challenges to state structures for financing public education. In particular, the heavy reliance on locally raised funds based upon the real property tax has led to great disparities in the total dollar amount spent on a per-pupil basis. Many have claimed that the more prosperous communities, which have the ability to devote more of their local money to education, have benefitted, while often the urban, poorer areas have not been able to provide the same educational opportunities. The Supreme Court rejected a challenge based on the Federal Equal Protection Clause, holding that education is not a federally protected right that warrants strict scrutiny.[6] The Court held that the financing system involving a combination of state and local support bears a rational relationship to a legitimate state purpose. Other challenges brought in state courts have alleged unconstitutionality based on both state constitutional equal protection[7] and state responsibility[8] clauses. These have succeeded in the courts of some states and have failed to be adopted by others.[9] Other issues have been raised in these cases that question the equity of school financing apart from the value of the real property tax base. The ability of some local governments, particularly heavily populated cities, to devote a proportionate amount of their budgets to education is much less than other local governments with similar tax bases, because the cities have heavier competing demands for other services and they have disproportionately higher education costs.[10] This argument has not been particularly successful but the impact of all school-financing cases has been enormous. Most states have addressed educational financing and significant changes have been adopted in many states.

---

[6] San Antonio Indep. Sch. Dist. v. Rodriguez, 411 U.S. 1 (1973).

[7] Serrano v. Priest, 487 P.2d 1241 (Cal. 1971); Robinson v. Cahill, 303 A.2d 273 (N.J. 1973).

[8] Helena Elementary Sch. Dist. No. 1 v. State, 769 P.2d 684 (Mont. 1989); Rose v. Council for Better Educ., 790 S.W.2d 186 (Ky. 1989).

[9] See § 10.4 infra for further discussion on financing education by revenue raised from the local real property tax.

[10] Bd. of Educ., Levittown Union Free Sch. Dist. v. Nyquist, 439 N.E.2d 359 (N.Y. 1982). Referred to as municipal overburden, the cities were able to show that they spent 28% of their budget for schools while other local governments spent 45%. They also demonstrated that they had a much higher proportion of students with special needs. This is referred to as educational overburden. The New York Court denied relief, finding that the state constitution only required that the state provide a sound basic education.

The reliance on state constitutional clauses, combined with increasing concern about the quality of education in this country, has directed the focus in more modern cases toward the adequacy of public education. The Kentucky Court invalidated the state's total educational system, holding that the creation, implementation and financing did not meet its state constitutional mandate to "provide an efficient system of common schools throughout the state."[11] However, there is still reticence among some state courts to find unconstitutionality, primarily because they do not read the education mandates in their state constitutions to require educational equity or a certain quality of education. The courts are concerned about separation of powers and their role in defining standards of education.

Unless provided otherwise in its constitution, a state may be responsible for drawing school district boundaries or providing for their creation at the local level. A state may also delegate this responsibility to local governments. A school's relationship to the local government in which it exists varies from state to state and may even vary within states. Some schools are subject to local land use and building regulations while others are exempt. Some must pay special utility assessments; others do not. Often, a local government will be responsible for collecting and paying to schools taxes that are imposed by the school. The permutations of the relationships between school districts and local governments are varied and have developed over many years. They often reflect historical origins that may not be the most efficient but survive because they are entrenched and difficult to change. However, the state may reasonably create, dissolve or change the boundaries and functioning of schools as it deems appropriate because education is a state responsibility. The only limitations on the exercise of state authority to control the structure and operation of its schools are those restrictions that may be based upon the state or federal constitutions.

The federal government has a significant impact on public education. In addition to federal aid, there are numerous federal laws that protect the individual rights of students, school officers and employees. These federal laws address school action as it affects speech and religion, desegregation, elections and voting rights, and discrimination based on race, gender, disability, or age. Many federal statutes have been enacted which directly impact the operation of local schools.

Using its delegated constitutional authority, Congress has adopted legislation that requires school authorities to provide assistance to those who have language barriers.[12] It also has prohibited school districts from excluding or discriminating against disabled individuals in any program or activity receiving federal financial assistance.[13] The Individuals With Disabilities Education Act[14] conditions the grant of federal assistance by

---

[11] Rose v. Council for Better Educ., 790 S.W.2d 189 (Ky. 1989). *See also* Edgewood Indep. Sch. Dist. v. Kirby, 777 S.W.2d 391 (Tex. 1989).

[12] EQUAL EDUCATIONAL OPPORTUNITIES ACT, 20 U.S.C. § 1701 *et seq.* (1999).

[13] REHABILITATION ACT AND AMERICANS WITH DISABILITIES ACT, 29 U.S.C. § 794 (1999).

[14] 20 U.S.C. § 1400 (1999).

requiring that schools receiving such aid provide all children with disabilities a free appropriate public education. To comply, a school must develop an individualized education plan (IEP) based upon the child's needs. There has been a great deal of litigation surrounding this legislation, with various courts interpreting its requirements in great detail.[15]

Section 1983 of the Federal Civil Rights Act has provided a very effective remedy for those who have been denied their federally protected rights by actions attributable to school districts or their officers and employees. If a school has an official custom or policy, or if it acts with deliberate indifference to an individual's federally protected rights, liability may be imposed under § 1983.[16] The Supreme Court has held that school board members and administrators have at most a qualified immunity from liability.[17]

Local schools have experienced a great deal of controversy in their effort to balance the protections found in the First Amendment's prohibition against the establishment of religion and its protection of an individual's right to the free exercise of religion. Questions have been raised under the Establishment Clause about the use of textbooks,[18] public transportation[19] and school facilities, and government vouchers for private religious schools. At the same time, a school's refusal to permit student-initiated prayer before public school activities or the use of school facilities for Bible study have raised corresponding questions of an infringement of students' rights under the Free Exercise Clause.

The Supreme Court has established a test to be used to determine whether a government action or policy violates the Establishment Clause. In *Lemon v. Kurtzman*,[20] the Court held that the action or policy is constitutional if it has a secular purpose, its primary effect neither advances nor inhibits religion, and it does not excessively entangle government with religion. In a subsequent application of the test, the Supreme Court held that public school employees could be permitted to provide instructional services in a nonpublic school if the assistance is distributed using neutral, secular criteria and is made available to both religious and secular schools on a nondiscriminatory basis. In another application of the test, the

[15] For cases and information discussing the *Individuals With Disabilities Education Act, see* SANDRA M. STEVENSON, ANTIEAU ON LOCAL GOVERNMENT LAW, Second Ed., § 46.05[6][c] (2001).

[16] 42 U.S.C. § 1983. For further discussion, *see* § 9.6 *infra*.

[17] Wood v. Strickland, 420 U.S. 308 (1975). For further discussion, *see* § 8.6 *infra*.

[18] Bd. of Educ. of Cent. Sch. Dist. No. 1 v. Allen, 392 U.S. 236 (1968) (holding that if the texts are designated for use in public schools, the loan does not violate the Establishment Clause).

[19] Everson v. Bd. of Educ. of Ewing Township, 330 U.S. 1 (1947) (stating that school districts may provide transportation to children attending religious schools). *But see* Wolman v. Walter, 433 U.S. 229 (1977) (finding that transportation for school field trips violates the Establishment Clause due to excessive entanglement).

[20] U.S. v. Mitchell, 403 U.S. 602 (1971). The Court reaffirmed this test in Agostini v. Felton, 521 U.S. 203 (1997).

Supreme Court upheld the redistribution of federal funds by a state to local education agencies which loaned computers and media materials to public and private schools for "secular, neutral and nonideological" programs.[21] The Court said that it did not have a primary effect of advancing or inhibiting religion because it was offered to a broad range of entities without consideration of their religion. Their eligibility was determined on a neutral basis and the aid was allocated based on the private choices of parents. The Court specifically rejected arguments that the aid must not go directly to the schools or be capable of being diverted to a religious use. However, the Supreme Court has held unconstitutional direct financial aid to church-related schools,[22] reimbursement of salaries for those teaching secular subjects,[23] or reimbursement for testing required by state law.[24]

The question of whether public funds may be used to aid a student in paying tuition to attend a religious school is currently an issue in many states. The debate is focused on the use of vouchers in order to permit a child to choose to attend a private school instead of a public school and whether this violates the federal or state establishment clauses. The Supreme Court has sustained a state's program which gave parents financial assistance to choose to enroll their children in private or public, religious or secular schools, instead of the demonstrably failing public school they were attending.[24.1] The program also provided an option of financial assistance for tutors if the parents chose not to remove their children from the public school. The Court found a valid secular purpose of providing children with an adequate educational opportunity which was available on a neutral, nonreligious basis to all low-income families within the school district. The religious schools only received the public funds if the parents chose to send their child to them, a truly private choice. Many state courts have sustained various assistance programs. The Arizona Court upheld a state tax-credit scheme against an Establishment Clause challenge[25] and the Wisconsin[26] and Ohio[27] Courts have sustained school voucher programs for low-income families.

The issue of religious freedom under the First Amendment has been raised in many recent cases. A student's right to read a religious story to his classmates led to an equal split by the Third Circuit Court of Appeals on the First Amendment issue.[28] But nothing has been as controversial as the question of prayer in public schools. The Supreme Court held that prayers composed by public officials could not be said during the regular

---

[21] Mitchell v. Helms, 1530 U.S. 793 (2000).

[22] Marburger v. Public Funds for Public Sch., 417 U.S. 961 (1974).

[23] Lemon v. Kurtzman, 403 U.S. 602 (1971).

[24] Levitt v. Committee for Pub. Educ. and Religious Liberty, 413 U.S. 472 (1973).

[24.1] Zelman v. Simmons-Harris, 536 U.S. 639 (2002).

[25] Kotterman v. Killian, 972 P.2d 606 (Ariz. 1999).

[26] Jackson v. Benson, 578 N.W.2d 602 (Wis. 1998).

[27] Simmons-Harris v. Goff, 711 N.E.2d 203 (Ohio 1999).

[28] C.H. v. Oliva, 226 F.3d 198 (3d Cir. 2000).

school day.[29] It extended the holding to include a ban on clergy offering prayers as part of an official public school graduation.[30] The rationale of the Court was that the decision that prayers should be given and the school's selection of religious participants, as well as direction that the prayer be nonsectarian, were factors that indicated government involvement. In response to this, a school adopted a policy of permitting student-led prayer, after a vote. If the vote was in favor of the prayer, then the students elected the student who was to give the nonsectarian, non-proselytizing prayer prior to school football games. Again, the Supreme Court said no.[31] The policy has both a perceived and actual endorsement of religion. In yet another case, the Supreme Court considered whether "silent meditation" violated the Establishment Clause.[32] The Court found that it did because it was motivated by an attempt to return voluntary prayer to the public schools. It failed the secular-purpose requirement of the *Lemon* test.[33] Various federal courts have also determined that a period of silence violates the Establishment Clause.[34]

The use of public school facilities for religious purposes has received varied results in the courts. Some have held that schools must permit students to have prayer and religious discussion groups in order to respect their free-exercise rights, but when the group grew large and actively proselytized, the school could implement a policy prohibiting student groups from meeting for religious purposes on school property immediately before or after school.[35] Congress entered the debate with enactment of the Equal Access Act[36] which requires equal access to students who wish to conduct a meeting and prohibits denial on the basis of religious, political, philosophical or other content of the speech. It applies to all public secondary schools receiving federal financial assistance which have a limited open forum that permits noncurriculum related student groups to meet on school premises during noninstructional times. Schools that choose not to permit access to noncurriculum related groups are not affected by the statute. School officials are expressly forbidden from participating in the meetings of student religious groups. The Supreme Court has upheld the statute, finding that it does not violate the Establishment Clause.[37]

Community religious organizations often request to use school facilities. If the school does not let any external group use its facilities then it is not

---

[29] Engell v. Vitale, 370 U.S. 421 (1962).

[30] Lee v. Weisman, 505 U.S. 577 (1991).

[31] Santa Fe Indep. Sch. Dist. v. Doe, 530 U.S. 290 (2000).

[32] Wallace v. Jaffree, 472 U.S. 38 (1985).

[33] *Lemon, supra* note 14 at 616.

[34] May v. Cooperman, 780 F.2d 240 (3d Cir. 1985), *appeal dismissed sub nom.*, Karcher v. May, 484 U.S. 72 (1987) (dismissed on jurisdictional grounds); Walter v. West Va. Bd. of Educ., 610 F. Supp. 1169 (S.D. W. Va. 1985). *But see* Bown v. Gwinnett County Sch. Dist., 895 F. Supp. 1564 (N.D. Ga. 1995).

[35] Clark v. Dallas Indep. Sch. Dist., 671 F. Supp. 1119 (N.D. Tex. 1987).

[36] 20 U.S.C. § 4071 *et seq.*

[37] Bd. of Educ. of Westside Community Schools v. Mergens, 496 U.S. 226 (1990).

required to make an exception for the religious use. However, the Supreme Court has held that if the school does permit others to use the buildings, it may not discriminate against the religious organization on the basis of the content of the speech.[38] Some schools have limited the use of school facilities to activities involving certain groups or discussion of certain topics. The Supreme Court has sustained this use of a limited-access forum and has held that the restriction must be reasonable and may not discriminate against speech based on the viewpoint of the organization seeking to use the school facility. When a school district precludes an organization from presenting films because they are based on a religious perspective,[39] or a university refuses to fund a student publication because it addresses issues from a religious perspective,[40] it violates the free speech rights of the participants. The Supreme Court has determined that permitting speech from a religious viewpoint on school grounds does not violate the Establishment Clause. It insures neutrality toward religion.[41] A school that prohibited use of its facilities because the participants expressed themselves through live storytelling and prayer was unconstitutional viewpoint discrimination.[42]

Many state constitutions have clauses that are identical or substantially similar to the Establishment and Free Exercise of Religion Clauses. The state courts may choose to interpret their provisions differently than the Federal Constitution but they may not violate a person's federal rights.[43] Some state constitutions have various bans upon the use of state funds for nonpublic purposes. What may be permitted under the Federal Constitution may not be permissible under state law.

§ 6.3   Special Improvement Districts

States have addressed many governmental concerns by creating or permitting local governments or residents to create special districts. The term "special district" is confusing because states vary in their use of the term. In this section, special improvement district refers to the specialized entity that provides a needed improvement or service to all or part of a local government. Unlike a local government, it is not a general purpose government with general governing authority. It is most often created to serve a single function and it usually has authority to perform the service and impose a tax or levy special assessments or user charges. To understand it, it is necessary to explain what it is not. It is not a special assessment district, created to provide an infrastructure improvement in a defined area, to be funded by special assessment of the costs upon the property that has

---

[38] Lamb's Chapel v. Center Moriches Union Free Sch. Dist., 508 U.S. 384 (1993).

[39] *Id.*

[40] Rosenberger v. Rector and Visitors of Univ. of Va., 515 U.S. 819 (1995).

[41] Good News Club v. Milford Central School, 533 U.S. 98 (2001).

[42] *Id.*

[43] Chittenden Town Sch. Dist. v. Dep't of Educ., 738 A.2d 539 (Vt. 1999), *cert. denied*, Andrews v. Vt. Dep't Educ., 528 U.S. 1066 (1999).

been improved.[1] It is not the public benefit corporate entity that is also created to perform a public service but is typically referred to as an authority.[2] Neither does the term special improvement district include school districts, which are truly independent governmental units that operate to provide their particular service without any direct connection to the county, town, city, village, or borough in which they are located.[3]

The special improvement district's strength and popularity comes from the flexibility it affords to local government to provide a specific service to a designated portion of the community and to impose the costs solely on those residing within the district boundaries. It is a means of providing services on less than a community-wide basis and limiting the cost to those areas receiving the benefit. Since the geographic reach of a special district is defined by the perceived need or desire to provide a service to a group of residents, it is not unusual for various special districts that provide different services to have boundaries that overlap. The independent authority to provide the service may permit a degree of flexibility that leads to efficiencies that exceed those of a local government providing the same service.

Special improvement districts may usually be created either by action of the local governing board or by petition of local residents requesting the creation in order to obtain a desired service. The services that have been provided through the use of the special improvement district are extremely varied, ranging from sewerage disposal, water supply, sidewalks, conservation, libraries, parking, and lighting to extremely localized needs such as mosquito control and duck sludge disposal districts.

The special improvement district is not always considered a totally separate unit of government but usually has a degree of independence from the administrative structure of the local government. It may have fiscal independence in managing its assets and assessing taxes, user charges and fees. However, they are not generally independent of local government oversight, which will periodically review their management and finances. In some special districts, the local government itself will provide the funds for the capital structure needed by the special district to provide the service. The local government may issue revenue bonds[4] in order to obtain necessary funds. The potential revenue to be raised from user fees or charges will be dedicated to the repayment of the indebtedness.

Management of the special improvement district is provided by the members of a governing board, who are usually appointed by the local executive or legislative body. The special improvement district is unlike authorities or public-benefit corporations and independent school districts where there may be an even greater separation in the management and finances from the local government.

---

[1] Special assessments for improvements are discussed in § 10.7 *infra*.

[2] Authorities are discussed in § 6.4 *infra*.

[3] School districts are discussed in § 6.2 *supra*.

[4] For a discussion of revenue bonds, *see* § 10.12 *infra*.

Although states vary in their adaptation of this form of providing services, local governments have widely and increasingly used the special improvement district for developing and providing services to their residents. The proliferation of the special district as a provider of local services has led to criticism that it has created a confusing array of governance. Overlapping districts and a lack of direct electoral accountability by appointed governing boards have left some local residents confused and unhappy with this form of government. On the other hand, as its proponents note, it has led to a decrease in incorporations of general purpose governments because people can obtain a needed service, and pay for its cost, without incurring the expense of establishing and supporting another local government.

The business improvement district (BID) is a district that is in some ways even less complicated than the typical special improvement district. It is composed of a defined geographical region but may have little or no government structure and no authority. It is a commercial area that has voluntarily chosen to have an assessment or tax imposed upon it, in addition to the normal taxes paid, in order to gain the benefits of additional improvements or services. Whether road or sidewalk improvements, or a general upgrade in security, landscaping or parking, the goal is to improve the economic fortunes of the defined commercial area. Businesses have chosen to pay extra taxes for such things as additional police services, landscaping, or other improvements in order to encourage patrons to frequent their establishments. In other ways, its governance may be more complicated than special improvement districts because it usually includes a high degree of resident participation. The continual decision-making process should reflect the wishes of those who are benefitted.

§ 6.4   Public Authorities

Public authorities are sometimes called districts, boards, or even commissions, but probably the most accurate title is public benefit corporations. In many respects they resemble special improvement districts[1] but there are significant differences. Authorities are similar to special districts in that both are usually created to provide a single public service but neither are given the broad governing authority of a local government. The powers and duties of an authority are specified in the legislation by which it was created. Authorities are very independent entities that usually have less direct contact with the local government than special districts. The local control of the authority may be limited to the power to appoint members of the governing board and by a requirement that the authority issue periodic reports to the state or local government it is serving.

The service provided by an authority is often one that requires a large-scale capital expenditure such as a power plant, an airport, or a transportation system. Unlike a special district, it is not usually limited to providing

---

[1] Special Improvement Districts are discussed in § 6.5 *infra*.

that service to a defined geographical part of the local government. Frequently, the service may be provided on a regional basis to people both within and outside the local government. The creation of an authority also permits local governments to work collaboratively to provide one service to many local governments. It can serve to bridge jurisdictional differences.

A major difference between many special improvement districts and authorities is that authorities do not have the power to impose a tax. This is a reflection of their independent status. In most jurisdictions it would be an unconstitutional delegation to attempt to empower a special benefit corporation with the governmental authority to tax. Typically, the authority issues its own bonds to obtain development costs. It imposes tolls or user charges for the service it provides to obtain revenue to repay the bonds and cover its operating expenses. For this reason, authorities are generally used to develop a facility or perform a service that will generate revenue to pay its costs. Public funds are preserved intact because tax dollars will not be needed to pay development or operating costs.

A strong incentive for the use of the authority is the avoidance of state or local government debt limitations and restrictions. The authority, or public benefit corporation, is usually delegated authority to incur its own debt and enter into contracts in order to accomplish its purposes. Since an authority is viewed as independent of state and local governments, and is usually prohibited from pledging the full faith and credit of the state or local government to its creditors, its debt is not considered a state or local debt. It is the authority's own debt and is subject to any limitations and restrictions that have been imposed on it. Those extending credit to the authority realize that it is the obligation of the authority to repay and must carefully analyze the soundness of the business model that supports the anticipated revenues which will provide funds for repayment. For state or local governments with debt limitations or voter approval requirements, the creation of an authority may be a practical way to provide a needed service. Often, voters do not like to incur debt for unpopular expenditures such as prisons, or for major capital expenditures that will not benefit them directly.

Public benefit corporations have other attributes that may be unique when compared to traditional government agencies. Many have greater flexibility in management decisions because the legislation that creates them does not require that they adhere to civil service laws that apply to traditional state and local agencies. Greater flexibility may also be found in their ability to contract without competitive-bidding requirements, or required approvals by local and state agencies. These features have also led to much criticism of the authority model, primarily because they are less accountable for their actions. Again, it should be noted that there are tremendous variations in the restrictions that are placed on these independent entities, not only from state to state, but within states. The organic legislation that created the entity will most likely define these conditions.

States have addressed many needs for governmental facilities or services by creating state authorities. They have been used to manage natural resources, construct public highway systems, develop and manage public utilities and provide a host of other state services on both a statewide and regional basis. Some have been encouraged and subsidized by an inflow of federal funds, such as public housing authorities. The authority that is often credited with opening the door to the use of the authority model for providing public services is the Port Authority of New York and New Jersey, which was created in 1921. Established by an interstate compact and ratified by Congress, it was used to enable two highly independent state governments to work together to develop major water and air transportation facilities that benefit both states. Just as significantly, the Authority was structured so it would generate sufficient revenue to cover its own costs.

Since this mechanism worked so well for the state, it has been applied at the local government level. Either created by the state or by the local government pursuant to state authorization, authorities now address regional and local needs. The local authority is an agency structure that permits multiple local governments to work toward a common goal to produce a regional benefit. In other words, local political and geographical boundaries that would be difficult to overcome are bypassed by creating a new mechanism that is focused on regional needs. It is a smaller pattern of why the Port Authority was created, but similar in its result. The local authority may be a regional airport, transportation system, land use plan, or it may address a common environmental concern. At the same time, many authorities have been created that are purely local, addressing a particular need within a single local government. These independent agencies have been used to assist in local economic development, the creation and operation of public utilities, hospitals, recreation, transportation, and many other kinds of local services.

The public benefit corporate structure has provided other important benefits. Since an authority, or public benefit corporation, is considered by the courts to have many of the attributes of a traditional government agency, it has many of the traditional advantages. Its property and bonds are exempt from state and local taxation, and possibly from federal taxation.[2] Since those lending the authority money receive a tax exemption on the interest, the authority is able to borrow money at a lower-than-market interest rate. This ability to borrow funds at a lower cost has been used by state and local government authorities to assist private development that will benefit the state or the local government. Many state and local governments have used authorities or public benefit corporations to borrow funds for the financing of private developments that will lead to socially beneficial activities such as education, health care, manufacturing, recreational and sports activities. The public purpose is to improve the health, safety and welfare of a community by encouraging economic growth and the development of needed services. Sometimes these assisted developments are also exempt from related state and local taxes, such as sales and real property taxes. As a state or local government entity, an authority is

---

[2] For a discussion of tax exemptions for local government bonds, see § 10.12 infra.

not required to pay taxes. Often this has translated into an ability to provide an exemption to private entities seeking their assistance. In many areas, local independent agencies have required that payments in lieu of real property taxes be paid by the companies receiving their aid. There are also other possibilities of exemption from fees and taxes, such as fees imposed on the transfer of real property or mortgage taxes.

§ 6.5   Privatization of Services or Assets

Privatization simply means transferring responsibility for all or part of a function to the private sector. One of the rationales behind all types of privatization is that it encourages the development or delivery of better services or products at a lower cost. A federal report appears to confirm this by finding that state and local governments have saved substantially, with the degree of economy depending on the type of service that is provided.[1] Another incentive for privatizing is that it may provide a means for local government to acquire a kind of expertise that it does not currently possess, with sophisticated information technology as a typical example.

Privatization is accomplished by the local government contracting with a private entity to provide the service to the public, or by transferring a public asset through sale or lease. In transfer of an asset, the local government discontinues the service and generally retains no management or supervisory responsibility. Some states and local governments have adopted a third form of privatization called managed competition. Here, public entities compete with private entities to submit the best plan for providing a public service.[2]

The most commonly used method of privatizing takes place when a local government contracts with a private service provider. It is a flexible method, in that it may involve a portion of one type of service or it may involve the entire range of activities. For instance, a local government could contract for the provision of jail facilities but retain responsibility for providing all other required services needed in the criminal detention process. When a service is privatized by contract, most often the local government retains responsibility for seeing that the contractor abides by the terms of the contract and lawfully provides the service.

A form of privatization that is different from the contractual format but bears some similarity is the use by local governments of private schools and landlords to meet public needs for education[3] and housing.[4] In both situations, local governments have provided vouchers or other forms of financial assistance to private individuals who qualify for public assistance to be given to private service providers.

---

[1] JOINT ECONOMIC COMM. STAFF REPORT, *The $7.7 Billion Mistake: Federal Barriers to State and Local Privatization* (Feb. 1996).

[2] This process is similar to competitive bidding with specifications drawn and a structure created whereby a winner can be designated after review of the submitted proposals.

[3] For a discussion on education vouchers, *see* § 6.2 *supra*.

[4] For a discussion on the use of public subsidies for private housing, *see* § 6.8 *infra*.

In a form of privatization that involves the transfer of a public asset to a private entity, the local government will be compensated for the value of the property or the right to the benefits of the asset. This form of privatization typically involves a proprietary function or a financial asset of the local government. It might involve the sale or lease of property, such as an arena, or a right to future income, such as the government debt on student education loans or the future income due the local government from a massive tobacco settlement.[5] It is easy to see that this may result in an immediate infusion of much-needed capital to the local government. It also can be used to return public property to the tax rolls or relieve the local government of liabilities that are draining its operating resources.

The third form of privatization, managed competition, has public agencies competing with private entities to see which can best provide the service. Perhaps its strongest benefit is the leverage it may provide government as a employer to obtain greater efficiencies from the public workforce. By injecting a competitive element, there is an incentive for public employees to develop a plan to provide a given service more efficiently than counterparts in the private sector.

Criticisms and concerns about the effects of privatization are numerous. Concerns are raised about the effect it may have on both government employees and members of the public alike. Other questions are targeted at the particular type of privatization that is being used. For instance, if privatization is by contract, it is noted that once a contract is in place, there is often little room to amend even when there are changes needed in the service. Consideration must often be given to transaction and monitoring responsibilities. If it is a managed competition, there are tremendous difficulties in precisely drawing the specifications and then fairly comparing costs of public providers with costs of private providers.

Since privatization is still at a very early developmental stage, governments are experimenting with various methods and they are developing information about potential uses and effects. Some states have established commissions that are responsible for examining processes to both assess its use and to assist in its implementation.[6] In addition, the U.S. General Accounting Office has investigated and reported on some state experiences.[7]

Several key issues have already been identified that raise particularly tough questions in the use of privatization. One strong concern is about its potential impact on the civil service protections afforded most government employees. Although privatization is an increasingly popular method

---

[5] For information about the Master Settlement Agreement between tobacco companies and governments, *see* § 3.5 *supra*.

[6] *Kansas Council on Privatization, Privatize, Eliminate, Retain or Modify: A Strategy for Competitiveness in Government* (1995).

[7] GAO REPORT GAO/GGD-97-48, *Privatization: Lessons Learned by State and Local Governments* 1 (1997).

of providing local services,[8] it has not yet had a major impact on the public sector workforce.[9] The courts that have considered whether privatization violates state constitutional, statutory or local mandates for a civil service system have offered differing conclusions. Some, like California,[10] have identified problems, while others have not.[11] Even where obstacles have been identified, exceptions have been recognized for certain types of privatization.[12] For instance, California has found few problems when the privatized service involves a new function and there is no displacement of workers currently protected by civil service.[13]

Courts have also differed in their decisions regarding collective bargaining agreements that may or may not prevent privatization.[14] Because many questions have been raised, some states have enacted legislation that defines when it is permissible for an agency to engage in privatization. This has permitted them to address potentially troublesome issues. For example, it can be provided that there must be no loss of civil service employment as a result of privatization.[15]

One of the most challenging issues raised by privatization is the definition of the legal status of the private provider. When local government provides a service there are responsibilities and liabilities, including constitutional rights and remedies that protect people from unlawful government conduct. When the service is privatized, what happens to those rights and remedies? In other words, it must be determined whether a contractor, acting on behalf of a local government, is bound by the statutory, charter, and constitutional laws that govern local government action. These questions are beginning to be addressed. For instance, the Florida court

---

[8] For an excellent discussion of this topic, *see* Featherston, Thornton, and Correnti, *State and Local Privatization: An Evolving Process*, 30 PUBLIC CONTRACT LAW JOURNAL, No. 4, Summer 2001.

[9] *See* John D. Donahue, *Privatization and Public Employment: An Essay on the Current Status and the Stakes*, 128 FORDHAM URBAN L.J. 1693 (2001).

[10] Professional Engineers v. Dept. of Transportation, 936 P.2d 473 (Cal. 1997); Colorado Ass'n of Pub. Employees v. Dep't of Highways, 809 P.2d 988 (Colo. 1991); Horrell v. Dep't of Admin., 861 P.2d 1194 (Colo. 1993); Konno v. County of Hawaii, 937 P.2d 397 (Haw. 1997); University of Nevada v. State of Nevada Employees Ass'n., 520 P.2d 602 (Nev. 1974); Washington Federation of State Employees v. Dep't of Social and Health Services, 966 P.2d 322 (Wash. Ct. App. 1998).

[11] Moore v. Dep't of Transportation and Pub. Facilities, 875 P.2d 765 (Alaska 1994); Corwin v. Farrell, 100 N.E.2d 135 (N.Y. 1951); Haub v. Montgomery Co., 727 A.2d 369 (Md. 1999); State *ex rel.* Sigall v. Aetna Cleaning Contractors of Cleveland, Inc., 345 N.E.2d 61 (Ohio 1976), *aff'd*, 345 N.E.2d 61 (Ohio Ct. App. 1976); Vermont State Employees' Ass'n, Inc. v. Vermont Criminal Justice Training Council, 704 A.2d 769 (Vt. 1997).

[12] Kennedy v. Ross, 170 P.2d 904 (Cal. 1946); California State Employees Ass'n v. Williams, 86 Cal. Rptr. 305 (Cal. Ct. App. 1970).

[13] *California State Employees Ass'n, supra* note 12 at 310.

[14] Johanson v. Dep't of Social and Health Servs., 959 P.2d 1166 (Wash. Ct. App. 1998); City of Belvidere v. Illinois State Labor Relations Bd., 670 N.E.2d 337 (Ill. App. Ct. 1996), *aff'd*, 692 N.E.2d 295 (Ill. 1998).

[15] *See* Featherston, *supra* note 8, for a discussion of these statutes.

held that a lessee of a public hospital had to comply with Florida's Public Records Law.[16]

There is also a question of tort liability. Private providers may not be able to claim any tort immunity that was previously applicable to the local government. The Supreme Court, in an opinion carefully limited to its facts, held that a prison guard, employed by a private company that had contracted with government to provide the service, could not claim the qualified immunity that had applied to a publicly employed guard.[17]

PART II PROTECTION, ASSISTANCE AND SERVICES TO INDIVIDUALS

§ 6.6   Local Liability for Law Enforcement and Fire Protection

Most local governments provide services and perform regulatory activities for the protection of their residents. These typically include fire and police protection, and various inspection and licensing programs that include land use regulations and building codes.

The question of local liability for harm that results when local officers or employees either fail to act or are negligent in carrying out these activities is of great importance to local governments. For many years, local governments were immune from tort liability while acting within their governmental capacity, and liable for torts committed while acting in a proprietary capacity. Although all courts have had difficulty defining what actions fall in which category, when a local government provides police and fire protection services, or is implementing its inspection and licensing programs, it is usually deemed to be acting in its governmental capacity.[1] This characterization, however, may no longer determine whether there is tort liability. Many jurisdictions have waived their common-law tort immunity. It may still be an important distinction where the waiver of sovereign immunity provides that the local government is to be liable just as an individual is liable.[2] Since individuals do not normally have a duty to voluntarily assist anyone, imposing liability on a local government for failing to act may be found to be treating a local government differently than a private individual.

State courts and legislatures have increasingly imposed liability on local governments for torts committed in either a proprietary or governmental

---

[16] Memorial Hospital-West Volusia, Inc. v. News-Journal Corp., 729 So. 2d 373 (Fla. 1999).

[17] Richardson v. McKnight, 521 U.S. 399 (1997). *See also* Jensen v. Lane County, 222 F.3d 570 (9th Cir. 2000).

[1] For police immunity, *see* Poole v. City of Louisville, 130 S.E.2d 157 (Ga. Ct. App. 1963); Allen v. City of Ogden, 499 P.2d 527 (Kan. 1972); Wilford v. City of Jacksonville Beach, 79 So. 2d 516 (Fla. 1955); Parks v. Town of Princeton, 8 S.E.2d 217 (N.C. 1940). For fire protection immunity, *see* Reynolds Boat Co. v. City of Haverhill, 260 N.E.2d 176 (Mass. 1970); Motyka v. City of Amsterdam, 204 N.E.2d 635 (N.Y. 1965).

[2] N.Y. COURT OF CLAIMS ACT § 8 (McKinney's 1989).

activity. This expansion of local tort liability is prompted by the availability of insurance coverage for local government negligence,[3] combined with general disaffection for local government immunity. Many have chosen to enact statutes that impose tort liability for negligence that occurs during the performance of specific types of government functions. A common example is the negligent operation of a publicly owned vehicle while the operator is acting within the scope of his or her government employment. Other statutes impose liability on the local government for its negligence in the maintenance of public property or for negligence in the condition, design or defects in public streets and sidewalks. Some states take a broader approach by declaring that local governments are immune only if it is specifically provided for a particular activity.

In examining how these changes have affected tort liability for local services or regulatory activities, consideration must be given to the public duty rule. It is a broad exception to local tort liability that has been adopted by many jurisdictions. It provides that while local governments owe a duty to the entire community, they do not owe a duty to every individual in the community.[4] In other words, a failure to assist an individual does not result in negligence liability. When local governments have failed to maintain an adequate water supply or working fire hydrants, resulting in destruction by fire, most courts have refused to impose liability.[5] A local government will not be liable for failure to enforce subdivision regulations.[6] The practical reasons given to support the interpretation of limited local liability include concerns about the fiscal impact of imposing a heavy burden on the taxpayers and inappropriate interference by the judicial branch with the allocation of local resources.[7] It has also been held that local police, fire, or emergency medical assistance personnel are not required to respond and assist those in need outside the local government boundaries, even if they had the capacity to do so.[8]

There are significant exceptions to the public duty rule, generally based upon the existence of a special relationship between the local government and the individual who has suffered an injury. This special relationship involves the assumption of a duty by the service provider. It is created

---

[3] Some courts have held that when a local government obtains insurance it has impliedly waived its immunity. See Clark v. Scheld, 117 S.E.2d 838 (N.C. 1961); My Sister's Place v. City of Burlington, 433 A.2d 275 (Vt. 1981); Thomas v. Broadlands Community Consolidated School district, 109 N.E.2d 636 (Ill. Ct. App. 1952). Some statutes authorizing local governments to purchase insurance provide that at least to the extent of the coverage, such purchase constitutes a waiver. Two may be seen at MINN. STAT. § 466.06 (2001) and KAN. STAT. ANN. 74-4707 (2001). Other courts have held that the mere purchase of insurance does not waive immunity. See Barad v. Jefferson Co., 178 N.W.2d 376 (Iowa 1970).

[4] DeHoney v. Hernandez, 595 P.2d 159 (Ariz. 1979)

[5] Reynolds Boat Co. v. City of Haverhill, 260 N.E.2d 176 (Mass. 1970); Stang v. City of Mill Valley, 240 P.2d 980 (Cal. 1952).

[6] Stillwater Condominium Ass'n v. Town of Salem, 668 A.2d 38 (N.H. 1995).

[7] Riss v. City of New York, 240 N.E.2d 860 (N.Y. 1968).

[8] Canade, Inc. v. Town of Blue Grass, 195 N.W.2d 734 (Iowa 1972); Valevais v. City of New Bern, 178 S.E.2d 109 (N.C. Ct. App. 1970).

through promises or actions by local officers or employees with their knowledge that failure to act could lead to the individual's harm. It may require direct contact between the individual and the local government, followed by the individual's justifiable and detrimental reliance on the government's assurance of assistance.[9] A special relationship may also be created by the status of the individual. For instance, a government informer who has responded to a request for law enforcement assistance may be owed a duty of care if it is foreseeable that his or her safety is threatened.[10] Some states have rejected the public duty rule, finding it imposes too great a limitation on local liability.[11]

Although there is a great deal of inconsistency in the holdings of the various states, courts have generally responded more favorably to plaintiffs who allege that a local government has acted in a negligent manner, an act of commission as opposed to an omission to act. Courts have held that if the local government officer chooses to act, even in a governmental capacity, he or she must act reasonably.[12] Liability can be imposed if the police, fire, or medical emergency department acts in a negligent manner, just as it would if a private individual assumed a duty to act and was negligent. However, some jurisdictions have held that even in acts of commission, police and fire personnel are engaged in exercising discretion in choosing how they carry out their functions and thus the local government is immune from liability.[13] Other courts have based their holdings on the character of the act. If the act is governmental, then there is immunity unless the individual is left in worse condition than before the government action. However, if the police, fire, or emergency medical equipment is being used for a proprietary purpose, liability may be found. A fire engine that negligently harmed someone as it was driven back from a parade resulted in liability.[14]

Courts have held that local governments may be liable for negligence in selecting, training and supervising local personnel when their actions deprive individuals of their federal statutory or constitutional rights. Recovery may be granted under § 1983 of the Civil Rights Act. It must be shown that the local government's failure to act reasonably amounts to a deliberate indifference to the plaintiff's rights.[15]

---

[9] Grieshaber v. City of Albany, 720 N.Y.S.2d 214 (3d Dep't 2001), *appeal denied*, 759 N.E.2d 370 (N.Y. 2001).

[10] Schuster v. City of New York, 219 N.Y.S.2d 955 (N.Y. App. Div. 1961).

[11] Doucette v. Town of Bristol, 635 A.2d 1387 (N.H. 1993); Leake v. Cain 720 P.2d 152 (Colo. 1986).

[12] Bernadine v. City of New York, 62 N.E.2d 604 (N.Y. 1945); Ziegler v. City of Millbrook, 514 So. 2d 1275 (Ala. 1987).

[13] City of Daytona Beach v. Palmer, 469 So. 2d 121 (Fla. 1985).

[14] Radobersky v. Imperial Volunteer Fire Dep't, 81 A.2d 865 (Pa. 1951).

[15] City of Canton v. Harris, 489 U.S. 378 (1989). This remedy is discussed further in § 9.6 *infra*. Liability for the negligence of government employees is also discussed in § 9.2 *infra*.

§ 6.7 Public Assistance

Although there is no common law government obligation to do so, many state constitutions and statutes require government to provide assistance to its needy. This assistance is deemed to be for a public purpose and does not violate the typical constitutional prohibition against gifts or loans of public moneys to private individuals. Although all three levels of government are participants in the process of providing assistance, the local governments have traditionally assumed a major role. In this area, as in all others, unless state law provides otherwise, local governments are subject to state preemption and their programs cannot conflict with state requirements.

Since the federal government provides a significant percentage of the funds used in assistance programs, it has exercised a great deal of control by imposing conditions on the voluntary acceptance of the funds by the state and local governments. The federal welfare system was completely revised by the Personal Responsibility and Work Opportunity Reconciliation Act of 1996 (PRWORA).[1] With a focus on requiring recipients to seek employment, it imposes certain time limits, including a five-year lifetime limit on welfare benefits. It replaced the Aid to Families with Dependent Children with a block grant program called Temporary Assistance for Needy Families (TANF). It also gives the states a great deal of flexibility in further shortening time limits, exempting some of their cases from the federal limits, and the ability to use their federal funds to achieve the goal of moving recipients off welfare.

The new approach adopted by PRWORA has presented both challenges and opportunities for local governments. The statutory mandate that encourages increased employment by the needy has been implemented at the same time that job opportunities are declining in urban areas.[2] Industry and employment opportunities are moving to the suburbs where job growth is increasing. This has created a problem because the greater concentration of welfare recipients is in the urban areas where job growth is declining. Linkage between the people who must obtain employment and the location of the jobs presents a major transportation challenge. Mass transportation systems were not designed to transport people to jobs in the suburbs. Most have limited routes and hours of operation, and the cost of using the systems is too expensive for most welfare recipients. Some local governments have met the challenge by using some of the federal welfare funds for transportation subsidies, modification of routes, and adoption of new programs to meet the need for transportation from the inner cities to the suburbs.[3] Some cities have introduced van service to transport low-income

---

[1] Personal Responsibility and Work Opportunity Reconciliation Act of 1996, Pub. L. No. 104-193, 110 Stat. 2105 (codified as amended in scattered sections of 42 U.S.C.).

[2] George E. Peterson & Wayne Vroman, Urban Labor Markets and Economic Opportunity, Urban Labor Markets and Job Opportunity 1 (Peterson and Vroman eds. 1992).

[3] See Monica Oui Frazer, License to Drive: Getting Welfare Recipients from the City to the Jobs, 7 Georgetown Journal on Poverty Law and Policy 1 (Winter 2000).

individuals and welfare recipients to jobs in the suburbs. Federal grants to operate transportation services have been made available to private, not-for-profit organizations.

All government programs must be administered in a constitutionally valid manner that does not violate any personal liberties. Guarantees of equal protection, due process, and the right to privileges and immunities in the federal and individual state constitutions must be met. A state or local government is prohibited from providing assistance in a discriminatory manner unless a compelling governmental purpose is established. The equal protection clauses prevent invidious discrimination against particular individuals or classes of people.[4]

Similarly, the federal and state due process clauses prohibit government from arbitrarily or unreasonably denying benefits to someone after it establishes an assistance program.[5] Government may not terminate assistance without observing due process rights. The Supreme Court has held that notice and a fair hearing are required prior to such termination.[6] The Court said that this includes a timely and adequate notice of reasons for the termination, and an effective opportunity to defend by confronting adverse witnesses and presenting arguments and evidence in at least an administrative process. The decision must be made by someone who did not participate in the initial determination to terminate and it must be based on the evidence produced at the hearing.

Courts have relied upon both equal protection and the privileges and immunities clauses to invalidate residency requirements that have been imposed by various states. Local governments can require that applicants for assistance currently reside within the community.[7] However, in 1969 the Supreme Court held that a requirement that a person reside within the community for one year before receiving assistance violated both constitutional liberties.[8] Subsequently, the Court reiterated its holding, stating that a local government could not use residency requirements to inhibit the migration of needy people into its jurisdiction. It also declared unconstitutional a federal law that permitted states to limit the amount of the benefit a person receives to that which he or she would have received in the state from which they moved, if they have lived in the granting state less than a year.[9] Any classification that imposes a penalty on the right to travel is unconstitutional unless justified by a compelling governmental purpose. The right to travel is a privilege and immunity that includes the

[4] Califano v. Aznavorian, 439 U.S. 170 (1978); Dandridge v. Williams, 397 U.S. 471 (1970).

[5] Graham v. Richardson, 403 U.S. 365 (1971).

[6] Goldberg v. Kelly, 397 U.S. 254 (1970).

[7] McCarthy v. Philadelphia Civil Serv. Comm'n, 424 U.S. 645 (1976).

[8] Shapiro v. Thompson, 394 U.S. 618 (1969), *overruled in part sub nom.*, Edelman v. Jordan, 415 U.S. 651 (1974). *See also* Memorial Hosp. v. Maricopa County, 415 U.S. 250 (1974) (holding that it is unconstitutional to impose a one-year county residence requirement before receipt of public medical care assistance).

[9] Saenz v. Roe, 526 U.S. 489 (1999).

right to enter and leave, the right to be treated as a welcome visitor while in a state, and the right to be treated like other citizens. New residents have the right to be treated like other citizens, with the same privileges and immunities. Just as importantly, the Court held that a state's legitimate interest in saving money is not a compelling governmental purpose that justifies discriminating between people who have lived in a state for less than a year and those who have lived there longer.

Over the years, states have defined who is needy in varying contexts. It is common to have limitations on people receiving assistance if they own property or have income. In many states, an applicant must be willing to work, and some states require that close relatives support needy persons before public assistance is given. First and Fourth Amendment protections, along with their state constitutional counterparts, must be respected in government assistance programs. State and local governments cannot require that these rights be waived as a condition to receiving aid. The Supreme Court has sustained state requirements of home visits by social workers, holding that such visits do not violate the Fourth Amendment's prohibition of unreasonable searches.[10]

By imposing limitations on restrictions for those governments using federal funds in their assistance programs, the federal government exercises a great deal of control over qualifications for assistance. The Supreme Court has upheld this use of federal authority, holding that local governments must comply with federal restriction limits whenever federal funds are used even partially to finance the program.[11] They have prohibited governments from refusing public assistance to children when the parents do not provide a suitable home, unless the state provides for their removal and adequate care.[12]

Section 1983 of the Civil Rights Act[13] may provide a mechanism for challenging assistance programs. Since the basis for the use of this federal remedy is the violation of a federal right, a plaintiff is not required to first exhaust state or local administrative remedies.

§ 6.8   Housing

Affordable housing is a major concern of local governments because of their efforts to provide assistance to those who are unable to find adequate accommodations. In addition to state involvement, the federal government is a dominant partner with local governments in providing funds and regulatory oversight. The Federal Housing Act, as amended by the Quality Housing and Work Responsibility Act of 1998 (QHWRA),[1] provides federal

---

[10] Wyman v. James, 400 U.S. 309 (1971).

[11] King v. Smith, 392 U.S. 309 (1968).

[12] See Turnboo v. Santa Clara Co., 301 P.2d 992 (Cal. Ct. App. 1956).

[13] 42 U.S.C. § 1983 (1994).

[1] PUB. L. NO. 105-276, tit. V, 112 Stat. 2461, 2514-2670 (codified as amended in scattered sections of 42 U.S.C.) (1999).

assistance to Public Housing Agencies (PHA), which are defined as ". . .any state, county, municipality or other governmental entity or public body authorized to engage in or assist in the development or operation of low-income housing."[2]

The adoption of QHWRA signaled a significant change in housing policy by facilitating mixed-income communities and adopting a goal of decreasing concentrations of poverty in public housing. It eliminated a restriction that occupancy in public housing be limited to people with incomes at or below 30 percent of the locality's median income level. Instead, PHAs may establish income-mix criteria so that they are able to rent a limited number of apartments to tenants with incomes exceeding the federal poverty level.[3]

Some of the federal funds are to be used by the local PHA to build and maintain housing properties. By accepting the assistance, the PHA must agree to abide by federal regulations that focus upon the selection and assignment of tenants and the possible termination of a tenant's right to inhabit the facilities. The PHA is required to submit annual plans detailing housing needs of low-income families (including the elderly and disabled) and their plan for addressing those needs.[4] The plans must also include a broad range of information on PHA finances, means of addressing programmatic needs of tenants, tenant safety plans, and its operating procedures. As explained in the federal regulations, the plan is to provide a framework for local accountability. It is also designed to provide information for participants about the PHA's policies, rules and requirements for its operations, programs, and services.[5]

Public housing in this country has not been viewed as an overwhelming success. There has been a great deal of criticism directed toward the concept of PHA-owned housing developments. It has been argued that it is substantially more costly to build and maintain, and is often poorly maintained.[6]

Under Section 8 of the federal law, federal funds are also available to subsidize rent paid by needy individuals or families to private landlords. The funds are given to a qualifying PHA which then issues rent-subsidy certificates to qualified individuals. Tenants who qualify to participate in a Section 8 Program will pay a portion of their income to the private landlord. The PHA will make an additional "Assistance Payment" to the private landlord so that the total received by him or her meets market-level rents.[7]

The Section 8 program has also been criticized for not producing new housing and because of administrative inefficiencies. The PHA must

---

[2] 42 U.S.C. § 1437(b)–(d) (1994).

[3] 42 U.S.C. § 1437(n) (1994).

[4] 42 U.S.C. § 1437(c)(1) (2001).

[5] 24 C.F.R. § 903.1(b) (1999), 64 Fed. Reg. 8181 (Feb. 18, 1999).

[6] William H. Simon, *The Community Economic Development Movement*, Vol. 2002 WISC. L. REV. 377, 392 (2002), adapted from WILLIAM H. SIMON, THE COMMUNITY ECONOMIC DEVELOPMENT MOVEMENT (Duke Univ. Press 2001).

[7] 42 U.S.C. § 1437(f) (1994).

estimate the market value of apartments in a given area in order to calculate the rent subsidies. If it is overestimated, then taxpayer money is wasted. If it is underestimated, participants will have difficulty in finding rentable space. It does not appear to have been met with accolades of overwhelming success. However, there is hope for a new approach.

Variations from both the PHA-owned housing and the Section 8 certificate programs have been adopted. There is a growing belief that the concept of Community Economic Development (CED), discussed in § 6.11 *infra*, holds the most promise. It views the needs of a community from a broad perspective with a basic goal of developing suitable housing and employment for low-income individuals by using a mixture of public and private sector involvement. It differs from earlier governmental programs because it does not separate housing needs from other needs. The CED movement is also based on greater participation by those being assisted. One approach encourages greater participation in the management by creating tenant councils to help in the management of the public housing. The government has also promoted home ownership, including the sale of PHA housing to tenants. Yet another focus has been programs of services or financial assistance to encourage economic self-sufficiency with government grants for job training, day care and counseling services.

Responding to an increase in crime associated with or near public housing facilities, congressional attention has been focused on concern about safety in public housing developments. As a result, local governments have been given a great deal of discretionary authority to impose reasonable restrictions on access to public housing and to regulate tenant conduct. Local agencies which receive federal assistance are required to include a clause in their tenants' leases that provides for the possibility of termination under certain circumstances. The lease may be terminated if a tenant, any member of the tenant's household or any guest or other person under the tenant's control, engages in any criminal activity that threatens health and safety, or the right to peaceful enjoyment of the premises by other tenants. Occupancy may also be terminated if one or more of these same individuals engage in any drug-related criminal activity on or off the premises. Local housing agencies are permitted to consider alternative remedies other than termination.

The use of the authority to terminate has resulted in several legal challenges. One challenge asked whether there was, or had to be, an implied requirement that the tenant knew or should have known of the forbidden conduct. An additional question was whether it must be shown that the tenant actually had the ability to exercise some control over the actor. After differing responses from lower courts, the Supreme Court held that the plain language in the statute required the inclusion of lease terms that gave the PHAs the absolute right to terminate a lease when the offending activity exists, whether or not the tenant knew, or should have known of the unlawful conduct.[8] Further, the Court held that this did not violate any

---

[8] Dep't of HUD v. Rucker, 535 U.S. 125 (2002).

constitutional rights of the tenants. The local agency was acting as a landlord, not attempting to criminally punish or civilly regulate the tenant. It was a legitimate term of a lease that was agreed to by the tenant.[9]

The PHA must respect all requirements of the federal and state constitutions, statutes and regulations and cannot violate their tenants' First Amendment rights of free speech and association.[10] They must comply with statutory requirements that protect the disabled members of society.[11] At the same time, local governments owe their tenants the same protections that are owed by private landlords. This means that they must maintain their properties in reasonable repair and in accordance with the minimal standards established by state or local regulations and sanitary codes.[12]

Applicants for public housing assistance are protected from arbitrary discrimination in the approval and selection process by the Due Process and Equal Protection Clauses of the federal and state constitutions. Local governments must act reasonably when they seek to terminate an existing tenancy. The tenant must be given timely and adequate notice detailing the reasons for a proposed termination and an opportunity to respond by confronting and cross-examining adversarial witnesses. The tenant has a right to have the assistance of an attorney, appear before an impartial decision-maker and receive a reasoned decision based on the law.

There are other federal statutes which directly impact the regulation of local housing. Title VI of the Civil Rights Act of 1964 prohibits discrimination in federally-assisted programs.[13] Title VIII of the Civil Rights Act of 1968, which is known as the Fair Housing Act[14] and is discussed in § 9.7 *infra*, imposes other requirements, including the prohibition of retaliation against fair-housing advocates.[15] The statute prohibits discrimination in the sale or rental of housing on the basis of race, creed, color and against disabled individuals, except for the sale or rental of a single-family dwelling

---

[9] *See* Memphis Hous. Auth. v. Thompson, 38 S.W.3d 504 (Tenn. 2001) (limiting the exercise of its local agency's discretion by holding that an eviction of a tenant is appropriate based upon the drug-related criminal activity of a "guest or other person under the tenant's control," if the tenant knew or should have known of the illegal drug-related activity and failed to take reasonable steps to prevent or halt it).

[10] McKenna v. Peekskill Hous. Auth., 647 F.2d 332 (2d Cir. 1981) (holding that a PHA rule requiring tenants to register and obtain prior approval of overnight visitors impinged tenants' First Amendment rights of association and privacy); Vasquez v. Hous. Auth. of City of El Paso, 271 F.3d 198 (5th Cir. 2001) (providing that a PHA cannot ban door-to-door political campaigning by nonresident political volunteers because it is a violation of the tenants' First Amendment rights).

[11] Green v. Hous. Auth. of Clackamas Co., 994 F. Supp. 1253 (D.Or. 1998). *See also* Bronk v. Ineichen, 54 F.3d 425 (7th Cir. 1995).

[12] Perez v. Boston Hous. Auth., 400 N.E.2d 1231 (Mass. 1980); Johnson v. District of Columbia, 728 A.2d 70 (D.C. 1999).

[13] Hardy v. Leonard, 377 F. Supp. 831 (N.D. Cal. 1974); Green Street Ass'n v. Daley, 373 F.2d 1 (7th Cir. 1967); Taylor v. Cohen, 405 F.2d 277 (4th Cir. 1968).

[14] 42 U.S.C. §§ 3533, 3535, 3601-19, 3631 (1995).

[15] Walker v. City of Lakewood, 272 F.3d 1114 (9th Cir. 2001).

by an owner.[16] It also requires reasonable accommodations in rules, policies, practices, and services as needed to afford disabled persons an equal opportunity to use and enjoy housing.

Often local governments have been criticized for using their authority to zone to either exclude low-cost housing or concentrate it in one or more locations within the community. The Fair Housing Act does not permit the exclusion of all low-cost housing within a community. However, when challenged that a community's zoning was in effect excluding minority populations, the Supreme Court refused to infer a discriminatory intent from a refusal to re-zone.[17] It held that the mere presence of a discriminatory effect does not prove a discriminatory intent.

§ 6.9   Local Response to Changes and Disasters

Most local governments have been given home-rule or specific statutory authority to address the changing needs and expectations of their residents. The need to adopt new regulations or provide new services is a normal ongoing process for local governments. For instance, with an anticipated increase in the proportionate number of older persons, many local governments are planning and developing an array of housing, services, and activities that address the needs of senior citizens.

Examples of changes in local regulatory programs include an increase in emphasis on land use controls. As areas become subject to greater development pressures, there is an expectation that local government will respond with adequate protection in order to preserve a certain perceived quality of life. Local zoning is the most common motivation for the creation of new local governments, so it is to be expected that existing local governments will be particularly sensitive to the land-use concerns of their residents. They also want local government to address their concerns about such things as the regulation of facilities and businesses that cater to adult uses. Many of the concerns that are expressed by residents have required that local governments be adept at balancing the First Amendment rights of some citizens with competing demands by others who disagree about the appropriate use of land.

There are also changes in what is believed to be the appropriate role of local government. The distinction between governmental and proprietary actions has never been clearly defined because the role of government is expected to change and respond to new needs and demands. What once may have been considered proprietary may soon be considered one of the tasks that is clearly governmental. No longer do citizens merely expect to be provided with water, sewerage service, police and fire protection. Many local governments have met the increasing demand of their residents for sports and entertainment by building and operating stadiums and entertainment complexes. Often this is done by the creation of an independent public

---

[16] 42 U.S.C. § 3615 (1995).

[17] Village of Arlington Heights v. Metropolitan Hous. Dev. Corp., 429 U.S. 252 (1977).

benefit corporation or through contracts with private management companies. Public subsidies to attract or retain sport franchises, whether through capital improvements or otherwise, have become viewed as an expenditure of public funds for a public purpose.

The provision of sophisticated transportation systems, including rail, bus, and air facilities, is a service that has led to regional cooperation with several local governments establishing one entity to benefit the region. The interaction with the federal government and the requirements attached to federal funds have challenged local entities to creatively solve complex issues of intergovernmental cooperation.

State and local governments have attempted to obtain compensation for some of their public expenditures from members of the private sector who are responsible for governmental costs. With a greater awareness of harm caused by cigarette smoking, many state and local governments have successfully sought and received compensation from the tobacco industry for health and welfare costs they incurred in caring for their residents who have suffered harm.[1] This experience taught many local governments the value of sharing resources and working with other state and local governments in order to obtain a mutually-shared goal.

The development of new technology has created roles for local governments in siting and permitting the use of public right-of-ways. Cable and cellular technology has made local governments partners with the federal government in its commitment to the rapid dissemination of its benefits. Communication and media infrastructure to deliver services to people and homes has also provided a source of revenue to many local governments through the fees charged for use of their public right-of-ways.[2]

The development of the Internet has also produced opportunities for all levels of government to provide information and services to their residents. The E-Government Act of 2002[3] was adopted by Congress to encourage this process and many states are responding with their own versions.[4] Local governments are increasingly developing electronic sites to provide information to their constituents.

Inevitably, some local governments will face a major natural or human-induced disaster. All states have statutes that provide procedures to be followed in emergency situations, with many allowing the governor to declare that a particular situation qualifies as a disaster.[5] This declaration may qualify the local government for state resources and assistance. In some jurisdictions this authority has been delegated to the local chief

---

[1] *See* § 10.8 *infra.*

[2] For further discussion of telecommunications, *see* § 3.11 *supra.*

[3] 44 U.S.C. § 36.

[4] VA. CODE ANN. § 2.1–7.4 (Cum. Supp. 1999).

[5] For a complete list of the states and their statutes, *see* Howard D. Swanson, *The Delicate Art of Practicing Municipal Law Under Conditions of Hell and High Water*, 76 NORTH DAKOTA L. REV. 487 (2000).

executive. Local governments also often have provisions that must be followed, often prescribing emergency powers and how they are to be used. State statutes may delegate emergency powers to the local government and these may supplement basic home rule authority. Those local attorneys who have guided their communities through disasters offer very practical advice when they suggest that local government attorneys should review all applicable legislation, charter and local enactments in advance.[6] They also emphasize the need for participation by counsel in the disaster planning and response processes.[7]

The federal government may assist local governments suffering disasters by acting pursuant to the Robert T. Stafford Disaster Relief and Emergency Assistance Act (Stafford Act).[8] This federal statute authorizes the President of the United States to provide technical assistance to the states and to allocate funds to update state disaster-assistance plans. If a disaster has occurred, the governor of a state may request that the President declare a "major disaster" pursuant to the Stafford Act provisions.[9] The Federal Emergency Management Agency (FEMA) will then become involved in reviewing the request and recommending action to the President. If the President decides to declare a major disaster, there is potential for substantial federal assistance to support state and local efforts to respond to the disaster. In addition, the Stafford Act provides for mitigation assistance to the state to help prevent the recurrence of the same kind of damage in the future.

§ 6.10 Local Courts and Dispute Resolution

Local governments do not have inherent authority to create a judicial system. They are usually dependent upon direct state action for the creation of courts to deal with disputes or violations of laws or regulations. Where local courts are created by the state constitution, the legislature must respect its provisions. However, even in strong home-rule states, the administration of justice is usually considered a matter of state concern. States have obliged by creating local courts, specifying their jurisdiction and procedure. These courts are called by many different names, including justice courts, police courts, magistrates courts, recorder courts, and municipal courts. Their jurisdiction varies a great deal from state to state. Often a state constitution will impose limitations on their jurisdictional authority.

The field of criminal law is a matter of state concern and local governments have authority to act only if it is delegated to them by the state.

---

[6] See Roger A. Nowadzky, *Lawyering Your Municipality Through a Natural Disaster or Emergency*, INSTITUTE ON PLANNING, ZONING, AND EMINENT DOMAIN, PLANNING, ZONING & EMINENT DOMAIN, Chapter 5, 5-1 (1995).

[7] See Swanson *supra* note 5.

[8] 42 U.S.C. §§ 5121–5195 (1994).

[9] See David G. Tucker and Alfred O. Bragg, III, *Florida's Law of Storms: Emergency Management, Local Government, and the Police Power*, 30 STETSON L. REV. 837 (2001).

However, since the duty of maintaining the peace primarily resides at the local level, local governments are generally held to have implied authority to impose penalties for breaches of local enactments.[1]

Some local courts are limited to civil cases, and others include both civil and criminal authority. Typically, a local court's criminal jurisdiction will be limited to misdemeanors. Authority to hear tort and contract actions is most often limited to disputes involving less than a specified monetary amount. Most local courts have been given authority to review local legislative violations which may be criminal or civil. States differ in their grants of jurisdiction to local courts to hear allegation of criminal activity that has occurred extraterritorially, with some giving local courts jurisdiction over actions outside but close to the territory of a local government.

It is rare that a local court will have any equitable power, so it is seldom that one can enjoin or restrain activities through local court action. An exception is landlord and tenant questions. It is not unusual for a local court to have eviction authority for its use when it decides occupancy questions.

Qualifications for local judges and the method of choosing them, whether by election or appointment, varies from state to state. It is not always necessary for one to have a law degree but a frequent requirement is that he or she be a resident of the community. The right of trial by jury and the means of choosing jurors also varies. In many states, there is no jury trial if the issue is ordinance violation with no possibility of imprisonment. Procedural rules are often specified in state statutes. However, some states have local court codes that specify the pleading, practice and procedural forms for use in local courts. Some local governments are permitted to promulgate their court rules, provided they do not conflict with general state statutes.

Rights of appeal are typically provided by statute and vary from state to state. In many states, an appeal from a local court will result in a trial *de novo*, with the reviewing court sometimes having the authority to increase the penalty imposed by the local court. Fines imposed by local courts may go into the local coffers but some states require that particular types of fines be transferred to the state.

There are continuing local efforts to foster the resolution of disputes between individuals through the use of court-ordered or voluntary negotiation, mediation, or arbitration. These methods of handling disputes, which are an alternative to the traditional legal process, have been very successful. Many not-for-profit organizations have worked with local governments or state court agencies to foster their use because of cost savings and a commitment to the quality of the results. There is a general recognition that often they lead to a better long-term solution with less harmful residual effects. Many states have adopted statutes or regulations providing for the integration of their use as part of the legal process.

---

[1] Ulrich v. City of St. Louis, 20 S.W. 466 (Mo. 1892).

Some local governments are seeking to integrate alternative dispute resolution techniques into public disputes. Although used extensively for many years in labor disputes, the processes and techniques involved in negotiation, mediation and arbitration are extended to disagreements involving contracts, environmental concerns, setting standards, and issuing permits.[2]

PART III COMMUNITY AND ECONOMIC DEVELOPMENT

§ 6.11 Community Development

The community economic development (CED) movement is a new approach to revitalizing areas within a local government. It often replaces government programs that have not worked well in the past, and its multifaceted approach is rapidly growing in acceptance and use. The CED movement views the needs of a community in a broad manner with a basic goal of developing suitable housing and employment for low-income individuals by using a mixture of public and private resources. It differs from earlier governmental programs because it does not compartmentalize community needs into discrete categories. Instead, CED requires that concern for housing, jobs and business opportunities be considered in a single framework because they are connected. It emphasizes, and most often requires, participation by and accountability to those living in the community. Finally, it seeks to combine the resources of both government and private organizations as major participants in a concerted effort to improve neighborhoods and the lives of those living in them.[1]

CED is in many respects a refinement and improvement on earlier efforts to address urban decay and poverty. It builds upon and corrects certain flaws found in the earlier government programs established by federal housing legislation such as the National Housing Act of 1949.[2] This statute was enacted to provide assistance to local communities in their efforts to clean up blighted areas through "urban renewal." The process then in place involved the development of an improvement plan by a government agency and private developers, using public and private funds. Although by outward appearances this approach may have been successful, it did not

---

[2] *See* Tanya Peacock, *Using Alternative Dispute Resolution in Local Government*, COMMUNITY DEVELOPMENT REPORTS, RESEARCH BRIEFS & CASE STUDIES, CORNELL COMMUNITY AND RURAL DEVELOPMENT INSTITUTE, Vol. 1, No. 3 April 1993; Robert J. MacPherson, *In Your Face ADR: New York City's Construction Contract Dispute Procedure*, 25 PUBLIC CONTRACT L. JOURNAL 301 (1996); David T. Douthwaite, *Why Procure Construction by Negotiation?*, 25 PUBLIC CONTRACT L. JOURNAL 423 (1996).

[1] For an excellent and thorough discussion of CED, its successes and history, *see* William H. Simon, *The Community Economic Development Movement*, adapted from William H. Simon, *The Community Economic Development Movement* (Duke Univ. Press 2001), Vol. 2002, Number 2, WISCONSIN L. REV. 377 (2002).

[2] 42 U.S.C. §§ 1441-90 (1990).

help the needy who had resided within the targeted areas long before they were "renewed." Often urban renewal displaced original residents by destroying the only housing and commercial property that they could afford. They were replaced with residents who could afford what had become very desirable properties. So-called "gentrification" had a devastating effect on the original inhabitants who could no longer afford to live in their original communities.

Changes in federal and state laws have facilitated the growth of the CED movement. The federal funds for community redevelopment were redirected in 1974 when the Community Development Block Grant program (CDBG) was adopted to give local governments greater flexibility in deciding how to spend the funds.[3] Although the funds could still be used for redevelopment, the flexibility in the new program permitted local governments to address their greater recognition of the needs of displaced people and businesses. In addition, there have been other changes imposed by state legislation[4] and some through federal law.[5] Statutes have been adopted that require payment of relocation or displacement costs to tenants and businesses who can no longer live in the community.[6] Other statutes have required that if low-or moderate-income housing is destroyed, replacement housing must be provided for displaced persons.[7]

Accompanying these changes, there has been substantial growth in various resident or neighborhood-group participation in the process. They have registered demands that local government meet their needs for better public facilities, while minimizing land-use decisions that they view as unfavorable.[8] Local government initiatives funded by CDBG have encouraged this development of citizen participation. It has been implemented by requiring the development of a plan by those living within an area seeking assistance. The community-based organizations are to be named in the application for the grant. The requirement that the people affected be partners in the implementation of the development plan is a direct response to the criticisms of earlier government programs that failed to address the well-being of the people who lived in the community.[9]

There is also an added emphasis on social services for the affected area. This is fostered by the complementary Community Services Block Grant program which provides funds for local governments to work cooperatively with neighborhood organizations to address broad community needs.

---

[3] 42 U.S.C. § 5301 *et seq.*

[4] *See* CAL. HEALTH & SAFETY CODE § 33385 (1999).

[5] 24 C.F.R. § 42.350(b) (2000).

[6] *See* UNIFORM RELOCATION ASSISTANCE AND REAL PROPERTY ACQUISITION POLICIES ACT, 42 U.S.C. §§ 4601-55; CAL. GOV'T CODE § 7260 (West 1995).

[7] 42 U.S.C. § 1453. A requirement has also been adopted that destroyed housing must be replaced within a specified period of time. *See* 24 C.F.R. § 42.375.

[8] *See* Simon, *supra* note 1 at 388. A study indicated that CDBG encouraged community activism. *See* JEFFREY M. BERRY ET AL., THE REBIRTH OF URBAN DEMOCRACY (1993).

[9] 26 U.S.C. § 1391(f)(2)(B) (1994).

Other federal programs have also served to increase consideration of the needs of an impoverished area. The HOME Investment Partnerships Program provides federal funds to local governments for affordable housing.[10] Job creation has received support in state and federal programs that designate economic development zones. This designation of a geographically-defined area that is in economic distress provides a wide array of benefits. Developers and employers within its boundaries may be eligible for grants, low-cost financing through the use of tax-exempt bonds, and tax benefits for hiring residents living within the zone.[11]

§ 6.12   Economic Development

Although it is a relatively new function when compared to other governmental responsibilities, local governments are increasing their efforts to work with the private sector to provide economic prosperity for their communities. These public-private partnerships have led to many creative ways of improving the economic well-being of a community. It is increasingly common for local governments to prepare economic development plans that set out strategies and activities to help them achieve their goals. The public purpose of providing better neighborhoods, employment opportunities, and an increasingly strong tax base to support government services justifies the use of local powers to tax, borrow and spend.

A goal that is increasing in importance is the encouragement of community economic development in neighborhoods that need revitalization. The focus on downtown development is often comprised of public and private partnerships aimed at assisting low-income areas which have not often benefitted from traditional economic development efforts. Community development corporations (CDC) have been formed as part of the community economic development (CED) movement[1] to foster capital investment and job training in low-income areas. These have been funded primarily by non-profit organizations with other public and private support.

Obtaining the small amount of funds needed to begin a neighborhood business is often beyond the reach of people residing within these communities. Some local governments offer revolving loan funds to such individuals to assist in their efforts to establish a small neighborhood enterprise. Microenterprise programs that provide small amounts of capital and training to help low-income individuals start their own businesses are growing in the low-income inner cities and rural areas.[2] The attempts to bring economic growth to needy areas have also taken advantage of federal and state programs. Local governments have used the designation of

---

[10] 12 U.S.C. §§ 12741-12756.

[11] 42 U.S.C. § 9901 (Supp. 2000).

[1] Discussed in § 6.8 *supra*.

[2] Mildred Warner, *Local Government Support for Community-Based Economic Development*, THE MUNICIPAL YEAR BOOK (2001), International City/County Management Association, pages 21, 25 (2001).

economic development zones to direct tax breaks and subsidies to encourage development. Federal welfare reform, with its emphasis on employment,[3] has encouraged local governments to provide job training, day care, and transportation to assist the needy in their transition from welfare to work.[4]

Using the general police power that has been delegated to local governments through grants in their state constitutions, charters or by legislative enactments, much has been done to revitalize urban areas while assisting businesses in expanding or locating facilities that provide tax revenue, jobs and commercial growth. Although one goal of economic development is attracting new businesses to communities, it is now matched or exceeded by a goal of retaining existing businesses and assisting in their expansion and growth. Infrastructure improvements are often undertaken to make a location more attractive for private development. This can include a broad range of projects, from new or improved roads; development of fiber optic capabilities; and downtown streetscapes to construction of performing arts facilities.

Where authorized, local governments can levy special assessments for infrastructure improvements that result in a special benefit to business property. For instance, if additional parking is needed, a local government can designate an area as a special assessment district, build a parking facility, and pay for it with fees assessed against the surrounding business property.[5] The assessment will be sustained if the benefit is at least equal to the cost imposed.[6] Existing businesses have also been assisted by the creation of business improvement districts.[7]

An increasingly popular method for financing local improvements is tax increment financing (TIF). An area is improved by using revenue obtained through the sale of local tax exempt bonds. They are repaid by the additional tax revenue that is produced by the increase in the assessed value of the property after the improvements by private investment that is attracted to the area. In other words, the private development that occurs as a result of the public investment in infrastructure improvements will increase the value of the property. This increase in value is reflected in a higher assessed value. The taxes produced by the increase in value are dedicated to the repayment of the bonds. This method of financing local improvements has been sustained by the courts.[8]

Some local governments have sought to ease the regulatory process for businesses by adopting one-stop programs that make it easier to obtain

---

[3] *See* § 6.7 *supra.*

[4] Workforce Investment Act of 1998, PUB. L. No. 105-220, 112 Stat. 936 (codified in scattered sections of 29 U.S.C.)

[5] City of Whittier v. Dixon, 24 Cal.2d 664, 151 P.2d 5 (1944).

[6] Reams v. City of Grand Junction, 676 P.2d 1189 (Colo. 1984); Tocci v. City of Three Forks, 216 Mont. 159, 700 P.2d 171 (1985).

[7] *See* § 6.3 *supra.*

[8] Meierhenry v. City of Huron, 354 N.W.2d 171 (S.D. 1984); Tribe v. Salt Lake City Corp., 540 P.2d 499 (Utah 1975).

permits and other government approvals. Others have provided assistance to private developers by identifying and obtaining sites and buildings, or by the sponsorship of industrial parks and business incubator programs.

The forms of local government assistance that are criticized the most are the financial arrangements between the local government and a developer for substantial tax incentives, low-interest loans, commitments for improved infrastructure, low utility rates, government-sponsored job-training programs, and even cash.[9] Although it has been argued that they are ineffective when all costs and benefits are considered, state and local governments continue to use them. Some communities have found that the businesses attracted by these devices may not meet their promises of job creation or retention, and may leave the community after receiving the benefits.[10]

If economic incentives are used, there are suggested ways to protect the community.[11] There should be a valid contract that may be enforced in a cost-efficient manner. It has also been suggested that the contract include mechanisms which permit the local government to adjust the incentives, based upon the performance of the business in meeting its express goals of contributing positively to the growth of the community. Another possibility is to permit recapture of financial benefits if the business does not remain in the community.[12]

Marketing efforts by local governments include the traditional forms of conveying information through print and film. Increasingly, local governments have internet web sites that contain information about the community to both encourage and facilitate a business decision to locate in the area.

---

[9] Scott J. Ziance, *Making Economic Development Incentives More Efficient*, 30 THE URBAN LAWYER 1, page 33 (1998).

[10] City of Yonkers v. Otis Elevator Co., 844 F.2d 42 (2d Cir. 1988); Charter Twp. of Ypsilanti v. General Motors Corp., No. 92-43075-CK slip op. at 6 (Washtenaw Co. Cir. Ct. Feb. 9, 1993). *See also* Halle Fine Terrion, *Charter Township of Ypsilanti v. General Motors: The Politics of Promissory Estoppel Run Amok*, 43 CASE W. RES. L. REV. 1475 (1993).

[11] *See* Ziance, *supra* n. 9.

[12] *Id.*

Chapter 7

Public Access to Information and Right to Vote

§ 7.1 Introduction and Chapter Overview

Access to government information and government meetings has been thought to be a citizen's First Amendment right. However, the Supreme Court has not accepted that argument, and has held that there is no general public right to access government information or sources of information within the government's control.[1] Access to information is to be decided by the legislative branch of government, not the judiciary.

The Federal Constitution does protect the right of individuals to receive information and ideas.[2] The Supreme Court has held that a major purpose of the First Amendment is to protect the free discussion of governmental affairs.[3]

The right of the Press to disseminate information that is available is protected by the First Amendment; but, this does not imply any right to the information in the first place.[4]

The legislative branches of the federal and state governments have responded to the question of access to government records and meetings by adopting statutes or constitutional provisions that give citizens very broad rights. A citizen's right to obtain public records possessed by local governments is well established by these various acts of legislation. They reflect the premise that governments exist to serve people's needs and information that it obtains or produces belongs to those for whom it was collected or developed. People also have a right to know how their government is functioning and the information on which its decisions are made. Most cases today do not concern the question of access in general, but rather they involve interpretations of the legislation that affords access.

The implementation of this fundamental concept has not been without its bumps. There are some kinds of information that local governments have that should not be made public. It is understood that there is public information that, if known, may harm either specific individuals or the

---

[1] Houchins v. KQED, Inc., 438 U.S. 1 (1978).

[2] Stanley v. Georgia, 394 U.S. 557 (1969).

[3] Globe Newspaper Co. v. Superior Ct., 457 U.S. 596 (1982).

[4] *Houchins*, 438 U.S. 1 (1978), *citing* Grosjean v. American Press Co., 297 U.S. 233 (1936); Mills v. Alabama, 384 U.S. 214 (1966). The Court was concerned with the freedom of the media to communicate information once it is obtained; however, this does not intimate that government is compelled to provide the information or access to it. *Id.*

149

collective well-being of all the residents of a community. The state statutes or constitutional provisions that have been adopted to insure access to public information attempt to balance these competing concerns.

Local governments have no inherent authority to hold elections but have been delegated this responsibility through statutes, state constitutions, or local charters. The Equal Protection Clause, the Fifteenth Amendment and the Federal Voting Rights Act all insure that qualified voters will have equal access to vote and that each vote cast is equal to all others.

PART I ACCESS TO INFORMATION

§ 7.2   Freedom of Information

All states provide for public access to government information. These statutes are referred to as freedom of information laws (FOIL), or open records statutes. Many are patterned on the Federal Freedom of Information Act[1] which grants public access to federal records. One of the most important parts of these statutes is the definition section. It defines what is to be considered a public record and therefore available, and what is exempt or unavailable.

At common law, access to public records was usually restricted to persons who could show some personal interest or need for the information it contained. There was no commonly held belief that a member of the general public had a right to inspect public records.[2] However, over a period of time the courts did gradually expand the scope of interest that would justify access to public information. Today, many of the state statutes have shifted the focus toward a presumption that all public information is available and only that which is specifically excluded by statute will be inaccessible.[3]

Most state statutes provide a process whereby records may be requested and a procedure whereby a government agency must respond. Many have also established steps for administrative and judicial appeal of denials. The right of access generally includes the right to copy and the statute may prescribe the monetary amount that may be charged for providing this service.

State statutes have sought to balance the public's right to access government information with its equally strong concern that some information should not be available. If the government has records that contain information which is of a personal nature and could harm an individual, it is probably exempt from disclosure requirements under most statutes. Likewise, if release of the information would harm the public because it would compromise contemplated government action, it too is probably

---

[1] THE FREEDOM OF INFORMATION ACT, 5 U.S.C. § 552 (1976).

[2] CHARLES N. DAVIS & SIGMAN L. SPLICHAL, ACCESS DENIED, FREEDOM OF INFORMATION IN THE INFORMATION AGE, Iowa State Univ. Press, *The Right to Know* (2000) at 10.

[3] *See* NY PUB. OFF., Art. VI §§ 84-90 (1978); IND. CODE, § 5-14-3-1 (1977).

unavailable. The exemptions that have been written into the state laws are sometimes broad, exempting a whole category of government records, such as those relating to the legislative or judicial process. At other times they may be quite specific, recognizing many confidential materials which are exempted from public disclosure.[4]

Many interesting issues have arisen under these statutes. Since FOIL typically applies to existing records, government agencies will generally not be required to create a record. The format of a record has been questioned since individuals now seek computer disks or taped records. In *Brownstone Pub. Inc. v. New York City Department of Buildings*,[5] an appellate court required a state agency to provide an individual with the information in the requested electronic format. The government had it in that format and the person was willing to pay for its reproduction. Congress adopted the Electronic Freedom of Information Act[6] in 1996, encouraging federal agencies to provide records in the form or format requested if it can be readily reproduced in that format.

The question of public access to e-mail has become particularly relevant. Although in many respects it is akin to telephonic conversations, in actuality it creates a written record. Its availability may depend upon a state statute's protection or exemption of internal agency communications.[7]

Some restrictions on the release of information have been challenged on First Amendment grounds. In one case, the Supreme Court upheld a state restriction limiting public access to the addresses of people who had been arrested, to those who had a scholarly, journalistic, political, or governmental purpose or who were licensed private investigators involved in a relevant investigation.[8] When a publishing company was denied access to this information, it claimed its First Amendment right was violated. The Court, consistent with its earlier holdings, held that access to information is *not* an implied right under the First and Fourteenth Amendments. The restriction was not facially invalid under the First Amendment, nor did it prohibit a speaker from conveying information. It was nothing more than a government denial of access to information in its possession.[9] The Supreme Court distinguishes between a limited right of access to government information

---

[4] Florida Soc. of Newspaper Editors, Inc. v. Fla. Pub. Serv. Comm'n, 543 So.2d 1262 (Fla. Dis. Ct. App. 1989). There are numerous exceptions in Florida Statutes, including records of active criminal investigations, personal telephone and addresses of police and firemen, sealed bids for public works, pending civil rights complaints, welfare and patient records, child abuse reports prior to resolution, and governmental attorney work products.

[5] Brownstone Publishers, Inc. v. New York City Dep't of Bldgs., 560 N.Y.2d 642 (N.Y. A.D. 1990).

[6] PUB. L. No. 104-231 (codified as amended at 5 U.S.C. § 552 (1996)).

[7] *See* Robert J. Freeman, *The Impact of Technology on the Freedom of Information Law, a/k/a the "FOIL,"* 2 NYSBA GOVERNMENT, LAW AND POLICY JOURNAL, Spring 2000, Vol. 2, No. 1 (2000).

[8] Houchins v. KQED, Inc., 438 U.S. 1 (1978).

[9] L.A. Police Dep't v. United Reporting Publ'g Corp., 528 U.S. 32 (1999).

and the clearly protected First Amendment right of the citizen to disseminate information that is obtainable. First Amendment considerations are
discussed further in § 7.3 *infra*.

In an effort to encourage the elimination and correction of certain
highway hazards, the federal government adopted the Hazard Elimination
Program.[10] The legislation provides that information collected for federal
highway safety programs may not be discovered or admitted in certain
federal or state judicial proceedings. The Supreme Court has held that
litigants may obtain reports or records that have been collected in the
normal course of their regular record-keeping activities but Congress
validly exercised its Commerce Clause authority to prevent accessibility to
information compiled or collected by a local government specifically for its
participation in the federal programs.[11]

§ 7.3 Open Meetings

Although the Supreme Court has indicated that the public and the Press
have no absolute First Amendment right to gain *access* to government
information, it has held that the First Amendment requires that certain
types of government proceedings be open to the public. In particular, the
public has a right of access to criminal trials.[1] The Court has explained
that a major purpose of the First Amendment is to protect the free
discussion of governmental affairs,[2] but it has not yet determined the
extent of access beyond criminal proceedings.

The Court has established a test to be used in determining whether the
public has a constitutional right of access to a particular governmental
proceeding. It involves a consideration of two factors: first, whether the
place and process has historically been open to the press and public;[3] and
second, whether public access plays a significant and positive role in the
functioning of the particular process under review. The process that has
been considered most frequently by the courts involves access to court proceedings.[4] In applying the two-prong test established by the Supreme
Court, the courts have held that relevant issues to be considered include
whether access will promote informed discussion of governmental affairs;
whether access will promote a public perception of fairness; whether access
will provide a significant community therapeutic value; whether access will

---

[10] 23 U.S.C. § 152.

[11] Pierce Co. v. Guillen, 123 S.Ct. 720 (2003).

[1] Richmond Newspapers, Inc. v. Virginia, 448 U.S. 555 (1980).

[2] Globe Newspaper Co. v. Superior Court, 457 U.S. 596 (1982).

[3] Press-Enterprise Co. v. Superior Court, 478 U.S. 1 (1986); Capital Cities Media, Inc. v.
Chester, 797 F.2d 1164 (3d Cir. 1986); Whiteland Woods, L.P. v. Township of West Whiteland,
193 F.3d 177 (3d Cir. 1999).

[4] Publicker Industries, Inc. v. Cohen, 733 F.2d 1059 (3d Cir. 1984) (providing that access
is granted to civil trial).

serve as a check on corrupt practices; whether access will enhance the performance of all involved; and whether it will discourage perjury.[5]

In considering whether the Press had a First Amendment right to review a transcript of a preliminary hearing in a criminal prosecution, the Supreme Court held that while open criminal proceedings give assurances of fairness to both the public and the accused, in limited situations the right to a fair trial might be undermined by publicity. The trial court must determine whether the rights of the accused override the qualified First Amendment right of access.[6]

Beyond the question of access, the Supreme Court has recognized a constitutional right to *disseminate or receive* information that is available. It has held that the Constitution protects the right to receive information and ideas,[7] and a major purpose of the First Amendment is to protect the free discussion of governmental affairs.[8] In other words, there may be a protected right of the Press to disseminate information that is available, but not to obtain it. In *Houchins v. KQED, Inc.*,[9] the Supreme Court upheld a state statute that imposed a *restriction on access* to information. Distinguishing this from a *restriction on distribution*, the Court held that the state could selectively determine who could have access to information where there was no duty to disclose.[10]

The states have addressed the question of access to government proceedings by adopting open-meetings laws, sometimes referred to as "Sunshine Laws." Although they vary in scope and application, most require that local government meetings, where public business is transacted, be open to the public. So-called "executive sessions" must be open in many jurisdictions, with possible exceptions for matters that would invade an individual's privacy, such as in personnel discussions; matters that involve certain kinds of negotiations; and discussions in preparation for litigation. It is commonly accepted that local government action must be taken, or legislation adopted, in meetings open to the public. Prior notice must have been given and the action taken must be recorded in public records. Most cases today involve interpretations of the legislation.

---

[5] U.S. v. Simone, 14 F.3d 833 (3d Cir. 1994); Whiteland Woods, L.P. v. Township of West Whiteland, 193 F.3d 177 (3d Cir. 1999).

[6] *Press-Enterprise Co., supra* note 3 at 9. *See also* Whiteland Woods, L.P. v. Township of West, 193 F.3d 177 (3d Cir. 1999) *citing Press-Enterprise.*

[7] Stanley v. Georgia, 394 U.S. 557 (1969).

[8] Globe Newspaper Co. v. Superior Ct., 457 U.S. 596 (1982).

[9] Houchins v. KQED, Inc., 438 U.S.1 (1978), *citing* Grosjean v. American Press Co., 297 U.S. 233 (1936) and Mills v. Alabama, 384 U.S. 214 (1966). The Court was concerned with the freedom of the media to communicate information once it is obtained. However, this does not intimate that government is compelled to provide the information or access to it.

[10] For further discussion, *see* Daniel J. Solove, *Modern Studies in Privacy Law: Notice, Autonomy and Enforcement of Data Privacy Legislation: Access and Aggregation: Public Records, Privacy and the Constitution*, 86 MINN. L. REV. 1137 (2002).

§ 7.4 Protection of Privacy

State and local governments collect a great deal of information about individuals through the exercise of their powers. Local governments are authorized by statutes and charters to conduct investigations to collect information that is needed to make informed decisions about the exercise of local authority. Sometimes they also possess delegated authority to issue subpoenas to compel the production of witnesses and records. In exercising their investigatory authority, local governments must act reasonably. The Fourteenth Amendment protects those being investigated from local government requests for information that are unreasonably broad or vague. The extent to which the Fourteenth Amendment provides protection against a local government's unjustified disclosure of private information it has collected is unclear.[1]

As access to information has increased, there is also a growing concern about personal privacy. States vary in the degree of individual protection that is afforded through state constitutions and statutes. Although every state has some data protection, none are alike. As noted by one author, this is largely unchartered territory.[2] Some statutes do provide general and specific protection against the disclosure of information by local governments.

The Federal Government has exercised its constitutional authority to protect privacy. In 1974 it adopted the Privacy Act[3] which gives people the right to obtain information that has been collected about them from federal agencies. They have the right to correct it if it is wrong. The statute also limits the federal agency's right to collect, use, or disclose such information, without the written consent of the individual. Government liability for unlawful disclosure may be limited to actual damages.[4]

Congress has adopted very specific and limited legislation regulating the use of personal information by state and local governments. The federal Privacy Act provides that federal, state and local governments are prohibited from denying rights, benefits or privileges to anyone because of a refusal to disclose his or her social security number.[5] In 1994, Congress adopted the Driver's Privacy Protection Act which prohibits states from disclosing or otherwise making available information about individuals

---

[1] *See* Whalen v. Roe, 429 U.S. 589 (1977). "We therefore need not, and do not, decide any question which might be presented by the unwarranted disclosure of accumulated private data whether intentional or unintentional. . . ." *But see* Cooksey v. Boyer, 289 F.3d 513 (8th Cir. 2002). To establish a violation of a constitutional right to privacy by disclosure of personal information, it must be shown that the information revealed is a "shocking degradation or an egregious humiliation, or a flagrant breach of a pledge of confidentiality" that led to acquisition of the information.

[2] Paul M. Schwartz, *Privacy and Participation: Personal Information and Public Sector Regulation in the United States*, 80 IOWA L. REV. 553, 604 (1995).

[3] 5 U.S.C. § 552(a)(b) (2000).

[4] *See* Doe v. Chao, 306 F.3d 170 (4th Cir. 2002).

[5] 5 U.S.C. § 552(a) (2000).

obtained in connection with motor vehicle records.[6] The Supreme Court upheld the statute, finding it to be a proper exercise of Congress' Commerce Clause authority and holding that it does not violate Tenth Amendment principles of federalism.[7] The statute was subsequently amended in 1999 to prohibit states from assuming drivers were permitting the release of their information if they did not check a designated box on the renewal form. States may only do this by an "opt-in" action, or in other words, by requiring that a box be checked.

PART II LOCAL ELECTIONS AND CITIZEN RIGHT TO VOTE AND GOVERN

§ 7.5   Local Elections and Voter Eligibility

The Supreme Court has held that the Fifteenth Amendment and the Equal Protection Clause protect the rights of all qualified citizens to vote in state, federal and local elections.[1] No government can arbitrarily, unreasonably or invidiously deny a person's federal constitutional right to vote or be considered for public service.[2] As stated by the Court:

> The right to vote freely for the candidate of one's choice is of the essence of a democratic society, and any restrictions on that right strike at the heart of representative government.[3]

The qualification of people to vote in local elections is generally prescribed by state constitution or statute. The Equal Protection Clause prohibits the exercise of power in an arbitrary, unreasonable or invidiously discriminatory manner. This will not prevent state legislative action that treats individuals differently if it is shown that there is a reasonable basis for the classification or disparate treatment. On the other hand, if the classification is not reasonable because it discriminates improperly, it will not be permitted. Local governments cannot give the right to vote to some and deny it to others, unless it has a justifiable reason to create different classes of people for voting purposes. For instance, the Supreme Court found that a Hawaiian voting qualification based on ancestry violated equal protection because it was not adequately justified by the state's argument that it was needed in order to administer some proceeds held in trust for the sole benefit of native Hawaiians.[4]

Generally no government can restrict the right to vote to those who own property. A requirement that a person own property in the school district or have children in the district school in order to vote in school elections

---

[6] 18 U.S.C. § 2721(a) (2000).

[7] Reno v. Condon, 528 U.S. 141.

[1] *Ex parte Yarbrough*, 110 U.S. 651 (1884); Avery v. Midland County, 390 U.S. 474 (1968).

[2] Turner v. Fouche, 396 U.S. 346 (1970).

[3] Reynolds v. Sims, 377 U.S. 533 (1964).

[4] Rice v. Cayetano, 527 U.S. 1061 (1999).

was declared unconstitutional by the Supreme Court.[5] However, property ownership qualifications have at times been sustained for some special kinds of elections.[6] The Supreme Court has permitted governments to restrict the right to vote in a special district election to a defined group of property owners where the activities of the district are limited in nature and there is a disproportionately greater impact on a particular group. For instance, the Court upheld a voting plan that limited the right to vote for directors of a water district to property owners and permitted the district to weight the votes according to the value of the property.[7] In other words, the plan did not violate the Equal Protection Clause because the election was for a *special limited purpose*, not for the election of officials who would exercise general governmental authority, and the outcome of the water district election had a *disproportionately greater impact* on landowners as a group because the district costs are imposed directly on the landowners.

The New York Court similarly held that it was permissible for the state legislature to limit the right to vote to those living in Staten Island in an advisory referendum on the question of whether the borough of Staten Island wanted to secede from New York City. The Court held that there was a rational basis for the exclusion of other city residents from voting because even though the impact would affect all residents of the city, those permitted to vote would be primarily affected by the decision.[8]

However, any classification based on race, or shown to have been motivated by a racial purpose or unexplainable on other grounds, is constitutionally suspect and subject to strict scrutiny by the courts.[9] The Fifteenth Amendment prohibits any government from denying or abridging a citizen's right to vote on account of race, color, or previous condition of servitude.[10]

States vary a great deal in their regulation of the election process. Local governments do not have any inherent authority to hold elections. This authority is delegated, either expressly or impliedly, through state constitutions, statutes or charters. Local governments are usually authorized to provide for the registration of voters. In most states, a qualified voter who fails to register may be denied the right to vote. Likewise, the Supreme Court has recognized that the state has a legitimate interest in supervising ballots. Reasonable filing fees and nominating petition requirements that reflect a degree of support have been sustained when they did not deny a poor person the opportunity to be elected. Other proposed restrictions that

---

[5] Kramer v. Union Free Sch. Dist. No. 15, 395 U.S. 621 (1973).

[6] *See* § 7.6 *infra.*

[7] Salyer Land Co. v. Tulare Lake Basin Water Storage Dist., 410 U.S. 719 (1973). *See also* Ball v. James, 451 U.S. 355 (1981). Voting in election for directors could be limited to property owners and weighted according to the amount of acreage owned because the district's purpose is sufficiently specialized and narrow, and its actions disproportionately impact landowners.

[8] City of New York v. State, 562 N.E.2d 118 (N.Y. 1990).

[9] Miller v. Johnson, 515 U.S. 900 (1995); Shaw v. Reno, 509 U.S. 630 (1993).

[10] U.S. CONST., Amend. XV., Sect. 1: The right of citizens of the United States to vote shall not be denied or abridged by the United States or by any State on account of race, color, or previous condition of servitude.

have no rational relationship to a legitimate governmental interest have been held void.

Residency requirements are permissible if reasonable. State and local governments cannot impose a tax on the right to vote since the Supreme Court has determined that this would be an unconstitutional violation of the Equal Protection Clause.[11] The Court has also upheld a federal ban on the use of literacy tests in all government elections.[12] However, convicted felons and people adjudged insane may be denied the right to vote.[13]

The eligibility to vote in annexations, consolidations or mergers varies from state to state.[14]

§ 7.6 Local Elections and Reapportionment

The Supreme Court has held that the Fifteenth Amendment and the Equal Protection Clause protect the rights of all qualified citizens to vote in state, federal and local elections[1] and to have their votes counted.[2] A person's right to vote most often concerns actual access to the polls.[3] The right to have a vote counted focuses upon the drawing of election districts or the weight given to votes.

The Fifteenth Amendment provides that neither the United States nor any state may deny or abridge a citizen's right to vote on account of race, color, or previous condition of servitude.[4] This explicit protection is deemed superior to the basic principle that states may organize and create their systems of local governments in any manner they choose. When faced with the issue, the Supreme Court refused to recognize state authority to reshape a local government boundary when the result would be to deny minority citizens their right to vote in local elections by excluding their properties from the city.[5] The Court acknowledged that usually a state's exercise of its plenary power over local governments is insulated from federal judicial review. However, that insulation does not exist when the state power is used as a means of circumventing a federally protected right.

The Equal Protection Clause requires that votes that are cast be counted equally. In *Baker v. Carr*,[6] the Supreme Court held that this prohibits the

---

[11] Harper v. Va. State Bd. of Elections, 383 U.S. 663 (1966) (holding that the Twenty-Fourth Amendment bans such taxes in federal elections).

[12] Oregon v. Mitchell, 400 U.S. 112 (1970).

[13] Richardson v. Ramirez, 418 U.S. 24 (1974).

[14] For an excellent analysis and survey of cases, *see* DANIEL R. MANDELKER, DAWN CLARK NETSCH, PETER W. SALSICH, JR. & JUDITH WELCH WEGNER, STATE AND LOCAL GOVERNMENT IN A FEDERAL SYSTEM 793–796 (5th ed. 2002).

[1] *Ex parte Yarbrough*, 110 U.S. 651 (1884); Avery v. Midland County, 390 U.S. 474 (1968).

[2] U.S. v. Mosley, 238 U.S. 383 (1915); Reynolds v. Sims, 377 U.S. 533 (1964).

[3] *See* § 7.5 *supra*.

[4] U.S. CONST., Amend. XV., Sect. 1 (stating that the right of citizens of the United States to vote shall not be denied or abridged by the United States or by any State on account of race, color, or previous condition of servitude).

[5] Gomillion v. Lightfoot, 364 U.S. 339 (1960).

[6] 369 U.S. 186 (1962), *on remand*, 206 F. Supp. 341 (M.D. Tenn. 1962).

dilution of a citizen's vote by a state's wrongful apportionment of seats in its legislature. Two years later in *Reynolds v. Sims*,[7] the Court added further clarity when it established that apportionment was to be on a population basis with the constitutional standard of one person, one vote determining equality. Four years later in *Avery v. Midland County*,[8] the Court held that this is applicable to local entities as well. Since these cases were decided, the term reapportionment is most often used to refer to the issue of the weight given each person's vote.

Population is the starting point for considering whether there is a reapportionment problem. Electoral apportionment must be based on population equality in order to give voters equal representation in government. The Court has held that the Constitution does not permit any substantial variation from equal protection in drawing voting districts for local governments that have general governmental powers over the entire geographic area. At the same time, mathematical precision is not a constitutional requirement and the Supreme Court has shown flexibility in its review of apportionment plans, provided there is no built-in bias favoring particular political interests or geographic areas.[9]

The Supreme Court has noted that local governments may need considerable flexibility to meet changing societal needs, and an intent to preserve the integrity of political subdivisions may justify a reapportionment plan which departs from numerical equality. In reviewing local plans, the Court has also indicated a willingness to consider factors that are unique to each situation, such as historical policies and differences in impact on different groups of people, as reasons to uphold variations in the weighting of votes. For instance, it upheld a state's requirement of a double referendum, whereby a majority of rural voters in a county could veto the adoption of a county charter, even though a majority of the total voters in the county favored its adoption.[10] This was held to not violate the Equal Protection Clause.

Gerrymandering is the term that describes the act of drawing lines of voting districts in an irregular manner to give an advantage or disadvantage to particular groups of electors. When this is done in order to minimize the vote of minority citizens it is unconstitutional.[11]

§ 7.7   Equality and the Voting Rights Act

The Fifteenth Amendment provides that no government may deny or abridge a citizen's right to vote on account of race, color, or previous

---

[7] 377 U.S. 533 (1964), *reh. denied*, 379 U.S. 870 (1964).

[8] 390 U.S. 474 (1968).

[9] Abate v. Mundt, 403 U.S. 182 (1971).

[10] Town of Lockport v. Citizens for Cmty. Action at Local Level, Inc., 430 U.S. 259 (1977).

[11] Shaw v. Reno, 509 U.S. 630 (1993) (holding that deliberate segregation of voters into districts on the basis of race without compelling justification violates the Equal Protection Clause).

condition of servitude.[1] Congress enacted the Federal Voting Rights Act of 1965[2] (Act) as part of its responsibility to enforce the requirements of this constitutional mandate. Sections 2 and 5 of the Act are particularly important to local governments.

Section 2 of the Voting Rights Act contains a broad grant of standing for individuals, or for the federal Justice Department, to challenge any state or local government's voting practice that is based on race, color, or language minority status, if the practice results in a denial or abridgment of a right to vote. Section 2 is focused on the *results* of the challenged action. It is not necessary to show that the state or local government has a discriminatory intent. Most of the cases that have been brought under this Section are concerned with redistricting plans. Drawing the boundaries of a voting district to minimize the votes of minority voters, or gerrymandering, violates the Act.[3]

The courts are reluctant to find that a state or local government has authority in Section 2 of the Act to disregard the traditional concerns of government for compactness, population equality and political boundaries in order to meet a compelling state interest of increasing minority representation. Instead, the Supreme Court permits the government to consider race *as a relevant factor*, along with the traditional concerns, in drawing boundaries. The Court finds that even if the government is seeking to increase minority representation, equal protection problems arise when race is the predominant motive that prompts a government to draw its boundaries in a particular manner.[4] If it is shown that race is the predominant factor, the proposed boundaries will be subjected to strict scrutiny.[5] In further support of its position, the Supreme Court has held that a state's policy of adhering to traditional concerns will not support an inference of discrimination that can be used by the Justice Department as a basis for an objection to a proposed change in apportionment under Section 5 of the Act.[6]

The Supreme Court has established a framework for determining whether government action has resulted in an unlawful dilution of minority voting strength under Section 2.[7] It will consider whether the minority group is sufficiently large and geographically compact to constitute a majority in a single-member district, whether it is politically cohesive, and whether the white majority votes sufficiently as a bloc to enable it usually to defeat the minority's preferred candidate. If these factors exist, then a

---

[1] *See* Perkins v. Matthews, 400 U.S. 379 (1971).

[2] 42 U.S.C. § 1973 *et seq.*

[3] Ketchum v. Byrne, 740 F.2d 1398 (7th Cir. 1984), *cert. denied*, 471 U.S. 1135 (1985).

[4] Miller v. Johnson, 515 U.S. 900 (1995).

[5] Shaw v. Hunt, 517 U.S. 899 (1996), *citing* Wygant v. Jackson Bd. of Educ., 476 U.S. 267 (1986).

[6] *Id.*

[7] Thornburg v. Gingles, 478 U.S. 30 (1986).

"totality of the circumstances" test is applied to determine whether minorities have less opportunity to participate in the political process. Section 2 has also been used to challenge at-large election systems and multi-member districts on the grounds that they dilute minority voting strength.[8] Again, a results test will be used to determine if there is a discriminatory effect. They will be found to be unconstitutional when they are being used invidiously to minimize or cancel out the voting strength of racial groups.[9]

Section 5 of the Voting Rights Act is applicable to certain areas of the country that have a history of voting discrimination. Local governments subject to Section 5 must apply for and obtain federal preclearance before changing any voting qualification or prerequisite to voting, or standard, practice, or procedure.[10] The object of the requirement is to ensure that a proposed change will not have a discriminatory purpose or effect.[11] The local government must file an application for a change with the Attorney General of the United States or the District Court of the District of Columbia. A proposed voting change may be approved if it does not have the purpose and the effect of denying or abridging the right to vote on account of race or color.[12] The Supreme Court affirmed the dismissal by a lower court of a challenge to preclear which was based on a plaintiff's lack of standing because of a failure to allege either residence or property ownership within the local government.[13]

The Supreme Court has interpreted the Voting Rights Act, and Section 5 in particular, to prohibit only changes that are retrogressive.[14] The government's existing plan is the benchmark for comparison purposes. In other words, minority voters must be no worse off under a proposed change. The Supreme Court has also held that it is not sufficient to allege that a redistricting plan has a discriminatory purpose.[15] It is necessary to allege a retrogressive purpose or effect since Section 5 prohibitions are limited to those addressing retrogression and not discrimination in general. Section 5 prohibits a purpose or effect of worsening the position of minority voters. The Supreme Court has held that preclearance may not be denied because the effect would be to dilute minority voting strength as prohibited by Section 2. The two sections are to be viewed separately with no linkage between them.[16]

---

[8] Whitcomb v. Chavis, 403 U.S. 124 (1971) (multi-member districts are not per se unconstitutional).

[9] White v. Regester, 412 U.S. 755 (1973).

[10] The statute may be used to challenge annexations. *See* City of Pleasant Grove v. United States, 479 U.S. 462 (1987).

[11] For a discussion of the VOTING RIGHTS ACT, *see* SANDRA STEVENSON, ANTIEAU ON LOCAL GOVERNMENT LAW, § 86.02[3].

[12] Reno v. Bossier Parish Sch. Bd., 528 U.S. 320 (2000).

[13] Parker-Weaver v. Fordice, 525 U.S. 1064 (1999).

[14] *Reno, supra* note 12 at 328; Beer v. U.S., 425 U.S. 130 (1976).

[15] *Reno, supra* note 12 at 328.

[16] *Id.*

The Voting Rights Act is also applicable to local government annexations of property where there is a purpose or effect of vote dilution of minority voters. If the net effect of the annexation is a substantial enlargement of majority votes without an increase in the minority vote, it may be found to be an invalid local government action.[17] In these cases, the Supreme Court has considered the voting system that is used to determine whether it fairly reflects the minority population subsequent to the annexation.[18] In *City of Port Arthur v. United States*[19] the Supreme Court affirmed a lower court's rejection of a voting plan which provided for two of six council members to be elected at-large, with four elected from single-member districts. The Court held that the anticipated racial bloc voting would undervalue the political strength of the minority members of the community since only one-third of the council members would be elected from districts where they constituted a majority.

§ 7.8 Initiative and Referendum

The people residing within a state or local government have no inherent right to directly participate in the legislative process. However, some state constitutions and statutes have given members of the public the right to approve, enact, modify or repeal local legislation. The process of enacting legislation by citizen action is known as a local initiative. The process of voting to approve or disapprove of local enactments that are proposed, or have already been enacted by the local governing board, is known as a local referendum.

Almost all states have state constitutional provisions that authorize state referendums in at least some situations. Many also authorize them at the local government level. However, not as many residents of states and local governments have the right to initiate legislative action. States in the west have used these processes more frequently than states in other areas of the country.

Both processes are focused on legislative action and may not be used to effect administrative or executive functions. Legislative acts change or make new law, thereby establishing public policy. Administrators and executors are engaged in administrative action which implements the law or policy that has been adopted. Another limitation on the use of initiative and referendum is that it cannot be used to direct officials to exercise their ministerial or discretionary powers in a particular way, such as establishing specific rates for public utilities.[1]

Whatever right the people have to initiate, approve or disapprove of legislative action, it must be within the delegated authority of the local

---

[17] City of Rome v. United States, 446 U.S. 156 (1980).

[18] City of Richmond v. United States, 422 U.S. 358 (1975).

[19] 459 U.S. 159 (1982).

[1] McKinley v. Fraser, 114 N.W.2d 341 (Mich. 1962).

government.[2] Neither initiative or referendum can be used as a means of expanding the authority of the local legislative body.

There must be compliance with all procedural requirements when the processes of initiative and referendum are used. Typically, both are begun by the circulation of a petition to obtain a specified number of signatures, thus indicating that a substantial number of the voters desire certain action be taken. The language of the petition must be sufficiently clear so that voters will reasonably understand it. The circulators of the petitions must also comply with any requirement that they submit a verifying affidavit attesting to the validity of the signatures on the petitions.

The petitions are usually to be presented to a designated local official or board. If an individual changes his or her mind and wants to withdraw a signature, the general rule is that it may be done, if no final action has been taken.[3] However, some jurisdictions disagree, and do not permit withdrawal after the petitions have been filed with the appropriate person or board.[4] If all the procedural steps are met, the governing board will post a notice and call for a vote of the qualified electors within the community.

The rule that local legislative enactments must be consistent with general state legislation on matters of state concern also applies to action taken pursuant to initiative and referendum, unless the state constitution or statutes provide otherwise. Initiative action will be subjected to the same standards of review as local legislation. It cannot be arbitrary, unreasonable or discriminatory in a manner that violates protections afforded individuals.[5]

Restrictions on the use of initiative have been challenged on First Amendment grounds. For instance, a requirement that a person who circulates initiative petitions must be a resident of the state has been upheld. However, the Supreme Court has determined that a state violated a First Amendment right to political speech when it required that a person circulating an initiative petition must be a registered voter, wear an identification badge, and that initiators must file a list of names and addresses of all paid circulators with the amount paid to each one.[6]

Jurisdictions vary in their use of the referendum process. Some statutes, charters or local laws require the governing body to submit a particular kind of proposed legislative action for a public referendum before it is adopted. Occasionally, multiple referendums among different local governments may be required. New York has a state constitutional requirement that a proposed county charter be approved by a majority of voters residing within cities and a majority of those residing outside the cities.[7] This requirement has been sustained by the Supreme Court.[8]

---

[2] Municipality of Anchorage v. Frohne, 568 P.2d 3 (Alaska 1977).

[3] Birmingham Gas Co. v. City of Bessemer, 33 So.2d 475 (Ala. 1948).

[4] Fischer v. Bd. of Supervisors of Washtenaw Co., 120 N.W. 13 (Mich. 1909).

[5] City of Cleburne v. Cleburne Living Center, 473 U.S. 432 (1985).

[6] Buckley v. American Constitutional Law Foundation, Inc., 525 U.S. 182 (1999).

[7] N.Y.S. CONST., art. IX, § 1, cl. h.

[8] Town of Lockport v. Citizens for Cmty. Action, 423 U.S. 808 (1975).

Other referendum provisions provide for the process to be used after the local government board acts. Sometimes, it is provided that if local legislation is not repealed within an indicated time, it must be submitted for approval by the voters. Finally, a frequent delegation of the referendum authority in state constitutions, statutes or charters provides for a "permissive" referendum which requires a local governing body to call an election upon the petition of a designated number of voters. If the citizens do not petition, then there is no referendum.

Often, state statutes provide that successful attempts to enact legislation through the initiative process will block any attempts by the local legislative body to repeal or amend it for a specified period of time. Filing a petition for a referendum on local legislative action usually means that the local body cannot take action on it until the voters have spoken.[9] If the voters reject the legislative action, it is sometimes provided that the local legislative body may not take any similar action for a specified period of time.[10]

Some states have been reticent to entrust the people with these powerful means of governing, preferring that the task of legislating be reserved to duly elected representatives. Their belief is that if the people do not agree with the actions of legislators, they may register their disapproval at the polls when the officers stand for reelection.

---

[9] Burks v. City of Lafayette, 142 Colo. 61 (1960).
[10] Martin v. Smith, 1 Cal. Rptr. 307 (Cal. App. 1959).

Chapter 8

Local Officers and Employees

§ 8.1 Introduction and Chapter Overview

Local governments are a large source of employment for many people. According to the 1999 Census, there were approximately 10.7 million people employed by local government, exceeding federal and state workforces combined.[1] Because individuals who work in the public sector are compensated from public funds and perform tasks on behalf of the public, they are subject to regulations and restrictions that may be inapplicable to those in private employment. At the same time, many government officers and employees enjoy the benefits of civil service protections. They are also at times protected from personal liability for actions committed during the course of their employment.

Local qualifications for public office are often specified in state constitutions, statutes, charters, or local enactments. Where these are ambiguous, eligibility will ordinarily be resolved in favor of the applicant for the position. Many local government positions are also subject to civil service laws and regulations and individuals must meet specified criteria to qualify for them. A qualification that unreasonably discriminates on the basis of race, ancestry, age, disability or gender is unlawful and are subject to judicial review under varying standards, depending upon the type of discrimination that is alleged.[2]

Unless specified by the state, local governments are usually deemed to have the authority to define the duties of local personnel. At one time, local government employment was considered a privilege and the employer could impose restrictions and conditions with little concern of reversal.[3] However, the Supreme Court held that the Constitution protects the individual liberties of public employees and restriction upon their fundamental rights must be justified by a compelling need to protect a substantial public interest.[4] Many other federal and state statutes have also been adopted to expand the protection that is granted public employees.

Often statutes that regulate conduct of local government workers distinguish between officers and employees and courts have adopted different means of distinguishing the two categories. In some, state constitutions establish offices, often providing for elections to fill the positions. People

---

[1] 1999 U.S. Census, U.S. Census Bureau, U.S. Dep't of Commerce, http://www.census.gov/Press-Release/www/2000/cb00-127.htm/.

[2] See §§ 8.2 and 8.5 infra.

[3] McAuliffe v. Mayor & Bd. of Aldermen, 29 N.E. 517 (Mass. 1892).

[4] Pickering v. Bd. of Educ., 391 U.S. 563 (1968).

elected to fill these positions are normally considered officers. At other times, statutes and local charters are the source of local offices. There are few clearly defined rules to be applied in categorizing local employment and most often the decision will be based on an ad hoc analysis of the intent of the constitutional, statutory, or charter provision.[5] As a general rule, an officer will have responsibility and supervisory control over other persons. Chief executives such as mayors, members of the local legislative bodies, judges and school superintendents are examples of positions that are typically considered to be officers.[6] Members of the police and fire departments are usually considered officers, but may be considered employees for conditions of employment, including residency, salaries and civil service.[7]

Many local governments have adopted conditions of employment, such as residency requirements. Other requirements have long been recognized by the common law. These include restrictions on conduct, such as conflicts of interest, in fulfilling the responsibilities of the position. A personal interest in a position or decision would disqualify an individual from the post or from participation in the decision-making process.

PART I REQUIREMENTS FOR LOCAL OFFICERS AND EMPLOYEES

§ 8.2 Eligibility and Ethical Considerations

Eligibility requirements for local office may be established by state constitutions, statutes, charters or by local government action. The general rules of preemption apply, and priority of state constitutions over statutes, which in turn normally take precedence over local requirements, will determine the rules in the event of a conflict. If the local government maintains that its home-rule authority supersedes state statutes, the result may vary depending upon the jurisdiction.[1]

Most local governments have been given authority to establish reasonable qualifications for local office and employment.[2] They may not impose arbitrary or unreasonable conditions that deny the opportunity for public service; nor can they unreasonably discriminate against individuals or groups on the basis of race, ancestry and alienage, age, disability and gender. Any discrimination based on race will be subjected to strict scrutiny and only sustained if narrowly tailored to further a compelling governmental interest.[3] For instance, an affirmative action plan will only be upheld

---

[5] For more information, *see* SANDRA M. STEVENSON, ANTIEAU ON LOCAL GOVERNMENT LAW, § 76.01[1] (2d ed. 2002).

[6] *See* OSBORNE M. REYNOLDS, JR., LOCAL GOVERNMENT LAW, § 77, pp. 262–265 (2d ed. 2000).

[7] *Id.*

[1] *See* §§ 2.2–2.4 *supra.*

[2] Landes v. Town of N. Hempstead, 231 N.E.2d 120 (1967).

[3] Adarand Constructors, Inc. v. Pena, 515 U.S. 200 (1995).

if it is narrowly tailored to remedy past discrimination which is specific. It is not enough to allege past discrimination of a general nature.[4] A requirement that an officer or employee be a citizen of the United States must be justified on a rational basis if for political reasons,[5] and a compelling interest basis if for economic purposes.[6] In addition to constitutional equal protection restrictions, federal statutes prohibit unreasonable discrimination on the basis of age, disability and gender.[7]

If local government employment is available and an applicant meets all reasonable requirements, he or she has a protected right to public employment. The Supreme Court has recognized a federal right to be considered for government employment without a burden of invidiously discriminatory disqualifications.[8] Local governments must be prepared to show that their requirements are based on a real and substantial difference that has a reasonable relation to the object sought to be accomplished.[9] Physical requirements that are directly related to health and safety,[10] and denial of employment to individuals with drug dependencies[11] have been sustained by the courts. Disqualification from local employment because of a criminal record has been accepted by the courts as a legitimate limitation. In addition to constitutional protections, local governments must comply with the numerous federal and state statutes that protect individuals from discrimination in employment.[12]

A requirement that a local government employee reside within the community is generally upheld if there is a rational basis for it.[13] A claim that members of the police or fire department should be available for emergency services or that a member of the legislative board should have greater familiarity with the community easily justifies such a requirement. State courts have differed on whether a state may prohibit its local governments from imposing a residency requirement.[13.1]

---

[4] City of Richmond v. J.A. Croson Co., 488 U.S. 469 (1989).

[5] Cabell v. Chavez-Salido, 454 U.S. 432 (1982).

[6] Sugarman v. Dougall, 413 U.S. 634 (1973).

[7] See § 8.5 infra.

[8] Turner v. Fouche, 396 U.S. 346 (1970). See also Landes v. Town of N. Hempstead, 231 N.E.2d 120 (1967) (holding that there can be no arbitrary exclusions from office. If a classification is used, it must be nondiscriminatory and based on a real and substantial difference having reasonable relation to the object sought to be accomplished).

[9] Landes supra note 2 at 443.

[10] McCrea v. Cunningham, 277 N.W.2d 52 (Neb. 1979).

[11] NYC Transit Auth. v. Beazer, 440 U.S. 568 (1979).

[12] See §§ 8.5 and 9.8 infra.

[13] McCarthy v. Philadelphia Civil Serv. Comm'n, 424 U.S. 645 (1976). See also Wardwell v. Bd. of Educ., 529 F.2d 625 (6th Cir. 1976) (rule requiring all teachers to establish residency within school district within 90 days of employment is supported by a rational basis).

[13.1] City and Co. of Denver v. State, 788 P.2d 764 (Colo. 1990). It is a local concern and the state cannot limit the authority of home rule municipalities to require that its employees reside within its corporate limits as a condition of employment. But see Uniformed Firefighters Assoc. v. City of New York, 50 N.Y.2d 85, 405 N.E.2d 679 (N.Y. 1980). A local law imposing a residency requirement for local officers and employees is preempted by a state law that exempts certain employees and officers from residency requirements.

However, durational residency requirements, which require a person to have lived within the community for a period of time before eligibility, must meet a compelling-interest test. Equal protection, the right to travel, and the privileges and immunities protection found in the Federal Constitution may be used to challenge these restrictions.[14] Such a durational residency requirement will be unconstitutional if it is for an unreasonably long period of time and not supported by a compelling public purpose.[15]

Local governments are not generally permitted to impose a property ownership requirement. The Supreme Court held that such a requirement for membership on a local school board violated equal protection. It noted that the privilege of holding public office could not be based on distinctions that violate federal constitutional guarantees.[16] Nor did the Court permit the property ownership requirement to be imposed for membership on boards to develop reorganization plans for cities.[17]

If a person has fulfilled the duties of an officer but for some reason did not meet the qualifications and therefore had no valid claim to the position, he or she may be considered a *de facto* officer. The purpose of this characterization is to give validity to the acts he or she performed on behalf of the local government and thus insure local government stability.[18] In order to claim this status, the person must have acted in a manner consistent with an apparent right to the office, openly possessing it so that reasonable people would have assumed the possession to be lawful, and was engaged in discharging the duties of the office.[19]

Ethical considerations limit a person from holding a public office or job if he or she has a personal interest that might interfere with the impartial performance of public duties.[20] The disqualification is not dependent on actual proof of bias, but rather the appearance of impropriety is sufficient. There are many state statutes that address conflict of interest disqualifications. In some jurisdictions there is a common law doctrine regarding incompatible public offices. Such a doctrine may prevent one person from holding two public offices when duties of those offices cannot be executed with care and ability by the same person.[21] Other states have included state constitutional clauses that prohibit a person from holding more than one public office.[22]

---

[14] Wellford v. Battaglia, 485 F.2d 1151 (3d Cir. 1973); Barnard v. Thorstenn, 489 U.S. 547 (1989).

[15] Thompson v. Mellon, 507 P.2d 628 (Cal. 1973); Cowan v. City of Aspen, 509 P.2d 1269 (Colo. 1973).

[16] *Turner, supra* note 8 at 362-63.

[17] Quinn v. Millsap, 491 U.S. 95 (1989).

[18] Waite v. Santa Cruz, 184 U.S. 302 (1902).

[19] People *ex rel.* Hess v. Wheeler, 187 N.E. 146 (Ill. 1933).

[20] Brown v. Kirk, 355 N.E.2d 12 (Ill. 1976).

[21] City of Everett v. Curnane, 109 N.E.2d 135 (Mass. 1952).

[22] Matter of Sawyer, 594 P.2d 805 (Or. 1979).

Corrupt practices acts in many states disqualify candidates for offices and jobs if they seek to obtain the position by bribery or illegal expenditures. These acts are upheld, as are statutes that require the disclosure of campaign finances. While the Supreme Court has sustained the constitutionality of the federal disclosure statute which requires extensive disclosure and record keeping, and imposes contribution limits, it has not permitted the imposition of ceilings on the amount of money that could be expended on behalf of candidates or by the candidates themselves. It was found that such restrictions inhibit political expression which is protected by the First Amendment.[23]

A requirement that officers or employees take a loyalty oath has been sustained by the courts, as have disqualifications of people who in the past knowingly joined organizations committed to the violent overthrow of the government.[24] However, these requirements will be carefully scrutinized to insure that there is no unreasonable infringement upon First Amendment rights.

Local offices are deemed to be public trusts.[25] Public officers and employees are responsible for performing their duties for the benefit of the people. They are obligated to serve with good faith, honesty and integrity, uninfluenced by any adverse motives or interests. This high degree of trust requires that local officials refrain from outside activities or interests which interfere with their public duties. They must also refrain from anything which may create a proclivity to act in a manner that is antithetical to fulfilling their public trust. Even the appearance of conflicts of interest between an officer's personal and public interests are not to be tolerated. When a person accepts the responsibility of acting on behalf of the public, it is to be assumed that he or she will avoid private activities or interests that may appear to benefit from the exercise of discretion by the officer. Local government officials and employees cannot place themselves in a position where personal interest may conflict with public duty.[26]

Some courts have found that it is a violation of the fiduciary duty of a local officer to vote to increase his or her compensation.[27] Gifts may not be accepted from firms or persons doing business with the local government, nor may public officers and employees act on behalf of friends, relatives or private clients. Local officers and employees may not have an interest either directly or indirectly in any contract of their government. In many jurisdictions, if it is shown that there has been an improper interest in a contract, the contract it may be void or voidable at the option of the local government.[28]

---

[23] Buckley v. Valeo, 424 U.S. 1 (1976).

[24] Cole v. Richardson, 405 U.S. 676 (1972).

[25] State v. Weleck, 91 A.2d 751 (N.J. 1952).

[26] Josephson v. Planning Board of City of Stamford, 199 A.2d 690 (Conn. 1964).

[27] Baker v. Marley, 170 N.E.2d 900 (N.Y. 1960).

[28] *See* § 5.12 *supra.*

Conflicts of interests by local officers and employees may justify their removal from office. It may also be sufficient grounds to set aside any local government action influenced or taken by the individual. It is not necessary to base such action upon actual proof of dishonesty. However, personal interests that are only remote, speculative, uncertain, or insubstantial are usually insufficient to create a conflict of interest.[29]

If public officers fail to fulfill their responsibility of trust, they are accountable to the local government for public funds or property they have appropriated. Public officers are also responsible for interest and any profits they have received, even if the local government suffered no economic harm.[30] A constructive trust may be imposed and an accounting required.[31]

Many local governments have adopted codes of ethics for officers and employees, and courts have sustained them, provided they have authority to do so and the requirements are reasonable. These often require the public disclosure of financial interests of the officer and his immediate family. When courts have considered the requirements, they have generally concluded that the deterrence of corruption and conflicts of interest in order to enhance public confidence in the integrity of government furthers a substantial state interest. It outweighs any adverse effects upon the privacy rights of the officer or employee.[32] There are also many statutes that require full disclosure of any interest in contracts or other business of the local government which an officer or employee may have. Other statutes provide criminal penalties for those public officers and employees who abuse the public trust.

§ 8.3   Regulation of Activities and Conduct

A local government may generally regulate the duties and terms of office of local personnel, unless preempted by state constitution, statute or local charter. The recognition that an officer or employee retains his or her individual rights after accepting public employment has meant that the courts have examined many requirements that have been imposed by local governments. For instance, some local governments have sought to restrict employees to their residences when on sick leave. Courts have agreed that this has the potential to violate the right to travel, vote, and exercise freedom of religion. They have differed on whether it has been justified by a compelling government interest.[1] However, most have upheld requirements

---

[29] Wilson v. Long Branch, 142 A.2d 837 (N.J. 1958), *cert. denied*, 358 U.S. 873 (1958).

[30] Borough of Totowa v. American Surety Co. of New York, 188 A.2d 586 (N.J. 1963).

[31] Town of Myrtle Beach v. Suber, 81 S.E.2d 352 (S.C. 1954).

[32] Banny v. City of New York, 712 F.2d 1554 (2d Cir. 1983), *cert. denied*, 464 U.S. 1017 (1983).

[1] Pienta v. Village of Schaumburg, 710 F.2d 1258 (7th Cir. 1983) (finding that the restriction amounted to "house arrest"). *But see* Atterberry v. Police Comm'r of Boston, 467 N.E.2d 150 (Mass. 1984), *cert. denied*, 469 U.S. 1208 (1985); Bruno v. Dept. of Police, 451 So. 2d 1082, *aff'd*, 462 So. 2d 139 (La. 1985), *cert. denied*, 474 U.S. 805 (1985).

that the officer or employee give advance notification of intended absences or verify illness or injury with a doctor's opinion.

Unless prohibited by a statute or otherwise preempted, local governments are permitted to determine the hours of work for their officers and employees. Residency requirements have also been generally upheld, provided the local government has a rational basis to support it.[2] Bans against outside employment have been sustained also, if reasonably related to the ability of the officer or employee to perform the job.[3] Total bans that are not limited to restrictions on types or hours of outside employment are more difficult to defend as reasonably related to job performance and have met with disapproval.[4]

Local government restrictions on the political activity of officers and employees have at times been sustained.[5] At other times, they have been found to violate an officer's or employee's First Amendment rights of free speech and association.[6] The federal government and many states have adopted statutes regulating the political activity of personnel. Local governments have been permitted to impose restrictions on local officers and employees running for other public offices if supported by a rational basis.[7]

The Supreme Court has permitted local governments to regulate the appearance of its employees if there is a rational connection to the furtherance of a public purpose.[8] Cases have upheld restrictions on hair length, facial hair,[9] and jewelry,[10] provided the officers or employees do not establish that their activity is constitutionally protected religious or cultural expression.[11]

§ 8.4　Dismissal and Disciplinary Action

Although it is often stated that there is no property interest in a government job, statutes, contracts, or local enactments may create a property interest by causing an expectation that a particular employment relationship will continue unless certain defined events occur.[1] Employees who are not protected by civil service provisions or contracts, and who do

---

[2] See § 8.2 supra.

[3] Flood v. Kennedy, 190 N.E.2d 13 (N.Y. 1963); People ex rel. Masterson v. French, 18 N.E. 133 (N.Y. 1888).

[4] City of Crowley Firemen v. City of Crowley, 280 So. 2d 897 (La. 1973).

[5] Wachsman v. Dallas, 704 F.2d 160 (5th Cir. 1983), cert. denied, 464 U.S. 1012 (1983); Salt Lake City Fire Fighters Local v. Salt Lake City, 449 P.2d 239 (Utah 1969), cert. denied, 395 U.S. 906 (1969).

[6] City of Miami v. Sterbenz, 203 So. 2d 4 (Fla. 1967).

[7] Clements v. Fashing, 457 U.S. 957 (1982), reh. denied, 458 U.S. 1133 (1982).

[8] Kelley v. Johnson, 425 U.S. 238 (1976).

[9] Domico v. Rapides Parish Sch. Bd., 675 F.2d 100 (5th Cir. 1982).

[10] Rathert v. Vill. of Peotone, 903 F.2d 510 (7th Cir.), cert. denied, 498 U.S. 921 (1990).

[11] Id.; Mississippi Employment Sec. Comm'n v. McGlothin, 556 So. 2d 324 (Miss. 1990).

[1] Bishop v. Wood, 426 U.S. 341 (1976).

not have a property interest in their jobs, may be dismissed without cause. There is no due process requirement that the person be given notice or a hearing before dismissal. However, if an officer or an employee is found to have a property interest in a job, a local government will be found to violate due process if it arbitrarily dismisses the person.[2] He or she also has a due process right to notice of the dismissal charges and must be afforded a fair hearing.[3] Apart from the existence of a property right, a common law right to dismiss an employee where it becomes an economic necessity has been recognized in some jurisdictions.[4]

Local governments may not dismiss any officer or employee, whether or not he or she has a property interest, a contract, or civil service protection, for exercising his or her constitutional rights. This is discussed further in § 8.5 *infra*.

Local governments must comply with all prescribed rules and procedures in the dismissal process. Dismissal rules may often be found in state constitutions, civil service statutes, tenure statutes, other state statutes and in local charters and enactments. If using a civil service or tenure statute to challenge a dismissal, an employee or officer must first establish that he or she met those requirements in the appointment to the position.

Administrative review is frequently available to one who has been dismissed. Most often this remedy must be exhausted before a dismissed employee is able to seek judicial review. Courts generally sustain local government disciplinary action if it is neither arbitrary nor unreasonable, and if there is substantial evidence in the record to support the decision.

Local governments are generally permitted to conduct reasonable investigations of officer and employee conduct as it relates to their employment. Some local governments have been given authority to subpoena personnel to testify, and may require the production of written materials. However, local officers and employees are protected by the Fifth and Fourteenth Amendments against self-incrimination and may claim this privilege when their answers might incriminate them.[5] A local government cannot impose a requirement that failure to answer questions will result in loss of employment, unless it simultaneously grants immunity or provides that the answers given cannot be used against the officer or employee in subsequent criminal prosecutions. After it grants immunity, the local government can provide that refusal to answer questions may result in dismissal.[6] Local

---

[2] Cleveland Bd. of Educ. v. Loudermill, 470 U.S. 532 (1985).

[3] Perry v. Sindermann, 408 U.S. 593 (1972). *See* Macklin v. City of New Orleans, 293 F.3d 237 (5th Cir. 2002), *cert. denied*, 123 S.Ct. 967 (2003). The court held that an officer who had not been given a pre-suspension hearing was not denied due process. It stated that due process is satisfied when the employee receives "oral or written notice of the charges against him, an explanation of the employer's evidence, and an opportunity to present his side of the story."

[4] Hennessey v. City of Bridgeport, 569 A.2d 1122 (Conn. 1990); Small v. Bd. of Safety of Town of Monroeville, 513 N.E.2d 196 (Ind. App. 1987).

[5] Gardner v. Broderick, 392 U.S. 273 (1968); Garrity v. New Jersey, 385 U.S. 493 (1967).

[6] Lefkowitz v. Turley, 414 U.S. 70 (1973). *See also* Confederation of Police v. Conlisk, 489 F.2d 891 (7th Cir. 1973), *cert. denied*, Rochford v. Confederation of Police, 416 U.S. 956 (1973).

governments have been sustained in their claim that an officer or employee is insubordinate when he or she refuses to comply with its request for information about the public employment, when there is no danger of criminal prosecution.[7]

The common law recognizes an implied right to suspend an employee with pay until an investigation and determination of the legitimacy of charges against the individual can be undertaken. Sometimes this common law right is amended by statute. Some states have imposed limitations on the length of the suspension or have prohibited successive suspensions. Others specifically permit suspension without pay for a limited period, provided that after it expires the employee or officer is paid. Still others provide that pay is to be determined ultimately by the outcome of the investigatory process.

Local governments are generally authorized to respond in many ways to the misconduct of an officer or employee. Whatever action is taken, it must not be arbitrary or so disproportionate to the offense that it is shocking to a person's sense of fairness. The grounds for disciplinary investigation and action may be found in state constitutions, statutes, local charters, and local enactments. Local governments have inherent authority to suspend those who have been indicted for malfeasance in office. State constitutions and statutes may address specific misconduct issues as well. If there are no legislative requirements, local governments can suspend for any reason deemed sufficient for dismissal, since power to dismiss normally includes power to suspend.

Reviewing courts will sustain local disciplinary action if the reasons given indicate that the conduct being reviewed would impair the efficiency of the public service. There must be a substantial relation between the offending conduct and the efficient operation of public service. Punishment cannot be imposed for violation of invalid regulations.

An improper basis for punitive action may violate the First or Fourteenth Amendment rights of the individual officer or employee. As noted in § 8.5 *infra*, local government employees and officers are protected by the First Amendment. The Supreme Court has determined that they may not be dismissed for their comments on a matter of public concern, unless they know such comments to be false, or made them with reckless disregard of whether their statement is true or false. However, if the employer is able to show that the comments interfere with the efficient functioning of the workplace, this concern may outweigh the individual's right to free speech.[8] The Supreme Court has extended the protection of an employee's right of free speech and association to other areas of employer action, such as hiring and promotion.[9]

Local governments are not permitted to discharge individuals just because they are members of a particular political party, unless it is an

---

[7] Lybarger v. City of Los Angeles, 710 P.2d 329 (Cal. 1985).

[8] Pickering v. Bd. of Educ., 391 U.S. 563 (1968); Waters v. Churchill, 511 U.S. 661 (1994).

[9] Rutan v. Republican Party of Illinois, 497 U.S. 62 (1990).

appropriate requirement for the position.[10] Although party affiliation may be an acceptable requirement for some types of government employment, the hiring authority must demonstrate that it is an appropriate requirement for the effective performance of the job. Sometimes the person will be a "policymaker" or "confidential" employee, but not always.[11]

Generally, local governments have the right to freely transfer employees or officers to other positions if no demotion is involved and there is no punitive intent. If misconduct is involved, grounds for dismissal will certainly justify demotion. It is recognized that less is required to be shown for demotion than is needed for dismissal.

PART II PROTECTION AND LIABILITY FOR LOCAL OFFICERS AND EMPLOYEES

§ 8.5 Constitutional and Statutory Civil Rights Protections

The right of local government to control the actions of its officers and employees has changed markedly over the years. In 1892, when Justice Holmes said that ". . .there may be a constitutional right to talk politics, but there is no constitutional right to be a policeman," public employment was clearly considered a privilege.[1] Today, it is well established that government employees are protected by the Federal Constitution and by many federal and state constitutions and statutes. It is well known that any local government that imposes rules or regulations upon the exercise of an officer's or employee's fundamental rights must show a compelling public need to do so.[2]

The Supreme Court has held that the discharge of officers or employees for partisan political reasons infringes First Amendment rights unless party affiliation is an appropriate requirement for the effective performance of the job.[3] The First Amendment also protects an officer or employee against politically motivated hiring or promotion decisions, except where party affiliation is an appropriate requirement for the position.[4]

Attempts to control the speech of officers and employees that is critical of the local government or its personnel is circumscribed by the First Amendment. An improper basis for punitive action may violate the First or Fourteenth Amendment rights of the individual officer or employee. The Supreme Court has determined that officers or employees may not be dismissed for their comments *on a matter of public concern*, unless they

---

[10] Elrod v. Burns, 427 U.S. 347 (1976).

[11] Branti v. Finkel, 445 U.S. 507 (1980).

[1] McAuliffe v. City of New Bedford, 29 N.E. 517 (Mass. 1892).

[2] Pickering v. Bd. of Educ., 391 U.S. 563 (1968).

[3] Branti v. Finkel, 445 U.S. 507 (1980).

[4] Rutan v. Republican Party of Illinois, 497 U.S. 62 (1990).

know that the statement is false, or they spoke with reckless disregard of whether the statement is true or false. However, if the local government is able to show that the comments interfere with the efficient functioning of the workplace, this concern may outweigh the individual's right to free speech.[5] The Supreme Court held that such expression cannot be controlled or result in penalties to the employee, unless the expression destroys the efficiency of the public service, impairs discipline, destroys harmony with co-workers, or prevents successful service under a government leader.[6] The Court has adopted a process for determining whether an officer or employee has been improperly punished for such protected speech. The employee's right is to be balanced with the government interests. If the Court favors the right of the employee then it must be shown that the detrimental employment decision was taken because of the speech. If the employee meets this responsibility, then liability is imposed *unless* the local government shows, by a preponderance of the evidence, that it would have taken the same action in the absence of the speech.[7] The Supreme Court has extended the protection of an employee's right of free speech and association to other areas of employer action, such as hiring and promotion.[8]

The Fourth Amendment's protection against an unreasonable search and seizure has been interpreted by the Supreme Court to apply to mandatory drug testing of government employees. A flexible test is to be used to determine whether reasonable cause exists for the testing program. If the government establishes that there is a special need for testing, it does not have to show probable cause or even individualized suspicion of drug abuse. In *Skinner v. Railway Labor Executives Ass'n,*[9] the Court found that the government's compelling interest in regulating the conduct of railroad employees was such a special need. A general test requirement for employees involved in certain train accidents, or for those violating certain safety rules, is reasonable. The Supreme Court found a similar justification for a drug testing program adopted by the U.S. Customs Service for applicants for transfers or promotions to positions involving the interdiction of drugs, or for carrying firearms.[10] Public safety and a public interest in safeguarding borders outweighed the privacy interest of employees. However, the Court found that a state could not require candidates for certain state offices to certify that they had been tested within thirty days prior to qualifying for nomination or election. It was "symbolic" and the diminishment in personal privacy was not justified.[11]

The Fourteenth Amendment Due Process Clause prohibits dismissals for violations of arbitrary rules and regulations, or for ones that are so vague

---

[5] *Pickering, supra* note 2 at 564; Waters v. Churchill, 511 U.S. 661 (1994).

[6] Pickering v. Bd. of Educ. 391 U.S. 563 (1968).

[7] *Id.*

[8] *Rutan, supra* note 4 at 73.

[9] Skinner v. Ry. Labor Executives' Ass'n, 489 U.S. 602 (1989).

[10] Nat'l Treasury Employees Union v. Von Raab, 489 U.S 656 (1989).

[11] Chandler v. Miller, 520 U.S. 305 (1997).

that people of common intelligence must guess at their meaning.[12] Officers and employees are also entitled to procedural due process. However, the degree of protection is to be determined by the facts of each case. The Supreme Court has upheld the immediate suspension of a local school employee without a hearing and without pay, after it was revealed that he had been charged with a drug felony.[13] The Court noted that due process is flexible. It requires procedural protections as demanded by a particular situation.

Employees and officers are protected by the Equal Protection Clause from discriminatory enforcement of employment rules. A local government is not permitted to enforce a rule against some employees and not require compliance from others who are similarly situated.

The Federal Civil Rights Act provides protection to local officers and employees. Title VII[14] prohibits discrimination based on the employee's race, color, religion, sex, or national origin in hiring, discharge, compensation, terms, conditions, or privileges of employment. The Supreme Court has determined that the protection is broad and not limited to terms and conditions in the narrow sense.[15] For instance, where sexual harassment is so severe or pervasive that it creates an environment that is both objectively and subjectively offensive, Title VII is violated.[16] The local government, as an employer, may also be found liable for the acts of its supervisory personnel when it fails to take corrective action.[17] It may raise the affirmative defense that it exercised reasonable care to prevent and promptly correct any sexually harassing behavior and that the plaintiff unreasonably failed to take advantage of any preventive or corrective opportunities provided by the employer to avoid the harm.

The Supreme Court has also determined that same-gender sexual harassment is actionable under Title VII. The gender or motivation of the perpetrator is not relevant.[18] It is the offensive conduct and the context in which it occurs that is addressed by Title VII.

There are federal statutes that prohibit discrimination based on age or disability. The Supreme Court has determined that the Eleventh Amendment prevents Congress from providing for private lawsuits seeking damages against states for violations of the Age Discrimination in Employment Act[19] or the Americans With Disabilities Act.[20] However, since the

---

[12] Some courts have voided regulations that require "conduct unbecoming an officer" but the Supreme Court upheld such a standard in the UNIFORM CODE OF MILITARY JUSTICE against a vagueness challenge in Parker v. Levy, 417 U.S. 733 (1974).

[13] Gilbert v. Homar, 520 U.S. 1102 (1997).

[14] 42 U.S.C. § 2000e-2(a)(1) (1994).

[15] Faragher v. City of Boca Raton, 141 L.Ed.2d 662 (1998).

[16] Harris v. Forklift Systems, Inc., 510 U.S. 17 (1993); Meritor Savings Bank, FSB v. Vinson, 477 U.S. 57 (1986).

[17] Faragher, supra note 15 at 807.

[18] Oncale v. Sundowner Offshore Servs., Inc., 523 U.S. 75 (1998).

[19] Kimel v. Florida Board of Regents, 528 U.S. 62 (2000).

[20] Garrett v. University of Alabama, 531 U.S. 356 (2001).

Eleventh Amendment does not apply to local governments,[21] they may be sued by individuals in private actions for their violations of both statutes.[22] These are discussed in § 9.8 *infra*.

Although § 1983 of the Civil Rights Act[23] does not create new rights, it provides the means for an employee or officer to seek a remedy for the infringement of a federal constitutional or statutory right.

§ 8.6 Personal Liability and Qualified Immunity

An individual will be personally responsible for the repayment of any public funds that he or she has misappropriated. If a local government suspects that public funds or properties have been taken for personal use, it may require an officer or employee to account for that which he or she has improperly received.[1] The court may also award interest as part of the compensation. Many states have provided statutory remedies for misappropriation and these enactments frequently authorize taxpayers to seek repayment on behalf of the local government. Those who wrongfully steal public funds are also criminally liable under larceny statutes in most states.

If the officer or employee has not appropriated the money or property for personal use, but instead unlawfully disbursed it to someone else, he or she may still be personally liable for its return.[2] Some courts have been more sympathetic and have refused to impose liability if the misappropriation was not for the employee's benefit and there was no wrongful intent.[3] If an officer or employee has merely lost public funds, most often liability will be imposed with the courts holding the person strictly liable for funds entrusted to his or her care.[4] However, some jurisdictions are more lenient, finding that local officials must exercise ordinary diligence, and no personal liability will be imposed if that duty is met.[5]

Common law concepts of malfeasance (unlawful act), misfeasance (wrongful and injurious exercise of lawful authority), misconduct (corrupt misbehavior that breaches a public trust), and nonfeasance or neglect of duty (neglect or refusal to perform a duty of office) are generally governed by statute in many states, and most are punishable by criminal prosecution. States also have statutes that criminally punish officers and employees who solicit or accept bribes in connection with their government work.

---

[21] Mount Healthy City School Bd. of Educ. v. Doyle, 429 U.S. 274 (1977).

[22] For a discussion of Eleventh Amendment immunity, *see* § 1.3 *supra*.

[23] 42 U.S.C. § 1983.

[1] McWhorter v. Richmond, 514 S.W.2d 678 (Ky. 1974).

[2] City of Princeton v. Baker, 35 S.W.2d 524 (Ky. Ct. App. 1931); Stevenson v. Bay City, 26 Mich. 44 (1872); Pugnier v. Ramharter, 81 N.W.2d 38 (Wis. 1957).

[3] Adams v. Bryant, 370 S.W.2d 432 (Ark. 1963); McCarty v. City of St. Paul, 155 N.W.2d 459 (Minn. 1967).

[4] Bird v. McGoldrick, 14 N.E.2d 805 (N.Y. 1938).

[5] Edwards v. Hylbert, 118 S.E.2d 347 (W. Va. 1961).

When states waived their sovereign immunity, local government officers and employees became personally liable for their torts under the common law.[6] Their liability became similar to that of private sector workers, with some major exceptions. Generally, they are not liable for discretionary acts performed within the scope of their duties.[7] This means that when a government officer or employee performs an act that involves choice, judgment, or decision-making, he or she will not usually be civilly liable if harm results.[8]

On the other hand, if a government official or employee is performing a task that does not involve discretion but is ministerial in nature, the ordinary rules of tort law will usually apply. An act is ministerial if the law has prescribed and defined the duty to be done with such precision and certainty that nothing is left to the exercise of discretion or judgment. If it is found that the nondiscretionary task has been performed in a negligent manner, the government employee is personally liable to those who have been harmed as a result of his or her action.[9]

The question of what is discretionary and what is ministerial is answered on a case-by-case basis. Courts have hesitated to apply formulas or unhelpful characterizations such as "operational" as distinguished from "planning" decisions. Many jurisdictions have also refused to recognize personal immunity when the officer's conduct was ultra vires or unauthorized,[10] or done in bad faith, maliciously or with wrongful intent, regardless of the characterization of the act as discretionary or not.

Some courts have refused to impose personal liability where the alleged negligence is based on a failure of the officer or employee to act, as opposed to an affirmative act of negligence. The rationale is similar to that used by courts which have adopted the public-duty rule to limit local government tort liability where a duty is owed to the public at large.[11] They hesitate to impose personal liability on officers or employees for nonfeasance or failure to act.[12]

Personal liability is generally not imposed vicariously on those who supervise officers or employees of a local government. The courts have held that such liability will only be found if the supervisor directed or participated in the wrongful act, or knew of it and did nothing to correct it, or indicated his or her ratification or approval of the conduct.[13]

The courts have held that certain officials have absolute immunity when performing certain functions. Judges are immune from tort liability for

---

[6] See Chapter 9 *infra* for a discussion of Local Government Liability.

[7] Blalock v. Johnston, 185 S.E. 51 (S.C. 1936); Elder v. Anderson, 23 Cal. Rptr. 48 (Dist. Ct. 1962).

[8] Churchill v. McKay, 163 F. Supp. 339 (Alaska 1958).

[9] For a discussion of local government tort liability, *see* § 9.2 *infra*.

[10] Shellburne, Inc. v. Roberts, 238 A.2d 331 (Del. 1967).

[11] For a discussion on this, *see* § 9.3 *infra*.

[12] Montanick v. McMillin, 280 N.W. 608 (Iowa 1938).

[13] Jordan v. Kelly, 223 F. Supp. 732 (W.D. Mo. 1963).

their actions if they acted at least colorably within the scope of their responsibilities.[14] If they have acted totally outside their jurisdiction, the courts have held that immunity does not apply.[15] The Supreme Court has recognized the common law rule of absolute immunity of judges for acts within the judicial role, even if malicious or corrupt. The Court has not, however, extended this immunity to a judge's administrative decisions, such as hiring and firing of court personnel.[16] Some states, such as New York, have also limited judicial immunity by finding it inapplicable to purely ministerial acts.[17]

Local prosecutors are absolutely immune when acting as advocates in the criminal process. The Supreme Court has recognized this common law immunity and has held that prosecutors have full immunity from suits under the Federal Civil Rights Act.[18] The public policy behind these grants of immunity is a concern that unfounded litigation would deflect the efforts of judicial personnel from public duties and interfere with the independence of judgment required by the public trust placed in these officials. This immunity is extended to decisions by prosecutors to file charges that are alleged to be vindictive, reckless, without jurisdiction, and involving conspiracy.[19]

Local legislators are also absolutely immune from tort liability when engaged in legislative duties.[20] Individual members of a governing body or board are also immune from suit, provided they are performing discretionary as opposed to ministerial tasks.[21] Officers and employees are sometimes held to have only qualified or partial immunity for the tort of defamation. However, local legislators and other officials are immune when speaking at a duly called meeting or during the necessary exercise of the duties of office.

Local officers and employees may be subject to civil and criminal liability when they have violated someone's federal constitutional or statutorily protected rights, unless they are found to have qualified immunity. These claims are typically brought pursuant to § 1983 of the Civil Rights Act.[22] Under this statute, it must be shown that the officer or employee deprived someone of a right, privilege or immunity secured by federal law. Other wrongs, such as a claim for harm caused by negligence, may not be brought under § 1983. The Supreme Court has held that the Due Process Clause

---

[14] Calhoun v. Little, 106 Ga. 336, 32 S.E. 86 (Ga. 1898).

[15] Stump v. Sparkman, 435 U.S. 349 (1978); Nelson v. Kellogg, 123 P. 1115 (Cal. 1912); Osbekoff v. Mallory, 188 N.W.2d 294 (Iowa 1971).

[16] Forrester v. White, 484 U.S. 219 (1988).

[17] Scott v. Niagara Falls, 407 N.Y.S.2d 103 (N.Y. Sup. Ct. 1978).

[18] Imbler v. Pachtman, 424 U.S. 409 (1976).

[19] Myers v. Morris, 810 F.2d 1437 (8th Cir. 1987), *cert. denied*, Lallak v. Morris 484 U.S. 828 (1987).

[20] Tenney v. Brandhove, 341 U.S. 367 (1951); Bricker v. Sims, 259 S.W.2d 661 (Tenn. 1953).

[21] Clark v. Ferling, 151 A.2d 137 (Md. 1959).

[22] 42 U.S.C. § 1983 (1994).

does not protect individuals from the negligence of government officials. Therefore, litigants who seek recovery for negligent acts of government officers or employees must resort to state tort claims. They cannot use § 1983 because a negligent act does not form a basis for a federal constitutional or statutory right.[23] The Due Process Clause protects individuals from abuse of power by government officials or employees but does not protect them from a lack of due care.

Local officers and employees may claim qualified immunity in § 1983 suits if they acted in good faith and did not know, or should not reasonably have known, that their action violated the plaintiff's federal rights.[24] It is an affirmative defense that must be pleaded by the defendant official. In addressing immunity for the local officer or employee, the Supreme Court has indicated that qualified immunity will be decided based on the facts of each case. The Court has held that the officer will be immune from liability for civil damages if his or her conduct did not violate clearly established statutory or constitutional rights which a reasonable person, in the place of the officer or employee, would have known at the time.[25] The Court will use an objective test that considers whether there were clearly-established rights and it will examine the facts existing at the time the official acted. Whether the facts of the case are novel and dissimilar is not determinative. The issue is whether the officers had fair warning that their conduct violated federal law.[26] In other words, immunity from liability for damages is available if the official reasonably believed that his or her conduct was lawful in light of clearly established law and the information that he or she possessed at the time of the act.[27] Even if an act subsequently is determined to violate constitutional rights, the grant of immunity is decided on the law and facts at the time of the act. On the other hand, an officer or employee may not claim immunity solely on the basis that the local government trained or instructed him or her to perform something that is unconstitutional, where the unlawfulness of the act was clearly established when it was done.

Local officials and employees may be liable for punitive damages under § 1983 and Title VII of the Civil Rights Act. Under § 1983, it must be shown that the official acted with reckless or callous disregard for the plaintiff's rights with intent to violate federal law.[28] Punitive damages may be imposed pursuant to Title VII without a showing of egregious misconduct. It must be established that the defendant discriminated against the plaintiff, even though there was a perceived risk of violating federal law.[29]

---

[23] Daniels v. Williams, 474 U.S. 327 (1986); Davidson v. Cannon, 474 U.S. 344 (1986).

[24] Wood v. Strickland, 420 U.S. 308 (1975), *reh'g denied*, 421 U.S. 921 (1975).

[25] Saucier v. Katz, 121 S.Ct. 2151 (2001) (holding if an officer made a reasonable mistake as to what the law required, then the officer was entitled to the defense of qualified immunity).

[26] Hope v. Pelzer, 122 S.Ct. 2508 (2002).

[27] Anderson v. Creighton, 483 U.S. 635 (1987).

[28] Smith v. Wade, 461 U.S. 30 (1983).

[29] Kolstad v. American Dental Ass'n, 527 U.S. 526 (1999).

Many states have modified their common law tort rules of personal liability by enacting statutes. Some impose liability on local government officials for conduct that is corrupt, malicious, unauthorized, or for failure to perform certain duties. In addition, there are many statutes that require local governments to provide legal assistance to officers and employees who are sued for injuries arising out of their good faith performance of duty. Some require reimbursement of costs, or indemnification for local officers and employees who are held liable for acts committed in good faith performance of their duties. [30] These statutes vary, and some require reimbursement of costs only if the defendant officer or employee is successful in defending against a claim.

§ 8.7 Civil Service

Many state constitutions, statutes and local charters provide for the regulation of local employment by a civil service or "merit" system. The primary purpose for creating any civil service structure is to foster the objective of hiring qualified individuals for government positions, and eliminate, as far as practicable, the bias, partisanship and favoritism that may result from an appointive system. There is a long history of its use in both federal and state governments.

Often, certain local positions will be exempt from civil service and officers will be elected or appointed by the executive or legislative bodies. [1] This would include those with a specified term of office. In addition, frequently it includes those who are supervisors, or professionals with a particular expertise, and those individuals with an impermanent status. [2] The dismissal of existing employees for political reasons is discussed in § 8.4 *supra*.

Where local civil service commissions regulate the rules of employment, they have generally been delegated wide-ranging authority which they cannot exceed. [3] Typically, the local agencies are subject to state regulations and oversight. Although there is a great deal of variance in local civil service structures, many local commissions classify positions, describe their duties, and develop hiring criteria that may or may not include competitive examinations. If an examination is developed and administered by the local agency, courts will sustain it if it is reasonable [4] and the reasonable procedures prescribed for its administration have been followed. [5] Oral exams are generally sustained, provided the local agency can demonstrate a need for it because the job requires certain traits. It must be administered in the most objective manner possible. [6]

---

[30] Titus v. Lindberg, 228 A.2d 65 (N.J. 1967).

[1] City and County of Denver v. Rinker, 366 P.2d 548 (Colo. 1961).

[2] Civil Service Technical Guild v. LaGuardia, 44 N.Y.S.2d 860 (N.Y. Sup. Ct. 1943), *aff'd*, 55 N.E.2d 49 (N.Y. 1944).

[3] Mullin v. Ringle, 142 A.2d 216 (N.J. 1958).

[4] Short v. Kissinger, 168 N.W.2d 917 (Neb. 1969).

[5] State v. Auburn, 375 P.2d 499 (Wash. 1962).

[6] Kelly v. Civil Serv. Comm'n, 181 A.2d 745 (N.J. 1962).

Usually, local commissions will certify lists of eligible appointees to the local government office with a vacancy. A person is then selected to fill the position from an indicated number of those ranked highest on the list.[7] Persons included on the list do not have a right to be appointed, but are assured that only those eligible may be appointed, for as long as the list is valid.[8] State or local requirements may provide for hiring preferences to be given to veterans. Courts have sustained these when the veteran is otherwise qualified and the degree of preference is reasonable.[9]

Courts have given a wide degree of latitude to civil service commissions, sustaining their classifications and tests if there is a reasonable basis for their determinations.[10] If they wrongfully discriminate, the courts will not hesitate to enjoin the implementation of their decisions.[11] They must act fairly and abide by their own lawfully adopted regulations. The job classifications, requirements and examinations must be reasonably related to job performance. Objective criteria and examinations are generally preferred because they enable effective judicial review and reduce the possibility of subjective bias. However, oral examination and subjective criteria have been sustained by the courts, provided that the qualities sought and tested for are appropriate for the position.[12]

With the growth of privatization of government services, there is much concern about its potential impact on the civil service protections afforded most government employees. A current study indicated that it has not yet had a major impact on the public sector workforce.[13] Courts that have considered whether privatization violates state constitutional, statutory or local mandates for a civil service system have offered differing conclusions. Some, like California,[14] have identified problems, while others have not.[15] As indicated in § 6.5 *supra*, it may depend upon whether the privatized

---

[7] Bloodworth v. Suggs, 60 So. 2d 768 (Fla. 1952).

[8] Schroder v. Kiss, 181 A.2d 41 (N.J. Super. Ct. App. Div. 1962).

[9] McNamara v. Director of Civil Serv., 110 N.E.2d 840 (Mass. 1953).

[10] Dillon v. Nassau Co. Civil Serv. Comm'n, 373 N.E.2d 1225 (N.Y. 1978); Brady v. Dep't of Personnel, 693 A.2d 466 (N.J. 1997).

[11] Jones v. New York City Human Resources Admin., 528 F.2d 696 (2d Cir. 1976), *cert. denied*, 429 U.S. 825 (1976).

[12] *Kelly, supra* note 6 at 750.

[13] *See* John D. Donahue, *Privatization and Public Employment: An Essay on the Current Status and the Stakes*, FORDHAM URBAN LAW JOURNAL, Vol. XXVIII, page 1693 (2001).

[14] Professional Engineers in California Government, 63 Cal. Rptr. 2d 467; Colorado Ass'n of Pub. Employees v. Dep't of Highways, 809 P.2d 988 (Colo. 1991); Horrell v. Dep't of Admin., 861 P.2d 1194 (Colo. 1993); Konno v. Co. of Hawaii, 937 P.2d 397 (Haw. 1997); University of Nevada v. State of Nevada Employees Ass'n, 520 P.2d 602 (Nev. 1974); Washington Federation of State Employees v. Dep't of Social and Health Services, 966 P.2d 322 (Wash. Ct. App. 1998).

[15] Moore v. Dep't of Transp. and Pub. Facilities, 875 P.2d 765 (Alaska 1994); Corwin v. Farrell, 100 N.E.2d 135 (N.Y. 1951); Haub v. Montgomery Co., 727 A.2d 369 (Md. 1999); State *ex rel.* Sigall v. Aetna Cleaning Contractors of Cleveland, Inc., 345 N.E.2d 61 (Ohio 1976), *aff'd*, 345 N.E.2d 61 (Ohio Ct. App. 1976); Vermont State Employees' Ass'n, Inc. v. Vermont Criminal Justice Training Council, 704 A.2d 769 (Vt. 1997).

service is a new function that does not involve any displacement of existing workers.[16] Courts have also differed in their decisions regarding its impact on collective bargaining agreements.[17] Some states have enacted legislation to address potentially troublesome issues. It is possible that many states will reconcile concerns by enacting a statute that there must be no loss of civil service employment as a result of privatization.[18] This solution may still present a conflict with state constitutions, statutes and charters that require government functions to be fulfilled by workers protected by a civil service system.

---

[16] California State Employees Ass'n v. Williams, 86 Cal. Rptr. 305 (Cal. Ct. App. 1970).

[17] Johanson v. Dep't of Soc. and Health Servs., 959 P.2d 1166 (Wash. Ct. App. 1998); City of Belvidere v. Illinois State Labor Relations Bd., 670 N.E.2d 337 (Ill. App. Ct. 1996), aff'd, 692 N.E.2d 295 (Ill. 1998).

[18] For an excellent discussion of this topic, see Featherston, Thornton, and Correnti, State and Local Privatization: An Evolving Process, PUBLIC CONTRACT LAW JOURNAL, Vol. 30, No. 4, Summer 2001.

Chapter 9

Local Government Liability

§ 9.1 Introduction and Chapter Overview

After the American Revolution, the common law provided a shield for the federal government and the states from tort liability. The newly created federal structure of government had assumed the sovereignty that had previously belonged to the King.[1] As a result, most courts held that government would not be liable for the wrongful conduct of its officers and employees. This was based on the old English doctrine that "the King can do no wrong" and whatever the government did was lawful. Any person acting on its behalf that did commit a wrongful act was acting outside the scope of his or her delegated responsibilities.

Local governments, as creations of the states, were also deemed immune when they were engaged in governmental activities.[2] However, over the years, both the legislative and judicial branches have exhibited dissatisfaction with the concept of sovereign immunity. Through both statutes and court opinions, both branches of government have, in most jurisdictions, largely abolished or greatly limited immunity, except for legislative or judicial functions[3] and actions involving the exercise of discretion by local officers.

When immunity was waived, local governments became subject to causes of action based on common law torts that include nuisance, negligence, trespass and inverse condemnation. Today, local governments are also frequently sued under § 1983 of the federal Civil Rights Act. This federal statute does not create a new substantive right but it permits individuals to seek compensation or remedies for harm caused by a local government when it violated their federal rights. This applies to federal constitutional rights and the many statutes that have been enacted to protect against racial, gender, ethnic, age, and disability discrimination. The type of remedy available, whether damages or injunctive relief, and its applicability as either retrospective or solely prospective, has presented some of the more interesting questions for the Supreme Court.

Since it was a choice of government to waive its sovereign immunity, courts have recognized that it is government's prerogative to determine conditions that must be met in pursuing a legal remedy. The plaintiff must

---

[1] *See* OSBORNE M. REYNOLDS, JR., LOCAL GOVERNMENT LAW (2d ed. 2000) *citing* Borchard, *Governmental Responsibility in Tort*, 36 YALE L.J. 1 (1926).

[2] Local governments were first judicially deemed immune in England in 1798 in Russell v. Men of Devon, 2 Term Rep. 667, 100 Eng. Rep. 359 (1798).

[3] *See* § 8.6 *supra.*

strictly comply with notification requirements, filing deadlines, and other steps that are prescribed by the government that is being sued. The courts have dismissed many actions for failure to meet these procedural requirements.

PART I TORT CLAIMS

§ 9.2　Immunity and Liability for Acts of Officers, Employees and Independent Contractors

The early recognition by the courts of common law tort immunity for local governments was generally limited to those actions done by its officers or employees when performing a governmental function. In contrast, courts held local governments responsible for torts committed when the act was done in its proprietary capacity.[1] This attempt to characterize actions into one of these two categories has admittedly caused a great deal of confusion. Even the Supreme Court, in addressing a federalism question, dismissed as unworkable the classification of actions into governmental or proprietary categories.[2] Fortunately, most states have responded to the perceived inequity created by common law tort immunity and have either waived it, requiring that government shall be liable to the same extent as a private individual,[3] or expressly provided for liability or immunity for specific activities.[4]

Although the distinction between governmental and proprietary actions has diminished in importance, it still remains important in some jurisdictions and in other contexts. When a local government engages in activities that have been performed by the private sector, it will most likely be found to be acting in a proprietary capacity. The rationale is that since it is acting as a private party, the local government should be treated the same as a private individual. Thus, it is subject to tort liability, just as a private actor. If there are fees attached to the service, such as for use of a local parking garage, it is generally a proprietary action. Some examples of services that are considered proprietary include sewage disposal, health care facilities and garbage disposal services.[5] In contrast, government functions will typically include such things as legislative activities, enforcement of local requirements, police and fire protection, and the provision of education.[6] Jurisdictions have disagreed in their attempts to classify actions and have themselves changed their designations from time to time.

---

[1] Bailey v. City of New York, 3 Hill 531 (N.Y. 1842).

[2] Garcia v. San Antonio Metropolitan Transit Auth., 488 U.S. 889 (1998).

[3] NY CT. OF CLAIMS ACT Art. II § 8 (McKinney's 1989).

[4] See Narvocki v. Macomb Co. Rd. Comm'n, 615 N.W.2d 702 (Mich. 2000)

[5] City of Miami v. Brooks, 70 So. 2d 306 (Fla. 1954); McGuire v. City of Cedar Rapids, 189 N.W.2d 592 (Iowa 1971); Peters v. City of Medford, 818 P.2d 517 (Or. Ct. App. 1991).

[6] For further discussion, see SANDRA M. STEVENSON, ANTIEAU ON LOCAL GOVERNMENT LAW § 35.07 (2d ed. 1999).

One of the common law concepts that has been used to limit local government tort liability is a declaration of no liability when the officer or employee acts outside his or her delegated authority.[7] The rationale is that if the act was ultra vires, the local government should not be held responsible for the harm that occurs. This is distinguished from a finding of local government liability for authorized acts that were executed in an unreasonable manner. The failure to find liability is solely based on the fact that there was no local authority for the act in the first place. This concept has been adopted by some states and rejected as illogical or unfair by others.[8]

A similar limitation for local liability is based on the doctrine of respondeat superior. If a local government officer or employee negligently causes harm, the local government will generally not be held liable if it is found that the person was acting beyond the scope of his or her employment.[9] The factual determination of what is within the scope of employment is usually decided by a consideration of the job description, the time and space parameters, and whether the act that caused the harm was done with a purpose to serve the local government.

Even when sovereign immunity is abolished the local government may not be liable because there are two major exceptions to local tort liability. They are recognized in most jurisdictions. First, courts have found local immunity from tort liability for acts of officers and employees that are discretionary as opposed to ministerial. An act is discretionary if it involves the use of discretion or judgment by the officer or employee. It requires the exercise of policy evaluation, judgment and expertise.[10] This immunity is consistent with the judicial reluctance to impose personal liability on the officer or employee who has exercised discretion in the performance of a public duty. As explained in § 8.6 *supra*, when a local government officer or employee performs an authorized act that involves choice, judgment or decision-making, he or she will not usually be held personally liable for harm that is caused by the act. In contrast, an act is ministerial when it is prescribed and defined with such precision and certainty that nothing is left to the exercise of discretion or judgment. The allegation is that the officer or employee had authority to act but did not perform the duty in a reasonable manner. There is both personal and local government liability for this action. The policy supporting the tort liability exception for discretionary actions is that honest officers and employees should not be discouraged in their quest to perform their public responsibilities by concerns of potential liability.

---

[7] Posey v. Town of North Birmingham, 45 So. 663 (Ala. 1907); Cunningham v. County Court of Wood County, 134 S.E.2d 725 (W. Va. 1964).

[8] Krantz v. City of Hutchinson, 196 P.2d 227 (Kan. 1948).

[9] Patterson v. City of Phoenix, 436 P.2d 613 (Ariz. 1968).

[10] Some jurisdictions have used limiting language to prevent the inclusion of so-called "operational" activities, granting immunity for discretionary activities that involve "planning," or those acts that involve conscious balancing of risks and advantages. *See* Johnson v. State, 447 P.2d 352 (Cal. 1968). Another prevalent characterization is whether the negligent act is committed while in pursuit of a governmental or proprietary purpose. If the latter, then the negligence of the officer or employee may be imposed upon the local government.

The second major exception to local tort liability is the public duty rule. As explained in § 6.6 *supra*, it recognizes that some duties are owed to the general public, but not to every individual in the community.[11] In other words, a failure to assist or provide adequate protection to an individual does not necessarily result in negligence liability. A local government will not be liable for failure to enforce subdivision regulations,[12] or for its failure to maintain an adequate water supply or working fire hydrants.[13] The policy rationale is based on judicial concern about the fiscal impact of imposing a heavy burden on the taxpayers and inappropriate interference by the judicial branch with the allocation of local resources.[14]

There are significant exceptions to the public-duty rule, generally based upon the existence of a special relationship between the local government and the individual who has suffered an injury. This special relationship involves the assumption of a duty by the service provider. It is created through promises or actions by local officers or employees with their knowledge that failure to act could lead to the individual's harm. It may require direct contact between the individual and the local government, followed by the individual's justifiable and detrimental reliance on the government's assurance of assistance.[15] A special relationship may also be created by the status of the individual. For instance, a government informer who has responded to a request for law enforcement assistance may be owed a duty of care if it is foreseeable that his or her safety is threatened.[16] Some states have rejected the public-duty rule, finding it imposes too great a limitation on local liability.[17]

Litigants have raised the issue of local liability based on the actions of third parties who are not officers or employees of the local government. As a general rule, local governments will not be liable for wrongful acts committed by these individuals. Local governments are not normally responsible for the torts of their independent contractors.[18] However, the Supreme Court has recognized an exception when a special relationship is created between a local government and an individual who is subsequently harmed by a third party. For instance, liability may be found if the plaintiff suffers harm at the hands of a third party while his personal liberty has been restrained by the local government. In that situation, the plaintiff did not have an ability to provide for his or her own personal needs and is dependent on the local government for safekeeping. The restraint that most

---

[11] DeHoney v. Hernandez, 122 Ariz. 367, 595 P.2d 159 (1979)

[12] Stillwater Condominium Ass'n v. Town of Salem, 668 A.2d 38 (N.H. 1995).

[13] Reynolds Boat Co. v. City of Haverhill, 357 Mass. 668, 260 N.E.2d 176 (1970); Stang v. City of Mill Valley, 38 Cal.2d 486, 240 P.2d 980 (1952).

[14] Riss v. City of New York, 240 N.E.2d 860 (1968).

[15] Grieshaber v. City of Albany, 720 N.Y.S.2d 214 (3d Dep't 2001), *appeal denied*, 759 N.E.2d 370 (2001).

[16] Schuster v. City of New York, 154 N.E.2d 534 (1958).

[17] Doucette v. Town of Bristol, 635 A.2d 1387 (N.H. 1993); Leake v. Cain 720 P.2d 152 (Colo. 1986).

[18] Walker v. City of Cedar Rapids, 103 N.W.2d 727 (Iowa 1960).

often creates such a special relationship is government incarceration or involuntary placement in an institution. In defining the extent of this responsibility, the Supreme Court held that such a special relationship was not created when a county department of social services supervised a child who was harmed while in the custody of his father.[19] The Court found this situation differed from taking someone into custody and holding the person against his or her will. In the latter case, the local government has assumed a responsibility for safety because the restraint makes it impossible for the person to care for himself or herself.

§ 9.3 Negligence

A plaintiff must meet the same burden of establishing the elements of a negligence action that he or she would have to meet if suing a private person or entity. These include the establishment of a duty owed by the government, breach of that duty, and harm that is proximately caused by the breach of duty. However, the determination of whether a duty exists is different. In a private tort action, a duty is most often found if the defendant could foresee injury coming to the plaintiff as a result of his or her conduct. The same is usually true of a local government, if it is the *performance of an act* that forms the basis for the claim of negligence. However, if the claim of negligence is based on a *failure to act*, in most cases the courts have hesitated to find a duty. In other words, a duty is more readily found for acts of commission than for an omission to act. This difference is most frequently reflected in cases alleging a failure to provide protection, whether it be through police, fire, or inspection services.[1]

In cases where a plaintiff claims that an officer or employee negligently performed an act within the scope of his or her employment, the basic rules of tort liability apply. The local government is not an insurer of an individual's safety but is merely required to act reasonably. In addition, a plaintiff must establish that the negligent act was the cause of his or her harm. If the harm would have occurred without the negligent act, then liability will not be imposed upon the local government, even though the officer or employee did in fact act negligently. Furthermore, the negligent act must be the proximate cause of the harm. In most jurisdictions, this means that there must be no intervening, superseding cause between the local government's act and the plaintiff's harm, and the type of harm that occurred could have been anticipated when the negligent act was performed.

In cases alleging that an officer or employee was negligent because he or she failed to do something, the plaintiff must pass the hurdle of establishing that the local government in fact owes a duty to the plaintiff. For instance, most jurisdictions have held that it is unreasonable to find that a local police or fire department has a duty to protect every member

---

[19] DeShaney v. Winnebago County Dep't of Social Services, 489 U.S. 189 (1989).

[1] *See* § 6.6 *supra.*

of the public. The duty to provide police or fire protection is owed to the public at large and not to a particular person. The courts have indicated that to find a duty owed to each individual would interfere with the executive or legislative functions of allocating public resources. This *public duty* rule recognizes that determining how local funds are spent, whether on greater police and fire protection or on other types of public services, is not the responsibility of the judiciary. It is sometimes argued that state constitutional or statutory waivers of governmental immunity may call for this result. Many provide that the government is to be liable for its conduct, just as a private party.[2] Since the common law does not require a private individual to render assistance to a person in need, even if it could be done without risk of harm to the rescuer, there is no private corollary to a requirement that local government officers and employees act to provide protection. The public-duty rule is treating government in the same manner as private individuals.

However, there is an exception to the public-duty rule. The courts have imposed liability for inadequate police protection when they have found that a *special duty* is owed to a particular plaintiff. This special duty exception requires that a plaintiff show that the local government has assumed a duty of care for a particular plaintiff. In other words, there is a special relationship between the individual and the government service provider.[3]

All jurisdictions agree that when it is shown that a local government has assumed a duty, it will be held liable for harm that is caused by its failure to act reasonably. It should also be remembered that states can and frequently have changed the common law rules of local government liability by enacting statutes that impose duties or prescribe how liability is to be imposed. Many states have regulated portions of local tort liability by legislative enactments. Often these enactments have raised questions as to whether a particular plaintiff was within the class of individuals that the legislature intended to protect when it enacted the statute.[4]

Defenses that are available to private defendants in torts actions will generally be available to local governments. Most jurisdictions have adopted comparative negligence provisions that will be applied to these cases. A comparison of the degree of negligence between the two parties will result in an apportionment of liability. Thus, the local government will be responsible for only a portion of the damages if it is found that the plaintiff's actions contributed to the harm that occurred.

---

[2] *See* NY CT. OF CLAIMS ACT § 8 (McKinney's 1989).

[3] DeLong v. County of Erie, 457 N.E.2d 717 (N.Y. 1983); Zibbon v. Town of Cheektowaga, 382 N.Y.S.2d 152 (N.Y. A.D. 1976); Greishaber v. City of Albany, 720 N.Y.S.2d 214 (3d Dep't 2001). For further discussion, *see* § 9.2 *supra*.

[4] Garrett v. Holday Inns, Inc., 447 N.E.2d 717 (N.Y. 1983).

§ 9.4   Nuisance, Trespass and Unconstitutional Taking of Property

One of the oldest and most flexible remedies against harm caused by local governments is nuisance. Although courts have admitted that it is difficult to define,[1] a nuisance is generally referred to as an unreasonable condition that unreasonably and substantially interferes with another person's right to use and enjoy his or her land. Local governments are liable for their creation or maintenance of a nuisance, just as an individual would be liable.

Nuisance is a tort action that can usually be brought against a local government without the usual concerns about local government immunity. Courts grant recovery whether the local government has created or maintained a nuisance by an action characterized as proprietary, governmental, ministerial, or discretionary.[2]

Local government nuisances have included the creation or maintenance of sewage lagoons which polluted the water and air,[3] the flow of raw sewage onto adjoining private property,[4] the operation of a garbage disposal facility,[5] or the diversion of water.[6] The nuisance remedy has also been used to address problems created by odors and noises emanating from local government facilities.[7]

While various states have responded differently in their development of the common law tort of nuisance, most recognize the cause of action and allow some form of recovery for both property or personal injury that has been caused by local action.[8] There are courts that have found nuisance liability if the local government has taken some action that resulted in the nuisance, but refused recovery if the wrong was alleged to be based on a local government's failure to act.[9] In other words, failure to remedy a dangerous condition that the local government did not create did not lead to liability.

Some courts have found a property owner estopped from claiming a nuisance if it existed prior to the owner's acquisition of the property, was known or should have been known to the owner, and the offending activity

---

[1] City of Bowman v. Gunnells, 256 S.E.2d 782 (Ga. 1979).

[2] Thompson v. City of Eau Claire, 69 N.W.2d 239 (Wis. 1955); McCuistion v. Huachuca City, 594 P.2d 1037 (Ariz. Ct. App. 1979); Nestle v. City of Santa Monica, 496 P.2d 480 (Cal. 1972). However, an occasional case has held that local governments are not liable if the activity can be labeled governmental. *See* Dionne v. City of Trenton, 261 N.W.2d 273 (Mich. Ct. App. 1977).

[3] Hartzler v. Town of Kalona, 218 N.W.2d 608 (Iowa 1974); Kriener v. Turkey Valley Community School District, 212 N.W.2d 526 (Iowa 1973).

[4] City of Columbus v. Myszka, 272 S.E.2d 302 (Ga. 1980); Dempsey v. City of Souris, 279 N.W.2d 418 (N.D. 1979).

[5] Milan v. City of Bethlehem, 94 A.2d 774 (Pa. 1953).

[6] Walton v. City of Bozeman, 588 P.2d 518 (Mont. 1978); Anderson v. Columbus, 264 S.E.2d 251 (Ga. Ct. App. 1979).

[7] Edge v. City of Booneville, 83 So. 2d 801 (Miss. 1955).

[8] DeGarmo v. City of Alcoa, 332 F.2d 403 (6th Cir. 1964).

[9] Wright v. Brown, 356 A.2d 176 (Conn. 1975).

has not changed unexpectedly in its scope.[10] Other jurisdictions have by statute, constitution, or common law, limited liability in certain situations.[11] Limitations have excluded nuisance liability for certain conditions on local government land, or have imposed a requirement that there must be a continuous or repetitious act by the local government in order to find a nuisance.[12]

Although jurisdictions differ on how they handle this tort, courts have awarded both injunctive and monetary relief in nuisance actions. The assessment of the amount of compensable damages for permanent property depreciation caused by the nuisance will most likely be based on the difference in market values. Where temporary, it may be based on the decrease in rental or usable value. An amount may be added to both as compensation for the personal inconvenience or annoyance suffered by the plaintiff.

Local governments are also liable for their trespasses, whether caused by a proprietary or governmental action.[13] If local officers or employees enter upon private property, without any right to do so and even for a governmental purpose, the local government may be liable.[14]

Courts have sometimes used the label of "continuing trespass" where a local government has unlawfully built or installed something on private property. For instance, when a local government installed a storm sewer on private property without the owner's permission, the court found that it was continuing trespass and the government was liable to a subsequent owner of the land.[15] They have also been held liable under a trespass cause of action for diverting waters and flooding private lands where it was found that the local government caused the intrusion of the water onto the person's land.[16]

The federal and state constitutions require that just compensation be paid when private property is taken by a local government for a public purpose. Private property is taken by local governments when there is a physical occupation,[17] or a regulation that deprives an owner of the economically viable use of land,[18] or a regulation that fails to substantially

---

[10] Champeau v. Vill. of Little Chute, 81 N.W.2d 562 (Wis. 1957).

[11] Bragg v. City of Dallas, 605 S.W.2d 669 (Tex. Civ. App. 1980) (holding that a condition on local government land that is dangerous or hazardous to persons coming on the land is not a "nuisance" within the exception to the rule of governmental liability in the state constitution).

[12] City of Bowman v. Gunnells, 256 S.E.2d 782 (Ga. 1979); Trussell Servs., Inc. v. City of Montezuma, 386 S.E.2d 732 (Ga. Ct. App. 1989).

[13] Hathaway v. Osborne, 55 A. 700 (R.I. 1903); City and County of Denver v. Talarico, 61 P.2d 1 (Colo. 1936).

[14] *Hathaway*, 55 A. 700.

[15] Rosenthal v. City of Crystal Lake, 525 N.E.2d 1176 (Ill. Ct. App. 1988).

[16] Starcevich v. City of Farmington, 443 N.E.2d 737 (Ill. Ct. App. 1982); Corrington v. Kalicak, 319 S.W.2d 888 (Mo. App. 1959).

[17] Loretto v. Teleprompter Manhattan CATV Corp., 458 U.S. 419 (1982).

[18] Keystone Bituminous Coal Ass'n v. DeBenedictis, 480 U.S. 470 (1987), *quoting* Agins v. City of Tiburon, 447 U.S. 255 (1980).

advance a legitimate government interest.[19] Some state constitutions also require payment when private property is damaged.[20]

Local governments can take private property in different ways. It can be taken through the exercise of *eminent domain* or by government actions that do not comply with such formalities. The latter is often referred to as *inverse condemnation*. Some examples of actions that have led to this characterization are physical invasions, including permanent flooding of private land during the construction of a dam,[21] and repeated flights over private land by low-flying airplanes.[22] Whether the physical appropriation fosters a public purpose or whether it deprives the owner of all economically valuable use of the land is irrelevant to a determination of whether this is an unconstitutional taking that requires compensation. Once it is established that part or all of someone's property has been physically taken by a local government, there is a duty to pay compensation. The Supreme Court refers to these physical takings as *categorical takings*.[23]

Property can also be taken when a local government uses its regulatory authority in a manner that unconstitutionally deprives the owner of its use. The *regulatory taking* presents difficult issues because local governments have been delegated authority to adopt reasonable and constitutionally sound regulations of the use of private property. The question to be answered in determining whether a regulatory taking has occurred is whether the regulation imposes such a restriction on the use of the property that it produces nearly the same result as a direct taking. This is discussed in § 4.5 *supra*.

The Supreme Court has held that temporary regulatory takings, which deny a property owner all use of the property for a temporary period of time, are not different in kind from permanent takings. For instance, when a county prohibited construction in an area on an interim basis, the Court found that compensation could be claimed for that temporary time period.[24]

PART II CONSTITUTIONAL, CIVIL RIGHTS AND ANTITRUST CLAIMS

§ 9.5 Constitutional Claims

The Federal Constitution and the individual state constitutions provide strong protection for individuals from governmental power exercised in an

---

[19] Nollan v. California Coastal Comm'n, 483 U.S. 825 (1987).

[20] Elliott v. Los Angeles County, 191 P. 899 (Cal. 1920); Johnson v. Steele Co., 60 N.W.2d 32 (Minn. 1953).

[21] United States v. Lynah, 188 U.S. 445 (1903).

[22] Griggs v. Allegheny County, 369 U.S. 84 (1962).

[23] Tahoe-Sierra Preservation Council, Inc. v. Tahoe Regional Planning Agency, 535 U.S. 302 (2002).

[24] First English Evangelical Lutheran Church of Glendale v. Los Angeles County, 482 U.S. 304 (1987).

arbitrary or impermissible manner. A federal statute, § 1983 of the Civil Rights Act,[1] provides an effective remedy for those who seek redress of violations of their federal constitutional and statutory rights from local governments.[2]

Local enactments are presumed to be constitutional and reasonable unless they limit basic constitutional freedoms of individuals, or create suspect classifications of people. The courts will review local action with increased strictness if the regulation is such that it is applied differently to members of a particular group of people, or if it restricts activities specifically protected by constitutional provisions such as the First and Fifteenth Amendments.[3]

The Privileges and Immunities, Due Process, and Equal Protection Clauses shield against the unreasonable or impermissibly discriminatory exercise of governmental authority. Together, they require that restrictions on individual conduct must be narrowly and clearly tailored, and justified by a legitimate government purpose. The Privileges and Immunities Clause gives people the right to enjoy the same privileges and immunities as others within the same community. It was successfully used to prevent a state from imposing a one-year residency requirement before a family was eligible for maximum welfare benefits. However, it does not prevent reasonable residency requirements for activities such as voting, obtaining hunting licenses, divorces or lower tuition charges.[4]

The broad sweep of the Commerce Clause prohibits local government restrictions on interstate commerce that create undue burdens, are unreasonable, or improperly discriminate between out-of-state and in-state commerce. Typically, the local government cases have been concerned with regulations that treat local citizens or businesses preferentially to those who live outside the jurisdiction. An example is the imposition of a commuter tax on non-city residents that was found to violate the Commerce Clause.[5]

The Equal Protection Clause shelters citizens from the arbitrary, unreasonable or invidiously discriminatory exercise of local power. The Supreme Court has held that the purpose of equal protection is to protect against intentional and arbitrary discrimination in express terms of a law or by improper execution of authority by government officers or employees. Local governments may classify and even discriminate if the differentiation of treatment is reasonable.[6] However, the Supreme Court held that even a *single* individual, who has been intentionally treated differently from others who are similarly situated, has a cause of action against a local government

---

[1] 42 U.S.C. § 1983 (1994).

[2] *See infra* § 9.6 for a discussion of § 1983.

[3] *See supra* § 2.4 for further discussion of constitutional protections.

[4] Saenz v. Roe, 526 U.S. 489 (1999).

[5] City of New York v. State, 730 N.E.2d 920 (N.Y. 2000).

[6] Johnson v. Transp. Agency Santa Clara County, 480 U.S. 616 (1987).

if there is no rational basis for the difference in treatment.[7] The Court said that it is not necessary to show discrimination against a *group* of people.

The Equal Protection Clause also provides a very important substantive right to participate in the electoral process on an equal basis with other qualified voters. This right, in tandem with the Fifteenth Amendment, has had an enormous impact on the way that local governments must apportion their communities for local elections. It insures that each person's vote is of equal worth.[8]

The First Amendment gives citizens the right to seek the court's protection against local government action that unreasonably deprives them of their right to communicate, associate or worship as they choose. This protects those who frequent adult-entertainment establishments,[9] as well as those who engage in public protests.[10] The right to free speech is sometimes referred to as a "preferred" right because it is afforded more extensive protection from government infringement than some other rights.[11] Regulations that impinge on this freedom by seeking to control the content of speech are subjected to strict scrutiny review, requiring that they be narrowly tailored to meet a compelling governmental interest.[12] Those that impose less intrusive restrictions by regulating the time, place and manner of speech must be reasonable and narrowly drawn to serve a substantial government interest.[13] In addition, local regulations must not be overly broad or vague.[14] Local requirements for permits and licenses to exercise First Amendment rights must also be reasonable, narrowly drawn, without prohibitory fees or charges, and not subject to the unbridled discretion of the issuing officer.[15]

The Fifth and Fourteenth Amendments prohibit local government from taking private property without compensation or depriving a person of his or her property without due process of law.[16] This applies to both physical and regulatory takings. If a local government arbitrarily denies a license or permit to an applicant, it may be found to have deprived an individual

---

[7] Village of Willowbrook v. Olech, 528 U.S. 562 (2000).

[8] *See supra* § 7.6 for further discussion of the Fifteenth Amendment and the Equal Protection Clause in the context of local elections and the citizen right to vote.

[9] *See supra* § 3.4 for further discussion of the local regulation of adult use activities and the First Amendment.

[10] *See supra* § 3.6 for further discussion of the local regulation of speech and movement of individuals and the First Amendment.

[11] Murdock v. Pennsylvania, 319 U.S. 105 (1943).

[12] Police Dep't of Chicago v. Mosley, 408 U.S. 92 (1972). *See also* Boos v. Barry, 485 U.S. 312 (1988) (stating that content-based restriction on political speech in a public forum must be subjected to the most exacting scrutiny). *But see* Burson v. Freeman, 504 U.S. 191 (1992) (sustaining regulation that met the test).

[13] Ward v. Rock Against Racism, 491 U.S. 781 (1989).

[14] Broadrick v. Oklahoma, 413 U.S. 601 (1973).

[15] Forsyth County v. Nationalist Movement, 505 U.S. 123 (1992).

[16] *See supra* §§ 4.5 and 9.4 for further discussion of unconstitutional taking of property by local governments.

of property without due process of law.[17] A remedy may be sought by the aggrieved party who claims a violation of substantive due-process rights. Likewise, a local officer or employee, who is not afforded a hearing or a right to confront witnesses against him or her before losing a job, may be able to successfully seek a remedy by claiming a violation of procedural due-process rights if it is found that he or she has a constitutionally protected property interest in continued employment.[18]

Claims of federal constitutional violations that are brought against local governments are typically brought under § 1983 of the Civil Rights Act, discussed in § 9.6 *infra*. In addition to injunctive relief, the full range of compensatory damages may be awarded. However, the Supreme Court has held that an abstract value for the loss of constitutional rights is not an appropriate element of the compensation amount.[19] Punitive damages are not imposed on local governments. They may be awarded against officers or employees, as individuals, if there is evidence of an intentional action taken with malice or reckless indifference to the federal rights of a person.[20] The court, in its discretion, may award reasonable attorney's fees to a prevailing party in a § 1983 action.[21]

§ 9.6　Section 1983 Actions

Often plaintiffs will sue local governments in federal court under the Federal Civil Rights Act, and particularly, § 1983 which provides:

> Every person who, under color of any statute, ordinance, regulation, custom or usage, of any state or territory, subjects, or causes to be subjected, any citizen of the United States or other person within the jurisdiction thereof to the deprivation of any rights, privileges or immunities secured by the Constitution and laws, shall be liable to the party injured in an action at law, suit in equity, or other proper proceeding for redress.[1]

Since this statute applies to "persons," it does not provide a remedy against wrongful action done by a state government. The Supreme Court has determined that state officers and employees may be sued in their official capacity for injunctive relief.[2] However, the Court has held that local governments, as independent legal entities, are "persons" within the meaning of the statute and are subject to suit for violations of federal rights.[3] Similarly, as discussed in § 8.6 *supra*, individual local officers and employees may be found personally liable for harm caused by their actions.

---

[17] Town of Orangetown v. Magee, 643 N.Y.S.2d 21 (N.Y. 1996); Villager Pond, Inc. v. Town of Darien, 56 F.3d 375 (2d Cir. 1995).

[18] Small v. Inhabitants of City of Belfast, 796 F.2d 544 (1st Cir. 1986).

[19] Memphis Cmty. Sch. Dist. v. Stachura, 477 U.S. 299 (1986).

[20] Kolstad v. American Dental Ass'n, 527 U.S. 526 (1999).

[21] THE CIVIL RIGHTS ATTORNEY'S FEES AWARDS ACT OF 1976, 42 U.S.C. § 1988 (1994).

[1] 42 U.S.C. § 1983 (1994).

[2] Will v. Michigan Dep't of State Police, 491 U.S. 58 (1989).

[3] Monell v. Dep't of Soc. Servs. of City of New York, 436 U.S. 658 (1978).

Section 1983 does not create a new substantive right. It simply provides a powerful remedy for the violation of federal constitutional or statutory rights. In using it, a plaintiff may seek monetary, declaratory or injunctive relief from an official government policy or custom that deprives him or her of a right, privilege or immunity that is secured by federal law.[4]

In order to recover in a § 1983 action brought against a local government, a plaintiff must establish that the offending act was done under color of law, it deprived the plaintiff of a federally protected right, and the deprivation caused injury to the plaintiff. To meet the first requirement, the Supreme Court has held that local governments can be held liable only when the harm has been caused by the execution of a local government policy or custom.[5] It is not enough that a local officer or employee deprived plaintiff of a federal right. The local governments are not liable under a respondeat superior theory.[6] For liability, the officer or employee must have acted pursuant to a local government policy or custom.

In determining what action qualifies as a policy or custom, it has been held that it must have been established by legislators or by those whose edicts or acts may fairly be considered to represent official policy.[7] In more simple terms, a local government is liable for violations that result from decisions of its legislative body or of local officials whose acts are fairly considered those of the local government.[8]

There are many cases that address the question of whether an officer's action reflects a policy or custom of the local government. The Supreme Court has cautioned that rigorous standards of culpability and causation must be used in order to prevent the government from being held liable for actions that are solely those of its employee.[9] It has been held that only officials who have authority to make final policy, as determined by state law, may subject local governments to liability under § 1983. However, the Supreme Court has also determined that it may be sufficient to show that a policymaker made a single decision that resulted in a constitutional violation.[10] In the case that presented the issue, a county sheriff hired his nephew's son, in spite of said individual's previous questionable record. The nephew's son proceeded to violate an individual's constitutional rights. The Court indicated that where inadequate screening is alleged, a plaintiff will have to meet an extremely high burden by showing that it would have been plainly obvious that the person hired would inflict the harm that occurred.[11]

---

[4] Maine v. Thiboutot, 448 U.S. 1 (1980) (providing that a violation of any federal law may give rise to a § 1983 action).

[5] *Monell, supra* n. 3 at 690.

[6] Jett v. Dallas Indep. Sch. Dist., 491 U.S. 701 (1989), *on remand,* 7 F.3d 1231 (5th Cir. 1993); City of Phoenix v. Yarnell, 909 P.2d 377 (Ariz. 1995).

[7] *Monell, supra* n. 3 at 694; City of Canton v. Harris, 489 U.S. 378 (1989).

[8] Board of County Comm'rs of Bryan Co. v. Brown, 520 U.S. 397 (1997).

[9] Pembaur v. City of Cincinnati, 475 U.S. 469 (1986).

[10] *Board of County Comm'rs of Bryan Co., supra* n. 8 at 404.

[11] *Id.*

If there is a written policy of a local government that violates an individual's constitutional rights, the "color of law" requirement is met.[12] In addition, even if an action has not been formally approved by the local government or reduced to writing, the existence of a pattern of local government conduct that violates constitutional rights may be found to be a custom or policy that will subject the local government to liability.[13]

Another means of meeting the "color of law" requirement is for a plaintiff to establish that the local government has failed to train, supervise, or discipline its employees. This failure is used to indicate a deliberate indifference by the local government of the likelihood that a non-policymaking employee would commit a constitutional violation. In *City of Canton v. Harris*,[14] the Supreme Court held that inadequate training can be found to be a local "policy" where it amounts to a deliberate indifference to the rights of people.[15] It can form the basis for a § 1983 action where the need for more or different training is so obvious and the inadequacy so likely to result in a violation of rights that the policymakers have been deliberately indifferent to the need. This means that they knew or should have known that a failure to train, supervise, or discipline would lead to a constitutional violation of someone's rights. Deliberate indifference has also been shown by the characteristics of the government activity. If it is obvious that a lack of training in a particular area may lead to deprivation of constitutional rights, then a failure to provide it may lead to local government liability. In other situations, deliberate indifference is shown by a pattern of constitutional violations that preceded the act that violated the plaintiff's rights. In other words, the local government should have known that some training, supervision or discipline was needed and it was not forthcoming.

As a further safeguard for local governments, the Supreme Court has required that there be a direct causal link between a policy or custom of the local government and the harm that occurred.[16] Even if deliberate indifference to the constitutional rights of people is established, the plaintiff will still have to show that the specific inadequacies in training caused the harm that was sustained.[17]

Since the Supreme Court has held that there is no federal due process right to be free from the negligence of government officials, § 1983 may not be used to pursue negligence claims. They must be brought under state tort laws.[18] Similarly, the Court has also determined that the Due Process

---

[12] *Monell, supra* n. 3 at 682.

[13] Bordanaro v. McLeod, 871 F.2d 1151 (1st Cir. 1989), *cert. denied*, 493 U.S. 820 (1989) (holding that even if there is no proof of actual knowledge of a policy, it may be sufficient if there is evidence of constructive knowledge of a widespread and longstanding practice).

[14] *City of Canton, supra* n. 7.

[15] *Id.* at 388.

[16] *Jett, supra* n. 6 at 735-36.

[17] Kibbe v. City of Springfield, 777 F.2d 801 (1st Cir. 1985).

[18] Daniels v. Williams, 474 U.S. 327 (1986); Davidson v. Cannon, 474 U.S. 344 (1986).

Clause does not require that local governments provide a workplace that is free of unreasonable risks.[19] Nor does it require that local government provide its citizens protective services or when it chooses to do so that it be done in a competent or adequate manner. However, there is a Substantive Due Process violation when the manner in which a local service is provided shocks the conscience.[20]

Courts have held that an unreasonable and arbitrary denial or revocation of a permit or license may be considered a deprivation of property without due process that supports a § 1983 action.[21]

There are no specific statutes of limitations governing federal civil rights actions. The Supreme Court has held that courts should use state statutes of limitations for personal injury actions. State or local immunity enactments and notice of claim requirements are inapplicable to this federal remedy. A plaintiff is not required to exhaust administrative or other state remedies before filing a § 1983 claim, unless specifically required by statute.[22] Compensatory damages and attorney's fees may be available whether the action is brought in state or federal court.

§ 9.7　Other Federal Civil Rights Acts

Federal legislation adopted to prevent unfair competition or discrimination on the basis of race, age, gender or disabilities has affected the operation and activities of local government in many ways. The Supreme Court has determined that individuals have a private right of action against a government entity that has or is violating a civil right created by federal statute, if that right is established by Congress. It cannot be created by a federal agency in its promulgation of a regulation.[1] Some of the most frequently used federal civil rights legislation are 42 U.S.C. §§ 1981, 1982, 1983 and 1985(3).

Section 1981 of the Civil Rights Act[2] prohibits intentional racial discrimination[3] in the right to contract. It has been frequently used to challenge local government employment decisions and public housing regulations. It is necessary to establish a basis for the action that indicates an unlawful policy or custom of the local government, since it may not be based solely on a respondeat superior relationship between the offending officer or employee and the local government.[4]

---

[19] Collins v. Harker Heights, 503 U.S. 115 (1992).

[20] Co. of Sacramento v. Lewis, 523 U.S. 833 (1997). *See also* Douglas v. Commonwealth of Pa. Dept. of Health Emergency Medical Servs Training Inst., 318 F.3d 473 (3d Cir. 2003).

[21] Town of Orangetown v. Magee, 643 N.Y.S.2d 21 (1996); Shaw v. California Dep't of Alcoholic Beverage Control, 788 F.2d 600 (9th Cir. 1986).

[22] Booth v. Churner, 532 U.S. 731 (2001).

[1] Alexander v. Sandoval, 531 U.S. 1049 (2000).

[2] 42 U.S.C. § 1981 (1994).

[3] General Building Contractors Ass'n, Inc. v. Pennsylvania, 458 U.S. 375 (1982).

[4] Jett v. Dallas Indep. Sch. Dist., 491 U.S. 701 (1989).

Section 1982 similarly prohibits discrimination in the right to inherit, purchase, lease, sell, hold and convey real and personal property.[5] It has been used to challenge racially restrictive covenants in housing subdivisions and is used in conjunction with the Fair Housing Act.

Section 1985(3)[6] is similar to § 1983 in that it does not create a new substantive right. It creates a means of seeking a remedy against those who conspire, with a racial purpose or motive, to deprive others of their civil rights. The Supreme Court held that to recover using it, one must have been injured in his person or property or deprived of any right or privilege by a conspiracy that was motivated by racial discrimination or by another class-based invidiously discriminatory purpose.[7] It has a second provision that provides a remedy for conspiracies to prevent or hinder government from giving or securing the equal protection of the laws.

Section 1986,[8] with its one-year statute of limitations, creates a cause of action that may be brought against a person who could have prevented or aided in the prevention of a § 1985 violation, but knowingly refused to do so.[9] This has been used against law enforcement authorities and other public officials.[10]

Title II of the Civil Rights Act of 1964[11] prohibits discrimination on the basis of race, color, religion, or national origin in overnight accommodations, restaurants, and recreational facilities. It is applicable to private entities subject to regulation under the Commerce Clause, and to governments.

Title VI[12] prohibits all discrimination based on race, color, or national origin in programs or activities that receive federal funding. The local activities that are most affected by this include employment, education, housing, and public services. The Supreme Court has determined that individuals may recover compensatory damages under Title VI for intentional discrimination, but there is no private right of action to enforce regulations promulgated by federal agencies.[13]

One of the most frequently used Civil Rights Act provisions is Title VII, which prohibits discrimination based on race, color, religion, sex, or national origin against individuals in the hiring, firing, compensation, terms, conditions or privileges of employment.[14] Illegal discrimination in employment may be shown either by "disparate treatment," which is intentional

---

[5] 42 U.S.C. § 1982 (1994).

[6] 42 U.S.C. § 1985(3) (1994).

[7] Griffin v. Breckenridge, 403 U.S. 88 (1971); Bray v. Alexandria Women's Health Clinic, 506 U.S. 263 (1993).

[8] 42 U.S.C. § 1986 (1994).

[9] Clark v. Clabaugh, 20 F.3d 1290 (3d Cir. 1994).

[10] Farmer v. Brennan, 511 U.S. 825 (1994).

[11] 42 U.S.C. § 2000(a) (1994).

[12] 42 U.S.C. § 2000(d) (1994).

[13] *Alexander, supra* n. 1 at 280.

[14] 42 U.S.C. §§ 2000(e)–2000(e)(15) (1994).

discrimination of a particular individual, or by "disparate impact," which relieves the plaintiff from establishing intent to discriminate but requires that it be shown that the employer's conduct had that effect. If intent can be shown, both Title VII and the Equal Protection Clause may be used to seek a remedy. The statute provides an employer a defense to work policies or rules that facially discriminate in hiring on the basis of gender, religion or national origin, on the grounds that one of these characteristics is a "bona fide occupational qualification."[15] It must be related to a trait that goes to the "essence" of the business and have a high correlation to the employee's ability to perform a particular job.[16]

If the plaintiff relies on a disparate impact argument, instead of intent to discriminate, then Title VII must be used instead of the Equal Protection Clause. A prima facie case is shown by evidence indicating that what may appear to be a facially-neutral employment practice has, in fact, a discriminatory impact because its effect is significantly different on a particular class of people. If the defendant can rebut this by showing that the practice is manifestly related to the employment or is a business necessity,[17] the plaintiff then will be required to establish that the employer's action was a mere pretext for discrimination.[18] Title VII was amended by the Civil Rights Act of 1991 so that a plaintiff does not have to disprove other reasons given for the practice,[19] nor does he or she have to show that a particular employment practice results in the disparate impact if the employer's decision-making process has intertwined factors.[20] This statute also provides that where prohibited discrimination is a motivating factor for the employment practice, the practice is unlawful even if there are other factors that also motivate it.

The Supreme Court has held that Title VII prohibits sexual harassment which is so severe or pervasive that it alters the conditions of the employment and creates an abusive working environment.[21] Title VII has often been successfully used to challenge employment decisions that have been tainted with unlawful discrimination based on gender. As amended in 1991, an employment decision motivated in part by such discrimination violates

---

[15] 42 U.S.C. § 2000e-2 (1994).

[16] Western Air Lines, Inc. v. Criswell, 472 U.S. 400 (1985); U.A.W. v. Johnson Controls, 499 U.S. 187 (1991) (holding that the limitation must apply to the particular position, not just be essential to the business as a whole).

[17] A Supreme Court decision, Antonio v. Wards Cove Packing Co., Inc., 513 U.S. 809 (1994), interpreted the requirement so that an employer need only show a business justification for the practice, but the CRA of 1991 amended the Act to require that an employer show a business necessity after a plaintiff establishes disparate impact.

[18] Griggs v. Duke Power Co., 401 U.S. 424 (1971); Connecticut v. Teal, 457 U.S. 440, (1982); Albemarle Paper Co. v. Moody, 422 U.S. 405 (1975).

[19] 42 U.S.C. § 2000e-2(k)(1)(A)(i) (1994).

[20] 42 U.S.C. § 2000e-2(k)(1)(B)(i) (1994).

[21] Meritor Savings Bank, FSB v. Vinson, 477 U.S. 57 (1986). See also SANDRA M. STEVENSON, ANTIEAU ON LOCAL GOVERNMENT LAW § 76.19 (2d ed. 2002) for further discussion on Sexual Harassment liability.

Title VII even though an employer can show that the same decision would have been made for other reasons.[22]

Affirmative action plans that have been adopted by local governments have raised an issue of reverse discrimination and have been subject to challenge under the Equal Protection Clause and Title VII. The Supreme Court has permitted them, on a limited basis, as a means of remedying illegal past discrimination. All plans that involve racial classifications must be reviewed with strict scrutiny to determine whether the means chosen to reach a goal are specifically and narrowly drawn. They cannot be used to remedy general societal discrimination that has occurred in the past. There must be some showing of prior discrimination by the government unit now involved in seeking a remedy.[23] In reviewing a minority contractor set-aside plan, the Court held that it had not been shown that the city's construction industry had discriminated in the past and, therefore, the local government failed to demonstrate a current compelling purpose in apportioning public contracts on the basis of race.[24] In addition to showing a particular reason for an affirmative action plan, the Court also held that such plans must be temporary and have a defined goal as a termination point.[25] Courts have broad equitable authority under Title VII to remedy violations. The Civil Rights Act of 1991[26] authorized jury trials and compensatory and punitive damages for intentional violations.

Title VIII of the Civil Rights Act of 1968 is known as the Fair Housing Act,[27] which is also discussed in § 6.8 *supra*. It prohibits discrimination in a broad range of activities relating to housing, including financing and brokerage services, zoning practices, and the provision of public services. In 1988, amendments to the Act added a prohibition against discrimination based on disabilities.[28] The Supreme Court has determined that in the absence of special circumstances the Act does not impose vicarious liability upon the owners or officers of a residential real estate corporation for the discriminatory acts of employees who typically act on behalf of the corporation.[29]

Title IX of the Civil Rights Act prohibits sex discrimination in educational programs receiving federal funds.[30] It is applicable to all activities of a local government if any part receives federal financial assistance.

---

[22] 42 U.S.C. § 2000e-2(m) (1994).

[23] Wygant v. Jackson Bd. of Educ., 476 U.S. 267 (1986).

[24] City of Richmond v. J.A. Croson Co., 488 U.S. 469 (1989).

[25] Johnson v. Transp. Agency Santa Clara County, 480 U.S. 616 (1987).

[26] Pub. L. No. 102-166, 105 Stat. 1071 (codified at 42 U.S.C. § 1981).

[27] 42 U.S.C. § 3601 *et seq.* (1995).

[28] 42 U.S.C. § 3604 (1995).

[29] Meyer v. Holley, 123 S.Ct. 824 (2003).

[30] 20 U.S.C. § 1681 *et seq.* (1999).

§ 9.8   Americans With Disabilities and Age Discrimination in Employment Act

Many federal statutes prohibit discriminatory conduct against certain classes of vulnerable individuals. The Americans With Disabilities Act (ADA) prohibits discrimination against qualified individuals on the basis of their disabilities in any of the terms, conditions, or privileges of employment; public services and transportation; public accommodations; and telecommunications.[1] The ADA protects not only those who currently are disabled, but also those who are discriminated against because of a past disability or a perceived disability. Homosexuality, bisexuality, compulsive gambling, kleptomania and pyromania are not considered disabilities. Illegal drug users are not included in the protections unless an individual has completed or is participating in a supervised rehabilitation program and is no longer using drugs.

A person is considered disabled under the ADA if he or she has a physical or mental impairment that substantially limits one or more major life activities. The Supreme Court, in clarifying who is to be considered disabled, held that an impairment must prevent or restrict a person from performing tasks that are of central importance to most people's daily lives. The analysis cannot be limited to a class of manual tasks, such as those involved in a lower court's erroneous determination that a person was disabled because she was unable to do repetitive work with her hands and arms extended at or above shoulder level because she had carpal tunnel syndrome.[2]

The Supreme Court has also determined that before someone is considered disabled, consideration must be given to corrective measures. Two nearsighted applicants for airline pilot positions were found not to be disabled because their vision was normal when wearing corrective lenses.[3] In addition, the Court noted that the ADA permits an employer to prefer some physical attributes and the position of pilot is only one job among a broad range of jobs. The argument that a person has been unlawfully discriminated against because of an inability to qualify for a particular position has not received sympathetic treatment by the courts.

The ADA requires that employers make reasonable accommodations for disabled job applicants and for employees in order to enable them to perform essential functions of the job, unless it would result in undue hardship. This requirement has led to a great deal of litigation. An employee who was an airlines cargo handler requested a transfer to a job in the mail room and the employer refused because it would have been inconsistent with its seniority policy. The Supreme Court sustained the employer's refusal by holding that, ordinarily, it is unreasonable to require

---

[1] 42 U.S.C. § 12112 (1995).

[2] Toyota Motor Mfg., Ky., Inc. v. Williams, 534 U.S. 184 (2002).

[3] Sutton v. United Airlines, Inc., 527 U.S. 471 (1999). *See also* Murphy v. United Parcel Service, Inc., 527 U.S. 516 (1999) (stating that high blood pressure that can be controlled by medication did not substantially limit one or more major life activities).

an employer to adopt an accommodation that is in conflict with its seniority rules.[4]

Disability-based harassment against a qualified individual is also prohibited by the ADA. An action may be brought, based on discrimination in the terms, conditions, and privileges of employment.[5]

The Act also prohibits discrimination against the disabled in the areas of public services, accommodations, transportation and telecommunication services. The Supreme Court has held that the isolation and segregation of the disabled is prohibited. States must provide community-based treatment for the mentally disabled when it is determined to be appropriate, not opposed by the affected person, and it can be reasonably accommodated considering the public resources available and the needs of others with mental disabilities.[6]

The Supreme Court has also interpreted the prohibition of discrimination in public accommodations to require the nonprofit Professional Golf Association to permit a disabled golfer to use a golf cart in its activities.[7] Even though there was a requirement that participants walk, the Court held that it was not a modification that would fundamentally alter the nature of the events.

In many respects the ADA is similar to Title VII of the Civil Rights Act. The same enforcement provisions of Title VII apply.[8] Courts may award back pay, require that certain people be hired and have discretion to grant other equitable remedies deemed appropriate. Attorney fees may also be awarded to a prevailing party in a judicial or administrative action.

The Age Discrimination in Employment Act (ADEA) prohibits discrimination based on age against employees over forty years old, with exceptions that include firefighters and law enforcement officers.[9] The statute also permits age restrictions based on bona fide occupational qualifications or restrictions based upon reasonable factors other than age. An employer may raise these as a defense.

Plaintiffs who bring ADEA cases meet their burden of establishing age discrimination if they can prove an intent to discriminate. However, most do not have direct evidence and must rely on circumstantial evidence. Courts have relied on a test established in a Title VII discrimination case to define the division of burdens and standards of proof in the ADEA cases.[10] Plaintiff must first establish a prima facie case by showing that he or she was

---

[4] U.S. Airways, Inc. v. Barnett, 535 U.S. 391 (2002).

[5] Fox v. General Motors Corp., 247 F.3d 169 (4th Cir. 2001); Flowers v. Southern Regional Physician Services Inc., 247 F.3d 229 (5th Cir. 2001). *But see* Cannice v. Norwest Bank Iowa, N.A., 189 F.3d 723 (8th Cir. 1999).

[6] Olmstead v. L.C., 527 U.S. 581 (1999).

[7] PGA Tour, Inc. v. Casey Martin, 532 U.S. 661 (2001).

[8] 42 U.S.C. § 12117(a) (1995).

[9] 29 U.S.C. § 621 *et seq.* (1999).

[10] McDonnell Douglas v. Green, 411 U.S. 792 (1973).

discharged, qualified for the job, was within the protected class at the time of the discharge, and was replaced by someone outside the protected class or by someone younger in the class. The burden then shifts to the defendant employer to rebut the presumption of discrimination with a legitimate reason for the rejection or dismissal. If this is met, then the plaintiff has the burden of proving that the reason is a pretext for the alleged age discrimination. The Supreme Court has held that a plaintiff's prima facie case, combined with sufficient evidence that the employer's justification is false, may be sufficient without additional evidence of discrimination.[11]

The Supreme Court has determined that the Eleventh Amendment prevents Congress from providing for private lawsuits seeking damages against states for violations of the ADEA[12] or the ADA.[13] However, since the Eleventh Amendment does not apply to local governments,[14] they may be sued by individuals in private actions for their violations of both statutes.

§ 9.9 Antitrust

In 1943, the Supreme Court held that the federal antitrust laws do not prevent a state "as sovereign" from imposing regulations that may be prohibited to persons under the Sherman Act.[1] However, in 1978, the Court held that local governments are not states, they are "persons" subject to the antitrust laws.[2] The Court explained that the Parker doctrine exempts only anti-competitive conduct engaged in as an act of government by the state as a sovereign ". . . or by its subdivisions, pursuant to State policy. . . ."[3]

Many of the cases that were decided following this pronouncement held the local governments liable under the federal statute. A local government was subject to the Act when it granted a cab monopoly at a local airport.[4] A city's practice of hiring only fire department personnel to operate ambulance services was subject to it.[5]

However, the Supreme Court clarified its earlier holding when it decided *Town of Hallie v. City of Eau Claire*.[6] This antitrust action challenged a city's monopoly over the provision of sewage services. The Court found that the state statute delegating authority to the local government evidenced a clearly articulated and affirmatively expressed state policy to displace competition with regulation. Although not explicitly stated, the Court said

---

[11] Reeves v. Sanderson Plumbing Products, Inc., 530 U.S. 133 (2000).

[12] Kimel v. Florida Board of Regents, 528 U.S. 62 (2000).

[13] Garrett v. University of Alabama, 531 U.S. 356 (2001).

[14] Mount Healthy City School Bd. of Educ. v. Doyle, 429 U.S. 274 (1977).

[1] Parker v. Brown, 317 U.S. 341, 63 S.Ct. 307 (1943).

[2] City of Lafayette v. Louisiana Power & Light Co., 435 U.S. 389, 98 S.Ct. 1123 (1978).

[3] *Id.* at 413.

[4] Woolen v. Surtran Taxicabs, Inc., 461 F. Supp. 1025 (N.D. Tex. 1978).

[5] Neyens v. Roth, 326 N.W.2d 294 (Iowa 1982).

[6] 471 U.S. 34, 105 S.Ct. 1713 (1985).

that it was a foreseeable result of the statutory powers given the city to construct sewerage systems and determine the area to be served. Subsequently, the Court in another case held that a local government's unquestioned zoning power over size, location and spacing of billboards, delegated to it by the state, provided immunity to the local government.[7]

Congressional concern about increasing costs to local governments from antitrust litigation led to the enactment of the Local Government Antitrust Act of 1984.[8] This federal law precludes the recovery of money damages and attorney fees from general purpose and special function units of government. The restriction also prevents recovery from local officials or employees acting in an official capacity. It does not prohibit injunctive remedies.

Many states have enacted statutes that have attempted to exempt their local governments from federal antitrust liability. It is questionable whether this state action can serve to protect local governments from federal statutory liability.

PART III PROCEDURAL REQUIREMENTS

§ 9.10 Notice of Injury and Intent to File a Claim

If an individual suffers harm as a result of the action of local government or of its officers or employees, he or she may be required to give notice of the injury shortly after it occurs. In addition, notice may be required of a subsequent intention to file a claim. These requirements must be met to preserve the right to pursue legal action against the local government.

Notification requirements are usually imposed by statutes, state constitutions, charters, or local enactments. Reasonable notice requirements have been upheld by the courts and justified on the grounds that they permit the local government to gain information in a timely manner, correct a problem that may be potentially dangerous to others, and permit the negotiation and settlement of legitimate claims without the costs associated with litigation.[1] Unreasonable requirements will be found to violate due-process requirements of federal and state constitutions.[2] Those that create arbitrary classifications will be held to violate the equal protection clauses.[3]

Courts have disagreed on whether notice requirements, in general, may be imposed selectively on some individuals and not on others. For instance, courts have differed on whether notice can be required for claims brought against government entities when it is not required for claims against

---

[7] City of Columbia v. Omni Outdoor Advertising Co., 499 U.S. 365 (1991).

[8] 15 U.S.C. §§ 34-36 (1984).

[1] Allbritton v. City of Birmingham, 150 So. 2d 717 (Ala. 1963).

[2] Brown v. Town of Montgomery, 242 S.E.2d 476 (W. Va. 1978); Grubaugh v. City of St. Johns, 180 N.W.2d 778 (Mich. 1970).

[3] Kossak v. Stalling, 277 N.W.2d 30 (Minn. 1979); Lorton v. Brown Co. Community Unit School Dist., 220 N.E.2d 161 (1966); Gleason v. City of Davenport, 275 N.W.2d 431 (Iowa 1979).

private parties.[4] A court held unconstitutional a notice requirement for claims against a school district when there was none for claims brought against other local governments.[5] A requirement that notice be given within a thirty-day period for some local governments, while a sixty-day notice applied to others was also found to be unconstitutional.[6]

Notice of injury is usually required to be given in writing, specifying the time, place, and cause of the injury. It is also generally specified that the notice is to be given to a particular officer or office of the local government. There are many cases interpreting these requirements, with some exhibiting little flexibility and finding only strict compliance acceptable.[7] Others have found that substantial compliance is sufficient, focusing more on whether the intent of the requirement has been satisfied.[8]

Often, notice of an intention to file a claim must be given to the local government prior to filing suit. The accepted rationale is that it permits the local government to evaluate the claim and make a decision to settle if it wants to avoid the time and expense of litigation. Although the notice of claim is considered mandatory and failure to comply will usually bar a tort action, substantial compliance with the requirements of the contents of the notice may be sufficient in some jurisdictions. For instance, if an incomplete address is given but it is sufficient to permit the local government to contact the complainant, it may survive a challenge for noncompliance.[9] Some courts have found substantial compliance where a local government has actually investigated an accident or had knowledge of it.[10]

Contents of the notice of claim typically include the location of the place where the tort occurred. The courts have excused imperfect descriptions, provided the information given reasonably identifies the location. It must be definite enough to permit the local government, with reasonable certainty and diligence, to identify it without other information.[11] A failure by plaintiff to comply by inaccurately identifying the facts and date of the alleged tortious conduct will defeat the claim if it misleads the local government in its investigation or preparation for trial.[12] Similarly, failure to comply by failing to give a general description of the injuries has led to dismissal of the claim. Some facts, such as the extent of injuries, will not be deemed to limit a plaintiff's claim.

---

[4] Anderson v. Hinton, 242 S.E.2d 707 (W. Va. 1978). *But see* Reich v. State Highway Dep't, 194 N.W.2d 700 (Mich. 1972).

[5] *Lorton, supra* n. 3 at 163–64.

[6] *Gleason, supra* n. 3 at 433.

[7] Tucker v. Eaton, 393 N.W.2d 827 (Mich. 1986).

[8] Vermeer v. Sneller, 190 N.W.2d 389 (Iowa 1971).

[9] Elmore Co. Comm'n v. Ragona, 540 So. 2d 720 (Ala. 1989); Bush v. City of Albany, 188 S.E.2d 245 (Ga. Ct. App. 1972); Sandak v. Tuxedo Union Sch. Dist., 124 N.E.2d 295 (N.Y. 1954).

[10] Oakley v. State, 505 P.2d 1182 (Haw. 1973).

[11] West Plains v. Loomis, 279 F.2d 564 (8th Cir. 1960).

[12] Baldridge v. City of Ashland, 613 S.W.2d 430 (Ky. Ct. App. 1981); Anniston v. Rosser, 158 So. 2d 99 (Ala. 1963).

Where a plaintiff has a claim based upon a deprivation of a federal right he or she will not generally be barred by a failure to comply with state or local notice requirements.[13] Notice requirements may also be found inapplicable where the remedy sought is based on an equitable action to enjoin a continuing tort.

§ 9.11   Time Limitations and Damages

The requirement that notice of intent to file a claim be given within a specified period of time has been strictly construed in many jurisdictions, with even a one-day delay foreclosing suit against a local government.[1] Even those courts which have permitted some flexibility have generally required at least substantial compliance. They have usually noted that the local government was not prejudiced by the delay and had ample opportunity to fully investigate the circumstances that produced the claim.[2] Still others have accepted actual notice by the local government as sufficient.[3]

Jurisdictions differ in their interpretation of whether minors must comply with notice requirements. Some hold that there must be compliance and have refused to extend any time restrictions.[4] Others hold that notice requirements are not binding upon minors.[5] Statutes that extend the time in which minors can bring actions have been held to impliedly extend the time to file notice of intent as well.[6]

Some states have adopted statutes that give courts the authority to accept late filings where reasonable.[7] In these jurisdictions it is particularly helpful if the plaintiff can establish that the local government has not been disadvantaged and there is a good reason for the delay.[8] Occasionally, some courts will even hold that if a local government has knowledge of the intention to sue, it has waived or is estopped from asserting the notice requirement. However, most courts hold that local governments do not have the authority to modify a statutory requirement.

---

[13] *See* SANDRA STEVENSON, ANTIEAU ON LOCAL GOVERNMENT LAW (2d ed.) § 12.07 (1999).

[1] Gale v. Santa Barbara County, 257 P.2d 1000 (Cal. Ct. App. 1953). *See also* Hoffman v. City of Palm Springs, 337 P.2d 521 (Cal. Ct. App. 1959).

[2] Dubin v. Southeastern Pa. Transp. Auth., 281 A.2d 711 (Pa. Super. 1971); Stevenson v. Monroe County, 473 N.E.2d 237 (N.Y. 1984).

[3] Jenkins v. Bd. of Education, 228 N.W.2d 265 (Minn. 1975).

[4] Independent School District of Boise City v. Callister, 539 P.2d 987 (Idaho 1975); Fox v. City of Overland Park, 499 P.2d 524 (Kan. 1972); George v. Town of Saugus, 474 N.E.2d 169 (Mass. 1985).

[5] McCrary v. Odessa, 482 S.W.2d 151 (Tex. 1972); Wills v. Metz, 231 N.E.2d 628 (Ill. Ct. App. 1967).

[6] City Barnesville v. Powell, 183 S.E.2d 55 (Ga. Ct. App. 1971); Scott v. School Bd. of Granite School Dist., 568 P.2d 756 (Utah 1977).

[7] Begin v. City of Auburn, 574 A.2d 888 (Me. 1990); Speer v. Armstrong, 402 A.2d 963 (N.J. Super. Ct. App. Div. 1979).

[8] Jenkins v. Bd. of Education, 228 N.W.2d 265 (Minn. 1975).

Statutes of limitations for bringing tort actions may be shorter for suits against local governments than against private parties. The public policy reason most often given is that the shorter period will assist the local government in planning its budget. Actions against local governments must be brought within the specified time period or they will be dismissed.[9]

Rules for awarding damages against local governments are generally the same as those applicable in private tort actions. Unless provided otherwise by statute, compensatory damages will be governed by the same rules.[10] However, statutes have been adopted in some states that limit the amount that may be awarded against local governments.[11] If the local government is derivatively liable because of the negligence of an officer or employee, damages are limited to the amount recoverable from the employee.

Punitive damages are not generally available against a local government unless specifically authorized by statute.[12] Failure by a local government to pay a judgment within a reasonable time may result in a deprivation of property without due process because the delay deprived the plaintiff of the right to use his or her property.[13]

---

[9] Harris v. City of Montgomery, 435 So. 2d 1207 (Ala. 1983); Tubbs v. Southern Cal. Rapid Transit Dist., 433 P.2d 169 (Cal. 1967).

[10] Fuller v. Birmingham, 377 So. 2d 957 (Ala. 1979); Wollaston v. Burlington Northern Inc., 612 P.2d 1277 (Mont. 1980).

[11] Hale v. Port of Portland, 783 P.2d 506 (Or. 1989); Smith v. City of Philadelphia, 516 A.2d 306 (Pa. 1986), *appeal dismissed*, 479 U.S. 1074 (1987).

[12] Shore v. Mohave County, 644 F.2d 1320 (9th Cir. 1981); Michaud v. Bangor, 203 A.2d 687 (Me. 1964); Chappell v. City of Springfield, 423 S.W.2d 810 (Mo. 1968).

[13] Evans v. City of Chicago, 689 F.2d 1286 (7th Cir. 1982).

Chapter 10

Local Finances

§ 10.1 Introduction and Chapter Overview

Local governments need revenue to support their activities and maintain their physical resources. Although they look to the federal and state governments as sources of funding, they remain responsible for raising a substantial portion of their revenue through taxation, special assessments, and various user fees and charges. *The Municipal Year Book 2002* reports that local governments raise more than 65% of their own revenues, with the property tax producing the largest portion of this, and other revenue coming from sales tax, individual income tax (only permitted in 15 states), and various charges and fees. Most of the remaining funds needed by the local government come from federal and state aid.[1]

In one sense, local finances are simple. A local government develops a budget for future expenses, subtracts from this total the amount of state and federal assistance it will receive, and the balance is the amount it will need to raise from its own local sources. It then establishes property taxes and user chargers to raise the needed amount of revenue. The reality is that it is far from simple. The political consequences are an enormous consideration and weigh heavily in both budgetary and revenue decisions. In addition, local governments must abide by limitations imposed by federal and state constitutions and statutes on the type, amount and the methods in which revenue can be raised. Perhaps most perplexing, they also must accept variations in state and federal assistance, while complying with the mandates that are imposed on them by the other two levels of government. A local government cannot levy excess taxes because the creation of a cash surplus is inconsistent with acceptable taxing policy.

Local governments are often considered to be both impliedly and specifically authorized to spend their public funds for local purposes. Historically, taxation is viewed as an essential power of every local government.[2] However, in actuality, taxation is not an inherent local power, and local governments must find authority in state constitutions, statutes or charter provisions in order to impose taxes. The courts require strict compliance with these provisions.

A local tax is constitutional only if it is for a public purpose, and many states have expressly provided this in their state constitutions and statutes. There are also state limitations on the kinds of local taxes that can be

---

[1] David R. Berman, *State-Local Relations: Authority, Finances, Cooperation*, MUNICIPAL YEAR BOOK 2002, B1 (2002).

[2] United States v. New Orleans, 98 U.S. 381 (1878).

imposed and numerous exemptions exist for particular goods or services. In addition, local taxation may be deemed preempted because it conflicts with a state tax or because the state tax has occupied the field so completely that it impliedly preempts local action.

Local governments do not have inherent authority to grant exemptions from local taxation. Such authority may be delegated to them and local authorities have used such exemptions in an effort to attract and encourage economic growth for their communities. The states have also provided directly for numerous real property tax exemptions which usually include property used for religious and educational purposes. State and federal properties and activities are not generally subject to local taxation. In some jurisdictions, property belonging to other local governments when considered "governmental" in nature is generally exempt from local taxation while property of a "proprietary" nature may be taxed.

When an expenditure cannot be met by current funds, local governments are often authorized to incur local indebtedness. Most states have debt limitations and strict procedures that carefully prescribe how borrowing is to be done. Particular types of expenditures may require state approval or comment. There are also competitive bidding requirements that seek to assure responsible use of funds.

PART I LOCAL REVENUE

§ 10.2 Federal and State Aid

Local governments receive federal aid for programs that include such areas as medical assistance for the needy, education, highway improvement, and public housing. Over the years, this assistance has increased substantially, particularly when the country's economy is thriving. According to the *Municipal Year Book 2002*,[1] federal assistance accounted for around 17% of total local spending in 1997. Some of this federal aid was given to the states, to be subsequently directed to local governments to fund local programs. Other federal assistance was given directly to the local governments. The percentage of aid that is given directly to local governments, bypassing the state governments, has increasingly declined between 1978 and 2002, from 29% down to 11%. This trend has raised concerns among some local governments who fear that, as states face economic pressure, they may not transfer as many funds to the local level.[2]

In the 1960s and 1970s, federal assistance was given primarily for specific programs and was referred to as a "categorical grant." However, the federal government eventually moved toward a system of revenue sharing where it distributed substantial sums to state and local governments, giving them broad discretion in the use of these funds. This form of revenue-sharing

---

[1] David R. Berman, *State-Local Relations: Authority, Finances, Cooperation*, 45, MUNICIPAL YEAR BOOK 2002, B1 (2002).

[2] State *ex rel.* Tyler v. McMonagle, 494 N.E. 1144 (Ohio 1986).

ended for local governments in 1986. It has been replaced with assistance in the form of block grants. These differ from the earlier categorical grants because state and local governments have more flexibility to use them within broad programmatic areas, and much of the government "red tape" has been eliminated. There are fewer planning, auditing and reporting requirements.

Recipients of federal funds are subject to federal statutes that require compliance with their terms by governments receiving any kind of federal assistance.[3] Other grants of assistance have their own individual conditions that must be met by the recipient. An example is the increasing federal role in public education with the adoption by Congress of the *No Child Left Behind Act of 2001*[4] (NCLB). This federal law imposes increased levels of accountability for states, school districts, and schools receiving federal education funds. It requires statewide standards, annual testing and annual statewide progress objectives.[5] This form of federal control over state and local activity, by offering a carrot with strings attached, has consistently been held to be a legitimate exercise of federal authority if certain factors are present. It must be shown that the spending is in furtherance of the general welfare; the states may knowingly accept or reject the funds; the conditions imposed are reasonably related to the federal interest in the particular program; and there is no constitutional bar to the conditional grant of these funds.[6]

States have questioned whether there is, in fact, a voluntary choice to be made since they depend upon federal assistance to carry out their governmental responsibilities. One state challenged the federal requirement that state recipients of Medicaid funds agree to provide emergency medical services to illegal aliens as a violation of the Tenth Amendment's protection of state sovereignty. The state alleged that although technically the program permitted it to choose whether or not to accept federal funding, as a practical matter it had no choice because its medical system would collapse without the federal assistance. The Court of Appeals for the Ninth Circuit rejected the argument, noting that the coercion argument has always been unsuccessful.[7] A similarly unsuccessful argument was made when a state questioned the conditioning of federal highway funds on the acceptance of a national speed limit.[8] The Supreme Court has also upheld

---

[3] For instance, Title VI of the Civil Rights Act of 1964, 42 U.S.C. § 2000D, prohibits discrimination in *federally-assisted programs. See* discussion in § 9.7 *supra.*

[4] Pub. L. 107–110 (H.R.1). This was part of the reauthorization of the ELEMENTARY AND SECONDARY EDUCATION ACT of 1965.

[5] *See* discussion *supra* § 6.2.

[6] South Dakota v. Dole, 483 U.S. 203 (1987); State of California v. U.S., 104 F.3d 1086 (9th Cir. 1997); King v. Smith, 392 U.S. 309 (1968).

[7] State of Cal. v. U.S., 104 F.3d 1086 (9th Cir. 1997).

[8] State of Nev. v. Skinner, 884 F.2d 445 (9th Cir. 1989).

the right of the federal government to enforce the terms of a grant against a local government.[9]

Most local governments also receive substantial assistance from their state governments. As noted in the *Municipal Year Book 2002*,[10] local governments are active lobbyists within their states for more revenue, greater authority, more state aid and extended discretion in their ability to choose how to spend funds. States give their local governments both restricted grants, for targeted areas such as education and transportation, and general unrestricted grants. Local governments also often share in tax revenues that are collected by the state, such as the income, gasoline, and sales taxes.

Local government dependence on state aid has increased as federal assistance has declined. However, the generosity of the state in providing funds to local governments usually reflects the health of the general economy. When the state is struggling because of shrinking state revenue, local governments typically receive decreased financial support. During such times, local governments have been forced to meet their responsibilities with creative and cost-effective programs, including specific tax increases, interlocal agreements with other local governments to provide services and goods more efficiently, and by contracting out public services.[11]

Any determination of whether there is adequate state assistance for a local government to meet its financial responsibilities must include consideration of the overall division of financial responsibility between a state and its local governments. Some states have assumed responsibility for providing funding for courts, the criminal justice system, and public health and welfare assistance. In shifting the cost of major services to the state, the local government is better able to meet the costs of its local programs.

§ 10.3 Constitutional and Statutory Limitations on Local Taxation

The overwhelming view is that there is no inherent authority to impose a tax and each local government must have delegated authority to do so. This authority is usually found in state constitutions, statutes, or charters.[1] Courts are inclined to strictly interpret the authority, resolving any ambiguities by finding a limited authority.[2] Frequently, the delegation of

---

[9] U.S. v. Northern Pac. Ry. Co., 256 U.S. 51 (1921); City of Columbia v. Board of Health & Environmental Control, 355 S.E.2d 536 (S.C. 1987); U.S. v. Harrison County, Miss., 399 F.2d 485 (5th Cir. 1968).

[10] David R. Berman, *State-Local Relations: Authority, Finances, Cooperation*, 46, MUNICIPAL YEAR BOOK 2002, B1 (2002).

[11] *Id.* at 51.

[1] Town of Hackleburg v. Northwest Alabama Gas Dist., 170 So. 2d 792 (Ala. 1964); People *ex rel.* Metropolitan St. R. Co. v. State Bd. of Tax Comm'rs, 67 N.E. 69 (N.Y. 1903).

[2] State *ex rel.* Woodruff v. Centanne, 89 So. 2d 570 (Ala. 1956); City of Tampa v. Birdsong Motors Inc., 261 So. 2d 1 (Fla. 1972); Consolidated Diesel Elec. Corp. v. City of Stamford, 238 A.2d 410 (Conn. 1968).

authority to local governments is for a particular type of tax. In reviewing local implementation, courts will examine the operation and effect of the tax to see if it is consistent with the delegated authority, but will not examine the wisdom of the local officials in adopting it.[3]

The Federal Constitution imposes many limitations on state and local taxation. For instance, the ports of New Orleans and New York City had fees invalidated because Article I, § 10 provides that no state shall lay any duty of tonnage without the consent of Congress.[4] If the assessment was for a service rendered, such as a pilotage or wharfage fee, it would have been acceptable, but a fee imposed for the mere privilege of arriving and departing is not. The Constitution also prohibits state and local governments from imposing import taxes on goods.[5] However, the Supreme Court has permitted a tax on imported goods stored in warehouses when the goods are no longer in transit. The tax is then considered a property tax and not an import tax.[6] The same Constitutional provision bars taxation of exports which have begun their movement into foreign commerce. However, if they have not begun their journey, then they may be taxed.[7]

The Commerce Clause prohibits the taxation of goods moving in interstate or foreign commerce. This does not prevent a local government from taxing goods while they are stored, or even destined for commerce. Until actually on their way, they are fair game for taxation.[8] Local governments are also permitted to tax property used by motor carriers in interstate commerce, provided that the charge is reasonable compensation for the use of local roads. The Supreme Court looks at the effect of the local tax and, if it is discriminatory against foreign producers and favors local producers, it will be found to violate the Commerce Clause. Those that exempt local producers while imposing taxes on foreign ones will most often be held void. Similarly, local taxes that discriminate either against persons engaged in or products of interstate commerce will be found unconstitutional.

The Commerce Clause is of particular concern today because of an increasing local government interest in requiring that nonresidents pay locally imposed taxes. The Supreme Court adopted a test in 1977 that examines the actual effect of a tax rather than its legal terminology. Taxes may be imposed on out-of-state activity that has a substantial nexus with the taxing government; is fairly apportioned and nondiscriminatory; and fairly relates to the services provided by the government.[9]

---

[3] Lurie v. City of Indianapolis, 198 N.E.2d 755 (Ind. 1964).

[4] U.S. CONST. Art. I, § 10, Cl. 2. See Southern S.S. Co. v. Portwardens, 73 U.S. 31 (1867); Inman S.S. Co. v. Tinker, 94 U.S. 238 (1876).

[5] U.S. CONST. Art. I, § 10, cl. 2.

[6] Michelin Tire Corp. v. Wages, 423 U.S. 276 (1976); R.J. Reynolds Tobacco Co. v. Durham County, 479 U.S. 130 (1986).

[7] See Empresa Siderugica v. County of Merced, 337 U.S. 154 (1949).

[8] Coe v. Town of Errol, 116 U.S. 517 (1886).

[9] Complete Auto Transit, Inc. v. Brady, 430 U.S. 274 (1977), quoted in American Trucking Ass'ns., Inc. v. Scheiner, 483 U.S. 266 (1987), limited by American Trucking Ass'ns., Inc. v. Smith, 496 U.S. 167 (1990).

The Due Process Clause requires that all taxes imposed must be for a public purpose.[10] This requirement has also been specifically included in many state constitutions. The Due Process Clause is also relevant in the taxation of interstate businesses. The Supreme Court has held that there must be some nexus between the entity imposing the tax and the activities subject to the tax. In other words, the entity subject to the tax was receiving a benefit from the government imposing the tax, even if the benefit was simply the enjoyment of the privileges of living in that community. The tax must also be reasonable in light of the connection.[11]

The Due Process Clause also requires that tax enactments be clear and certain, with individuals able to determine with a reasonable degree of certainty whom and what the local government intends to tax. If the complaint against a tax is that it is too great, the courts have indicated that it will be found to be unconstitutional when the tax is so unreasonable and oppressive that it is confiscatory. Merely stating that it is too high is insufficient.[12]

The Equal Protection Clause protects against the use of the taxing power in an unreasonable, arbitrary or invidiously discriminatory manner.[13] Classification is possible if supported by a rational basis, but unequal treatment of taxpayers within classes is unconstitutional. The court will also determine whether the difference in treatment between the classes rationally furthers a legitimate government interest.[14]

A local government cannot impose a tax that directly discourages the exercise of First Amendment rights to religion, speech and press. However, this does not prevent the taxation of publishers of printed materials such as newspapers,[15] unless the tax is found to be discriminatory because they are treated differently than similarly-situated publications.[16]

Many state constitutions have uniformity-of-taxation provisions which typically provide that all taxes shall be uniform upon the same class of property. Although states vary in application of these provisions, most states apply this requirement solely to those taxes that are imposed directly on property and not to other types of taxes. It is usually interpreted to mean that the assessments are fair and equal and the tax rate applied to the assessment is uniform for all property. In other words, similar people and

---

[10] Cremer v. Peoria Housing Authority, 78 N.E.2d 276 (Ill. 1948).

[11] See Moorman Mfg. Co. v. Bair, 437 U.S. 267 (1978); Container Corp. of America v. Franchise Tax Bd., 463 U.S. 159 (1983).

[12] Fox Bakersfield Theatre Corp. v. City of Bakersfield, 222 P.2d 879 (Cal. 1950).

[13] Township of Hillsborough v. Cromwell, 326 U.S. 620 (1946).

[14] Nordlinger v. Hahn, 505 U.S. 1 (1992). Taxpayers who should reasonably, naturally and properly be considered part of the same class are not to be treated differently from others in the same class.

[15] Grosjean v. American Press Co., 297 U.S. 233 (1936); Murdock v. Pennsylvania, 319 U.S. 105 (1943).

[16] See Minneapolis Star & Tribune Co. v. Minnesota Comm'r of Revenue, 460 U.S. 575 (1983).

property must be taxed the same. The imposition of a residential dwelling-unit fee that was imposed upon apartment owners was held unconstitutional because it did not apply to other property owners.[17]

Classifications and variation in treatment, if they are reasonable, are permitted in states with a uniformity clause. As a practical matter, there does not have to be absolute equality. One state imposed a tax on businesses based upon an ability to pay and upon the government cost in providing it protection.[18] When a business argued that it was disproportionately impacted by a business and occupation tax because it paid seventy percent of the tax collected but accounted only for fifty percent of the revenue, it was denied relief. Absolute equality is not required by uniformity provisions.[19] Classifications may be based on differences that are generally recognized, or upon reasonable considerations of public policy. All courts agree, however, that members of the classes created must be treated the same.

Sometimes it is necessary to distinguish a regulatory fee from a tax when reviewing whether the uniformity provision has been violated. It is usually held to be a regulatory fee if the primary purpose is to regulate or to collect revenue to finance public improvements if the tax is segregated and allocated to regulating the entity, and if there is a direct relationship between the rate charged and the service rendered.[20] The uniformity requirement is not applicable to the regulatory fee.

Many local governments are restricted in their power to impose taxes by very specific provisions in their state constitutions or statutes. These restrictions most often impose limitations on the real property tax and were adopted when similar limitations were imposed on the overall power of local governments to incur local debt. These provisions were seen originally as a means of curtailing government expenditures but have often evolved to meet other needs, such as the reduction in existing taxes imposed on real property. Eventually, some states used statutory restrictions to impose limits on the amount of revenue that can be raised through the use of the property tax in order to protect residents from rapidly rising real property values. It was followed by a wave of initiatives to amend state constitutions and statutes to limit real estate taxes.[21]

§ 10.4   Real Property Tax

The real property tax is the largest source of locally raised revenue for local governments, although regions of the country vary in their reliance

---

[17] Harbour Village Apts. v. City of Mukilteo, 989 P.2d 542 (Wash. 1999).

[18] Pharr Road Inv. Co. v. City of Atlanta, 164 S.E.2d 803 (Ga. 1968).

[19] Citizens Bank of Weston, Inc. v. City of Weston, 544 S.E.2d 72 (W. Va. 2001). The Court cited Washington v. Davis, 426 U.S. 229 (1976), which had earlier rejected this kind of analysis.

[20] Samis Land Co. v. City of Soap Lake, 980 P.2d 805 (Wash. App. 1999).

[21] Proposition 13 was adopted by California voters in June 1978. This tax revolt by citizens was soon followed by citizens and legislators in many other states. CAL. CONST. ART. XIII A §§ 1–7.

on it. It is also a source of revenue that is not used by the federal government, nor generally by most state governments. According to the *Municipal Year Book 2002*, the real property tax accounts for about 26% of total local revenues, increasing nationally the total revenue produced between 1980 and 1990 by 128%.[1] This is one of the most unpopular taxes, and the increasing number of complaints from property owners have now slowed its growth. Some states have taken steps to relieve public pressure against this tax by providing greater state funding for local programs or by shifting the financing of services like education to other taxes, such as the sales tax.[2]

The use of the real property tax to finance public school education remains controversial because of the disparity in the value of the real property tax base from one school district to another. The reality is that wealthier districts can provide greater resources to their schools than can poorer districts. When challenged on federal equal protection grounds, the Supreme Court held that the right to an education is not a fundamental right guaranteed by the Constitution and, therefore, disparities in funding do not violate the Equal Protection Clause.[3] However, many state courts have found this form of financing unconstitutional as a matter of state law, based on state constitutional equal protection grounds, or specific educational guarantees in state law.[4] Other state courts have disagreed, finding no state constitutional guarantee of educational quality or finding that the courts should not interfere in what is essentially a legislative determination. A few states have created a statewide property tax to address funding inequities in an effort to move toward equalizing per pupil spending across the state.[5]

The collection of the real property tax involves a multi-step process. Although states vary in their requirements, a typical process begins with the creation of an assessment role, listing and describing all the properties in the jurisdiction that are subject to the tax. Next, an assessed value is assigned to each parcel, reflecting its fair market value. Notification to property owners and an opportunity for them to protest the inclusion, description or assessment is generally required by due process concerns.

---

[1] David R. Berman, *State-Local Relations: Authority, Finances, Cooperation*, 52, MUNICIPAL YEAR BOOK 2002, B1 (2002).

[2] *Id.* Michigan did this in 1994. Wisconsin put a freeze on local property taxes and increased state funding. South Carolina and Minnesota reduced property taxes by increasing state aid to education. Washington voters adopted an initiative limiting property tax increases to 1% per year without voter approval. New Jersey raised its property tax rebate and the South Carolina legislature ratified a constitutional amendment that was approved by the voters to allow counties, with voter approval, to replace certain personal property taxes with a sales tax of up to two cents.

[3] San Antonio Indep. Sch. Dist. v. Rodriguez, 411 U.S. 1 (1973).

[4] Robinson v. Cahill, 303 A.2d 273 (N.J. 1973); Serrano II, 557 P.2d 929 (Cal. 1977); Rose v. Council for Better Educ., 790 S.W.2d 186 (Ky. 1989). However, in contrast, *see* Matanuska-Susitna Borough Sch. Dist. v. State, 931 P.2d 391 (Alaska 1997); Coalition for Adequacy & Fairness v. Chiles, 680 So. 2d 400 (Fla. 1995); Milliken v. Green, 212 N.W.2d 711 (Mich. 1973).

[5] Berman, *supra* n.1 at 55.

The local government's legislative body levies a tax that is imposed on a proportionate basis that relates to the value of each taxable parcel. The tax is collected and failure to pay by a property owner most often results in a local government lien imposed on the property, with strict foreclosure procedures. From an enforcement perspective, it is a very efficient tax. A property owner can resort to the courts for review of the local action after he or she has exhausted all administrative remedies.

In order to challenge the levy or imposition of the tax, a plaintiff usually must show that the prescribed process has not been followed or that an unequal burden has been placed upon his or her property. Proof of invidious discrimination will void an assessment or levy, but it is not enough to show that other kinds of property are assessed differently.[6] Many states have chosen to classify property by its use. For instance, business property may be treated differently than residential property. As explained in § 10.3 *supra*, this classification does not violate equal protection, provided that it is supported by a rational basis and there is equal treatment of taxpayers within each class. Business property is often assessed and taxed at a higher rate than residential property. The Supreme Court has even permitted a state to adopt an assessment method that taxes property based on the purchase price of the property rather than current value. The Court held that the state did not violate equal protection because it had a rational basis to adopt this method, with its intent to limit the overall amount of taxes paid and to restrain year-to-year increases.[7]

State constitutions and statutes often reduce the number of local properties that are subject to taxation by providing for many exemptions of particular types of property. Most states exempt property owned by religious organizations from local real property taxation if the property is used for religious purposes. The Supreme Court has decided that this is permissible and it does not violate the Establishment Clause of the Federal Constitution.[8] There are many cases questioning whether certain uses of property owned by religious organizations should be included in this exemption. Courts usually hold that all properties reasonably necessary or conducive to religious use may be included. However, these holdings have differed, with some finding that such ancillary uses as parking lots and parks may qualify.[9] Other decisions have excluded them and have held that the exemption should be limited to property actually used in religious worship and as housing for the clergy.[10]

---

[6] *See* discussion *supra* § 10.3.

[7] Nordlinger v. Hahn, 505 U.S. 1 (1992).

[8] Walz v. Tax Comm'n of New York, 397 U.S. 664 (1970).

[9] Immanuel Presbyterian Church v. Payne, 265 P. 547 (Cal. App. 1928); Supervisor of Assessments of Baltimore County v. Keeler, 764 A.2d 821 (Md. 2001).

[10] Second Church of Christ Scientist of Philadelphia v. City of Philadelphia, 157 A.2d 54 (Pa. 1960) (a state constitutional provision limited the exemption to actual places of religious worship); General Ass'n Branch Davidian Seventh Day Adventist v. McLennan County Appraisal Dist., 715 S.W.2d 391 (Tex. Ct. App. 1986).

In addition to religious property, other common exemptions include the properties of charitable, educational, hospital, scientific and other not-for-profit organizations. In some jurisdictions, specific types of property are temporarily or permanently exempt from local taxation. Homestead exemptions also exist in some states, while property used for low-cost housing or farming has also benefitted from special treatment. Veterans and elderly residents are often recipients of exemptions. Temporary reductions in taxes have been used by some communities to attract economically or socially beneficial development.

In defining the property that is attributable to these exempt uses, the courts look to the actual use of the property. They are interested in determining whether the property is in fact used for the stated purpose. Only the property that is an integral part of the exempt activity will be included, and any excess property will be excluded. Courts generally interpret exemptions very narrowly, expressing the view that taxation is the rule and exemption is an exception.

Property belonging to foreign governments, the United States, or the state in which the local government is located, is not generally subject to local taxation without their consent.

§ 10.5 Sales and Use Taxes

The sales tax generates a great deal of revenue for local governments and serves as an alternative or supplement to other taxes such as the real property tax. Collected by the vendor, it is a relatively easy tax to impose and administer. However, there is opposition to the tax because of its regressive nature, imposing the greatest burden on those least able to pay it. According to the *Municipal Year Book 2002*, the sales tax produces approximately 5% of local revenue with thirty-three states authorizing its use by their local governments.[1] Some jurisdictions are increasing their use of the sales tax in order to address growing opposition to the use of the real property tax.[2] Other institutional supporters have sought increases in order to afford greater revenue to activities such as public education. The *Municipal Year Book 2002* also notes that in recent years states have generally increased the authority of local governments to diversify their local taxes by permitting them to impose new sales taxes and fees for police, fire, and ambulance services.[3]

The sales tax must meet the requirements of due process, equal protection and public purpose that apply to other local taxes.[4] It has long been found to be a constitutionally sound tax, and local governments are not prevented from taxing, in their jurisdiction, the sales of goods that have

---

[1] David R. Berman, *State-Local Relations: Authority, Finances, Cooperation*, 54, MUNICIPAL YEAR BOOK 2002, B1 (2002).

[2] *See* discussion in § 10.4 *supra*. Michigan did this in 1994.

[3] Berman, *supra* note 1.

[4] *See* discussion in § 10.3 *supra*.

been imported through interstate commerce.[5] Many cases have approved the imposition of a sales tax in various situations with an emphasis on the importance of delivery of the sold item within the taxing local government.[6] In 1977, the Supreme Court held that taxation of interstate business is not unconstitutional if it is applied to an activity with a substantial nexus with the taxing state, is fairly apportioned, does not discriminate against interstate commerce, and is fairly related to the services provided by the taxing government.[7]

Local governments are generally authorized to require that vendors collect the sales tax. If the sales tax is imposed upon the purchaser, the vendor who collects the taxes does not have standing to oppose the tax or sue for refunds of illegally collected taxes.[8]

Closely related to the sales tax is the use tax. The purpose of the tax is to capture the lost sales tax revenue that results from sales that are accomplished by purchasing a product out of state. If authorized by the state constitution, statute, or charter, local governments can tax the goods or properties as long as they are no longer in the channel of interstate commerce. In other words, if items are purchased out of state, for resale within the state, the sales tax will be applied when the items are subsequently resold within the state. There can be no imposition of a use tax.[9]

Application of the use tax must meet the Supreme Court's test established in *Complete Auto Transit, Inc. v. Brady*.[10] Taxes may be imposed on out-of-state activity that has a substantial nexus with the taxing government; is fairly apportioned and nondiscriminatory; and fairly relates to the services provided by the government. However, the Supreme Court struck down on equal protection grounds a state tax on the purchase and use of motor vehicles when the taxing government gave a credit to state residents, but not to nonresidents who subsequently became residents, even though they had paid sales tax in the state of the purchase.[11] There has to be a sufficient nexus with the state, and it has been held that solicitations for mail orders where there are no offices or representatives within the state is insufficient.[12] The Supreme Court held that a physical presence is not

---

[5] Woodruff v. Parham, 75 U.S. 123 (1868); Muhammed Temple of Islam — Shreveport v. City of Shreveport, 387 F. Supp. 1129 (W.D. La. 1974), *aff'd*, 517 F.2d 922 (5th Cir. 1975) (Commerce Clause does not prohibit a state from imposing a nondiscriminatory tax upon the sale of goods since the sale occurs after interstate commerce has ended).

[6] Jagels v. Taylor, 21 N.E.2d 526 (N.Y. 1939), *aff'd*, Jagels v. Taylor, 309 U.S. 619 (1940).

[7] Complete Auto Transit, Inc. v. Brady, 430 U.S. 274 (1977).

[8] Krauss Co. v. Develle, 110 So. 2d 104 (La. 1959).

[9] Kansas City Royals Baseball Corp. v. Director of Revenue, 32 S.W.3d 560 (Mo. 2000).

[10] 430 U.S. 274 (1977), *quoted in* American Trucking Ass'ns., Inc. v. Scheiner, 483 U.S. 266 (1987), *limited by* American Trucking Ass'ns., Inc. v. Smith, 496 U.S. 167 (1990). *See* Brown's Furniture, Inc. v. Wagner, 665 N.E.2d 795 (Ill. 1996).

[11] Williams v. Vermont, 472 U.S. 14 (1985).

[12] Nat'l Bellas Hess, Inc. v. Dep't of Revenue of State of Ill., 386 U.S. 753 (1967); L.L. Bean, Inc. v. Commonwealth Dep't of Revenue, 516 A.2d 820 (Pa. Commw. Ct. 1986).

required by the more flexible Due Process Clause,[13] but may be required by the Commerce Clause and its "substantial nexus" requirement.[14]

The future impact of electronic commerce on sales tax revenue is of particular concern to state and local governments. If a tax cannot be imposed on purchases from out-of-state vendors who do not maintain a physical presence within the state because there is an insufficient nexus,[15] there is potential for a significant reduction in sales tax revenue. The development of commerce using the Internet presents complicated questions involving jurisdictional issues and the possibility of double taxation of the same products.[16] Congress adopted the Internet Tax Freedom Act of 1998 which imposes a three-year moratorium on new taxes on Internet products and services. The act is supposed to foster the federal policy to encourage the development of the Internet and to provide a period of time to resolve many of the questions of state and local taxation. The moratorium was extended in 2001, and is now set to expire after November 1, 2003.[17]

§ 10.6   Income, Gross Receipts, and Personal Property Taxes

Although local governments have no inherent authority to impose income or earnings tax on individuals, such power has been delegated to local governments in fifteen states.[1] It has been given primarily to large cities, but other forms of local governments use it as well. This tax has been sustained as constitutional when applied to individuals who work within the taxing community but live elsewhere.[2] It is often referred to as a commuter tax. There is recognition that those individuals who commute to work benefit from such government services as fire and police protection and that they use the government infrastructure of roads and other facilities.[3] In recognition of the fact that commuters also pay property taxes to their own local governments, some local income tax structures assess nonresidents at a lower rate than residents. Double income tax liability is not generally a problem because most often the authority to impose the tax has been given by a state to only one type of local government. The income tax may be

---

[13] Quill Corp. v. North Dakota, 504 U.S. 298 (1992) (the test is whether a defendant's contacts with the state makes it reasonable to require that it defend a suit in that state).

[14] Id.

[15] Nat'l Bellas Hess, Inc. v. Dep't of Revenue of State of Ill., 386 U.S. 753 (1967).

[16] See W. Hellerstein, State and Local Taxation of Electronic Commerce: Reflections on the Emerging Issues, 52 U. MIAMI L. REV. 691 (1998).

[17] PUB. L. NO. 107–75.

[1] David R. Berman, State-Local Relations: Authority, Finances, Cooperation, 52, MUNICIPAL YEAR BOOK 2002, B1 (2002). This accounts for 2% of total local government revenue.

[2] American Commuters Ass'n v. Levitt, 279 F. Supp. 40 (D.C.N.Y. 1967), aff'd, 405 F.2d 1148 (2d Cir. 1969). See also Shaffer v. Carter, 252 U.S. 37 (1920).

[3] Kiker v. City of Philadelphia, 31 A.2d 289 (Pa. 1943), cert. denied, 320 U.S. 741 (1943). But see City of New York v. State, 730 N.E.2d 920 (N.Y. 2000) (the imposition of the tax solely on commuters is not permissible).

imposed upon the income earned by state or federal employees who work within the local government,[4] just as it is upon other wage earners.[5]

Many states have delegated authority to local governments to tax the gross receipts on the total revenues of businesses and individuals. In some jurisdictions the authority is limited to certain businesses, and it is frequently applied to public utilities. This tax has been upheld by the courts.[6] It has also been applied to those individuals engaged in professions, such as contractors[7] and attorneys.[8]

Some local governments have been authorized to impose a tax on personal property. This authority will be strictly construed in favor of the taxpayer and, if a statute lists certain personal property, others will be deemed to have been excluded.[9] A constitutional due process concern limits the implementation of a tax to those tangible items that are situated within the geographical limits of the local government. Disagreements have been resolved by permitting the imposition of the tax on items located at the residence of the owner or at a place within the local government where it has "acquired a situs." This location requirement indicates that the property being taxed has benefitted from sufficient governmental protections to justify the levy. For property that moves about, the courts have been willing to consider its home as the place where it is generally kept, unless it is proven otherwise.[10] Occasionally, the issue is resolved by state legislation which specifies the location for taxation purposes.

§ 10.7　Fees and Special Assessments

User fees are widely used by local governments to finance services such as water, sewerage, garbage collection, recreational facilities, and transportation. They differ from taxes because they are compensation paid to a local government for a service or product.[1] Taxes are usually imposed to generate revenue for the support of government. The distinction is important because if a charge is a tax, the local government must be delegated the authority necessary to impose it. Generally, a fee may be imposed by a local government as an exercise of its general police powers. The difference is significant because, typically, local governments have been given very limited authority to tax but have been delegated broad police powers. However, there is a limitation that accompanies the use of the police power. If the fee is

---

[4] Helvering v. Gerhardt, 304 U.S. 405 (1938).

[5] Graves v. People ex rel. O'Keefe, 306 U.S. 466 (1939).

[6] Tamiami Trail Tours v. City of Tampa, 31 So. 2d 468 (Fla. 1947).

[7] O.H. Martin Co. v. Borough of Sharpsburg, 102 A.2d 125 (Pa. 1954).

[8] Franklin v. Peterson, 197 P.2d 788 (Cal. App. 1948).

[9] *Appeal of Dixon*, 11 A.2d 169 (Pa. Super. 1940).

[10] Liquid Carbonic Corp. v. Michigan Tax Comm'n, 145 N.W.2d 278 (Mich. App. 1966); Annis Furs, Inc. v. City of Detroit, 58 N.W.2d 907 (Mich. 1953). *See also* Levin-Townsend Computer Corp. v. City of Hartford, 349 A.2d 853 (Conn. 1974) (personal property can be taxed only at the owner's residence or where it has acquired a situs).

[1] City of Gary v. Indiana Bell Telephone Co., Inc., 732 N.E.2d 149 (Ind. 2000).

imposed as an exercise of this authority rather than an authority to tax for revenue, the amount charged must not greatly exceed the cost of the regulatory activity.[2] It cannot be an effort by the local government to generate revenue or it will be considered a tax.

A local government can charge nonresidents higher rates of user fees if the costs of providing those services are greater. Included in the justification for higher rates may be the hidden or potential costs that local residents have that nonresidents do not have, as well as contributions that they alone have made toward the provision of the service.[3]

Increasingly, local governments are expecting new developers of private property to share in the public costs that accompany their development. Developers are often assessed impact fees by local governments. This revenue is used to offset the public cost of infrastructure, such as roads, sewers, schools, fire stations and parks, that will be needed because of the growth produced by the development. Development impact fees have raised the question of whether these are in fact a tax or a regulatory fee. To address this concern, most local governments are careful to identify the burden imposed by the development, whether it be roads, water and sewer systems, or other needed improvements, and to specifically identify where the impact will be assessed and how the fee will be expended. Often, the burden is viewed incrementally because more than one developer will contribute to the total infrastructure needs. In this situation, there is an attempt by the local government to apportion the costs between current and future developments on a proportional basis.

A linkage fee is one that local governments have imposed on commercial developers for the additional public transportation or low-and moderate-income housing made necessary by the new development. These fees have been sustained where found to be authorized and where they are viewed as a reasonable exercise of local government's right to regulate the development of land. Courts have sustained linkage fees where reasonably related and limited to the increased services that are prompted by the new development.[4] The cost is determined most often by the size of the development.[5]

Local governments may also require that developers undertake specified improvements, or dedicate portions of land for public purposes, as a condition of receiving the permits needed to proceed with their project. This

---

[2] City of Seattle v. Paschen Contractors, Inc., 758 P.2d 975 (Wash. 1988). *See also* State of Florida v. City of Port Orange, 650 So. 2d 1 (Fla. 1994).

[3] Platt v. Town of Torrey, 949 P.2d 325 (Utah 1997).

[4] Russ Bldg. Partnership v. City and County of San Francisco, 234 Cal. Rptr. 1 (1987), *aff'd in part and rev'd in part on other grounds*, 750 P.2d 324, *appeal dismissed*, 488 U.S. 881 (1988). *But see* San Telmo Assocs. v. City of Seattle, 735 P.2d 673 (Wash. 1987). The requirement that developer replace low-income housing that was demolished during construction of commercial project, or contribute to a housing fund, is an unauthorized tax.

[5] *See* D. MANDELKER, LAND USE LAW §§ 9.20–9.23 (4th ed. 1997). *See also* discussion in §§ 6.7 and 6.8 *supra*.

has led to strong disagreement between developers and their local governments over the equity of shifting these costs. It has also raised questions about whether or not they are excessive.[6] For this reason, many states have enacted legislation that regulates the use of impact requirements. The goal is to see that the costs imposed are reasonable, and that they bear a reasonable relationship to the actual impact of the development.

License fees have been imposed by local governments for the right of doing business or engaging in a particular occupation. Some have taken the form of a charge for each billboard, a fee upon all fish caught, or a per-unit fee on the sale of condominiums.[7] License fees must be reasonable and operate uniformly upon all those within a particular class. Some local governments have opted for a license fee on all businesses, occupations, or professions.[8] Others have chosen to charge fees for particular occupations.

A special assessment is not a tax but a charge upon property that has been specially benefitted by a public improvement, in a manner and degree not benefitting the whole local government. It is in contrast to a general improvement which confers a substantially equal benefit to the property of the whole local government, or bestows a benefit to the public at large.[9] The benefit must be actual and real because it supports the legitimacy of the assessment.[10] Typical improvements that have been financed this way include water and sewer services, parks, streets, curbs, sidewalks, street lighting and water mains.

The special assessment may be made on a one-time basis, or the local government may choose to create an assessment district and impose fees for the maintenance and support of the facility or service. The special assessment that is charged each property owner within the district means that the property owners located in other areas of the local government do not assume the burden of paying the costs of the improvement. Each property owner must be benefitted in a manner and to a degree not enjoyed by the local government as a whole.[11] This targeted means of shifting costs to only those who directly benefit gives local governments greater flexibility in being responsive to the diverse needs of the community. Because it is not a tax, it is not subject to any state uniformity and equality of taxation requirement or to local government tax limitations.[12]

---

[6] See § 4.5 *supra* for a discussion of regulatory takings.

[7] City of Key West v. Marrone, 555 So. 2d 439 (Fla. Dist. Ct. App. 1990); City of Florissant v. Eller Outdoor Advertising Co., 522 S.W.2d 330 (Mo. Ct. App. 1975); Liberati v. Bristol Bay, 584 P.2d 1115 (Alaska 1978).

[8] City of Richmond v. Fary, 171 S.E.2d 257 (Va. 1969).

[9] Duncan Dev. Corp. v. Crestview Sanitary Dist., 125 N.W.2d 617 (Wis. 1964).

[10] Myles Salt Co. v. Bd of Comm'rs of Iberia & St. Mary Drainage Dist., 239 U.S. 478 (1916).

[11] Home Builders Ass'n of Central Arizona, Inc. v. Riddel, 510 P.2d 376 (Ariz. 1973).

[12] For an excellent discussion of problems in special assessment financing, *see generally* MANDELKER, ET AL, *supra* note 5, at 318–324.

§ 10.8 Other Taxes; Lotteries; and Recoupment of Public Costs From Tobacco and Gun Manufacturers

There are a variety of taxes that have been imposed by state and local governments on specific products, businesses or services. These include taxes on alcohol, tobacco products, motor vehicles, gasoline or motor fuel, hotel occupancy or accommodations. Some local governments have also imposed a tax upon admission to theaters and other amusement facilities.[1] Others permit the taxation of business or occupations.[2] These taxes have been sustained where there is clear authority delegated to the local government to impose such taxes and it has been done in a reasonable manner.[3]

All states, except two,[4] have some form of legalized gambling. As explained in the *Municipal Year Book 2002*,[5] gambling has contributed significant local revenue in several places. Louisiana's local governments receive 25% of the state taxes and fees on poker devices that are located in bars, restaurants, and truck stops. Many also receive entry fees of $2.50 per person for fifteen casino-style riverboats, while New Orleans receives revenue from a land-based casino. Many other states permit horse or dog races and approximately half permit casino gambling in selected cities.[6]

The most prevalent form of gambling that produces revenue for states are the numerous lotteries. This means of generating revenue is not viewed as a particularly efficient mechanism because there are very high administrative costs, and they require a significant capital investment to initiate. However, lotteries have been successful in generating revenue, with many states dedicating portions, or all, of the profits to a particular programmatic area, most often education or economic development. The lottery remains a controversial government undertaking, subject to criticism that they are regressive because they affect the poor more adversely than others. There are also issues of overall public welfare that are frequently raised. However, as noted in the *Municipal Year Book 2002*, as state and local finances become increasingly strained during downturns in the economy, the interest in producing revenue from gambling will increase.

A new source of revenue for many state and local governments has come from a settlement of litigation brought against the major tobacco manufacturers.[7] State and local governments joined together to bring legal action

---

[1] Wilson's Total Fitness Center, Inc. v. Dir. of Revenue, 38 S.W.3d 424 (Mo. 2001).

[2] Neal v. City of Huntington, 158 S.E.2d 223 (W.Va. 1967) (sustaining local tax upon those engaged in a profession).

[3] Fox Bakersfield Theatre Corp. v. City of Bakersfield, 222 P.2d 879 (Cal. 1950). *But see* City of St. Petersburg v. Florida Coastal Theaters, Inc., 43 So. 2d 525 (Fla. 1949).

[4] Hawaii and Utah.

[5] David R. Berman, *State-Local Relations: Authority, Finances, Cooperation*, 54, MUNICIPAL YEAR BOOK 2002, B1 (2002).

[6] *Id.*

[7] For further information, *see* SANDRA M. STEVENSON, ANTIEAU ON LOCAL GOVERNMENT LAW § 71.02[2] (2d ed. 2000).

seeking compensation for the increased public costs that resulted from the use of tobacco by their residents. In particular, governments argued that a high proportion of their Medicaid costs were related to the treatment of tobacco-related illnesses. An additional goal of the litigation was to gain commitments from the defendants to change their corporate practices.

A Master Settlement Agreement was reached in 1998 that provided for a sum, valued at $206 billion, to be paid to the states, with most of the money allocated according to a formula based upon size of the population and per-capita health care costs. In addition, certain regulatory concessions were granted. The payments are to be made in perpetuity and may vary according to changes in inflation or diminishment in cigarette sales. Local governments were included in the terms of the agreement releasing the tobacco companies from liability, and many will continue to receive the financial benefits for many years to come. As governments have found it increasingly difficult to find revenue to meet slowdowns in tax or grant revenue, there is increasing pressure to sell the rights to future settlement payments in order to obtain ready cash to close budget shortfalls.

Several local governments have attempted to recreate the success reflected in the tobacco litigation by bringing actions against gun manufacturers. They are seeking compensation for public health costs and want regulatory reform. However, it does not appear that this effort will gain the solidarity of state leadership that proved so potent in the tobacco litigation. Gun control is not an issue that appears to be as politically cohesive as tobacco. According to the *Municipal Year Book 2002*, some forty states have prohibited or restricted local gun control ordinances and most deny local governments the right to regulate the carrying of concealed weapons.[8] When several cities sued gun manufacturers to recover the public costs of violence caused by guns, thirteen states adopted legislation that prohibited their local governments from filing such lawsuits.

PART II LOCAL EXPENDITURES

§ 10.9 Public Purpose Requirement

Local governments cannot expend their local funds unless expressly or impliedly authorized to do so,[1] and the authority must apply to the particular property or service that is being purchased.[2] They may only expend funds for a public purpose. This requirement is expressed in some state constitutions,[3] and implied in all others.[4] It has also developed from

[8] Berman, *supra* note 5, at 51.

[1] Waters v. State *ex rel.* Schmutzer, 583 S.W.2d 756 (Tenn. 1979); Montgomery v. State, 153 So. 394 (Ala. 1934).

[2] City of Tacoma v. Taxpayers of Tacoma, 743 P.2d 793 (Wash. 1987); Ducey v. Inhabitants of Webster, 130 N.E. 53 (Mass. 1921).

[3] Town of Gila Bend v. Walled Lake Door Co., 490 P.2d 551 (Ariz. 1971).

[4] Oehmig v. Chattanooga, 80 S.W.2d 83 (Tenn. 1935).

court interpretations of federal and state constitutional due process clauses, as well as specific prohibitions against gifts and loans of property or credit to private entities. It simply means that public revenue cannot be used for the purely private or personal interests of any person or corporate entity.

Courts have said that a public purpose cannot be precisely defined, nor is there a rigid rule that can be used to determine its existence.[5] The decision in each case depends upon its own particular facts. The funds spent must promote the welfare of the local government and serve a public, rather than private, purpose. This does not exclude all private benefit. For instance, indirect economic benefits, such as reviving a city's commerce, creating jobs, and improving a local economy, do not change the public purpose of expending money to benefit the community by encouraging such growth.[6] Many cases have sustained local expenditures for advertisements of features of the community, and for the construction of buildings for lease to private industry. Local governments have also been sustained in their expenditures to care for the needy and for providing recreation and entertainment facilities.

Private entities that perform public functions, such as hospitals, museums, and zoos, have been recipients of local assistance, with the courts finding a public purpose in the expenditures. Courts have found the issue of public use to be primarily a question for the legislative branches of government and will not usually overturn a legislative declaration of public purpose, unless manifestly and palpably incorrect.[7]

A few state constitutions provide that only necessary expenditures can be made by local governments without a vote of approval from residents. Courts have differed in their interpretation of what is necessary. One state court found that expenditures for maintenance of an airport required electoral approval,[8] while another state found it to be a necessary expense and, therefore, no approval was needed.[9]

After a court has determined that a local government does, in fact, have the authority to make a particular purchase, it will not usually interfere with a decision that the expenditure is necessary or desirable.[10] It has been said that a challenger would have to show that the local officials acted in wanton disregard of the public good for a court to enjoin an expenditure.[11] Courts have also refused to order a local government to make a particular expenditure.[12]

---

[5] Wilmington Parking Auth. v. Ranken, 105 A.2d 614 (Del. Ch. 1954); Barnes v. Town of New Haven, 98 A.2d 523 (Conn. 1953).

[6] Maready v. City of Winston Salem, 467 S.E.2d 615 (N.C. 1996); Common Cause v. State, 455 A.2d 1 (Me. 1983).

[7] Barnes v. City of New Haven, 98 A.2d 523 (Conn. 1953); R.E. Short Co. v. City of Minneapolis, 269 N.W.2d 331 (Minn. 1978). *See also* Jones v. City of Portland, 245 U.S. 217 (1917).

[8] Vance Co. v. Royster, 155 S.E.2d 790 (N.C. 1967).

[9] City of Pocatello v. Peterson, 473 P.2d 644 (Idaho 1970).

[10] Geneva Co. Comm'n v. Tice, 578 So. 2d 1070 (Ala. 1991).

[11] Barbour v. Carteret Co., 120 S.E.2d 448 (N.C. 1961).

[12] State *ex rel.* Hauck v. Bachrach, 152 N.E.2d 311, *aff'd*, 153 N.E.2d 671 (Ohio 1958).

§ 10.10   Prohibited or Required Expenditures

Many state constitutions prohibit gifts of property to private individuals or lending of credit to either private or public entities. Although these provisions are often used in finding a requirement that an expenditure must be for a public purpose, they have also developed a jurisprudence of their own. They have prevented local governments from making voluntary payments to contractors or employees who have performed additional services beyond the terms of employment.[1] When a school district attempted to pay a teacher to leave her position in exchange for the remaining portion of the year's salary, it was found to be an unconstitutional gift of public money.[2]

However, some courts have provided greater leniency in interpreting the prohibitions. For instance, a local government was permitted to increase the amount of pension due a widow.[3] In another case, it was found that the purchase of development rights to preserve farmland and open space was constitutional, even though the same purpose could have been achieved through the use of local police powers.[4] These prohibitions are so broad that even the simple act of a police department decision to contribute unclaimed bicycles to a local children's organization must be considered for its potential to be an unconstitutional gift.

A government does not violate the constitutional prohibition of gifts of public funds to private individuals if the court finds that there is a moral obligation to do so. Even if there is no legal obligation, a government may do what ". . . a fine sense of justice and equity would dictate to an honorable individual."[5] Using this exception, local governments have been permitted to reimburse individuals who suffered losses caused by the local government,[6] reward people for heroic acts,[7] and pay claims which were no longer enforceable against the local government.[8]

Both federal and state constitutions prohibit state and local government action that establishes a religion. The establishment clauses prevent both direct local government assistance to religious organizations, and expenditures that aid religion, including religious schools. Local schools have frequently sought state or local assistance in the form of transportation and textbook assistance. This is discussed in 6.2 *supra*.

Because local governments are viewed as arms of the state, they must perform public services that are required by the state unless provided otherwise in the state constitution or by statute or charter. States have often

---

[1] McGovern v. New York City, 138 N.E. 26 (N.Y. 1923).

[2] Helen K. Boyd v. Collins, 195 N.Y.2d 153 (N.Y. Sup. Ct. 1960).

[3] Brummond v. City of Oakland, 244 P.2d 441 (Cal. App. 1952).

[4] Louthan v. King Co., 617 P.2d 977 (Wash. 1980).

[5] Ausable Chasm Co. v. State, 194 N.E. 843 (N.Y. 1935).

[6] City of New Orleans v. Clark, 95 U.S. 644 (1877).

[7] State *ex rel.* Morgan v. Rusk, 174 N.E. 142 (Ohio App. 1930).

[8] Opinion of the Justices, 238 N.E.2d 855 (Mass. 1968).

enacted legislation that imposes burdens on the local governments, whether it be requiring the implementation of a new program or changes to an existing one.[9] At times, the mandates are designed to carry out federal mandates that have been imposed on the states by the federal government.

The condition of the general economy has tended also to effect the imposition of mandates (or requirements for services) upon local governments. The federal and state governments have, at times, shown an inclination to cope with their own decrease in revenue by imposing unfunded mandates for services or programs on the next level of government. The federal government can impose mandates on the states and the states can impose them on the local governments. Since the local government is the last in the sequence of governmental units, it has been quite vocal in its complaints about unfunded mandates.

From a positive perspective, at times the requirements may relieve local officials from assuming responsibility for doing something that they feel is needed, but unpopular among their local residents. The greatest problem presented by mandates is that they may have a major impact on the local budget. If federal or state funding is not provided, the local government will have to find a way to fund the program. It may have to exercise its delegated authority to raise the needed revenue through local taxes, assessments, or fees.

Most states now require that state agencies develop a cost estimate of the financial impact on local governments for every proposed mandate. Some states have constitutional or statutory requirements that limit the ability of the state to impose local mandates, while some require full or partial state reimbursement of the costs. Congress enacted the Unfunded Mandates Reform Act of 1995[10] which requires that reports be attached to bills and joint resolutions containing mandates. The reports must identify and describe the mandate, estimate direct costs, have cost-benefit analyses, explain the effect upon the public and private sectors, and identify available federal assistance. Congress is prohibited from proceeding without a report and cannot consider a bill that has a direct cost in excess of $50 million without new budget authority equal to, or exceeding, the estimated cost.

§ 10.11 Expenditure Process

State constitutions, statutes and charters prescribe the process a local government must use in order to spend its revenue. Courts have held that

---

[9] It is reported that the problem of unfunded mandates varies from state to state. Ohio is said to have imposed them in one out of twelve laws enacted in recent years, while Tennessee did so in about one out of four enactments. *Id.*, pg. 49, *citing* State and Local Government Commission of Ohio, *Unfunded Mandates: Regaining Control at the Local Level* (Columbus, 8 December 1994) and Harry A. Green,"State Mandates to Local Governments," Memorandum to the Tennessee Advisory Commission on Intergovernmental Relations Commissioners, 28 August 1995.

[10] 2 U.S.C. § 1501 *et seq.*

there must be strict adherence to these requirements or the expenditure will be invalid.[1]

A local official is generally given responsibility for constructing a local budget which contains an estimate of revenues and expenditures for the coming year. This is typically done with budget requests obtained from the various departments and agencies within the local government. The proposed budget is submitted to the local government body. This body is usually required by law to adopt an annual budget and enact any appropriation needed for its implementation.

An appropriation is the process of setting aside, from general revenues, a certain sum of money for a specific object.[2] Most local governments are required to appropriate money for a particular purpose before it may be spent. In some states this is a constitutional requirement, and in others it is prescribed by statute. This is viewed as a method of insuring that the public has both information about proposed spending and an opportunity to have input before the funds are actually expended.

Budgets are usually required to be adopted by local legislative enactments after proper notice, and then they are often published. Courts have not interpreted appropriations requirements to mean that local governments must indicate every possible expense. Rather, taxpayers must be able to determine the amounts to be spent for various purposes in reasonably specific terms.[3] Generally, local spending is not valid unless it was included in the budget or appropriation enactment.

Local legislative bodies are generally given wide discretion in preparing the budget, and courts will reverse their action only if it is clearly arbitrary or capricious, or if it would unreasonably impair the ability of a public officer to fulfill his or her constitutional or statutory duties.[4]

The states have various requirements for the expenditure process. Some states have statutes that declare void any contract involving an expenditure that exceeds the amount budgeted or appropriated for the particular service or product. Contractors have been awarded the lesser amount that had been budgeted or appropriated at the time the local government entered into the contract.[5] In other states, local spending must be preceded by orders or resolutions of the local governing board that are entered on the records.[6] Yet others have required a roll call with "aye" and "nay" votes entered on the record before appropriations, and when not carried out, the transaction is void.[7]

---

[1] City of Quincy v. Brooks-Skinner Inc., 91 N.E.2d 206 (Mass. 1950).

[2] Illinois Municipal Retirement Fund v. City of Barry, 367 N.E.2d 1048 (Ill. App. 1977).

[3] Kotlikoff v. Township of Pennsauken, 331 A.2d 42 (N.J. 1974).

[4] Lovett v. Bussell, 249 S.E.2d 86 (Ga. 1978); Pinellas Co. v. Nelson, 362 So. 2d 279 (Fla. Dist. Ct. App. 1978).

[5] Bd. of County Comm'rs v. Central Nat'l Bank, 41 P.2d 853 (Okla. 1935).

[6] Smith v. McCoy, 533 S.W.2d 457 (Tex. Ct. App. 1976). The approval of the county auditor was a condition precedent to the ability to pay the claims. See also Earl Browder Inc. v. County Court, 102 S.E.2d 425 (W. Va. 1958).

[7] People ex rel. Smith v. Wabash Ry., 145 N.E.642 (Ill. 1924).

Once a budget or appropriation has specified funds for a particular purpose, the funds may not be transferred to another purpose unless the local government is specifically authorized to do so by statute or charter.[8] However, some state courts have indicated there is some flexibility in this rule.[9] Although taxpayers usually have standing to enjoin the diversion of funds from budgeted accounts into other accounts, they have at times been unable to contest the transfer of funds if they could not show damage from the reallocation.[10] Emergency situations have also provided grounds for exceptions and some states have provided for this by statute.

Often there is state involvement in the local budgeting process by the promulgation of rules, instructions, and even forms to be used. In some states, budgets must be approved by state departments.[11] In others, state officials have been given the power to audit and examine the books of local governments in order to check for compliance. Some have required that certain local action be taken if the local government's fiscal year ends with a deficit.[12] Still other states have provided that improper local government budgeting may result in a fine and may be cause for removal from office.[13]

States have provided statutory relief for taxpayers who want to challenge a proposed budget, expenditure or tax levy. Some even permit appeals to state boards.[14]

PART III LOCL INDEBTEDNESS

§ 10.12 Limitations on Borrowing

Local governments do not have inherent authority to borrow.[1] They must be delegated authority in the state constitution or by statute or local charter. This authority may be found to be implied by an authorization to purchase.[2] However, if the local government has been expressly authorized to borrow in a particular way, there must be compliance with the authorization and there is little flexibility to do it another way.[3]

---

[8] Keefe v. Adams, 143 So. 644 (Fla. 1932); McVeigh v. City of Jackson, 56 N.W.2d 231 (Mich. 1953)

[9] Town of Thornton v. Winterhoff, 92 N.E.2d 163 (Ill. 1950) (if the borrowed funds are returned to the fund from which they were borrowed and are available when demand is made, the practice of borrowing by one fund from another is not in itself illegal). See also Baldwin v. City of Martinsburg, 56 S.E.2d 886 (W. Va. 1949).

[10] Grand Rapids Indep. Publ'g Co. v. City of Grand Rapids, 56 N.W.2d 403 (Mich. 1953).

[11] N.J. Stat. Ann. § 40A:4-78.

[12] Mich. Comp. Laws Ann. § 141.921. The local government must develop a financial plan and submit it to the state treasury department.

[13] Kan. Gen. Stat. § 79-2919; Okla. Stat. Ann. § 17-211(c).

[14] Town of Mechanicsville v. State Appeal Bd., 111 N.W.2d 317 (Iowa 1961).

[1] Mayor and Recorder of Nashville v. Ray, 86 U.S. 468 (1873).

[2] Allen v. Intendant and Councilmen of LaFayette, 8 So. 30 (Ala. 1890).

[3] First Nat'l Bank v. Obion County, 3 F.2d 623 (W.D. Tenn. 1924); Denicore v. City of Burlington, 70 A.2d 582 (Vt. 1950).

Most local governments issue bonds to borrow the funds necessary to meet the infrastructure needs of their community. The authority to do this must be expressly delegated to the local government and it can only be used when the proceeds are to be used for a public purpose.[4] The authority to construct or purchase a public improvement does not ordinarily imply the authority to issue bonds, although occasionally, express authority to borrow has been held to do so.[5] Most often, states have given bonding authority to local governments for specified projects and have provided the process for its use.

The requirements for the process of issuing bonds are strictly construed by most courts.[6] Unless there is an exception for a particular kind of debt, bonds cannot be issued if such issuance will cause the local government to exceed its overall debt limitation which is usually found in the state constitution, a statute, or charter.

Two methods are most frequently used to limit local government debt. First, limits are placed on the total amount of debt a local government can owe at any one time. This may be expressed as a percentage of the total assessed valuation of property within the local government.[7] Some states provide a degree of flexibility by permitting the amount to be increased for certain activities.[8] At other times, the imposed limitation is based on the estimated local income and revenue for that year. Either way, the goal is to control the total amount of debt. The second method of debt limitation is a requirement that the voters must first approve a decision of the governing board to incur debt before the funds are actually borrowed. Some states have adopted both methods of controlling local debt. Others have adopted combinations of the two. For instance, one state prohibits debt in excess of the projected income and revenue for the year without the approval of the voters.[9] Others have set limits and, in addition, require voter approval for some debts.

Most states have constitutional or statutory debt limitations for at least some, if not all, of their local governments. These are adopted or enacted for the purpose of protecting the assets and property of a local government from any forced action against the community by debt holders seeking to obtain payment of a debt.[10] For this reason, the debt limitations are usually applicable only to the general obligation debt of the local government. This

---

[4] Van Eaton v. Town of Sidney, 231 N.W. 475 (Iowa 1930). For a discussion of public purpose, *see* discussion *supra* at § 10.9.

[5] Russell v. Middletown City Sch., 125 A. 641 (Conn. 1924).

[6] Shell v. Jefferson County, 454 So. 2d 1331 (Ala. 1984); Brown v. Longiotti, 420 So. 2d 71 (Ala. 1982).

[7] *See* IND. CONST. art. XIII and IOWA CONST. art. XI, § 3.

[8] ALA. CONST. art. XIII, § 225.

[9] CAL. CONST. art. XI, § 18. A vote of approval by two-thirds of the qualified voters is required.

[10] City of Redondo Beach v. Taxpayers, Property Owners, Citizens and Electors of Redondo Beach, 352 P.2d 170 (Cal. 1960).

debt is considered a charge against the general funds or revenues of the local government, which means the debt would be paid primarily from revenue received or collected from sources such as the real property tax.

When the local government issues general revenue bonds to obtain funds needed for a public purpose, it is promising to repay the debt from the taxes it collects from various sources, including the real property tax. These bonds are secured by the full faith and credit of the local government. This is in contrast to its issuance of revenue bonds. If money is borrowed through the issuance of revenue bonds, the debt is solely to be repaid from a designated source of local income and is not to be paid out of the general revenue of the local government. They are not secured by the full taxing authority of the local government. In most instances, the source of revenue that is designated to repay the loan is revenue produced by the facility or infra-structure that will be built with the proceeds from the sale of the bonds.

Local obligations incurred through the sale of general obligation bonds are considered debt for debt-limitation purposes. Most states have also authorized their local governments to issue revenue bonds; this kind of debt is not usually calculated in the determination of the total outstanding debt of a local government.[11] Local governments may be authorized to issue revenue bonds for commercial as well as industrial projects. They have been used for a vast array of projects, including transportation systems, recreational facilities and sports stadiums, and such things as the construction or expansion of a shopping center[12] and retail facilities.[13] Courts have found that these activities have a public purpose to benefit the local community. Often this kind of borrowing is not subject to voter approval.[14] This is discussed further in § 10.13 *infra*.

Among the states that have local debt limits, it is common to have exceptions for certain activities. The provision of water or sewerage services is often exempted from the calculation of total amount of debt.[15] Some states have also provided that a local government may increase its debt limit by a majority vote of the electors. Others have provided that a local government may exceed its debt limit to the extent of the value of a utility or industry for which the debt is to be incurred.[16] Some states provide that the debt limitation does not apply to the ordinary and necessary expenses authorized by the general laws of the state. The cost of police protection has been included in this category[17] but not payments for the building of nuclear power plants.[18] Emergencies that require the local government to

---

[11] Wickley v. Muscatine Co., 46 N.W.2d 32 (Iowa 1951).

[12] State *ex rel.* Ohio County Comm'n v. Samol, 275 S.E.2d 2 (W.Va. 1980).

[13] Marshall Field & Co. v. Village of South Barrington, 415 N.E.2d 1277 (Ill. App. 1981).

[14] State v. Jacksonville, 53 So. 2d 306 (Fla. 1951).

[15] Wis. Const. art. XI, § 3 (5); NYS Const., Art. VIII.

[16] Stark v. Jamestown, 37 N.W.2d 516 (N.D. 1949).

[17] Hanson v. City of Idaho Falls, 446 P.2d 634 (Idaho 1968).

[18] Asson v. City of Burley, 670 P.2d 839 (Idaho 1983), *cert. denied*, 469 U.S. 870 (1984).

incur debt are often permitted, although it may result in the local government exceeding its debt limit.[19]

Frequently, there is a question of whether local government contracts are to be included in the total-debt computation. Courts have reviewed many complex arrangements where it might appear that a contract was designed to avoid the problem of a debt limitation when a local government wanted to undertake a project to provide a needed service or product to the community. Generally, long-term contracts, for the provision of a service over a number of years, are not considered debts for debt-limitation totals if the payments are to be made annually for the services provided in that year.[20] However, a contract in which local governments agreed to make pro rata payments to a public utility district formed to finance, construct, own and operate electrical generating facilities, for electrical service, regardless of whether the service was ever received, was held invalid. The contract was held to be debt that exceeded the debt limitation of the local government and, as such, was unauthorized.[21] A similar local government contract with the same service provider was sustained as a valid service contract because it provided that the local government's obligations were payable solely from utility revenues that would be received from its customers.[22] There is disagreement among the states on whether contractual debt is to be included in the computation of a total debt ceiling of a local government, and each case is decided on the basis of its own facts.

If an obligation is to be included in the total debt limit, courts have held that the question of whether it exceeds the limit is to be determined as of the time the debt is authorized by the local government. If the obligation did not exceed the limit, the borrowing is still valid, even if it does exceed the maximum when the bonds are actually issued. However, if the amount of the borrowing exceeded the limit when authorized, it is invalid even if the amount of the bonds subsequently does not exceed the permitted limit when they are issued.[23]

A bond issuance that violates the debt limitation cannot be made valid by an act of ratification by the local government.[24] Courts, at times, have held that the bonds issued are valid up to the permitted debt limit amount, but anything beyond it is not a valid debt of the local government.[25] The

---

[19] Williams v. Barbourville, 246 S.W.2d 591 (Ky. 1952); City of Muskegon Heights v. Danigelis, 235 N.W. 83 (Mich. 1931).

[20] Thomas v. Alabama Mun. Elec. Auth., 432 So. 2d 470 (Ala. 1983); Protsman v. Jefferson-Craig Consol. Sch. Corp., 109 N.E.2d 889 (Ind. 1953).

[21] Asson v. City of Burley, 670 P.2d 839 (Idaho 1983), cert. denied, 469 U.S. 870 (1984); Chemical Bank v. Washington Pub. Power Supply Sys., 666 P.2d 329 (Wash. 1983).

[22] DeFazio v. Washington Pub. Power Supply Sys., 679 P.2d 1316 (Ore. 1984). See also City of Springfield v. Washington Pub. Power Supply Sys., 752 F.2d 1423 (9th Cir. 1985).

[23] Fisher v. City of Philadelphia, 116 A.2d 735 (Pa. 1955).

[24] Doon Township v. Cummins, 142 U.S. 366 (1892).

[25] City of Laredo v. Looney, 185 S.W. 556 (Tex. 1916); Holderman v. Hidalgo County Water Control and Improvement Dist. No. 12, 142 F.2d 792 (5th Cir. 1944).

debt limitations are to protect the local taxpayers; those who conduct business with local governments do so at their own risk.

Local governments have used various means of avoiding debt limitations. Many have been successful in their efforts to have their state legislatures create separate districts, boards, authorities and commissions to provide needed local infrastructure or services. Frequently, these entities can incur debt that will not be included as part of the local government debt. The constitutional debt limit may not be applicable, and the borrowing limit of the separate entity, if any, will frequently be established as part of the creating legislation. Often, one of these entities will issues bonds to construct a facility and enter into a long-term lease with the local government. It is understood that the lease payments will be used to pay off the bonds. The lease agreement may contain an option permitting the local government to purchase the facility during or after completion of the lease agreement. Many of these arrangements have been sustained, with courts finding that the debt of the separate entity is not to be added to the overall debt of the local government.[26]

Some local governments have conveyed governmental properties to private organizations which then built facilities to be leased back to the local government, often with purchase options.[27] These conveyances have been sustained if the lease creates no immediate indebtedness and confines local government liability to each yearly installment, which is for the consideration actually furnished that year. The courts do not generally consider the value of the entire lease as debt to be considered in computing the overall amount of local debt.[28] If the annual payments are in excess of reasonable rent, the arrangement is not likely to be sustained as a lease, but will probably be viewed as a purchase and considered as debt.[29]

When local governments have conveyed property for the construction of a public facility and there is an understanding that after the lease payments are completed the building will be conveyed to the local government, the lease has been held to be a purchase or a mortgage. This transaction is a debt and is to be considered within the debt limitations of the local government.[30] This is understandable since installment purchase agreements, where payments are made over a number of years, are generally treated as a lump sum debt, with the total of all the payments to be considered in the overall debt limitation amount.[31]

---

[26] Nations v. Downtown Dev. Auth. of Atlanta, 345 S.E.2d 581 (Ga. 1986); Eberhart v. Mayor and City Council of Baltimore, 433 A.2d 1118 (Md. 1981); Millar v. Barnett, 221 N.W.2d 8 (S.D. 1974); City of LaHabra v. Pellerin (Cal. App. 1963); Protsman v. Jefferson-Craig Consol. Sch. Corp., 109 N.E.2d 889 (Ind. 1953).

[27] City of Pocatello v. Peterson, 473 P.2d 644 (Idaho 1970).

[28] City of Los Angeles v. Offner, 122 P.2d 14 (Cal. 1942).

[29] Garrett v. Swanton, 13 P.2d 725 (Cal. 1932), *overruled in part by* City of Oxnard v. Dale, 290 P.2d 859 (Cal. 1955).

[30] Palmer v. City of Albuquerque, 142 P. 929 (N.M. 1914); City of Phoenix v. Phoenix Civic Auditorium & Convention Center Ass'n, 408 P.2d 818 (Ariz. 1965); Bachtell v. Waterloo, 200 N.W.2d 548 (Iowa 1972).

[31] Garrett v. Swanton, 13 P.2d 725 (Cal. 1932).

Long-term service contracts are not generally considered local government debt. If payments are made annually for services provided in that year, the courts do not usually find that the total must be considered in the overall debt limit.[32]

§ 10.13 Borrowing for Community Development

Most local governments are authorized to issue revenue bonds for projects that are owned or leased by private entities that meet the requirement of having a public purpose. States have created both state and local entities which issue revenue bonds to obtain funds that are used to assist private individuals or companies in their development of facilities and services that contribute to the welfare of the community. These private activities have included the construction of manufacturing facilities that create new jobs and provide increased tax revenue, the creation of housing for low- and moderate-income individuals, hospitals, educational facilities, and air and water pollution control facilities. The public purpose that justifies this government action is the contribution that the private activity will make toward the enrichment and well being of those individuals residing within the community.

During their early use, interest earned by the revenue bonds that were used to raise revenue for private development was exempt from federal income tax, as was the interest on bonds issued to assist in the development of direct government activities. This meant that funds could be borrowed at a lower rate of interest than the current market rate because the purchaser of the bond did not owe the taxes that would normally be paid on the interest. This significantly lowered the cost of obtaining needed capital for the private developer. However, with the popularity and rapid growth in the use of these private development bonds, the federal government, among other concerns, became concerned about lost tax revenue, and over the years has greatly restricted the qualifications for federal tax exemption.[1] While revenue bonds, used by governments to finance their public operations, retain their federal tax exempt status, the tax exempt status of private development bonds has been eliminated for most activities and restricted to a very few types of facilities.[2]

Many local governments continue to issue nonexempt revenue bonds in order to financially assist businesses that will meet the public purpose of providing a benefit to their communities. The use of revenue bonds to assist private economic development in local communities is usually undertaken by public entities, often known as industrial development agencies, created by state legislative action. The bonds that they issue are referred to most often as industrial development bonds. Although most interest on the bonds

---

[32] Thomas v. Alabama Mun. Elec. Auth., 432 So. 2d 470 (Ala. 1983).

[1] *See* TAX REFORM ACT of 1986, PUB. L. NO. 99-514, 100 Stat. 2085 (codified as amended in scattered sections of 26 U.S.C.).

[2] I.R.C. § 103(c) (1968).

is not exempt from federal income tax, some states grant exemptions from state and local taxes, thereby providing significant financial benefit to the private entities.

§ 10.14   Borrowing Procedure

State constitutions, statutes and charters prescribe the process that must be followed by local governments when they borrow money. Early courts held that local government bonds are not valid until they have been issued in accordance with these requirements.[1] However, substantial compliance and a determination that a particular provision is merely directory have saved some noncompliance actions.[2] State legislative action has also corrected and cured defects in local bond issuance when the defects were not constitutional.[3] Some states have enacted legislation validating all previous local bond issues.[4]

Most often the legislative body of the local government must pass a resolution of intention or a local enactment that provides basic information about the bond issuance. This is often required to be published and a public hearing held, permitting members of the public to express their opinions about the borrowing.

An election may be required; frequently, the borrowing proposal must be approved by more than a majority of those voting. If the borrowing proposal is for a revenue bond, with the proceeds of the improvement solely used to pay the debt, there is often no state requirement for an election. Another situation in which there is generally no election is where the bonds issued are those of an independent entity, and not those of the local government.

If there is an election, the right to vote must be nondiscriminatory. The Supreme Court has held that the right to vote may not be limited to property owners in either revenue bond[5] or in general obligation bond elections.[6] The form of the ballot is usually prescribed by the regulatory statute and it must clearly state the information that is necessary to inform the voter about the approval that is sought. It is typically required that a ballot only relate to the single purpose for which bonds are to be issued.

Reasonable delays in issuing bonds that have been approved are usually acceptable. It has been held that local officials can issue bonds at a lower interest rate, provided this does not conflict with state law.[7] However, local

---

[1] Portsmouth Savings Bank v. Village of Ashley, 52 N.W. 74 (Mich. 1892); Peterman v. City of Milford, 104 A.2d 382 (Del. Ch. 1954).

[2] Hitchins v. Mayor and City Council of Cumberland, 138 A.2d 359 (Md. 1958); State *ex rel.* Bd. of Educ. v. Maxwell, 60 N.E.2d 183 (Ohio 1945).

[3] Starmount Co. v. Ohio Sav. Bank & Trust Co., 55 F.2d 649 (4th Cir. 1932); Judith Basin Land Co. v. Fergus County, 50 F.2d 792 (9th Cir. 1931).

[4] *See* ALA. CODE § 11-81-31 (1997); IND. CODE ANN. § 5-1-1-1 (Michie 1995); N.J. STAT. ANN. § 8-6.1 *et seq.* (school districts) and § 19-1.1 (municipalities and counties) (West 1997).

[5] Cipriano v. City of Houma, 395 U.S. 701 (1969).

[6] City Phoenix v. Kolodziejski, 399 U.S. 204 (1970).

[7] Spitzer v. Bd. of Trustees for Regina Pub. Sch. Dist. No. 4 of Saskatchewan, 267 F. 121 (6th Cir. 1920), *cert denied*, 254 U.S. 653 (1920).

governments cannot use the proceeds obtained from the sale of the bonds for anything other than the approved purpose.[8]

Many states provide for pre-issuance validation proceedings which serve to add finality to any question of law or fact regarding validity of the bonds. This may also include the resolution of questions regarding the validity of proposed methods of financing their repayment, such as by lease or imposition of user charges.

The procedure for the sale of the bonds is prescribed by state constitution, statute or charter, and substantial compliance by the local government is required. States generally provide a mechanism for citizens to challenge the issuance of bonds, and there are usually somewhat short time limitations for this action.

---

[8] Wood v. City of Birmingham, 165 So. 2d 95 (Ala. 1964).

TABLE OF CASES

[References are to text sections]

A

A.A.T. Chem., Inc.; Brewer Environmental
   Industries, Inc. v. 5.6n54
Abate v. Mundt 7.6n51
Abbott v. Cape Canaveral, City of . . . . .
                     3.11n151
Abilene, City of v. FCC 3.11n141
Abrahams; People v. 3.3n22
Adams v. Bryant 8.6n87
Adams v. Colorado Springs, City of . . . . .
                     1.7n53
Adarand Constructors, Inc. v. Pena . . . . .
                5.6n64; 5.8n86
Adler v. Deegan 2.3n6
Adoption of (see name of party)
Aero Motors, Inc. v. Motor Vehicles Admin.
       . . . . 3.3n24
Aetna Cleaning Contractors of Cleveland,
   Inc.; Sigall, State ex rel. v. . . . 6.5n60;
                     8.7n129
Agins v. Tiburon, City of 4.3n27;
         4.5n69; 4.6n89; 9.4n44
Agostini v. Felton 6.2n20
Aiello; Spielvogel v. 5.6n62
Akron, City of; Osborn v. 4.9n140
Akron, City of; Zehenni v. 5.10n98
Alabama; Mills v. 7.1n4; 7.3n22
Alabama; South Central Bell Telephone
   Co. v. 3.9n122
Aladdin's Castle, Inc. v. N. Riverside, Village
   of 3.3n27
Alameda County; Moor v. 1.3n15
Albany, City of; Grieshaber v. . . . 6.6n75;
              9.2n18; 9.3n25
Albemarle Paper Co. v. Moody . . 9.7n110
Albuquerque; Coe v. 4.3n20
Albuquerque; Watson v. 4.8n115
Albuquerque, City of; Spray v. . . . 5.1n3
Alcoa, City of; DeGarmo v. 9.4n34
Alden v. Maine 1.3n11; 2.7n50
Alexander v. Sandoval 9.7n93
Alexandria Women's Health Clinic; Bray v.
                 . . . . 9.7n99
Alford v. Gadsden, City of 5.11n112
Algert; Imperial Beach, City of v. . . . . . .
                   4.8n124
Alleged Contempt of (see name of party)
Allegheny County; Griggs v. 4.5n64;
                   9.4n48
Allegheny County; Schenley Farms Co. v.
       . . . . 5.12n121

Allen; Bd. of Educ. of Cent. Sch. Dist. No. 1 v.
            . . . . 1.4n34; 6.2n18
Allen v. McGovern 3.6n77
Allen v. Ogden, City of 6.6n67
Allstate Ins. Co. v. Municipality of Anchorage
       . . . . 3.8n100
Alma, City of; Johnson v. 3.12n161
Almquist v. Marshan, Town of . . . 4.6n86
Alton, City of; Godfrey, Town of v. . . . . .
                   1.4n27
Amarillo, City of; Traylor v. 3.2n14
Ambler Realty Co.; Euclid, Village of v. . . .
                   4.3n14
American Commuters Ass'n v. Levitt . . . .
                  10.6n63
American Constitutional Law Foundation,
   Inc.; Buckley v. 7.8n75
American Dental Ass'n; Kolstad v. . . . . .
               8.6n113; 9.5n70
American Mini Theaters; Young v. . . . . .
                   4.3n31
American Press Co.; Grosjean v. . . 7.1n4;
             7.3n22; 10.3n28
American Surety Co. of New York; Borough of
   Totowa v. 8.2n37
American Trucking Ass'ns., Inc. v. Scheiner
           . . . . 10.3n22; 10.5n54
American Trucking Ass'ns., Inc. v. Smith
           . . . . .10.3n22; 10.5n54
Amsterdam, City of; Motyka v. . . . 6.6n67
Anchorage Equal Rights Comm'n; Thomas v.
                  3.8n95
Anderson v. Columbus 9.4n32
Anderson v. Creighton 8.6n111
Anderson; Elder v. 8.6n91
Andrews v. Vt. Dep't Educ. 6.2n43
Annis Furs, Inc. v. Detroit, City of . . . . .
                  10.6n71
Antonio v. Wards Cove Packing Co., Inc.
                 . . . . 9.7n109
Antrim v. Hohlt 4.4n58
Appeal of (see name of party)
Appeal of Estate of (see name of party)
Application of (see name of applicant)
Arcadia Dev. Corp. v. Bloomington, City of
                 . . . . . . 4.4n49
Arlington Heights, Village of v. Metropolitan
   Hous. Dev. Corp. 6.8n111
Arlington, Town of; Collura v. . . . 4.6n86
Armory Park Neighborhood Ass'n. v. Episco-
   pal Com. Servs. 3.2n7
Asbury Park, City of; 405 Monroe Co. v. . . .
                  5.13n136

[References are to text sections]

Ash Grove Cement Co. v. Jefferson 4.2n3

Ashburn, City of; Got-It Hardware & Gifts, Inc. v. 5.13n138

Aspen, City of; Cowan v. 8.2n22

Assad; Human Rights Comm'n of Worcester v. 3.8n100

AT&T Wireless PCS, Inc. v. Atlanta, City of 3.11n159

AT&T Wireless PCS, Inc. v. City Council of Virginia Beach 3.11n157

AT&T Wireless PCS, Inc. v. Winston-Salem Zoning Bd. of Adjustment . . . 3.11n158

Atlanta, City of; AT&T Wireless PCS, Inc. v. 3.11n159

Atlanta, City of v. J.A. Jones Constr. Co. 5.8n83

Atlanta, City of; Pharr Road Inv. Co. v. . . 10.3n31

Atlanta, City of; Steinberg v. . . . 4.9n131

Atterberry v. Police Comm'r of Boston . . . 8.3n40

Auburn; State v. 8.7n119

Auburn, City of v. Desgrosseillers 4.7n94

Aunt Hack Ridge Estates, Inc. v. Planning Comm'n 4.6n88

Aurora, City of; Dean Milk Co. v. 1.5n42

Aurora, City of; First Nat'l Bank v. 4.9n136

Austin v. Housing Auth. of City of Hartford 5.7n73

Austin, City of; Gopher Sales Co. v. 3.12n169

Austin, City of v. Southwestern Bell Video Svs., Inc. 3.11n146

Avery v. Midland County 7.5n29; 7.6n43; 7.6n50

Aznavorian; Califano v. 6.7n85

B

Baby Tam & Co., Inc. v. Las Vegas, City of 3.4n36

Bailey v. New York, City of 9.2n4

Bair; Moorman Mfg. Co. v. 10.3n24

Baker v. Carr 7.6n48

Baker v. Marley 8.2n34

Baker; Princeton, City of v. 8.6n86

Bakersfield, City of; Fox Bakersfield Theatre Corp. v. 10.3n25; 10.8n86

Ball v. James 7.5n35

Ballou; Litchfield, City of v. 5.12n114

Baltimore v. Chesapeake Marine Ry. Co. 4.8n126

Baltimore, City of; Marino v. 4.4n53

Banny v. New York, City of 8.2n39

Bantam Books, Inc. v. Sullivan . . 3.4n35

Barad v. Jefferson Co. 6.6n69

Barbourville, City of; Peoples Gas Co. of Kentucky v. 3.10n129

Barker Bros. v. Los Angeles, City of 2.7n43; 3.9n105

Barlow v. Friendship Heights Citizens' Comm. 2.4n10

Barnard v. Thorstenn 8.2n21

Barnes v. Dayton, City of 3.5n49

Barnes v. Glen Theatre, Inc. 3.4n37

Barnett; Bel-Nor, Village of v. . . . 3.3n25

Barnett; U.S. Airways, Inc. v. . . . 9.8n125

Barrett & Assocs., Inc.; Wiggins v. 5.13n137

Barry; Boos v. 9.5n62

Basiardanes v. Galveston, City of 3.4n44

Baton Rouge, City of v. Ewing . . . 3.6n71

Baton Rouge, City of; Herlitz v. . . 4.8n118

Battaglia; Wellford v. 8.2n21

Baxendale; Pierro v. 2.7n40

Baxley, City of; Staub v. 3.12n172

Bay City; Stevenson v. 8.6n86

Baycol, Inc. v. Downtown Development Authority 4.8n106

Bayonne, City of; Slurzberg v. . . . 5.4n36

Bd. of Adjustment of Ross Tp.; Kovacs v. 3.12n177

Bd. of County Comm'rs; Mt. Carmel Medical Ctr. v. 5.9n92

Bd. of County Comm'rs for Pennington County; Brown v. 4.8n112

Bd. of County Comm'rs of Queen Anne's Co.; Soaring Vista Properties, Inc. v. 4.3n18

Bd. of Comm'rs v. Gustafson 2.6n27

Bd. of Comm'rs; Hernandez v. . . 3.12n168

Bd. of Comm'rs of Chattanooga; Hughes v. 2.7n41

Bd. of Comm'rs of Edwards County v. Simmons 5.12n119, n120

Bd. of Comm'rs of El Paso County; McIntyre v. 4.8n120

Bd of Comm'rs of Iberia & St. Mary Drainage Dist.; Myles Salt Co. v. 10.7n81

Bd. of Comm'rs of Shawnee County; Kratina v. 4.8n107

Bd. of County Comm'rs; Champlin Petroleum Co. v. 1.2n6

Bd. of Educ. v. Allen 1.4n34

Bd. of Educ.; Brown v. 6.2n3

Bd. of Educ.; Goin v. 5.13n129

[References are to text sections]

Bd. of Educ. v. Hall 5.6n59
Bd. of Educ.; Pickering v. . . 8.1n4; 8.4n58;
                                        8.5n63, n67
Bd. of Educ., Levittown Union Free School
   District v. Nyquist 6.2n10
Bd. of Educ. of Central School Dist. No. 1 v.
   Allen 6.2n18
Bd. of Educ. of Ewing Township; Everson v.
   . . . .   6.2n19
Bd. of Educ. of Santa Fe Public Schools; Sena
   Sch. Bus Co. v. 5.3n27
Bd. of Educ. of Westside Community Schools v.
   Mergens 6.2n37
Bd. of Health of Barnstable; Tri-Nel Manage-
   ment, Inc. v. 3.5n56
Bd. of Oklahoma City v. Shanbour . . . . .
                                        4.4n57
Bd. of Pub. Works of Rolla v. Sho-Me Power
   Corp. 5.3n29
Bd. of Safety of Town of Monroeville; Small v.
   . . . .   8.4n54
Bd. of Supervisors; Curtis v. 1.6n46
Bd. of Supervisors of Albemarle County; 360
   Degrees   Communications   Co.   of
   Charlottesville v. 3.11n157
Bd. of Supervisors of Washtenaw County;
   Fischer v. 7.8n73
Bd. of Zoning Adjustment of Mobile v. Wil-
   liams 4.4
Bd. of Zoning Appeals of Lansing; Citizens
   Savings Bank, Matter of v. . . .   4.4n54
Bd. of Zoning Appeals of New Haven; Culi-
   nary Institute v. 4.4n54
Beach v. Planning & Zoning Comm'n. of Mil-
   ford 4.2n5; 4.2n8
Beard; Mayor, Councilmen & Citizens v. . .
                                        1.7n55
Beasy; Commonwealth v. 3.8n92
Beatrice, City of; Burger v. 4.8n106
Beatrice, City of; Day v. 5.2n12
Beazer; NYC Transit Auth. v. . . .   8.2n18
Beer v. U.S. 7.7n67
Begin v. Inhabitants of Sabattus . . . . .
                               2.7n34; 3.9n111
Bel Air, Town of; Beshore v. 5.2n19
Bel-Nor, Village of v. Barnett . . .   3.3n25
Belvidere, City of v. Illinois State Labor Rela-
   tions Bd. 6.5n63; 8.7n131
Benson; Jackson v. 6.2n26
Benton, City of; Center v. 4.8n122
Berinstein; Schaefer v. 5.2n22
Bernadine v. New York, City of . .   6.6n78
Beshore v. Bel Air, Town of 5.2n19
Bessemer, City of; Birmingham Gas Co. v.
   . . . .   .7.8n72

Bethlehem, City of; Milan v. 9.4n31
Bingle; Petka v. 2.6n28
Bird v. McGoldrick 8.6n88
Birdsong Motors Inc.; Tampa, City of v. . .
                                        10.3n15
Birmingham, City of; Paar v. . . .   4.9n133
Birmingham, City of; Shuttlesworth v. . . .
                                       3.12n173
Birmingham Gas Co. v. Bessemer, City of
   . . . .   .7.8n72
Bishop v. Wood 8.4n51
Black Brook, Town of v. State . . .   1.4n35
Blaisdell; Home Bldg. & Loan Ass'n v. . . .
                                      3.10n128
Blalock v. Johnston 8.6n91
Bloodworth v. Suggs 8.7n121
Bloomfield Planning Bd.; Graves v. . . . . .
                                        4.4n48
Bloomington, City of; Arcadia Dev. Corp. v.
   . . . .   .4.4n49
Blue Grass, Town of; Canade, Inc. v. . . . .
                                        6.6n74
Blumenthal v. Headland, Town of . . . . . .
                                       5.10n95
Board of County Comm'rs of Bryan Co. v.
   Brown 9.6n79
Board of Comm'rs of Bradley Beach; New
   Jersey Good Humor v. 2.4n8
Board of Education; Wardwell v. . .   8.2n20
Board of Health & Environmental Control;
   Columbia, City of v. 10.2n11
Board of Sup'rs of Fairfax County v. Horne
   . . . .   2.4n16
Boca Raton, City of; Faragher v. . .   8.5n76
Boise Artesian Hot & Cold Water Co. v. Boise
   City 3.10n125
Boise City; Boise Artesian Hot & Cold Water
   Co. v. 3.10n125
Bone v. Lewiston, City of 4.7n93
Bontatibus; Larkin v. 1.6n44
Booneville, City of; Edge v. 9.4n33
Boos v. Barry 9.5n62
Booth v. Churner 9.6n92
Bordanaro v. McLeod 9.6n84
Borough of Glen Rock; Home Owners Constr.
   Co. v. 5.4n35; 5.5n52
Borough of Mt. Ephraim; Schad v. . . . . .
                                        4.3n31
Borough of Oakland v. Roth 4.2n5
Borough of Sharpsburg; O.H. Martin Co. v.
   . . . .   10.6n68
Borough of Totowa v. American Surety Co. of
   New York 8.2n37
Boss Capital, Inc. v. Casselberry, City of
   . . . .   3.4n36

[References are to text sections]

Bossier Parish Sch. Bd.; Reno v. . . . 7.7n65
Boston Hous. Auth.; Perez v. 6.8n106
Bosworth v. Hagerty 5.12n113
Boulder Corp. v. Vann 4.2n6
Bowling Green-Warren County Airport Bd. v.
    Long 4.3n22
Bowman, City of v. Gunnells 9.4n27,
    n38
Bown v. Gwinnett County Sch. Dist. . . . .
    6.2n34
Boyce v. Gastonia, City of 3.10n131
Boyd v. Donelon 4.7n95
Bozeman, City of; Walton v. 9.4n32
Braaten v. Olson 5.5n44
Bradford; Wilmington Medical Center v. . .
    4.3n16
Brady; Complete Auto Transit, Inc. v. . . .
    10.3n22; 10.5, n51
Brady v. Dep't of Personnel 8.7n124
Bragg v. Dallas, City of . . 4.9n140; 9.4n37
Brandhove; Tenney v. 8.6n104
Branson School Dist. RE-82 v. Romer . . .
    1.4n33
Branti v. Finkel 8.4n61; 8.5n64
Braunfeld v. Brown 3.3n21
Bray v. Alexandria Women's Health Clinic
    . . . . .9.7n99
Breckenridge; Griffin v. 9.7n99
Breier; Peters v. 3.6n80
Brennan; Farmer v. 9.7n102
Brent; Fracasse v. 5.12n119
Brewer v. Claypool 4.8n124
Brewer Environmental Industries, Inc. v.
    A.A.T. Chem., Inc. 5.6n54
Bricker v. Sims 8.6n104
Bride v. Slater, City of 5.3n26
Bridgeport, City of; Hennessey v. . . . . . .
    8.4n54
Bristol Bay; Liberati v. 10.7n78
Bristol, Town of; Doucette v. 6.6n77;
    9.2n20
Broadlands Community Consolidated School;
    Thomas v. 6.6n69
Broadrick v. Oklahoma 9.5n64
Broderick; Gardner v. 8.4n55
Bronk v. Ineichen 6.8n105
Brookpark Entertainment, Inc. v. Taft . . .
    2.8n53
Brooks; Miami, City of v. 9.2n8
Brown v. Bd. of Co. Comm'rs for Pennington
    County 4.8n112
Brown v. Bd. of Educ. 6.2n3
Brown; Board of County Comm'rs of Bryan
    Co. v. 9.6n79
Brown; Braunfeld v. 3.3n21

Brown v. Chicago, City of 3.5n60
Brown; Kinney v. 4.8n113
Brown v. Kirk 8.2n27
Brown; Parker v. 1.3n17; 9.9n136
Brown; Wright v. 4.9n139; 9.4n35
Brown's Furniture, Inc. v. Wagner . . . . .
    10.5n54
Brownstone Pub. Inc. v. New York City De-
    partment of Buildings 7.2n9
Brownstone Publishers, Inc. v. New York City
    Dep't of Bldgs. 7.2n9
Bruno v. Dept. of Police 8.3n40
Bryant; Adams v. 8.6n87
Brzonkala v. Virginia Polytechnic and State
    Univ. 2.5n24
Buckley v. American Constitutional Law
    Foundation, Inc. 7.8n75
Buckley v. Valeo 8.2n30
Buffalo; Harbison v. 4.4n43
Burbank, City of; Burbank-Pasadena Airport
    Auth. v. 1.4n33
Burbank-Pasadena Airport Auth. v. Burbank,
    City of 1.4n33
Bureau of Licenses; Fink v. . . . 3.12n177
Burger v. Beatrice, City of 4.8n106
Burger v. Springfield, City of 5.1n3;
    5.3n26
Burgess v. Concord, City of 4.2n1
Burks v. Lafayette, City of 7.8n78
Burlington Broadcasters Inc.; Freeman v.
    . . . . 3.11n150
Burlington, City of; Eno v. 3.2n13
Burlington, City of; My Sister's Place v. . . .
    6.6n69
Burns; Elrod v. 8.4n60
Burson v. Freeman 9.5n62
Butler v. Michigan 3.4n31
Buxbom v. Riverside, City of 3.6n76
Buzzetti v. New York, City of . . . 3.4n40
Byrne; Ketchum v. 7.7n56

C

Cabell v. Chavez-Salido 8.2n12
Cabiness; Wilson-Jones v. 1.3n13
Cahill; Robinson v. 6.2n7; 10.4n38
Cahn v. Huntington, Town of 5.2n4
Cain; Leake v. 6.6n77; 9.2n20
Calhoun v. Little 8.6n98
Calhoun, City of; Cumberland Telephone &
    Telegraph Co. v. 3.12n165
Calif. Coastal Comm'n; Remmenga v. . . .
    4.6n88
Califano v. Aznavorian 6.7n85
California; Cohen v. 3.6n65
California; Miller v. 3.4n28

[References are to text sections]

California; Splawn v. 3.4n29
California Coastal Commission; Nollan v.
. . . . 4.6n90
California Coastal Comm'n; Nollan v. . . .
4.5n80; 9.4n45
California Dep't of Alcoholic Beverage Con-
trol; Shaw v. 9.6n91
California State Employees Ass'n v. Williams
. . . . 6.5n61; 8.7n130
California, State of v. U.S. . . . 10.2n8, n9
Call; Thomson v. 5.2n22; 5.12n113
Cameron v. Johnson 3.6n83
Canade, Inc. v. Blue Grass, Town of . . . .
6.6n74
Cannata v. New York, City of . . . 4.8n105
Cannice v. Norwest Bank Iowa, N.A. . . . .
9.8n126
Cannon; Davidson v. . . . 8.6n107; 9.6n89
Canton, City of v. Harris 6.6n81;
9.6n78, n85
Cape Canaveral, City of; Abbott v. . . . . .
3.11n151
Capital Cities Media, Inc. v. Chester . . . .
7.3n16
Carey; Ottawa, City of v. 2.4n9
Carl Bolander & Sons v. Minneapolis, City of
. . . . 5.8n84
Carr; Baker v. 7.6n48
Carruth v. Madera, City of 5.1n1
Carter; Shaffer v. 10.6n63
Carter Co. v. Elizabethton, City of . . . . .
5.13n139
Cascade, Town of; Iowa Elec. Co. v. . . . . .
5.6n58
Casey Martin; PGA Tour, Inc. v. . . . . . .
9.8n128
Casselberry, City of; Boss Capital, Inc. v.
. . . . 3.4n36
Cayetano; Rice v. 7.5n32
Cedar Bay Constr., Inc. v. Fremont, City of
. . . . 5.6n70
Cedar Falls, City of; Marco Dev. Corp. v.
. . . . .5.2n20; 5.12n117
Cedar Rapids, City of; McGuire v. . . 9.2n8
Cedar Rapids, City of; Walker v. . . 9.2n21
Centanne; Woodruff, State ex rel. v. . . . .
10.3n15
Center v. Benton, City of 4.8n122
Center Moriches Union Free Sch. Dist.;
Lamb's Chapel v. . . . 4.10n145; 6.2n38
Central Bitulithic Paving Co. v. Mt. Clemens,
City of 5.11n108
Central Hudson Gas & Electric Corp. v. Pub-
lic Service Commission of N.Y. . . . . . .
3.6n74

Central Nat'l Bank; Chicago, City of v. . . .
4.2n7, n9
Central Nat'l Bank; Peoria, City of v. . . . .
4.8n125
Century Holdings, Ltd.; Whatcom County
Water Dist. No. 4 v. 5.12n116
Cervase v. Kawaida Towers, Inc. . . 4.7n92
C.H. v. Oliva 6.2n28
Champeau v. Vill. of Little Chute . . . . . .
9.4n36
Champlin Petroleum Co. v. Bd. of County
Comm'rs 1.2n6
Chandler v. Miller 8.5n72
Chaplinsky v. New Hampshire . . . 3.6n64
Chapman v. New York, City of . . . 5.2n17
Chariton, City of; Midwest Inv. Co. v. . . .
3.2n9
Charlottesville, City of; Schleifer v. . . . . .
3.6n79
Charter Twp. of Ypsilanti v. General Motors
Corp., ... 6.12n143
Chavez-Salido; Cabell v. 8.2n12
Chavis; Whitcomb v. 7.7n61
Cheektowaga, Town of; Zibbon v. . . . . . .
9.3n25
Chemical Bank v. Washington Pub. Power
Supply System. 5.13n128
Chesapeake Marine Ry. Co.; Baltimore v.
. . . . .4.8n126
Chester; Capital Cities Media, Inc. v. . . . .
7.3n16
Chester, City of; United States v. . . . . . .
1.3n21
Chester, City of; U.S. v. 4.3n19
Chicago v. FCC 3.11n146
Chicago, City of; Brown v. 3.5n60
Chicago, City of v. Central Nat'l Bank . . .
4.2n7, n9
Chicago, City of; Chicago Food Management,
Inc. v. 5.13n138
Chicago, City of; Chicago Patrolmen's Ass'n v.
. . . . 5.4n36
Chicago, City of; Father Basil's Lodge v. . . .
3.9n102
Chicago, City of; Illinois Cigarette Serv.
Co. v. 3.5n55
Chicago, City of v. Morales 3.6n85
Chicago, City of; Villa v. 5.11n107
Chicago Food Management, Inc. v. Chicago,
City of 5.13n138
Chicago Land Clearance Comm'n v. White
. . . . .4.8n105
Chicago Patrolmen's Ass'n v. Chicago, City of
. . . . 5.4n36
Chiles; Coalition for Adequacy & Fairness v.
. . . . 10.4n38

[References are to text sections]

Chittenden Town Sch. Dist. v. Dep't of Educ. 6.2n43

Churchill v. McKay 8.6n92

Churchill; Waters v. 8.4n58; 8.5n66

Churner; Booth v. 9.6n92

Cincinnati, City of; McGuire v. . . . 2.4n19

Cincinnati, City of; Pembaur v. . . 9.6n80

Citizens Bank of Weston, Inc. v. Weston, City of 10.3n32

Citizens for Cmty. Action; Lockport, Town of v. 1.8n59; 7.6n52; 7.8n77

Citizens Savings Bank, Matter of v. Bd. of Zoning Appeals of Lansing 4.4n54

City v. (see name of defendant)

City and County of (see name of city and county)

City & County of San Francisco; Powell v. 2.4n17

City Council of City of Orange; J. Turco Paving Contractor, Inc. v. 5.6n61

City Council of Virginia Beach; AT&T Wireless PCS, Inc. v. 3.11n157

City & County of Honolulu; Pickard v. . . . 4.9n130

City of Charleston, State ex rel. v. Coghill 1.4n26

Civil Serv. Comm'n; Kelly v. . . . 8.7n120

Civil Service Technical Guild v. LaGuardia 8.7n116

Clabaugh; Clark v. 9.7n101

Clark v. Clabaugh 9.7n101

Clark v. Dallas Indep. Sch. Dist. . . 6.2n35

Clark v. Ferling 8.6n105

Clark v. Scheld 6.6n69

Clary; Haskins v. 5.2n9

Claypool; Brewer v. 4.8n124

Clayton v. Oak Park, Village of . . 3.8n98

Clear Lake, City of; Kelroy v. . . . 4.8n124

Clear Lake, City of; Page & Crane Lumber Co. v. 4.8n125

Cleburne, City of v. Cleburne Living Center 4.3n29; 7.8n74

Cleburne Living Center; Cleburne, City of v. 4.3n29; 7.8n74

Clements v. Fashing 8.3n46

Clermont; Walton v. 4.8n113

Cleveland Bd. of Educ. v. Loudermill 8.4n52

Clovis, City of; Latimer v. 4.9n137

County Comm'rs of Middlesex; Majestic Radiator Enclosure Co. v. 5.5n51

County of Hawaii; Konno v. 6.5n59; 8.7n128

County of Merced; Empresa Siderugica v. 10.3n20

Coalition for Adequacy & Fairness v. Chiles 10.4n38

Coast Cigarette Sales, Inc. v. Mayor of Long Branch 3.5n55

Cobb v. Pasadena City Bd. of Educ. 5.5n42

Cobb County v. Peavy 4.3n30

Coe v. Albuquerque 4.3n20

Coe v. Errol, Town of 10.3n21

Coghill; City of Charleston, State ex rel. v. 1.4n26

Cohen v. California 3.6n65

Cohen; Publicker Industries, Inc. v. 7.3n17

Cohen; Taylor v. 6.8n107

Coldwater, Town of; Mississippi Power & Light Co. v. 3.12n163

Cole v. Richardson 8.2n31

College Savings Bank; Florida Prepaid Postsecondary Education Expense Board v. 1.3n14

Collier County; First Assembly of God v. 3.9n117; 4.3n24

Collier Dev. Corp.; Naples Airport Auth., City of v. 4.3n21

Collins v. Harker Heights 9.6n90

Collura v. Arlington, Town of 4.6n86

Colorado Ass'n of Pub. Employees v. Dep't of Highways 6.5n59; 8.7n128

Colorado Springs, City of; Adams v. 1.7n53

Colorado Springs, City of v. Smartt 4.3n15

Columbia, City of v. Board of Health & Environmental Control 10.2n11

Columbia, City of v. Omni Outdoor Advertising Co. 9.9n142

Columbus; Anderson v. 9.4n32

Columbus, City of v. Myszka 9.4n30

Commission v. (see name of opposing party)

Commissioner v. (see name of opposing party)

Commissioner of Internal Revenue (see name of defendant)

Committee for Indus. Org.; Hague v. 2.7n45; 3.9n106

Committee for Pub. Educ. and Religious Liberty; Levitt v. 6.2n24

Common Council of Grand Rapids; Hawkins v. 2.4n13

Commonwealth v. (see name of defendant)

Commonwealth Dep't of Revenue; L.L. Bean, Inc. v. 10.5n56

Commonwealth ex rel. (see name of relator)

Commonwealth of Pa.; Murdock v. 2.7n33

[References are to text sections]

Comm'rs of Bethany Beach; Drexler v. . . . 2.4n12

Complete Auto Transit, Inc. v. Brady 10.3n22; 10.5, n51

Concord, City of; Burgess v. 4.2n1

Concord, City of; Flowerree v. . . . 4.4n46

Condon; Reno v. 2.5n25; 7.4n28

Confederation of Police v. Conlisk 8.4n56

Confederation of Police; Rochford v. 8.4n56

Conlisk; Confederation of Police v. 8.4n56

Connecticut v. Teal 9.7n110

Conservatorship of (see name of party)

Consolidated Box Co.; Tampa v. . . 4.3n20

Consolidated City of Indianapolis; Foley v. 5.2n8

Consolidated Diesel Elec. Corp. v. Stamford, City of 10.3n15

Consolidated Rail Corp. v. Smith 2.5n22

Container Corp. of America v. Franchise Tax Bd. 10.3n24

Continental Illinois Nat'l Bank & Trust Co. v. Middlesboro, City of . . 3.12n165

Continental Oil Co. v. Twin Falls, City of 3.12n166

Conyers, City of; Moon v. 4.8n112

Cook v. Navy Point, Inc. 5.3n29

Cook, County of; Santucci Const. Co. v. . . 5.7n72

Cooper; Kovacs v. 3.7n89

Cooperman; May v. 6.2n34

Copple v. Lincoln, City of 4.3n20

Coral Gables, City of v. Weksler 5.12n126

Coronado, City of v. San Diego Unified Port Dist. 1.4n31

Coronado Dev. Co. v. McPherson . . 4.6n87

Corrington v. Kalicak 9.4n42

Corsicana, City of v. Wilson 3.2n11

Corwin v. Farrell 6.5n60; 8.7n129

Council for Better Educ.; Rose v. 6.2nn8, 11; 10.4n38

Council of Borough of Munhall; Pa. Alliance for Jobs & Energy v. 3.9n115

County v. (see name of defendant)

County Court of Wood County; Cunningham v. 9.2n10

County of (see name of county)

Cowan v. Aspen, City of 8.2n22

Cox v. Louisiana 3.6n69

Cox v. New Hampshire . . . 3.9n112, n114, n120

Crabtree Co.; State v. 3.5n55

Cramton v. Cramton's Estate 2.4n11

Cramton's Estate; Cramton v. . . . 2.4n11

Craven, State ex rel. v. Tacoma, City of . . 3.12n170

Creighton; Anderson v. 8.6n111

Cremer v. Peoria Housing Authority 10.3n23

Crestview Sanitary Dist.; Duncan Dev. Corp. v. 10.7n80

Criswell; Western Air Lines, Inc. v. 9.7n108

Cromwell v. Ferrier 4.3n37

Cromwell; Township of Hillsborough v. . . 10.3n26

Crowley, City of; Crowley Firemen, City of v. 8.3n43

Crowley Firemen, City of v. Crowley, City of 8.3n43

Crystal Lake, City of; Rosenthal v. 9.4n41

Cuffley v. Mickes 3.6n72

Culinary Institute v. Bd. of Zoning Appeals of New Haven 4.4n54

Culver v. Dagg 4.3n24

Cumberland, City of; Schultz v. . . 3.4n34, n39

Cumberland Telephone & Telegraph Co. v. Calhoun, City of 3.12n165

Cunningham v. County Court of Wood County 9.2n10

Cunningham; McCrea v. 8.2n17

Curnane; Everett, City of v. 8.2n28

Curtis v. Bd. of Supervisors 1.6n46

Custody of (see name of party)

D

Dagg; Culver v. 4.3n24

Daley; Green Street Ass'n v. . . . 6.8n107

Dallas; Wachsman v. 8.3n44

Dallas, City of; Bragg v. . 4.9n140; 9.4n37

Dallas, City of; FW/PBS, Inc. v. . . 2.8n56; 3.4n36; 3.9n119

Dallas, City of; Gardner v. 5.2n19; 5.12n122

Dallas Indep. Sch. Dist.; Clark v. 6.2n35

Dallas Indep. Sch. Dist.; Jett v. . . 9.6n77; 9.7n96

Dalsin; St. Paul, City of v. 3.9n104

Dandridge v. Williams 6.7n85

Daniels v. Williams 8.6n107; 9.6n89

Darien, Town of; Villager Pond, Inc. v. . . . 9.5n67

Daves v. Longwood, City of 2.6n27

Davidson v. Cannon 8.6n107; 9.6n89
Davies v. Madelia, Village of 5.6n56
Davis v. Imlay Township 4.3n23
Davis; Washington v. 10.3n32
Day v. Beatrice, City of 5.2n12
Dayton, City of; Barnes v. 3.5n49
Dayton, City of; Frecker v. 3.9n108
Daytona Beach, City of v. Palmer . . . . . .
6.6n79
Dean Milk Co. v. Aurora, City of . . 1.5n42
DeBenedictis; Keystone Bituminous Coal
Ass'n v. 9.4n44
Decatur, City of; Georgia Power Co. v. . . .
3.10n137
Deegan; Adler v. 2.3n6
Defiance, City of; Ohio Oil Co., State ex rel. v.
. . . . 3.12n171
DeGarmo v. Alcoa, City of 9.4n34
DeHoney v. Hernandez 6.6; 9.2
DeKalb County; Southern Airways Co. v.
. . . . 5.12n121
Del E. Webb Development Co.; Spur Indus-
tries, Inc. v. 3.2n3
Del Monte Dunes at Monterey, Ltd.; Monte-
rey, City of v. 4.5n81
Del Sesto; Worrell v. 4.4n50
Delight Wholesale Co. v. Prairie Village, City
of 3.1n1
Delmarva Power & Light Co. v. Seaford, City
of 3.10n132
DeLong v. Erie, County of 9.3n25
Delony v. Rucker 3.10n129
Dempsey v. Souris, City of 9.4n30
Denio v. Huntington Beach, City of . . . . .
5.12n119
Denver, City and County of v. Rinker . . .
8.7n115
Denver, City and County of v. Talarico . . .
9.4n39
Dep't of Admin.; Horrell v. 6.5n59;
8.7n128
Dep't. of Community Affairs; N.J. State
League of Municipalities v. . . . 4.3n16
Dep't of Educ.; Chittenden Town Sch. Dist. v.
. . . . 6.2n43
Dept of Health, City of New York; S.H. Kress
& Co. v. 3.3n19
Dep't of Highways; Colorado Ass'n of Pub.
Employees v. 6.5n59; 8.7n128
Dep't of HUD v. Rucker 6.8n102
Dep't of Personnel; Brady v. 8.7n124
Dept. of Police; Bruno v. 8.3n40
Dep't of Revenue of State of Ill.; Nat'l Bellas
Hess, Inc. v. 10.5nn56, 59
Dept. of Soc. Svcs. of the City of N.Y.;
Monell v. 1.3n16

Dep't of Soc. and Health Serv.; Johanson v.
. . . . 8.7n131
Dep't of Social and Health Services; Washing-
ton Federation of State Employees v. . .
6.5n59; 8.7n128
Dep't of Social and Health Servs.; Johanson v.
. . . . 6.5n63
Dept. of Transportation; Professional
Engineers v. 6.5n59
Dep't of Transportation and Pub. Facilities;
Moore v. 6.5n60; 8.7n129
Derby, City of v. Di Yanno 4.8n107
Desgrosseillers; Auburn, City of v. . . . . .
4.7n94
DeShaney v. Winnebago County Dep't of So-
cial Services 9.2n22
Detroit, City of; Annis Furs, Inc. v. . . . . .
10.6n71
Detroit, City of; Hughes v. 2.8n55
Detroit, City of; Stratton v. 5.10n94,
n97
Develle; Krauss Co. v. 10.5n52
Dewitt Apparel, Inc. v. Four Seasons of Ro-
mar Beach Condominium Owner's Assoc.
. . . . 4.2n10
D.H.L. Associates, Inc. v. O'Gorman . . . .
3.4n41
Di Yanno; Derby, City of v. 4.8n107
Diedrich; Secrist v. 5.5n39; 5.6n59
Dillon v. Nassau Co. Civil Serv. Comm'n
. . . . 8.7n124
Dillon v. York City Sch. Dist. . . . 4.9n132
DiMa Corp. v. Hallie, Town of . . . 3.4n33
Dionne v. Trenton, City of 9.4n28
Dir. of Revenue; Wilson's Total Fitness Cen-
ter, Inc. v. 10.8n84
Director of Civil Serv.; McNamara v. . . . .
8.7n123
Director of Revenue; Kansas City Royals
Baseball Corp. v. 10.5n53
District of Columbia; Johnson v. . . . .
6.8n106
District of Columbia Bd. of Zoning Adjust-
ment; Hilton Hotels v. 4.7n94
Dixon; Whittier, City of v. 6.12n138
Doe; Plyler v. 6.2n3
Doe; Regents of the Univ. of Calf. v. . . . .
1.3n15
Doe; Santa Fe Indep. Sch. Dist. v. . . . . .
6.2n31
Doe, In re 3.6n81
Doerner; Mongiovi v. 5.5n45
Dolan v. Tigard, City of . . 4.3n27; 4.5n81
Dole; South Dakota v. 10.2n8
Domico v. Rapides Parish Sch. Bd. . . . . .
8.3n48

[References are to text sections]

Donelon; Boyd v. 4.7n95

Donrey Communications Co. Inc. v. Fayetteville, City of 4.4n43

Doucette v. Bristol, Town of 6.6n77;
9.2n20

Dougall; Sugarman v. 8.2n13

Downtown Development Authority; Baycol,
Inc. v. 4.8n106

Doyle; Mount Healthy City School Bd. of
Educ. v. 1.3n15; 8.5n82; 9.8n135

Drexler v. Comm'rs of Bethany Beach . . .
2.4n12

Duckworth v. Robertsdale 4.8n121

Duke Power Co.; Griggs v. 9.7n110

Duluth, City of; Sermon v. 3.12n161

Duncan Dev. Corp. v. Crestview Sanitary
Dist. 10.7n80

Duncan Parking Meter Corp. v. Gurdon, City
of 5.3n25

Dunlap v. Tift 4.8n127

Dupuis v. Submarine Base Credit Union . .
4.7n94

DuPuy; Lufkin, City of v. 4.8n110

Durango, City of v. Durango Transp. Inc.
. . . . 1.2n5

Durango Transp. Inc.; Durango, City of v.
. . . . 1.2n5

Durham County; R.J. Reynolds Tobacco
Co. v. 10.3n19

E

E. Chicago, City of; Goldblatt Bros. Corp. v.
. . . . 3.6n76

E. Greenbush, Town of; Thompson v. . . . .
3.12n167

East v. Wrightsville 4.8n111

Eastside Disposal Co. v. Mercer Island, City
of 5.6n68

Eau Claire, City of; Hallie, Town of v. . . .
9.9

Eau Claire, City of; Thompson v. . . . . . .
9.4n28

Edelman v. Jordan 6.7n89

Edge v. Booneville, City of 9.4n33

Edgewood Indep. Sch. Dist. v. Kirby . . . .
6.2n11

Edison Illuminating Co. v. Misch . . . . . .
4.8n117

Edmonds; Price v. 5.2n22

Edwards; Gainesville, City of v. . . . .
5.13n134

Edwards v. Hylbert 8.6n89

El Paso, City of v. Nicholson 5.9n89

El Paso Co.; Junglen v. 3.9n106

Elder v. Anderson 8.6n91

Elizabethton, City of; Carter Co. v. . . . . .
5.13n139

Eller Outdoor Advertising Co.; Florissant,
City of v. 10.7n78

Elliott v. Los Angeles Co. 9.4n46

Elrod v. Burns 8.4n60

Elwyn v. Miami, City of 4.4n56

Emmite; Harris Co. v. 5.10n93

Empire City Subway Co.; New York Elec.
Lines Co. v. 3.10n136

Employment Div., Dept of Human Resources
of Oregon v. Smith 3.8n96

Empresa Siderugica v. Co. of Merced . . . .
10.3n20

Engell v. Vitale 6.2n29

Enger v. Walker Field, Colo. Pub. Airport
Auth. 1.4n31

Eno v. Burlington, City of 3.2n13

Entrekin; Glasden, City of v. 4.7n99

Environmental Encapsulating Corp. v. New
York, City of 2.5n22

Episcopal Com. Servs.; Armory Park Neighborhood Ass'n. v. 3.2n7

Erie v. Pap's A.M. 3.4n39

Erie, City of v. Pap's A.M. 4.3n35

Erie, County of; DeLong v. 9.3n25

Errol, Town of; Coe v. 10.3n21

Est. of (see name of party)

Estate of (see name of party)

Euclid, Ohio v. Ambler Realty Corp. . . . .
4.3n14

Euclid, Village of v. Ambler Realty Co. . . .
4.3n14

Evans v. Just Open Gov't 4.3n19

Evanston, City of v. Regional Transp. Auth.
. . . . 4.3n19

Evansville, City of; Miller v. 5.4n33

Everds Bros. v. Gillespie 5.11n111

Everett, City of v. Curnane 8.2n28

Everson v. Bd. of Educ. of Ewing Township
. . . . 6.2n19

Ewing; Baton Rouge, City of v. . . . 3.6n71

Ex parte (see name of applicant)

Ex rel. (see name of relator)

Excelsior v. F.W. Pearce Corp. . . . 5.5n38

F

Fairfax, County of v. Southern Iron Works,
Inc. 2.8n57

Faragher v. Boca Raton, City of . . 8.5n76

Farmer v. Brennan 9.7n102

Farmington, City of; Starcevich v. . . . . . .
9.4n42

Farrell; Corwin v. 6.5n60; 8.7n129

Fary; Richmond, City of v. 10.7n79

[References are to text sections]

Fashing; Clements v. 8.3n46

Father Basil's Lodge v. Chicago, City of . . 3.9n102

Fayetteville, City of; Donrey Communications Co. Inc. v. 4.4n43

FCC; Abilene, City of v. 3.11n141

FCC; Chicago v. 3.11n146

FCC; Gulf Power Co. v. 3.11n148

FCC; New York, City of v. 2.5n22

FCC; Time Warner Entertainment Co. L.P. v. 3.11n156

Feiner v. New York 3.6n68

Felton; Agostini v. 6.2n20

Ferling; Clark v. 8.6n105

Ferrier; Cromwell v. 4.3n37

F.H. Myers Constr. Co. v. New Orleans, City of 5.6n61

Filler; Kenai, City of v. 5.13n129

Fine v. Galloway Township Comm. 4.2n9

Finelli Brothers; Whitemarsh Township Authority v. 5.6n67

Fink v. Bureau of Licenses 3.12n177

Finkel; Branti v. 8.4n61; 8.5n64

First Assembly of God v. Collier County . . 3.9n117; 4.3n24

First English Evangelical Lutheran Church of Glendale v. Los Angeles Co. 4.5n76, n78; 9.4n50

First Nat'l Bank v. Aurora, City of 4.9n136

Fiscal Court of Jefferson Co.; Louisville, City of v. 5.2n16

Fischer v. Bd. of Supervisors of Washtenaw Co. 7.8n73

Fla. Pub. Serv. Comm'n; Florida Soc. of Newspaper Editors, Inc. v. 7.2n8

Flint, City of; Schwartz v. 4.3n21

Flood v. Kennedy 8.3n42

Florida Board of Regents; Kimel v. 8.5n80; 9.8n133

Florida Coastal Theaters, Inc.; St. Petersburg, City of v. 10.8n86

Florida Prepaid Postsecondary Education Expense Board v. College Savings Bank . . 1.3n14

Florida Soc. of Newspaper Editors, Inc. v. Fla. Pub. Serv. Comm'n 7.2n8

Florida, State of v. Port Orange, City of . . 10.7n73

Florissant, City of v. Eller Outdoor Advertising Co. 10.7n78

Flowerree v. Concord, City of 4.4n46

Flowers v. Southern Regional Physician Services Inc. 9.8n126

Floyd, State ex rel. v. Noel 3.5n46

Foley v. Consolidated City of Indianapolis 5.2n8

Fontainebleau Hotel Corp., State ex rel.; Miami Beach, City of v. 3.12n171

Foote; State v. 5.2n17

Fordice; Parker-Weaver v. 7.7n66

Forest Const. Co. v. Planning & Zoning Comm'n of Town of Bethany . . 4.6n85

Forklift Systems, Inc.; Harris v. . . 8.5n77

Forrester v. White 8.6n100

Forsyth County v. Nationalist Movement 9.5n65

Fort Gratiot Sanitary Landfill, Inc. v. Michigan Dep't of Natural Resources 3.7n88

Fort Lauderdale, City of; Smith v. 3.6n84

Foss v. Spitznagel 5.12n127

Fouche; Turner v. 7.5n30; 8.2n15

Four Seasons of Romar Beach Condominium Owner's Assoc.; Dewitt Apparel, Inc. v. 4.2n10

426 Bloomfield Ave. Corp. v. Newark, City of 5.8n80

405 Monroe Co. v. Asbury Park, City of . . 5.13n136

Fourth Nat'l Bank; State for Use of Russell County v. 5.2n9

Fowler; Steele v. 4.8n123

Fox v. General Motors Corp. . . . 9.8n126

Fox Bakersfield Theatre Corp. v. Bakersfield, City of 10.3n25; 10.8n86

Fracasse v. Brent 5.12n119

Franchise Tax Bd.; Container Corp. of America v. 10.3n24

Frank v. Russell 4.4n61

Franklin v. Peterson 10.6n69

Franklin County v. St. Albans, City of . . . 4.4n45

Fraser; McKinley v. 7.8n70

Frecker v. Dayton, City of 3.9n108

Freedman v. Maryland 3.9n119

Freeman v. Burlington Broadcasters Inc. 3.11n150

Freeman; Burson v. 9.5n62

Fremont, City of; Cedar Bay Constr., Inc. v. 5.6n70

French; Masterson, People ex rel. v. 8.3n42

Friendship Heights Citizens' Comm.; Barlow v. 2.4n10

Frohne; Municipality of Anchorage v. 7.8n71

Ft. Meyers, City of v. Hospital Bd. of Directors of Lee Co. 5.9n90

[References are to text sections]

Fuller; Packard v. 4.8n107

FW/PBS, Inc. v. Dallas, City of . . 2.8n56;
　　　　　　　　　　　3.4n36; 3.9n119

F.W. Pearce Corp.; Excelsior v. . . . 5.5n38

G

Gadsden, City of; Alford v. 5.11n112

Gainesville, City of v. Edwards . . . .
　　　　　　　　　　　5.13n134

Galloway Township Comm.; Fine v. . . . . .
　　　　　　　　　　　4.2n9

Galveston; Hitchcock v. 5.2n13

Galveston, City of; Basiardanes v. . . . . .
　　　　　　　　　　　3.4n44

Gamewell v. Phoenix, City of 5.6n57

Garcia v. San Antonio Metropolitan Transit
　　Auth. 9.2n5

Gardner v. Broderick 8.4n55

Gardner v. Dallas, City of 5.2n19;
　　　　　　　　　　　5.12n122

Garrett v. Holday Inns, Inc. 9.3n26

Garrett v. University of Alabama . . . 8.5;
　　　　　　　　　　　9.8n134

Garrity v. New Jersey 8.4n55

Gary, City of v. Indiana Bell Telephone Co.,
　　Inc. 10.7n72

Gastonia, City of; Boyce v. 3.10n131

Gaudiya Vaishnava Society v. San Francisco,
　　City of 2.8n52

G.C. Murphy Co. v. Redevelopment Auth. of
　　City of Erie 4.8n119

General Ass'n Branch Davidian Seventh Day
　　Adventist v. McLennan County Appraisal
　　Dist. 10.4n44

General Building Contractors Ass'n, Inc. v.
　　Pennsylvania 9.7n95

General Elec. Co. v. Mobile, City of . . . . .
　　　　　　　　　　　5.5n47

General Motors Corp.; Fox v. . . . 9.8n126

Georgia; Stanley v. 7.1n2; 7.3n20

Georgia Power Co. v. Decatur, City of . . .
　　　　　　　　　　　3.10n137

Georgia Power Co.; Summerville, City of v.
　　. . . . . 3.12n162

Gerhardt; Helvering v. 10.6n65

Gerzof v. Sweeney 5.8n76

Gianturco; San Diego Unified Port Dist. v.
　　. . . . . 1.4n34

Gilbert v. Homar 8.5n74

Gilleo; Ladue, City of v. 4.3n38

Gillespie; Everds Bros. v. 5.11n111

Gingles; Thornburg v. 7.7n60

Ginsberg v. New York 3.4n30

Girves v. Kenai Peninsula Borough . . . . .
　　　　　　　　　　　2.4n8

Glasden, City of v. Entrekin 4.7n99

Glatstein v. Miami, City of 5.5n53;
　　　　　　　　　　　5.6n60

Glaze; People v. 2.7n36

Glen Theatre, Inc.; Barnes v. 3.4n37

Globe Newspaper Co. v. Superior Ct. . . . .
　　　　　　　　　　7.1n3; 7.3nn15, 21

Goddard, City of; Griggs v. 4.9n129

Godfrey, Town of v. Alton, City of . . . . . .
　　　　　　　　　　　1.4n27

Goff; Simmons-Harris v. 6.2n27

Goin v. Bd. of Educ. 5.13n129

Goldberg v. Kelly 2.8n58; 6.7n87

Goldblatt v. Hempstead, Town of . . . . . .
　　　　　　　　　　　4.5n71

Goldblatt Bros. Corp. v. E. Chicago, City of
　　. . . . . 3.6n76

Golden v. Ramapo, Town of 4.6n88

Golden State Transit Corp. v. Los Angeles,
　　City of 2.5n22; 3.10n138

Goldrush II v. Marietta, City of . . . .
　　　　　　　　　　　3.12n174

Gomillion v. Lightfoot . . . 1.4n28; 1.7n48;
　　　　　　　　　　　7.6n47

Good News Club v. Milford Central School
　　. . . . . .6.2n41

Gooding v. Wilson 3.6n66

Gopher Sales Co. v. Austin, City of . . . . .
　　　　　　　　　　　3.12n169

Gore v. Hicks 4.2n8

Goss v. Little Rock, Ark., City of . . 4.7n98

Got-It Hardware & Gifts, Inc. v. Ashburn,
　　City of 5.13n138

Graham v. Richardson 6.7n86

Graham, Town of v. Karpark Corp. . . . . .
　　　　　　　　　　5.2n21; 5.12n120

Granada Bldgs., Inc. v. Kingston, City of
　　. . . . . 5.2n14

Grand Forks, City of; Grand Forks Co. v.
　　. . . . . 5.9n91

Grand Forks Co. v. Grand Forks, City of
　　. . . . . 5.9n91

Grand Junction, City of; Reams v. . . . . .
　　　　　　　　　　　6.12n139

Grand Rapids, City of; Hoyt Bros. v. . . . .
　　　　　　　　　　　2.8n54

Grand Rapids, City of; Lewis v. . . 3.9n107

Grand Trunk W. Ry. v. South Bend, City of
　　. . . . . 3.10n126

Graves v. Bloomfield Planning Bd. . . . . .
　　　　　　　　　　　4.4n48

Graves v. O'Keefe, People ex rel. . . . . . .
　　　　　　　　　　　10.6n66

Greater New Orleans Broadcasting Ass'n,
　　Inc. v. U.S. 3.6n75

[References are to text sections]

Greco; State v. 3.5n45
Green v. Hous. Auth. of Clackamas Co. . .
6.8n105
Green; McDonnell Douglas v. . . . 9.8n131
Green; Milliken v. 10.4n38
Green v. Shaw 3.12n161
Green Street Ass'n v. Daley 6.8n107
Grieshaber v. Albany, City of . . . 6.6n75;
9.2n18; 9.3n25
Griffin v. Breckenridge 9.7n99
Griggs v. Allegheny County 4.5n64;
9.4n48
Griggs v. Duke Power Co. 9.7n110
Griggs v. Goddard, City of 4.9n129
Grimm v. Troy, City of 5.5n49
Griswold v. Ramsey Co. 5.8n80
Grosjean v. American Press Co. . . . 7.1n4;
7.3n22; 10.3n28
Guardianship of (see name of party)
Guion; Shaker Square Co., State ex rel. v.
. . . . .4.4n59
Gulf Power Co. v. FCC 3.11n148
Gulf Power Co.; National Cable & Telecom-
munications Assoc., Inc. v. . . . 3.11n149
Gunnells; Bowman, City of v. . . . 9.4n27,
n38
Gurdon, City of; Duncan Parking Meter
Corp. v. 5.3n25
Gustafson; Bd. of Comm'rs. v. . . . 2.6n27
Guste; Home Depot, Inc. v. 3.3n20
Guthrie, City of v. Pike & Long . . 3.9n104
Guttenberg, City of; Pearson v. . . 4.8n124
Gwinnett Co. Sch. Dist.; Bown v. . . . . . .
6.2n34

H

Hackleburg, Town of v. Northwest Alabama
Gas Dist. 10.3n14
Hagerty; Bosworth v. 5.12n113
Hague v. Committee for Indus. Org. . . . .
2.7n45; 3.9n106
Hahn; Nordlinger v. . . . 10.3n27; 10.4n41
Hale v. Port of Portland 1.2n6
Hall; Bd. of Educ. v. 5.6n59
Hall v. Lea County Elec. Co-Op. . . . . . .
4.10n141
Hallie, Town of; DiMa Corp. v. . . . 3.4n33
Hallie, Town of v. Eau Claire, City of . . .
9.9
Hampton, Town of; Marrone v. . . . 5.2n9;
5.11n102
Hand v. Rhodes 4.8n114
Harbison v. Buffalo 4.4n43
Harbour Village Apts. v. Mukilteo, City of
. . . . 10.3n30

Hardage v. Jacksonville Beach, City of . . .
3.5n46
Hardy v. Leonard 6.8n107
Harker Heights; Collins v. 9.6n90
Harper v. Va. State Bd. of Elections . . . .
7.5n39
Harrell, Ex parte 3.3n23
Harris; Canton, City of v. 6.6n81;
9.6n78, n85
Harris v. Forklift Systems, Inc. . . 8.5n77
Harris Co. v. Emmite 5.10n93
Harrisburg, City of; Schooling v. . . . . . .
4.8n125
Harrison v. Schwartz 1.3n21
Harrison Central Sch. Dist. v. Nyquist . . .
5.12n120
Harrison County, Miss.; U.S. v. . . 10.2n11
Hartford, City of; Levin-Townsend Computer
Corp. v. 10.6n71
Hartke; Oregon City v. 4.3n37
Hartzler v. Kalona, Town of . . . 4.9n138;
9.4n29
Haskins v. Clary 5.2n9
Hatch v. Maple Valley Township Unit School
. . . . 5.11n112
Hatcher v. Kentucky & W. Va. Power Co.
. . . . 3.10n123
Hathaway v. Osborne 9.4n39
Haub v. Montgomery Co. . 6.5n60; 8.7n129
Haulaway Trash Removal, Inc.; Ridley
Township v. 5.13n133
Haverhill, City of; Reynolds Boat Co. v. . .
6.6n67, n71; 9.2n16
Hawaii Housing Auth. v. Midkiff . . . . . .
4.8n102
Hawkins v. Common Council of Grand Rapids
. . . . 2.4n13
Haynes v. Mayor and Council of Borough of
Oradell 3.3n26
Headland, Town of; Blumenthal v. . . . . .
5.10n95
Heffron v. International Soc'y for Krishna
Consciousness, Inc. 4.3n39
Helena Elementary Sch. Dist. No. 1 v. State
. . . . .6.2n8
Helms; Mitchell v. 6.2n21
Helvering v. Gerhardt 10.6n65
Hempstead, Town of; Goldblatt v. . . . . .
4.5n71
Hennessey v. Bridgeport, City of . . 8.4n54
Henry; Neisius v. 5.12n115
Henry v. Rock Hill, City of 3.6n69
Henry Walker Park Ass'n v. Mathews . . .
4.8n114
Herlitz v. Baton Rouge, City of . . 4.8n118

[References are to text sections]

Hernandez v. Bd. of Comm'rs . . 3.12n168
Hernandez; DeHoney v. 6.6; 9.2
Hess v. Port Authority Trans-Hudson Corp.
. . . . 1.3n15
Hess, People ex rel v. Wheeler . . . 8.2n26
Hess Realty Corp.; Melbourne, City of v. . .
3.12n177
Hicks; Gore v. 4.2n8
Hill; Houston, City of v. 3.6n70
Hilton Hotels v. District of Columbia Bd. of
Zoning Adjustment 4.7n94
Hitchcock v. Galveston 5.2n13
Hoepker v. Madison Plan Comm'n, City of
. . . . 4.6n87; 4.7n100
Hohlt; Antrim v. 4.4n58
Holday Inns, Inc.; Garrett v. 9.3n26
Homan v. Lynch 4.4n53
Homar; Gilbert v. 8.5n74
Home Bldg. & Loan Ass'n v. Blaisdell . . .
3.10n128
Home Builders Ass'n of Central Arizona,
Inc. v. Riddel 10.7n82
Home Builders Ass'n of Greater Kansas
City v. Kansas City, City of . . . 4.6n88
Home Depot, Inc. v. Guste 3.3n20
Home Owners Constr. Co. v. Borough of Glen
Rock 5.4n35; 5.5n52
Hope v. Pelzer 8.6n110
Horn; State v. 3.5n58
Horne; Board of Sup'rs of Fairfax County v.
. . . . 2.4n16
Horrell v. Dep't of Admin. 6.5n59;
8.7n128
Hospital Bd. of Directors of Lee County; Ft.
Meyers, City of v. 5.9n90
Hospital Service Plan of N.J.; Johnson v.
. . . . 5.13n131
Hot Springs, City of; Lamar Bath House
Co. v. 5.12n123
Houchins v. KQED, Inc. . . 3.8n101; 7.1n1;
7.2n12; 7.3n22
Hous. Auth. of City of El Paso; Vasquez v.
. . . . 6.8n104
Hous. Auth. of Clackamas Co.; Green v. . .
6.8n105
Housing Auth. of City of Hartford; Austin v.
. . . . 5.7n73
Housing Auth. of Durham; Wm. Muirhead
Constr. Co. v. 5.1n2
Houston, City of v. Hill 3.6n70
Houston, City of v. Magnolia Park, City of
. . . . 1.7n49
Howe v. St. Louis, City of 3.8n97
Howlett v. Rose 1.3n16
Hoyt Bros. v. Grand Rapids, City of . . . .
2.8n54

Huachuca City; McCuistion v. . . . 9.4n28
Hughes v. Bd. of Comm'rs of Chattanooga
. . . . 2.7n41
Hughes v. Detroit, City of 2.8n55
Human Rights Comm'n of Worcester v. Assad
. . . . 3.8n100
Hunt; Shaw v. 7.7n58
Hunter v. Pittsburgh, City of . 1.4; 1.6n43
Huntington Beach, City of; Denio v. . . . .
5.12n119
Huntington, City of; Neal v. 10.8n85
Huntington Park, City of; Sieroty v. . . . .
3.6n76
Huntington, Town of; Cahn v. 5.2n4
Hurdis Realty, Inc. v. N. Providence, Town of
. . . . 5.9n91
Huron, City of; Meierhenry v. . . 6.12n141
Hutchinson; State v. 2.4n21
Hutchinson, City of; Krantz v. . . . 9.2n11
Hylbert; Edwards v. 8.6n89

I

Iacobucci; Newport, City of v. . . . 3.5n47
Idyllwild County Water Dist.; Riverside,
County of v. 5.2n15
Illinois Cigarette Serv. Co. v. Chicago, City of
. . . . 3.5n55
Illinois State Labor Relations Bd.; Belvidere,
City of v. 6.5n63; 8.7n131
Illusions on Peachtree Street, Inc. v. Young
. . . . 3.12n174
Imbler v. Pachtman 8.6n102
Imlay Township; Davis v. 4.3n23
Immanuel Presbyterian Church v. Payne
. . . . 10.4n43
Imperial Beach, City of v. Algert . . . . . .
4.8n124
Imperial Volunteer Fire Dep't; Radobersky v.
. . . . 6.6n80
In re (see name of party)
Incorp. Town of Mapleton v. Iowa Light, Heat
& Power Co. 3.12n164
Incorporated City of Humboldt v. Knight
. . . . 5.13n139
Indep. Dist. of Monroe; Seim v. . . . .
5.13n130
Indiana Bell Telephone Co., Inc.; Gary, City
of v. 10.7n72
Indianapolis, City of; Lurie v. . . . 10.3n16
Ineichen; Bronk v. 6.8n105
Ingleside, City of v. Stewart 5.9n88
Inhabitants of City of Belfast; Small v. . . .
9.5n68
Inhabitants of Sabattus; Begin v. . . . . . .
2.7n34; 3.9n111

[References are to text sections]

Inman S.S. Co. v. Tinker 10.3n17
Int'l Assoc. of Firefighters Local 1596 v. Law-
  rence, City of 2.6n30; 5.4n37
Int'l Soc'y for Krishna Consciousness, Inc.;
  Heffron v. 4.3n39
Iowa Elec. Co. v. Cascade, Town of . . . . .
  5.6n58
Iowa Light, Heat & Power Co.; Incorp. Town
  of Mapleton v. 3.12n164

J

J. Turco Paving Contractor, Inc. v. City Coun-
  cil of City of Orange 5.6n61
J.A. Croson Co.; Richmond, City of v. . . . .
  5.6n64; 5.8n86; 8.2n11; 9.7n116
J.A. Jones Constr. Co.; Atlanta, City of v.
  . . . . .5.8n83
Jackson v. Benson 6.2n26
Jackson Bd. of Educ.; Wygant v. . . . . . .
  7.7n58; 9.7n115
Jacksonville Beach, City of; Hardage v. . .
  3.5n46
Jacksonville Beach, City of; Wilford v. . . .
  6.6n67
Jacksonville, City of; Northeastern Florida
  Chapter of the Associated Gen. Contract v.
  . . . . 5.8n85
Jaffree; Wallace v. 6.2n32
Jagels v. Taylor 10.5n50
James; Ball v. 7.5n35
James; Wyman v. 6.7n91
James Cable Partners, L.P. v. Jamestown,
  City of 3.10n133
Jamestown, City of; James Cable Partners,
  L.P. v. 3.10n133
Jefferson; Ash Grove Cement Co. v. . . . .
  4.2n3
Jefferson Co.; Barad v. 6.6n69
Jensen v. Lane County 6.5n66
Jered Contracting Corp. v. NYC Transit
  Auth. 5.7n75
Jett v. Dallas Indep. Sch. Dist. . . 9.6n77;
  9.7n96
Johanson v. Dep't of Soc. and Health Services
  . . . . 6.5n63; 8.7n131
Johnson v. Alma, City of 3.12n161
Johnson; Cameron v. 3.6n83
Johnson v. District of Columbia . . 6.8n106
Johnson v. Hospital Service Plan of N.J. . .
  5.13n131
Johnson; Kelley v. 8.3n47
Johnson; Miller v. 7.5n37; 7.7n57
Johnson v. Opelousas, City of . . . 3.6n81
Johnson; Scharping v. 1.6n45
Johnson; Sioux City v. 4.8n124

Johnson v. State 9.2n13
Johnson v. Steele Co. 9.4n46
Johnson v. Transp. Agency Santa Clara
  County 9.5n56; 9.7n117
Johnson City, Village of; Waldo's Inc. v. . .
  4.8n104
Johnson Controls; U.A.W. v. . . . 9.7n108
Johnson County Bd. of County Commission-
  ers; Southwestern Bell Wireless Inc. v.
  . . . . 3.11n150
Johnston; Blalock v. 8.6n91
Johnston; Poynter v. 4.8n109
Jones v. New York City Human Resources
  Admin. 8.7n125
Joplin, City of v. Southwest Missouri Light
  Co. 3.10n134
Jordan; Edelman v. 6.7n89
Jordan v. Kelly 8.6n97
Josephson v. Planning Board of City of Stam-
  ford 8.2n33
Judiz; People v. 3.5n61
Junglen v. El Paso Co. 3.9n106
Just Open Gov't; Evans v. 4.3n19

K

Kalicak; Corrington v. 9.4n42
Kalona, Town of; Hartzler v. . . . 4.9n138;
  9.4n29
Kane v. Marion, City of 5.2n5
Kaneville, Town of v. Meredith . . 4.8n108
Kansas City; Marshall v. 3.8n92
Kansas City; Metropolitan Express Services,
  Inc. v. 5.6n55; 5.8n81
Kansas City, City of; Home Builders Ass'n of
  Greater Kansas City v. 4.6n88
Kansas City Royals Baseball Corp. v. Director
  of Revenue 10.5n53
Karcher v. May 6.2n34
Karpark Corp.; Graham, Town of v. . . . .
  5.2n21; 5.12n120
Katz; Saucier v. 8.6n109
Kawaida Towers, Inc.; Cervase v. . . . . . .
  4.7n92
Kawakami; Kunimoto v. 4.2n13
Keeler v. Mayor & City Council of Cumber-
  land 4.3n40
Keeler; Supervisor of Assessments of Balti-
  more County v. 10.4n43
Kekedakis; St. Paul, City of v. . . . 3.5n59
Kelley v. Johnson 8.3n47
Kellogg; Nelson v. 8.6n99
Kelly v. Civil Serv. Comm'n . . . 8.7n120
Kelly; Goldberg v. 2.8n58; 6.7n87
Kelly; Jordan v. 8.6n97
Kelroy v. Clear Lake, City of . . . 4.8n124

[References are to text sections]

Kenai, City of v. Filler 5.13n129
Kenai Peninsula Borough; Girves v. 2.4n8
Kennedy; Flood v. 8.3n42
Kennedy v. Ross 6.5n61
Kentucky & W. Va. Power Co.; Hatcher v. 3.10n123
Ketchum v. Byrne 7.7n56
Key West, City of v. Marrone . . . 10.7n78
Keystone Bituminous Coal Ass'n v. DeBenedictis 9.4n44
Kibbe v. Springfield, City of 9.6n88
Kiker v. Philadelphia, City of . . . 10.6n64
Killian; Kotterman v. 6.2n25
Kimel v. Florida Board of Regents 8.5n80; 9.8n133
King v. Smith 6.7n92; 10.2n8
Kingsport, City of; Penn-Dixie Cement Corp. v. 2.4n8
Kingston, City of; Granada Bldgs., Inc. v. 5.2n14
Kinney v. Brown 4.8n113
Kipperman v. Markham, City of 3.9n110
Kirby; Edgewood Indep. Sch. Dist. v. 6.2n11
Kirk; Brown v. 8.2n27
Kiss; Schroder v. 8.7n122
Kissinger; Short v. 8.7n118
Knapp v. Newport Beach, City of . . 3.2n8
Knight; Incorporated City of Humboldt v. 5.13n139
Knight; Leischner v. 2.4n14
Kohl; Trap Rock Indus., Inc. v. . . . 5.6n62
Kolender v. Lawson 3.6n85
Kollarik; State v. 5.5n39
Kolstad v. American Dental Ass'n 8.6n113; 9.5n70
Konkle; Paducah, City of v. 4.9n135
Konno v. Co. of Hawaii . . 6.5n59; 8.7n128
Koontz v. Superior, Town of 4.8n107
Kotterman v. Killian 6.2n25
Kovacs v. Bd. of Adjustment of Ross Tp. . . 3.12n177
Kovacs v. Cooper 3.7n89
KQED, Inc.; Houchins v. 3.8n101; 7.1n1; 7.2n12; 7.3n22
Kramer v. Union Free Sch. Dist. No. 15 . . 7.5n33
Krantz v. Hutchinson, City of . . . 9.2n11
Kratina v. Bd. of Comm'rs of Shawnee Co. 4.8n107
Krauss Co. v. Develle 10.5n52
Kriener v. Turkey Valley Community School District 9.4n29

Kunimoto v. Kawakami 4.2n13
Kunkle Water & Elec., Inc. v. Prescott, City of 5.5n39; 5.6n59
Kurpinski v. Vreeland 3.12n171
Kurtzman; Lemon v. 6.2n20, n23

L

L.A. Police Dep't v. United Reporting Publ'g Corp. 7.2n13
Ladue, City of v. Gilleo 4.3n38
Lafayette, City of; Burks v. 7.8n78
Lafayette, City of v. Louisiana Power & Light Co. 1.3n18; 9.9n137
LaGuardia; Civil Service Technical Guild v. 8.7n116
Lake Co. Bd. of Comm'rs; Sekerez v. 5.5n52
Lakewood, City of v. Plain Dealer Publ'g Co. 2.7n32; 3.9nn113, 118; 4.10n144
Lakewood, City of; Walker v. . . . 6.8n109
Lallak v. Morris 8.6n103
Lamar Bath House Co. v. Hot Springs, City of 5.12n123
Lambert v. New Haven, City of . . 4.9n132
Lamb's Chapel v. Center Moriches Union Free Sch. Dist. . . . 4.10n145; 6.2n38
Landes v. N. Hempstead, Town of 8.2n9, n15
Lane v. Mount Vernon, City of . . . 3.2n16
Lane County; Jensen v. 6.5n66
Larkin v. Bontatibus 1.6n44
Larkin Co. v. Schwab 3.12n169
Las Vegas, City of; Baby Tam & Co., Inc. v. 3.4n36
Las Vegas, City of; Lydo Entertainments, Inc. v. 3.4n42
Lathrop Co. v. Toledo, City of . . . 5.3n29
Latimer v. Clovis, City of 4.9n137
Lauderdale Co. Bd. of Supervisors; Telcom Sys. Inc. v. 5.5n48
Lawrence, City of; Int'l Ass'n of Firefighters v. 2.6n30; 5.4n37
Lawson; Kolender v. 3.6n85
Layman's Sec. Co. v. Water Works & Sewer Bd. of Prichard 5.5n46
L.C.; Olmstead v. 9.8n127
Lea County Elec. Co-Op.; Hall v. 4.10n141
Leake v. Cain 6.6n77; 9.2n20
Leavitt; Milwaukee, City of v. . . . 4.7n95
Lee; People v. 3.5n51
Lee v. Walker 4.8n125
Lee v. Weisman 6.2n30
Lefkowitz v. Turley 5.6n66; 8.4n56

[References are to text sections]

Leiby; Manchester, City of v. . . . 3.9n116

Leischner v. Knight 2.4n14

Lemon v. Kurtzman 6.2n20, n23

Leninski; Zoning Comm'n of Sachem's Head Ass'n v. 4.3n28

Leo; Puritan-Greenfield Improvement Ass'n v. 4.4n50

Leonard; Hardy v. 6.8n107

Levin-Townsend Computer Corp. v. Hartford, City of 10.6n71

Levitt; American Commuters Ass'n v. . . . 10.6n63

Levitt v. Committee for Pub. Educ. and Religious Liberty 6.2n24

Levy; Parker v. 8.5n73

Lewis v. Grand Rapids, City of . . 3.9n107

Lewiston, City of; Bone v. 4.7n93

Liberati v. Bristol Bay 10.7n78

License of (see name of party)

Lierman; Montgomery, People ex rel. v. . . 1.2n8

Lightfoot; Gomillion v. . . . 1.4n28; 1.7n48; 7.6n47

Lim v. Long Beach 3.4n43

Limestone College; Stanley Smith & Sons v. 5.1n2

Lincoln, City of; Copple v. 4.3n20

Lindberg; Titus v. 8.6n114

Liquid Carbonic Corp. v. Michigan Tax Comm'n 10.6n71

Litchfield, City of v. Ballou . . . 5.12n114

Little; Calhoun v. 8.6n98

Little Rock, Ark., City of; Goss v. 4.7n98

L.L. Bean, Inc. v. Commonwealth Dep't of Revenue 10.5n56

Lng v. Loqa 4.3n17

Lockport, Town of v. Citizens for Cmty. Action 1.8n59; 7.6n52; 7.8n77

Long; Bowling Green-Warren Co. Airport Bd. v. 4.3n22

Long Beach; Lim v. 3.4n43

Long Beach, City of; Los Angeles Dredging Co. v. 5.8n77

Long Branch; Wilson v. 8.2n36

Long Branch, City of; Tim v. 1.3n20

Longwood, City of; Daves v. 2.6n27

Lopez; United States v. . . 2.5n23; 3.5n62

Loqa; Lng v. 4.3n17

Loretto v. Teleprompter Manhattan CATV Corp. 9.4n43

Lorillard Tobacco Co. v. Reilly . . . 3.5n53

Los Angeles, City of; Barker Bros. v. 2.7n43; 3.9n105

Los Angeles, City of; Golden State Transit Corp. v. 2.5n22; 3.10n138

Los Angeles, City of; Lybarger v. . . . 8.4n57

Los Angeles, City of; Preferred Communications, Inc. v. 3.11n152

Los Angeles, City of; Welton v. . . . 3.2n15

Los Angeles Co.; Elliott v. 9.4n46

Los Angeles Co.; First English Evangelical Lutheran Church of Glendale v. 4.5n76, n78; 9.4n50

Los Angeles Dredging Co. v. Long Beach, City of 5.8n77

Loudermill; Cleveland Bd. of Educ. v. . . . 8.4n52

Louisiana; Cox v. 3.6n69

Louisiana Highway & Heavy Branch of Assoc. Gen. Contract; Parish Council of East Baton Rouge v. 5.6n58

Louisiana Power & Light Co.; Lafayette, City of v. 1.3n18; 9.9n137

Louisville, City of v. Fiscal Court of Jefferson Co. 5.2n16

Louisville, City of; Poole v. 6.6n67

Louisville, City of; Schwalk's Administrator v. 4.9n129

Louisville, City of v. Thomas 5.2n18

Louisville Extension Water Dist. v. Sloss 5.10n98

Lubelle v. Rochester Gas & Elec. Co. 4.10n141

Lucas v. South Carolina Coastal Council 4.5n70

Lufkin, City of v. DuPuy 4.8n110

Lurie v. Indianapolis, City of . . . 10.3n16

Lybarger v. Los Angeles, City of . . 8.4n57

Lydo Entertainments, Inc. v. Las Vegas, City of 3.4n42

Lykes v. Texarkana, City of 5.8n78

Lynah; United States v. . . 4.5n63; 9.4n47

Lynch; Homan v. 4.4n53

Lyons, City of v. Suttle 3.5n51

Lytle v. Payette-Oregon Slope Irrigation Dist. 5.9n90

M

M. & O. Disposal Co. v. Township of Middletown 5.11n109

M. & R. Enters, Inc. v. Zoning Bd. of Appeals of Southington 4.4n56

Macomb Co. Rd. Comm'n; Narvocki v. . . . 9.2

Madelia, Village of; Davies v. 5.6n56

Madera, City of; Carruth v. 5.1n1

Madison Plan Comm'n, City of; Hoepker v. 4.6n87; 4.7n100

Madison, Town of; Rockingham Square Shopping Ctr., Inc. v. . . . 5.2n19; 5.11n103; 5.12n122

[References are to text sections]

Madison Tp.; Midtown Properties v. 4.6n87

Magee; Orangetown, Town of v. . . 9.5n67; 9.6n91

Magnolia Park, City of; Houston, City of v. 1.7n49

Mahon; Pennsylvania Coal Co. v. 4.5n66, n67

Maine; Alden v. 1.3n11; 2.7n50

Maine v. Thiboutot 9.6n75

Maine Sch. Dist. Comm'n; School Admin. Dist. No. 3 v. 5.11n109

Majestic Radiator Enclosure Co. v. Co. Comm'rs of Middlesex 5.5n51

Mallory; Osbekoff v. 8.6n99

Manchester, City of v. Leiby . . . 3.9n116

Manchester, City of; R. Zoppo Co. v. 5.9n87

Manning v. Reilly 4.3n23

Maple Valley Township Unit School; Hatch v. 5.11n112

Marburger v. Public Funds for Public Sch. 6.2n22

Marco Dev. Corp. v. Cedar Falls, City of . . 5.2n20; 5.12n117

Maricopa County; Memorial Hosp. v. 6.7n89

Marietta, City of; Goldrush II v. 3.12n174

Marina Parks, Inc.; Volpe v. . . . 4.8n110

Marino v. Baltimore, City of 4.4n53

Marion, City of; Kane v. 5.2n5

Markham, City of; Kipperman v. 3.9n110

Marley; Baker v. 8.2n34

Marriage of (see name of party)

Marrone v. Hampton, Town of . . . 5.2n9; 5.11n102

Marrone; Key West, City of v. . . . 10.7n78

Marshall v. Kansas City 3.8n92

Marshan, Town of; Almquist v. . . 4.6n86

Martin v. Smith 7.8n79

Maryland; Freedman v. 3.9n119

Maryland; McGowan v. 3.3n21

Masters v. Pruce 4.3n25

Masterson, People ex rel. v. French 8.3n42

Matanuska-Susitna Borough Sch. Dist. v. State 10.4n38

Mathews; Henry Walker Park Ass'n v. 4.8n114

Matter of (see name of party)

Matthew v. Smith 4.4n51

Matthews; Perkins v. 7.7n54

May v. Cooperman 6.2n34

May; Karcher v. 6.2n34

Mayor and City Council of Cumberland; McKaig v. 5.2n7; 5.11n106

Mayor and Council of Borough of Oradell; Haynes v. 3.3n26

Mayor and Council of New Castle; New Castle Co. v. 5.2n21

Mayor & Bd. of Aldermen; McAuliffe v. . . 8.1n3

Mayor & City Council of Baltimore; Williams v. 1.4n29

Mayor & City Council of Cumberland; Keeler v. 4.3n40

Mayor & City Council of Ocean City; Windsor Resort Inc. v. 4.8nn113, 116

Mayor, Councilmen & Citizens v. Beard . . 1.7n55

Mayor of Long Branch; Coast Cigarette Sales, Inc. v. 3.5n55

McAuliffe v. Mayor & Bd. of Aldermen . . . 8.1n3

McAuliffe v. New Bedford, City of 8.5n62

McCall; Townsend v. 5.8n79

McCarthy v. Philadelphia Civil Serv. Comm'n 6.7n88; 8.2n20

McCarty v. St. Paul, City of 8.6n87

McCrea v. Cunningham 8.2n17

McCuistion v. Huachuca City 9.4n28

McDonnell Douglas v. Green . . . 9.8n131

McGlothin; Mississippi Employment Sec. Comm'n v. 8.3n50

McGoldrick; Bird v. 8.6n88

McGovern; Allen v. 3.6n77

McGowan v. Maryland 3.3n21

McGrew, Village of v. Steidley . . . 4.3n23

McGuire v. Cedar Rapids, City of . . 9.2n8

McGuire v. Cincinnati, City of . . . 2.4n19

McIntyre v. Bd. of Comm'rs of El Paso Co. 4.8n120

McKaig v. Mayor and City Council of Cumberland 5.2n7; 5.11n106

McKay; Churchill v. 8.6n92

McKenna v. Peekskill Hous. Auth. 6.8n104

McKinley v. Fraser 7.8n70

McKinney v. Ruderman 4.8n109

McKnight; Richardson v. 6.5n66

McLendon; Troy, City of v. 4.9n134

McLennan County Appraisal Dist.; General Ass'n Branch Davidian Seventh Day Adventist v. 10.4n44

McLeod; Bordanaro v. 9.6n84

McLintock; School Dist. No. 9 Fractional of Waterford and Pontiac Tps. v. . . . 5.2n10

[References are to text sections]

McLintock; School Dist. No. 9 v. . . . .
5.11n104
McMillin; Montanick v. 8.6n96
McMonagle; State, ex rel. Tyler v. . . . . .
10.2n4
McNamara v. Director of Civil Serv. . . . .
8.7n123
McPherson; Coronado Dev. Co. v. . . . . . .
4.6n87
McWhorter v. Richmond 8.6n85
Medford, City of; Peters v. 9.2n8
Medford, City of; Richard D. Kimball Co. v.
. . . . 5.3n29
Meierhenry v. Huron, City of . . 6.12n141
Melbourne, City of v. Hess Realty Corp. . .
3.12n177
Melhar Corp.; St. Louis, City of v. . . . . .
3.10n136
Mellon; Thompson v. 8.2n22
Members of City Council of City of Los
Angeles v. Taxpayers for Vincent . . . .
4.3n36
Memorial Hosp. v. Maricopa County . . . .
6.7n89
Memorial Hospital-West Volusia, Inc. v.
News-Journal Corp. 6.5n65
Memphis Cmty Sch. Dist. v. Stachura . . .
9.5n69
Memphis Hous. Auth. v. Thompson . . . . .
6.8n103
Menasha, City of; Probst v. 5.5n52
Menzl v. Milwaukee, City of 5.5n39
Mercer Island, City of; Eastside Disposal
Co. v. 5.6n68
Meredith; Kaneville, Town of v. . . 4.8n108
Mergens; Bd. of Educ. of Westside Commu-
nity Schools v. 6.2n37
Meritor Savings Bank, FSB v. Vinson . . .
8.5n77; 9.7n113
Merrill, City of v. Wenzel Bros., Inc. . . . .
5.7n74
Mesa, City of; Outdoor Sys. Inc. v
4.4n44
Metropolitan Express Services, Inc. v. Kansas
City 5.6n55; 5.8n81
Metropolitan Hous. Dev. Corp.; Arlington
Heights, Village of v. 6.8n111
Metropolitan St. R. Co., People ex rel. v. State
Bd. of Tax Comm'rs . . . 2.2n2; 10.3n14
Miami Beach, City of v. Fontainebleau Hotel
Corp., State ex rel. 3.12n171
Miami, City of v. Brooks 9.2n8
Miami, City of; Elwyn v. 4.4n56
Miami, City of; Glatstein v. 5.5n53;
5.6n60

Miami, City of v. Sterbenz 8.3n45
Michael v. Rochester, City of 5.2n24
Michelin Tire Corp. v. Wages . . . 10.3n19
Michigan; Butler v. 3.4n31
Michigan Dep't of Natural Resources; Fort
Gratiot Sanitary Landfill, Inc. v. . . . . .
3.7n88
Michigan Dep't of State Police; Will v. . . .
9.6n73
Michigan Tax Comm'n; Liquid Carbonic
Corp. v. 10.6n71
Mickes; Cuffley v. 3.6n72
Middlesboro, City of; Continental Illinois
Nat'l Bank & Trust Co. v. . . . 3.12n165
Midkiff; Hawaii Housing Auth. v. . . . . . .
4.8n102
Midland County; Avery v. 7.5n29;
7.6n43; 7.6n50
Midtown Properties v. Madison Tp. . . . . .
4.6n87
Midwest Inv. Co. v. Chariton, City of . . . .
3.2n9
Milan v. Bethlehem, City of 9.4n31
Milford Central School; Good News Club v.
. . . . 6.2n41
Milham, State ex rel. v. Rickhoff . . 1.2n5
Mill Valley, City of; Stang v. 6.6n71;
9.2n16
Millbrook, City of; Ziegler v. 6.6n78
Miller v. California 3.4n28
Miller; Chandler v. 8.5n72
Miller v. Evansville, City of 5.4n33
Miller v. Johnson 7.5n37; 7.7n57
Miller v. New York, City of 4.8n120
Milliken v. Green 10.4n38
Mills v. Alabama 7.1n4; 7.3n22
Millsap; Quinn v. 8.2n24
Milwaukee, City of v. Leavitt 4.7n95
Milwaukee, City of; Menzl v. 5.5n39
Milwaukee, City of v. Wilson 3.6n82
Minneapolis, City of; Carl Bolander & Sons v.
. . . . 5.8n84
Minneapolis, City of v. Minneapolis St. Ry.
Co. 3.10nn127, 135
Minneapolis St. Ry. v. Minneapolis, City of
. . . . 3.10nn127, 135
Minneapolis Star & Tribune Co. v. Minnesota
Comm'r of Revenue 10.3n29
Minnesota Comm'r of Revenue; Minneapolis
Star & Tribune Co. v. 10.3n29
Misch; Edison Illuminating Co. v. . . . . . .
4.8n117
Mississippi Employment Sec. Comm'n v. Mc-
Glothin 8.3n50
Mississippi Power & Light Co. v. Coldwater,
Town of 3.12n163

[References are to text sections]

Missouri International Investigators, Inc. v.
Pacific, City of 5.10n94
Missouri Utils. Co.; Sikeston, City of v. . .
3.12n162
Mitchell v. Helms 6.2n21
Mitchell; Oregon v. 7.5n40
Mitchell; U.S. v. 6.2n20
Mobile, City of; General Elec. Co. v.
5.5n47
Mobile, City of; Sammy's of Mobile, Ltd. v.
. . . . 3.5n48
Mobile, City of v. Waldon 4.6n88
Monell v. Dept. of Soc. Svcs. of the City of N.Y.
. . . . 1.3n16; 9.6n74
Mongiovi v. Doerner 5.5n45
Montana-Dakota Utils. Co.; Sheridan, City
of v. 3.12n162
Montanick v. McMillin 8.6n96
Monterey, City of v. Del Monte Dunes at
Monterey, Ltd. 4.5n81
Montezuma, City of; Trussell Servs., Inc. v.
. . . . 9.4n38
Montgomery Co.; Haub v. 6.5n60;
8.7n129
Montgomery, People ex rel. v. Lierman . .
1.2n8
Moody; Albemarle Paper Co. v. . . . .
9.7n110
Moody v. Transylvania County . . . 5.2n6;
5.3n25; 5.11n101
Moon v. Conyers, City of 4.8n112
Moor v. Alameda County 1.3n15
Moore v. Dep't of Transportation and Pub.
Facilities 6.5n60; 8.7n129
Moore v. Rochester, City of 4.4n61
Moorman Mfg. Co. v. Bair 10.3n24
Morales; Chicago, City of v. 3.6n85
Morris; Lallak v. 8.6n103
Morris; Myers v. 8.6n103
Morrison; United States v. 1.3n12;
2.5n24
Morristown Emergency and Rescue Squad,
Inc. v. Volunteer Dev. Co. . . . 3.10n123
Morton Grove, Village of; Quilici v. . . . . .
3.5n57
Mosley; Police Department of Chicago v. . .
9.5n62
Mosley; U.S. v. 7.6n44
Motor Vehicles Admin.; Aero Motors, Inc. v.
. . . . 3.3n24
Mott, City of; Munch v. 4.3n20
Motyka v. Amsterdam, City of . . . 6.6n67
Mount Healthy City School Bd. of Educ. v.
Doyle 1.3n15; 8.5n82; 9.8n135
Mount Prospect, Village of; Pioneer Trust &
Sav. Bank v. 4.6n88

Mount Vernon, City of; Lane v. . . 3.2n16
Mt. Carmel Medical Ctr. v. Bd. of Co. Comm'rs
. . . . 5.9n92
Mt. Clemens, City of; Central Bitulithic Pav-
ing Co. v. 5.11n108
Muhammed Temple of Islam — Shreveport v.
Shreveport, City of 10.5n49
Mukilteo, City of; Harbour Village Apts. v.
. . . . 10.3n30
Mullin v. Ringle 8.7n117
Munch v. Mott, City of 4.3n20
Mundt; Abate v. 7.6n51
Municipality of Anchorage; Allstate Ins.
Co. v. 3.8n100
Municipality of Anchorage v. Frohne . . . .
7.8n71
Murdock v. Pennsylvania 2.7n33;
3.9n120; 9.5n61; 10.3n28
Murphy; Plattsmouth, City of v. . . . .
5.11n111
Murphy v. United Parcel Service, Inc. . . .
9.8n124
My Sister's Place v. Burlington, City of . .
6.6n69
Myers v. Morris 8.6n103
Myles Salt Co. v. Bd of Comm'rs of Iberia &
St. Mary Drainage Dist. 10.7n81
Myrtle Beach, Town of v. Suber . . 8.2n38
Myszka; Columbus, City of v. 9.4n30

N

N. Charleston, City of v. N. Charleston Dist.
. . . . 5.11n105
N. Charleston Dist.; N. Charleston, City of v.
. . . . 5.11n105
N. Hempstead, Town of; Landes v. . . . . .
8.2n9, n15
N. Providence, Town of; Hurdis Realty,
Inc. v. 5.9n91
N. Riverside, Village of; Aladdin's Castle,
Inc. v. 3.3n27
Namer Inv. Corp., State ex rel. v. Williams
. . . . 2.7n39; 3.9n109
Naples Airport Auth., City of v. Collier Dev.
Corp. 4.3n21
Narvocki v. Macomb Co. Rd. Comm'n . . .
9.2
Nassau Co. Civil Serv. Comm'n; Dillon v.
. . . . .8.7n124
National Asphalt Pavement Ass'n v. Prince
George's County 3.8n99
Nat'l Bellas Hess, Inc. v. Dep't of Revenue of
State of Ill. 10.5nn56, 59
Nat'l Cable & Telecommunications Assoc.,
Inc. v. Gulf Power Co. 3.11n149

[References are to text sections]

Nationalist Movement; Forsyth County v.
. . . . 9.5n65
Nat'l Treasury Employees Union v. Von Raab
. . . . 8.5n71
Navy Point, Inc.; Cook v. 5.3n29
Neal v. Huntington, City of 10.8n85
Neisius v. Henry 5.12n115
Nelson v. Kellogg 8.6n99
Nelson; State v. 1.5n40
Nelson, Inc. v. Sewerage Comm'n of City of
Milwaukee 5.7n71
Nestle v. Santa Monica, City of . . 9.4n28
Nev., State of v. Skinner 10.2n10
Nevada Employees Ass'n., State of; Univer-
sity of Nevada v. 6.5n59; 8.7n128
New Bedford, City of; McAuliffe v. . . . . .
8.5n62
New Bern, City of; Valevais v. . . . 6.6n74
New Castle Co. v. Mayor and Council of New
Castle 5.2n21
New Hampshire; Chaplinsky v. . . 3.6n64
New Hampshire; Cox v. . . 3.9n112, n114,
n120
New Hampshire; Poulos v. 3.12n173;
4.10n143
New Hampshire, City of; Steinlage v. . . . .
4.7n101
New Haven, City of; Lambert v. . . . .
4.9n132
New Haven, City of v. New Haven Water Co.
. . . . 3.10n129
New Haven Water Co.; New Haven, City of v.
. . . . 3.10n129
New Jersey; Garrity v. 8.4n55
New Jersey; Newark v. 1.4n29
New Jersey; Philadelphia, City of v. . . . .
3.7n88
New Jersey; Trenton, City of v. . . 1.4n29
New Jersey Good Humor v. Board of Comm'rs
of Bradley Beach 2.4n8
New Jersey Power & Light Co.; Whelan v.
. . . . .5.5n40
New Orleans; United States v. . . . 10.1n2
New Orleans, City of; F.H. Myers Constr.
Co. v. 5.6n61
New Smyrna Beach, City of; Watson v. . .
5.12n124
New York; Feiner v. 3.6n68
New York; Ginsberg v. 3.4n30
New York; Saia v. 3.9n113
New York City; Penn Central
Transportation v. 4.5n73, n74
New York City Department of Buildings;
Brownstone Pub. Inc. v. 7.2n9
New York City Dep't of Bldgs.; Brownstone
Publishers, Inc. v. 7.2n9

New York City Human Resources Admin.;
Jones v. 8.7n125
New York, City of; Bailey v. 9.2n4
New York, City of; Banny v. 8.2n39
New York, City of; Bernadine v. . . 6.6n78
New York, City of; Buzzetti v. . . . 3.4n40
New York, City of; Cannata v. . . 4.8n105
New York, City of; Chapman v. . . 5.2n17
New York, City of; Environmental Encapsu-
lating Corp. v. 2.5n22
New York, City of v. FCC 2.5n22
New York, City of; Miller v. 4.8n120
New York, City of; New York State Club
Ass'n. v. 3.8n93
New York, City of; Penn Central Transp.
Co. v. 4.3n26
New York, City of; Riss v. . 6.6n73; 9.2n17
New York, City of; Schuster v. . . . 6.6n76;
9.2n19
New York, City of v. State 7.5n36;
9.5n55; 10.6n64
New York, City of; Stringfellow's of New York,
Ltd. v. 3.4n40
New York, City of; Time Warner Cable v.
. . . . .3.11n153
New York, City of; Vango Media, Inc. v. . .
2.5n22
New York Elec. Lines Co. v. Empire City
Subway Co. 3.10n136
New York State Club Ass'n. v. New York, City
of 3.8n93
Newark v. New Jersey 1.4n29
Newark, City of; 426 Bloomfield Ave. Corp. v.
. . . . 5.8n80
Newport Beach; Tischauser v. . . 4.8n110
Newport Beach, City of; Knapp v. . . 3.2n8
Newport, City of v. Iacobucci 3.5n47
News-Journal Corp.; Memorial Hospital-West
Volusia, Inc. v. 6.5n65
Neyens v. Roth 9.9n140
Niagara Falls; Scott v. 8.6n101
Nicholson; El Paso, City of v. 5.9n89
N.J. Power & Light Co.; Whelan v. . . . . .
5.5n52
N.J. State League of Municipalities v. Dep't.
of Community Affairs 4.3n16
Noel; Floyd, State ex rel. v. 3.5n46
Nokomis, City of v. Sullivan 3.2n12
Nollan v. California Coastal Comm'n . . . .
4.5n80; 4.6n90; 9.4n45
Nordlinger v. Hahn . . . 10.3n27; 10.4n41
Norfolk, City of v. Tiny House, Inc. . . . . .
3.5n49
Normandy Estates Ltd.; Normandy Estates
Metro. Recreation Dist. v. 5.2n11

[References are to text sections]

Normandy Estates Metro. Recreation Dist. v. Normandy Estates Ltd. 5.2n11

North Birmingham, Town of; Posey v. . . . 9.2n10

North Dakota; Quill Corp. v. . . . 10.5n57

North Palm Beach, Village of; State v. . . . 2.4n18

North Salt Lake Corp; Triangle Oil, Inc. v. 3.5n50

Northeastern Florida Chapter of the Associated Gen. Contract v. Jacksonville, City of 5.8n85

Northern Pac. Ry. Co.; U.S. v. . . 10.2n11

Northwest Alabama Gas Dist.; Hackleburg, Town of v. 10.3n14

Norwest Bank Iowa, N.A.; Cannice v. . . . 9.8n126

NYC Transit Auth. v. Beazer 8.2n18

NYC Transit Auth.; Jered Contracting Corp. v. 5.7n75

Nyquist; Bd. of Educ., Levittown Union Free School District v. 6.2n10

Nyquist; Harrison Central Sch. Dist. v. . . 5.12n120

O

Oak Park, Village of; Clayton v. . . 3.8n98

Oak Park, Village of; Utica State Savings Bank v. 5.12n118

Oberlin, City of; Porter v. 3.8n94

O'Brien; United States v. 3.4n38

Ogden, City of; Allen v. 6.6n67

O'Gorman; D.H.L. Associates, Inc. v. 3.4n41

O.H. Martin Co. v. Borough of Sharpsburg 10.6n68

Ohio Oil Co., State ex rel. v. Defiance, City of 3.12n171

O'Keefe, People ex rel.; Graves v. 10.6n66

Oklahoma; Broadrick v. 9.5n64

Oklahoma City v. Poor 3.12n175

Olech v. Willowbrook, Village of . . 2.7n42

Olech; Willowbrook, Village of v. . . 9.5n57

Oliva; C.H. v. 6.2n28

Olmstead v. L.C. 9.8n127

Olson; Braaten v. 5.5n44

Omaha, City of; Philson v. 5.6n58

Omni Outdoor Advertising Co.; Columbia, City of v. 9.9n142

Oncale v. Sundowner Offshore Servs., Inc. 8.5n79

Opelousas, City of; Johnson v. . . . 3.6n81

Orangetown, Town of v. Magee . . 9.5n67; 9.6n91

Oregon v. Mitchell 7.5n40

Oregon City v. Hartke 4.3n37

Orlando, City of; Tamiami Trail Tours, Inc. v. 3.9n102

Osbekoff v. Mallory 8.6n99

Osborn v. Akron, City of 4.9n140

Osborne; Hathaway v. 9.4n39

Otis Elevator Co.; Yonkers, City of v. 6.12n143

Ottawa, City of v. Carey 2.4n9

Otto v. Steinhilber 4.4n61

Outdoor Sys. Inc. v. Mesa, City of 4.4n44

Owen of Ga., Inc. v. Shelby Co. . . 5.8n82

Owensboro, City of v. Smith 3.9n103

P

Pa. Alliance for Jobs & Energy v. Council of Borough of Munhall 3.9n115

Paar v. Birmingham, City of . . . 4.9n133

Pachtman; Imbler v. 8.6n102

Pacific, City of; Missouri International Investigators, Inc. v. 5.10n94

Packard v. Fuller 4.8n107

Paducah, City of v. Konkle 4.9n135

Page & Crane Lumber Co. v. Clear Lake, City of 4.8n125

Palatka, City of; Southern Utils. Co. v. 3.10n130

Palazzolo v. Rhode Island . . 4.5n68, n75, n82

Palmer; Daytona Beach, City of v. 6.6n79

Pap's A.M.; Erie, City of v. 3.4n39; 4.3n35

Parham; Woodruff v. 10.5n49

Parish Council of East Baton Rouge v. Louisiana Highway & Heavy Branch of Assoc. Gen. Contract 5.6n58

Parker v. Brown 1.3n17; 9.9n136

Parker v. Levy 8.5n73

Parker-Weaver v. Fordice 7.7n66

Parkridge v. Seattle, City of 2.8n59

Parks v. Princeton, Town of 6.6n67

Pasadena City Bd. of Educ.; Cobb v. 5.5n42

Paschen Contractors, Inc.; Seattle, City of v. 10.7n73

Patterson v. Phoenix, City of 9.2n12

Payette-Oregon Slope Irrigation Dist.; Lytle v. 5.9n90

Payne; Immanuel Presbyterian Church v. 10.4n43

Pearson v. Guttenberg, City of . . 4.8n124

Peavy; Cobb County v. 4.3n30

[References are to text sections]

Peekskill Hous. Auth.; McKenna v. . . . . .
                                        6.8n104
Pelzer; Hope v. 8.6n110
Pembaur v. Cincinnati, City of . . . 9.6n80
Pena; Adarand Constructors, Inc. v. . . . .
                            5.6n64; 5.8n86; 8.2n10
Pence v. Rantoul, Village of 3.5n50
Penn Central Transp. Co. v. New York, City
    of 4.3n26; 4.5n73, n74
Penn-Dixie Cement Corp. v. Kingsport, City
    of 2.4n8
Pennsylvania; General Building Contractors
    Ass'n, Inc. v. 9.7n95
Pennsylvania; Murdock v. 3.9n120;
                          9.5n61; 10.3n28
Pennsylvania Coal Co. v. Mahon . . . . . .
                                   4.5n66, n67
People v. (see name of defendant)
People ex (see name of defendant)
People ex rel. (see name of defendant)
Peoples Gas Co. of Kentucky v. Barbourville,
    City of 3.10n129
Peoria, City of v. Central Nat'l Bank . . . .
                                        4.8n125
Peoria Housing Authority; Cremer v. . . . .
                                        10.3n23
Perez v. Boston Hous. Auth. . . . 6.8n106
Perkins v. Matthews 7.7n54
Perry v. Sindermann 3.6n73; 8.4n53
Peters v. Breier 3.6n80
Peters v. Medford, City of 9.2n8
Peterson; Franklin v. 10.6n69
Petition of (see name of party)
Petka v. Bingle 2.6n28
PGA Tour, Inc. v. Casey Martin . . . .
                                        9.8n128
Pharr Road Inv. Co. v. Atlanta, City of . .
                                        10.3n31
Philadelphia, City of; Kiker v. . . 10.6n64
Philadelphia, City of v. New Jersey . . . . .
                                        3.7n88
Philadelphia, City of; Second Church of
    Christ Scientist of Philadelphia v. . . . .
                                        10.4n44
Philadelphia, City of; United States v. . . .
                                        1.3n21
Philadelphia Civil Serv. Comm'n; McCarthy v.
    . . . . 6.7n88; 8.2n20
Philson v. Omaha, City of 5.6n58
Phoenix, City of; Gamewell v. . . .   5.6n57
Phoenix, City of; Patterson v. . . . 9.2n12
Phoenix, City of v. Yarnell 9.6n77
Pickard v. City & County of Honolulu . . .
                                        4.9n130
Pickering v. Bd. of Educ. . . 8.1n4; 8.4n58;
                                   8.5n63, n67

Piedmont, City of; Roman Catholic Welfare
    Corp. v. 2.7n38; 4.3n29
Pienta v. Schaumburg, Village of . . . . . .
                                        8.3n40
Pierro v. Baxendale 2.7n40
Pike & Long; Guthrie, City of v. . . . . . .
                                        3.9n104
Pilgrim; Rome, City of v. 4.7n101
Pinellas Park, City of; Zimring-McKenzie
    Constr. Co. v. 5.9n90
Pioneer Trust & Sav. Bank v. Mount Pros-
    pect, Village of 4.6n88
Pittsburgh, City of; Hunter v. . . 1.4; 1.6n43
Pittsfield Fire Dist.; Prout v. 2.4n10
Plain Dealer Publ'g Co.; Lakewood, City of v.
    . . . . . . 2.7n32; 3.9nn113, 118;
                                        4.10n144
Planning and Zoning Commission of Town of
    Milford; Beach v. 4.2n8
Planning Board of City of Stamford;
    Josephson v. 8.2n33
Planning Comm'n; Aunt Hack Ridge Estates,
    Inc. v. 4.6n88
Planning & Zoning Comm'n. of Milford;
    Beach v. 4.2n5
Planning & Zoning Comm'n of Town of Beth-
    any; Forest Const. Co. v. 4.6n85
Platt v. Torrey, Town of 10.7n74
Plattsmouth, City of v. Murphy . . . .
                                        5.11n111
Playboy Entertainment Group, Inc.; U.S. v.
    . . . . 3.11n154
Playtime Theaters, Inc.; Renton, City of v.
    . . . . 3.4n40; 4.3n31
Pleasant Grove, City of v. United States . .
                                        7.7n63
Plourde; Racine County v. 4.3n37
Plyler v. Doe 6.2n3
Police Comm'r of Boston; Atterberry v. . . .
                                        8.3n40
Police Dep't of Chicago v. Mosley . . . . . .
                                        9.5n62
Polk Township v. Spencer 5.2n23
Poole v. Louisville, City of 6.6n67
Poor; Oklahoma City v. 3.12n175
Poremba v. Springfield, City of . . 4.8n103
Port Authority Trans-Hudson Corp.; Hess v.
    . . . . 1.3n15
Port of Portland; Hale v. 1.2n6
Port Orange, City of; Florida, State of v. . .
                                        10.7n73
Porter v. Oberlin, City of 3.8n94
Portland, City of; Real Silk Hosiery v. . . .
                                        3.3n25
Portwardens; Southern S.S. Co. v. . . . . .
                                        10.3n17

[References are to text sections]

Posey v. North Birmingham, Town of . . .
    9.2n10
Potts v. Utica, City of 5.5n43
Poulos v. New Hampshire 3.12n173;
    4.10n143
Powell v. City & Co. of San Francisco . . .
    2.4n17
Poynter v. Johnston 4.8n109
Prairie Village, City of; Delight Wholesale
    Co. v. 3.1n1
Preferred Communications, Inc. v. Los Ange-
    les, City of 3.11n152
Prescott, City of; Kunkle Water & Elec.,
    Inc. v. 5.5n39; 5.6n59
Press-Enterprise Co. v. Superior Court . . .
    7.3n16
Price v. Edmonds 5.2n22
Priest; Serrano v. 6.2n7
Prince George's County; National Asphalt
    Pavement Ass'n v. 3.8n99
Prince George's County; Tuxedo Cheverly
    Volunteer Fire Co. v. 5.11n100
Princeton, City of v. Baker 8.6n86
Princeton, City of v. Princeton Elec., Light &
    Power Co. 3.12n165
Princeton Elec., Light & Power Co.; Prince-
    ton, City of v. 3.12n165
Princeton, Town of; Parks v. 6.6n67
Probst v. Menasha, City of 5.5n52
Professional Engineers v. Dept. of Transpor-
    tation 6.5n59
Prout v. Pittsfield Fire Dist. 2.4n10
Pruce; Masters v. 4.3n25
Public Funds for Public Sch.; Marburger v.
    . . . . 6.2n22
Public Service Commission of N.Y.; Central
    Hudson Gas & Electric Corp. v. . . . . .
    3.6n74
Publicker Industries, Inc. v. Cohen . . . . .
    7.3n17
Pugnier v. Ramharter 8.6n86
Puritan-Greenfield Improvement Ass'n v. Leo
    . . . . 4.4n50

Q

Quilici v. Morton Grove, Village of . . . . .
    3.5n57
Quill Corp. v. North Dakota 10.5n57
Quinn v. Millsap 8.2n24

R

R. Zoppo Co. v. Manchester, City of . . . . .
    5.9n87
Racine County v. Plourde 4.3n37

Racine Fire and Police Comm'n v. Stanfield
    . . . . 2.4n10
Radobersky v. Imperial Volunteer Fire Dep't
    . . . . 6.6n80
Rahway, City of; Riddlestorffer v. . . . . . .
    5.2n13; 5.13n131
Railway Labor Executives Ass'n; Skinner v.
    . . . . 8.5n70
Ramapo, Town of; Golden v. 4.6n88
Ramharter; Pugnier v. 8.6n86
Ramirez; Richardson v. 7.5n41
Ramsey Co.; Griswold v. 5.8n80
Rantoul, Village of; Pence v. 3.5n50
Rapid City v. Schmitt 2.7n35
Rapides Parish Sch. Bd.; Domico v. . . . . .
    8.3n48
Rathert v. Vill. of Peotone 8.3n49
R.A.V. v. St. Paul, City of 3.6n67
R.D. Anderson Constr. Co., Inc. v. Topeka,
    City of 5.6n58
Real Silk Hosiery v. Portland, City of . . .
    3.3n25
Reams v. Grand Junction, City of . . . . . .
    6.12n139
Rector and Visitors of Univ. of Va.;
    Rosenberger v. 6.2n40
Redevelopment Auth. of City of Erie; G.C.
    Murphy Co. v. 4.8n119
Reeves v. Sanderson Plumbing Products, Inc.
    . . . . 9.8n132
Regents of the Univ. of Calf. v. Doe . . . . .
    1.3n15
Regester; White v. 7.7n62
Regional Transp. Auth.; Evanston, City of v.
    . . . . 4.3n19
Reid; Commonwealth v. 2.4n8
Reilly; Lorillard Tobacco Co. v. . . . 3.5n53
Reilly; Manning v. 4.3n23
Remmenga v. California Coastal Comm'n
    . . . . 4.6n88
Reno v. Bossier Parish Sch. Bd. . . 7.7n65
Reno v. Condon 2.5n25; 7.4n28
Reno; Shaw v. 7.5n37; 7.6n53
Reno, City of v. Silver State Flying Service,
    Inc. 5.1n2
Renton, City of v. Playtime Theaters, Inc.
    . . . . 3.4n40; 4.3n31
Republican Party of Illinois; Rutan v. . . .
    8.4n59; 8.5n65
Reynolds v. Sims . . . 7.5n31; 7.6n44, n49
Reynolds Boat Co. v. Haverhill, City of . .
    6.6n67, n71; 9.2n16
Rhode Island; Palazzolo v. . . 4.5n68, n75,
    n82
Rhodes; Hand v. 4.8n114

[References are to text sections]

Rice v. Cayetano 7.5n32
Richard D. Kimball Co. v. Medford, City of
. . . . 5.3n29
Richardson; Cole v. 8.2n31
Richardson; Graham v. 6.7n86
Richardson v. McKnight 6.5n66
Richardson v. Ramirez 7.5n41
Richmond; McWhorter v. 8.6n85
Richmond, City of v. Fary 10.7n79
Richmond, City of v. J.A. Croson Co. . . . .
5.6n64; 5.8n86; 8.2n11; 9.7n116
Richmond Newspapers, Inc. v. Virginia . .
7.3n14
Rickhoff; Milham, State ex rel. v. . . 1.2n5
Riddel; Home Builders Ass'n of Central Ari-
zona, Inc. v. 10.7n82
Riddlestorffer v. Rahway, City of . . . . . .
5.2n13; 5.13n131
Ridley Township v. Haulaway Trash Re-
moval, Inc. 5.13n133
Ringle; Mullin v. 8.7n117
Rinker; Denver, City and County of v. . . .
8.7n115
Riss v. New York, City of . 6.6n73; 9.2n17
River Vale v. R.J. Longo Constr. Co. . . . .
5.6n70
Riverside, City of; Buxbom v. 3.6n76
Riverside, County of v. Idyllwild County Wa-
ter Dist. 5.2n15
R.J. Longo Constr. Co.; Township of River
Vale v. 5.6nn69, 70
R.J. Reynolds Tobacco Co. v. Durham County
. . . . 10.3n19
Roberts; Shellburne, Inc. v. 8.6n94
Robertsdale; Duckworth v. 4.8n121
Robinson v. Cahill 6.2n7; 10.4n38
Rochester Ass'n of Neighborhoods v. Roches-
ter, City of 4.7n93
Rochester, City of; Michael v. 5.2n24
Rochester, City of; Moore v. 4.4n61
Rochester, City of; Rochester Ass'n of
Neighborhoods v. 4.7n93
Rochester, City of, Matter of 1.5n38
Rochester Gas & Elec. Co.; Lubelle v. . . .
4.10n141
Rochford v. Confederation of Police . . . . .
8.4n56
Rock Against Racism; Ward v. . . . 9.5n63
Rock Hill, City of; Henry v. 3.6n69
Rockingham Square Shopping Ctr., Inc. v.
Madison, Town of . . 5.2n19; 5.11n103;
5.12n122
Rodriguez; San Antonio Indep. Sch. Dist. v.
. . . . 6.2n6; 10.4n37
Roe; Saenz v. 6.7n90; 9.5n54

Roman Catholic Welfare Corp. v. Piedmont,
City of 2.7n38; 4.3n29
Rome, City of v. Pilgrim 4.7n101
Romer; Branson School Dist. RE-82 v. . . .
1.4n33
Rose v. Council for Better Educ.
. . . . 6.2nn8, 11; 10.4n38
Rose; Howlett v. 1.3n16
Roselle v. Wright 2.7n37
Rosenberger v. Rector and Visitors of Univ. of
Va. 6.2n40
Rosenthal v. Crystal Lake, City of . . . . .
9.4n41
Ross; Kennedy v. 6.5n61
Roth; Borough of Oakland v. 4.2n5
Roth; Neyens v. 9.9n140
Roth v. United States 3.4n28
Rowland; Sheffield v. 4.3n18
Royal School Labs., Inc. v. Watertown, Town
of 5.10n96
Rucker; Delony v. 3.10n129
Rucker; Dep't of HUD v. 6.8n102
Ruderman; McKinney v. 4.8n109
Russ Bldg. Partnership v. San Francisco, City
and County of 10.7n75
Russell; Frank v. 4.4n61
Rutan v. Republican Party of Illinois . . . .
8.4n59; 8.5n65
Rutland Cable T.V. Inc. v. Rutland, City of
. . . . 3.12n160
Rutland, City of; Rutland Cable T.V. Inc. v.
. . . . 3.12n160
Ry. Labor Executives' Ass'n; Skinner v. . . .
8.5n70

S

Saenz v. Roe 6.7n90; 9.5n54
Saia v. New York 3.9n113
Salem, Town of; Stillwater Condominium
Ass'n v. 6.6n72; 9.2n15
Salisbury, Town of; Salisbury Water Supply
Co. v. 5.4n37
Salisbury Water Supply Co. v. Salisbury,
Town of 5.4n37
Salt Lake City; Salt Lake City Fire Fighters
Local v. 8.3n44
Salt Lake City Corp.; Tribe v. . . 6.12n141
Salt Lake City Fire Fighters Local v. Salt
Lake City 8.3n44
Salyer Land Co. v. Tulare Lake Basin Water
Storage Dist. 7.5n35
Samis Land Co. v. Soap Lake, City of . . .
10.3n33
Sammy's of Mobile, Ltd. v. Mobile, City of
. . . . 3.5n48

[References are to text sections]

San Antonio Indep. Sch. Dist. v. Rodriguez
. . . . 6.2n6; 10.4n37
San Antonio Metropolitan Transit Auth.;
Garcia v. 9.2n5
San Diego, City of; San Diego Gas & Elec.
Co. v. 4.3n27
San Diego Gas & Elec. Co. v. San Diego, City
of 4.3n27
San Diego Unified Port Dist.; Coronado, City
of v. 1.4n31
San Diego Unified Port Dist. v. Gianturco
. . . . .1.4n34
San Francisco, City and County of; Russ Bldg.
Partnership v. 10.7n75
San Francisco, City of; Gaudiya Vaishnava
Society v. 2.8n52
San Telmo Assocs. v. Seattle, City of . . . .
10.7n75
Sanderson Plumbing Products, Inc.; Reeves v.
. . . . 9.8n132
Sandoval; Alexander v. 9.7n93
Santa Clara Co.; Turnboo v. 6.7n93
Santa Cruz; Waite v. 8.2n25
Santa Fe Indep. Sch. Dist. v. Doe . . . . . .
6.2n31
Santa Monica, City of; Nestle v. . . 9.4n28
Santucci Const. Co. v. Cook, County of . . .
5.7n72
Saucier v. Katz 8.6n109
Sawyer, Matter of 8.2n29
Scarborough Properties Corp. v. Vill. of Briar-
cliff Manor 5.11n111
Schad v. Borough of Mt. Ephraim . . . . . .
4.3n31
Schaefer v. Berinstein 5.2n22
Scharping v. Johnson 1.6n45
Schaumburg, Village of; Pienta v. . . . . . .
8.3n40
Scheiner; American Trucking Ass'ns., Inc. v.
. . . . 10.3n22; 10.5n54
Scheld; Clark v. 6.6n69
Schenley Farms Co. v. Allegheny County
. . . . .5.12n121
Schleifer v. Charlottesville, City of . . . . .
3.6n79
Schmitt; Rapid City v. 2.7n35
School Admin. Dist. No. 3 v. Maine Sch. Dist.
Comm'n 5.11n109
School Dist. No. 9 v. McLintock . . . .
5.11n104
School Dist. No. 9 Fractional of Waterford and
Pontiac Tps. v. McLintock 5.2n10
Schooling v. Harrisburg, City of . . . .
4.8n125
Schroder v. Kiss 8.7n122

Schultz v. Cumberland, City of . . 3.4n34,
n39
Schuster v. New York, City of . . . 6.6n76;
9.2n19
Schwab; Larkin Co. v. 3.12n169
Schwalk's Administrator v. Louisville, City of
. . . . 4.9n129
Schwartz v. Flint, City of 4.3n21
Schwartz v. Harrison 1.3n21
Schwartz; Harrison v. 1.3n21
Scott v. Niagara Falls 8.6n101
Seabrook, Town of v. Vachon Management,
Inc. 4.7n97
Seaford, City of; Delmarva Power & Light
Co. v. 3.10n132
Seattle, City of; Parkridge v. 2.8n59
Seattle, City of v. Paschen Contractors, Inc.
. . . . 10.7n73
Seattle, City of; San Telmo Assocs. v. . . . .
10.7n75
Second Church of Christ Scientist of
Philadelphia v. Philadelphia, City of . .
10.4n44
Secrist v. Diedrich 5.5n39; 5.6n59
Seim v. Indep. Dist. of Monroe . . . .
5.13n130
Sekerez v. Lake Co. Bd. of Comm'rs . . . .
5.5n52
Sena Sch. Bus Co. v. Bd. of Educ. of Santa Fe
Public Schools 5.3n27
Sermon v. Duluth, City of 3.12n161
Serrano v. Priest 6.2n7
Sewerage Comm'n of City of Milwaukee; Nel-
son, Inc. v. 5.7n71
S.H. Kress & Co. v. Dept of Health, City of
New York 3.3n19
Shaffer v. Carter 10.6n63
Shaker Square Co., State ex rel. v. Guion
. . . . .4.4n59
Shanbour; Bd. of Oklahoma City v. . . . . .
4.4n57
Shapiro v. Thompson 6.7n89
Shaw v. California Dep't of Alcoholic Bever-
age Control 9.6n91
Shaw; Green v. 3.12n161
Shaw v. Hunt 7.7n58
Shaw v. Reno 7.5n37; 7.6n53
Shaw v. WaKeeney, City of 2.6n30
Sheffield v. Rowland 4.3n18
Shelby Co.; Owen of Ga., Inc. v. . . 5.8n82
Shellburne, Inc. v. Roberts 8.6n94
Sheridan, City of v. Montana-Dakota Utils.
Co. 3.12n162
Sho-Me Power Corp.; Bd. of Pub. Works of
Rolla v. 5.3n29

[References are to text sections]

Short v. Kissinger 8.7n118

Shreveport, City of; Muhammed Temple of Islam — Shreveport v. 10.5n49

Shuttlesworth v. Birmingham, City of . . . 3.12n173

Sieroty v. Huntington Park, City of 3.6n76

Sigall, State ex rel. v. Aetna Cleaning Contractors of Cleveland, Inc. 6.5n60; 8.7n129

Sikeston, City of v. Missouri Utils. Co. . . . 3.12n162

Silver State Flying Service, Inc.; Reno, City of v. 5.1n2

Simmons; Bd. of Comm'rs of Edwards Co. v. 5.12n119, n120

Simmons-Harris v. Goff 6.2n27

Simone; U.S. v. 7.3n18

Sims; Bricker v. 8.6n104

Sims; Reynolds v. . . . 7.5n31; 7.6n44, n49

Sindermann; Perry v. . . . 3.6n73; 8.4n53

Sioux City v. Johnson 4.8n124

Skillken & Co. v. Toledo 4.3n21

Skinner; Nev., State of v. 10.2n10

Skinner v. Ry. Labor Executives' Ass'n . . . 8.5n70

Slater, City of; Bride v. 5.3n26

Sloss; Louisville Extension Water Dist. v. 5.10n98

Slurzberg v. Bayonne, City of . . . 5.4n36

Small v. Bd. of Safety of Town of Monroeville 8.4n54

Small v. Inhabitants of City of Belfast . . . 9.5n68

Smartt; Colorado Springs, City of v. 4.3n15

Smith; American Trucking Ass'ns., Inc. v. 10.3n22; 10.5n54

Smith; Consolidated Rail Corp. v. 2.5n22

Smith; Employment Div., Dept of Human Resources of Oregon v. 3.8n96

Smith v. Fort Lauderdale, City of 3.6n84

Smith; King v. 6.7n92; 10.2n8

Smith; Martin v. 7.8n79

Smith; Matthew v. 4.4n51

Smith; Owensboro, City of v. . . . 3.9n103

Smith; Valatie, Village of v. 4.4n43

Smith v. Wade 8.6n112

Smith Setzer & Sons, Inc. v. South Carolina Procurement Review Panel . . . 5.6n63

Snyder v. Waukeska Co. Zoning Bd. of Adjustment 4.4n51

Soap Lake, City of; Samis Land Co. v. . . . 10.3n33

Soaring Vista Properties, Inc. v. Bd. of Co. Comm'rs of Queen Anne's Co. . . 4.3n18

Souris, City of; Dempsey v. 9.4n30

South Bend, City of; Grand Trunk W. Ry. v. 3.10n126

South Carolina Coastal Council; Lucas v. 4.5n70

South Carolina Procurement Review Panel; Smith Setzer & Sons, Inc. v. . . 5.6n63

South Central Bell Telephone Co. v. Alabama 3.9n122

South Dakota v. Dole 10.2n8

Southern Airways Co. v. DeKalb Co. 5.12n121

Southern Iron Works, Inc.; Fairfax, County of v. 2.8n57

Southern Regional Physician Services Inc.; Flowers v. 9.8n126

Southern S.S. Co. v. Portwardens 10.3n17

Southern Utils. Co. v. Palatka, City of . . . 3.10n130

Southwest Missouri Light Co.; Joplin, City of v. 3.10n134

Southwestern Bell Video Svs., Inc.; Austin, City of v. 3.11n146

Southwestern Bell Wireless Inc. v. Johnson County Bd. of County Commissioners . . 3.11n150

Sparkman; Stump v. 8.6n99

Spencer; Polk Township v. 5.2n23

Spielvogel v. Aiello 5.6n62

Spitznagel; Foss v. 5.12n127

Splawn v. California 3.4n29

Spray v. Albuquerque, City of 5.1n3

Springfield, City of; Burger v. 5.1n3; 5.3n26

Springfield, City of; Kibbe v. 9.6n88

Springfield, City of; Poremba v. . . 4.8n103

Spur Industries, Inc. v. Del E. Webb Development Co. 3.2n3

St. Albans, City of; Franklin County v. . . . 4.4n45

St. Cloud, City of; St. Cloud Pub. Serv. Co. v. 3.10n130

St. Cloud Pub. Serv. Co. v. St. Cloud, City of 3.10n130

St. Louis, City of; Howe v. 3.8n97

St. Louis, City of v. Melhar Corp. 3.10n136

St. Louis, City of; Ulrich v. . . . 6.10n121

St. Louis Co.; Wakely v. 5.11n108

St. Paul, City of v. Dalsin 3.9n104

St. Paul, City of v. Kekedakis . . . 3.5n59

St. Paul, City of; McCarty v. 8.6n87

[References are to text sections]

St. Paul, City of; R.A.V. v. 3.6n67
St. Paul, City of; Sutton v. 5.6n61
St. Petersburg Beach, City of; Star Island
 Assocs. v. 4.8n109, n114
St. Petersburg, City of v. Florida Coastal
 Theaters, Inc. 10.8n86
Stachura; Memphis Community Sch. Dist. v.
 . . . . 9.5n69
Stamford, City of; Consolidated Diesel Elec.
 Corp. v. 10.3n15
Stanfield; Racine Fire and Police Comm'n v.
 . . . . 2.4n10
Stang v. Mill Valley, City of 6.6n71;
 9.2n16
Stanley v. Georgia 7.1n2; 7.3n20
Stanley Smith & Sons v. Limestone College
 . . . . .5.1n2
Star Island Assocs. v. St. Petersburg Beach,
 City of 4.8n109, n114
Starcevich v. Farmington, City of . . . . . .
 9.4n42
State v. (see name of defendant)
State Bd. of Tax Comm'rs; Metropolitan St. R.
 Co., People ex rel. v. 10.3n14
State ex (see name of state)
State ex rel. (see name of state)
State, ex rel. Tyler v. McMonagle . . . . . .
 10.2n4
State for Use of Russell County v. Fourth
 Nat'l Bank 5.2n9
State of (see name of state)
Statesboro Pub. Co., Inc. v. Sylvania, City of
 . . . . 3.6n78
Staub v. Baxley, City of 3.12n172
Steele v. Fowler 4.8n123
Steele Co.; Johnson v. 9.4n46
Steidley; McGrew, Village of v. . . . 4.3n23
Steinberg v. Atlanta, City of . . . 4.9n131
Steinhilber; Otto v. 4.4n61
Steinlage v. New Hampshire, City of . . . .
 4.7n101
Sterbenz; Miami, City of v. 8.3n45
Stevenson v. Bay City 8.6n86
Stewart; Ingleside, City of v. 5.9n88
Stillwater Condominium Ass'n v. Salem,
 Town of 6.6n72; 9.2n15
Stratton v. Detroit, City of . . 5.10n94, n97
Strickland; Wood v. 6.2n17; 8.6n108
Stringfellow's of New York, Ltd. v. New York,
 City of 3.4n40
Stump v. Sparkman 8.6n99
Suber; Myrtle Beach, Town of v. . . 8.2n38
Submarine Base Credit Union; Dupuis v.
 . . . . 4.7n94
Sugarman v. Dougall 8.2n13

Suggs; Bloodworth v. 8.7n121
Sullivan; Bantam Books, Inc. v. . . 3.4n35
Sullivan; Nokomis, City of v. 3.2n12
Sullivan, Town of; Wolfe v. 4.8n123
Summerville, City of v. Georgia Power Co.
 . . . . 3.12n162
Sumner v. Teaneck Township . . . 3.8n97
Sundowner Offshore Servs., Inc.; Oncale v.
 . . . . .8.5n79
Superior Court; Press-Enterprise Co. v. . .
 7.3n16
Superior Court of Spokane Co.; State v. . .
 2.4n13
Superior Ct.; Globe Newspaper Co. v. . . .
 7.1n3; 7.3n21
Superior, Town of; Koontz v. . . . 4.8n107
Supervisor of Assessments of Baltimore
 County v. Keeler 10.4n43
Surtran Taxicabs, Inc.; Woolen v. . . . . . .
 9.9n139
Suttle; Lyons, City of v. 3.5n51
Sutton v. St. Paul, City of 5.6n61
Sutton v. United Airlines, Inc. . . 9.8n124
Sweeney; Gerzof v. 5.8n76
Sylvania, City of; Statesboro Pub. Co., Inc. v.
 . . . . 3.6n78

T

Tacoma, City of; Craven, State ex rel. v. . .
 3.12n170
Tacoma, City of; Turner v. 4.9n135
Taft; Brookpark Entertainment, Inc. v. . .
 2.8n53
Tahoe Regional Planning Agency; Tahoe-
 Sierra Preservation Council, Inc. v. . . .
 4.5, n65, n72, n74; 9.4n49
Tahoe-Sierra Preservation Council, Inc. v.
 Tahoe Regional Planning Agency . . 4.5,
 n65, n72, n74; 9.4n49
Talarico; Denver, City and County of v. . .
 9.4n39
Tamiami Trail Tours v. Tampa, City of . .
 10.6n67
Tamiami Trail Tours, Inc. v. Orlando, City of
 . . . . 3.9n102
Tampa v. Consolidated Box Co. . . 4.3n20
Tampa, City of v. Birdsong Motors Inc. . .
 10.3n15
Tampa, City of; Tamiami Trail Tours v. . .
 10.6n67
Tax Comm'n of New York; Walz v. . . . . .
 10.4n42
Tax Comm'rs; Metropolitan St. R.R., People
 ex rel. v. 2.2n2

[References are to text sections]

Taxpayers for Vincent; Members of City Council of City of Los Angeles v. 4.3n36
Taylor v. Cohen 6.8n107
Taylor; Jagels v. 10.5n50
TCG New York, Inc. v. White Plains, City of 3.11n142
Teal; Connecticut v. 9.7n110
Teaneck Township; Sumner v. . . . 3.8n97
Telcom Sys. Inc. v. Lauderdale Co. Bd. of Supervisors 5.5n48
Teleprompter Manhattan CATV Corp.; Loretto v. 9.4n43
Tenney v. Brandhove 8.6n104
Texarkana, City of; Lykes v. 5.8n78
Thiboutot; Maine v. 9.6n75
Thomas v. Anchorage Equal Rights Comm'n 3.8n95
Thomas v. Broadlands Community Consolidated School 6.6n69
Thomas; Louisville, City of v. 5.2n18
Thompson v. E. Greenbush, Town of 3.12n167
Thompson v. Eau Claire, City of . . 9.4n28
Thompson v. Mellon 8.2n22
Thompson; Memphis Hous. Auth. v. 6.8n103
Thompson; Shapiro v. 6.7n89
Thomsen-Abbott Constr. Co. v. Wausau, City of 5.5n52
Thomson v. Call 5.2n22; 5.12n113
Thornburg v. Gingles 7.7n60
Thorstenn; Barnard v. 8.2n21
Three Forks, City of; Tocci v. . . 6.12n139
360 Degrees Communications Co. of Charlottesville v. Bd. of Supervisors of Albemarle Co. 3.11n157
Tiburon, City of; Agins v. 4.3n27; 4.5n69; 4.6n89; 9.4n44
Tice; Commonwealth v. 5.5n41
Tift; Dunlap v. 4.8n127
Tigard, City of; Dolan v. . . 4.3n27; 4.5n81
Tim v. Long Branch, City of 1.3n20
Time Warner Cable v. New York, City of 3.11n153
Time Warner Entertainment Co. v. U.S. . . . 3.11n155
Time Warner Entertainment Co. L.P. v. FCC 3.11n156
Tinker; Inman S.S. Co. v. 10.3n17
Tiny House, Inc.; Norfolk, City of v. 3.5n49
Tischauser v. Newport Beach . . . 4.8n110
Titus v. Lindberg 8.6n114
Tocci v. Three Forks, City of . . . 6.12n139

Toledo; Skillken & Co. v. 4.3n21
Toledo, City of; Lathrop Co. v. . . . 5.3n29
Topeka, City of; R.D. Anderson Constr. Co., Inc. v. 5.6n58
Torrey, Town of; Platt v. 10.7n74
Townsend v. McCall 5.8n79
Township of Hillsborough v. Cromwell . . . 10.3n26
Township of Middletown; M. & O. Disposal Co. v. 5.11n109
Township of River Vale v. R.J. Longo Constr, Co. 5.6n69
Township of West; Whiteland Woods, L.P. v. 7.3n19
Township of West Whiteland; Whiteland Woods, L.P. v. 7.3n16, n18
Toyota Motor Mfg., Ky., Inc. v. Williams . . 9.8n123
Transp. Agency Santa Clara County; Johnson v. 9.5n56; 9.7n117
Transylvania County; Moody v. . . . 5.2n6; 5.3n25; 5.11n101
Trap Rock Indus., Inc. v. Kohl . . . 5.6n62
Traylor v. Amarillo, City of 3.2n14
Trenton, City of; Dionne v. 9.4n28
Trenton, City of v. New Jersey . . . 1.4n29
Tri-Nel Management, Inc. v. Bd. of Health of Barnstable 3.5n56
Triangle Oil, Inc. v. North Salt Lake Corp 3.5n50
Tribe v. Salt Lake City Corp. . . 6.12n141
Troy, City of; Grimm v. 5.5n49
Troy, City of v. McLendon 4.9n134
Trussell Servs., Inc. v. Montezuma, City of 9.4n38
Trust Estate of (see name of party)
Tulare Lake Basin Water Storage Dist.; Salyer Land Co. v. 7.5n35
Turkey Valley Community School District; Kriener v. 9.4n29
Turley; Lefkowitz v. 5.6n66; 8.4n56
Turnboo v. Santa Clara Co. 6.7n93
Turner v. Fouche 7.5n30; 8.2n15
Turner v. Tacoma, City of 4.9n135
Tuxedo Cheverly Volunteer Fire Co. v. Prince George's County 5.11n100
Twin Falls, City of; Continental Oil Co. v. 3.12n166

U

U.A.W. v. Johnson Controls 9.7n108
Ulrich v. St. Louis, City of 6.10n121
Union Free Sch. Dist. No. 15; Kramer v. . . 7.5n33
United Airlines, Inc.; Sutton v. . . 9.8n124

[References are to text sections]

United Parcel Service, Inc.; Murphy v. . . . 9.8n124
United Reporting Publ'g Corp.; L.A. Police Dep't v. 7.2n13
United States v. (see name of defendant)
University of Alabama; Garrett v. . . . 8.5; 9.8n134
University of Nevada v. Nevada Employees Ass'n., State of 6.5n59; 8.7n128
U.S.; Beer v. 7.7n67
U.S.; Cal., State of v. 10.2n8, n9
U.S. v. Chester, City of 4.3n19
U.S.; Greater New Orleans Broadcasting Ass'n, Inc. v. 3.6n75
U.S. v. Harrison County, Miss. . . 10.2n11
U.S. v. Mitchell 6.2n20
U.S. v. Mosley 7.6n44
U.S. v. Northern Pac. Ry. Co. . . . 10.2n11
U.S. v. Playboy Entertainment Group, Inc. 3.11n154
U.S. v. Simone 7.3n18
U.S.; Time Warner Entertainment Co. v. 3.11n155
U.S. Airways, Inc. v. Barnett . . . 9.8n125
Utica, City of; Potts v. 5.5n43
Utica State Savings Bank v. Oak Park, Village of 5.11n111; 5.12n118

V

Va. State Bd. of Elections; Harper v. 7.5n39
Vachon Management, Inc.; Seabrook, Town of v. 4.7n97
Valatie, Village of v. Smith 4.4n43
Valeo; Buckley v. 8.2n30
Valevais v. New Bern, City of . . . 6.6n74
Vango Media, Inc. v. New York, City of . . 2.5n22
Vann; Boulder Corp. v. 4.2n6
Vasquez v. Hous. Auth. of City of El Paso 6.8n104
Vermont; Williams v. 10.5n55
Vermont Criminal Justice Training Council; Vermont State Employees' Ass'n, Inc. v. 6.5n60; 8.7n129
Vermont State Employees' Ass'n, Inc. v. Vermont Criminal Justice Training Council 6.5n60; 8.7n129
Vill. of Briarcliff Manor; Scarborough Properties Corp. v. 5.11n111
Vill. of Forest View; Wilson v. . . 5.11n112
Vill. of Glen Ellyn; Young v. 5.5n48
Vill. of Little Chute; Champeau v. 9.4n36

Vill. of Oak Park; Utica State Savings Bank v. 5.11n111
Vill. of Peotone; Rathert v. 8.3n49
Villa v. Chicago, City of 5.11n107
Villager Pond, Inc. v. Darien, Town of . . . 9.5n67
Vinson; Meritor Savings Bank, FSB v. . . . 8.5n77; 9.7n113
Virginia; Richmond Newspapers, Inc. v. . . 7.3n14
Virginia Polytechnic and State Univ.; Brzonkala v. 2.5n24
Vitale; Engell v. 6.2n29
Volpe v. Marina Parks, Inc. 4.8n110
Volunteer Dev. Co.; Morristown Emergency and Rescue Squad, Inc. v. . . . 3.10n123
Von Raab; Nat'l Treasury Employees Union v. 8.5n71
Vreeland; Kurpinski v. 3.12n171
Vt. Dep't Educ.; Andrews v. 6.2n43

W

Wachsman v. Dallas 8.3n44
Wade; Smith v. 8.6n112
Wages; Michelin Tire Corp. v. . . . 10.3n19
Wagner; Brown's Furniture, Inc. v. 10.5n54
Waite v. Santa Cruz 8.2n25
WaKeeney, City of; Shaw v. 2.6n30
Wakefield Township; Webb v. . . 5.11n112
Wakely v. St. Louis Co. 5.11n108
Waldon; Mobile, City of v. 4.6n88
Waldo's Inc. v. Johnson City, Village of . . 4.8n104
Walker v. Cedar Rapids, City of . . 9.2n21
Walker v. Lakewood, City of . . . 6.8n109
Walker; Lee v. 4.8n125
Walker; People v. 3.3n27
Walker Field, Colo. Pub. Airport Auth.; Enger v. 1.4n31
Wallace v. Jaffree 6.2n32
Walter v. West Va. Bd. of Educ. . . 6.2n34
Walter; Wolman v. 6.2n19
Walton v. Bozeman, City of 9.4n32
Walton v. Clermont 4.8n113
Walz v. Tax Comm'n of New York 10.4n42
Ward v. Rock Against Racism . . . 9.5n63
Wards Cove Packing Co., Inc.; Antonio v. 9.7n109
Wardwell v. Bd. of Educ. 8.2n20
Warrenton; Yates v. 4.8n123
Washington v. Davis 10.3n32
Washington Federation of State Employees v. Dep't of Social and Health Services . . . 6.5n59; 8.7n128

[References are to text sections]

Washington Pub. Power Supply System.; Chemical Bank v. 5.13n128
Water Works & Sewer Bd. of Prichard; Layman's Sec. Co. v. 5.5n46
Waters v. Churchill 8.4n58; 8.5n66
Watertown, Town of; Royal School Labs., Inc. v. 5.10n96
Watson v. Albuquerque 4.8n115
Watson v. New Smyrna Beach, City of . . . 5.12n124
Waukeska Co. Zoning Bd. of Adjustment; Snyder v. 4.4n51
Wausau, City of; Thomsen-Abbott Constr. Co. v. 5.5n52
Webb v. Wakefield Township . . 5.11n112
Weisman; Lee v. 6.2n30
Weksler; Coral Gables, City of v. 5.12n126
Weleck; State v. 8.2n32
Wellford v. Battaglia 8.2n21
Welton v. Los Angeles, City of . . . 3.2n15
Wenzel Bros., Inc.; Merrill, City of v. 5.7n74
West Va. Bd. of Educ.; Walter v. . . 6.2n34
Western Air Lines, Inc. v. Criswell 9.7n108
Weston, City of; Citizens Bank of Weston, Inc. v. 10.3n32
Whatcom Co. Water Dist. No. 4 v. Century Holdings, Ltd. 5.12n116
Wheeler; Hess, People ex rel v. . . . 8.2n26
Whelan v. New Jersey Power & Light Co. 5.5n40
Whelan v. N.J. Power & Light Co. 5.5n52
Whitcomb v. Chavis 7.7n61
White; Chicago Land Clearance Comm'n v. 4.8n105
White; Forrester v. 8.6n100
White v. Regester 7.7n62
White Plains, City of; TCG New York, Inc. v. 3.11n142
Whiteland Woods, L.P. v. Township of West Whiteland 7.3n16, n18, n19
Whitemarsh Township Authority v. Finelli Brothers 5.6n67
Whittier, City of v. Dixon 6.12n138
Wiggins v. Barrett & Assocs., Inc. 5.13n137
Wilford v. Jacksonville Beach, City of . . . 6.6n67
Will v. Michigan Dep't of State Police . . . 9.6n73
Williams; Bd. of Zoning Adjustment of Mobile v. 4.4

Williams; California State Employees Ass'n v. 6.5n61; 8.7n130
Williams; Dandridge v. 6.7n85
Williams; Daniels v. 8.6n107; 9.6n89
Williams v. Mayor & City Council of Baltimore 1.4n29
Williams; Namer Inv. Corp., State ex rel. v. 2.7n39; 3.9n109
Williams; Toyota Motor Mfg., Ky., Inc. v. 9.8n123
Williams v. Vermont 10.5n55
Willis v. Woodruff, Town of . . . 3.12n176
Willowbrook, Village of v. Olech . . 9.5n57
Willowbrook, Village of; Olech v. . . 2.7n42
Wilmington Medical Center v. Bradford . . 4.3n16
Wilson; Corsicana, City of v. 3.2n11
Wilson; Gooding v. 3.6n66
Wilson v. Long Branch 8.2n36
Wilson; Milwaukee, City of v. . . . 3.6n82
Wilson v. Vill. of Forest View . . 5.11n112
Wilson-Jones v. Cabiness 1.3n13
Wilson's Total Fitness Center, Inc. v. Dir. of Revenue 10.8n84
Windsor Resort Inc. v. Mayor & City Council of Ocean City 4.8nn113, 116
Winnebago Co. Dep't of Social Services; DeShaney v. 9.2n22
Winston-Salem Zoning Bd. of Adjustment; AT&T Wireless PCS, Inc. v. 3.11n158
Wm. Muirhead Constr. Co. v. Housing Auth. of Durham 5.1n2
Wolfe v. Sullivan, Town of 4.8n123
Wolman v. Walter 6.2n19
Wood; Bishop v. 8.4n51
Wood v. Strickland 6.2n17; 8.6n108
Woodruff v. Parham 10.5n49
Woodruff, State ex rel. v. Centanne 10.3n15
Woodruff, Town of; Willis v. . . . 3.12n176
Woolen v. Surtran Taxicabs, Inc. 9.9n139
Worrell v. Del Sesto 4.4n50
Wright v. Brown 4.9n139; 9.4n35
Wright; Roselle v. 2.7n37
Wrightsville; East v. 4.8n111
Wygant v. Jackson Bd. of Educ. . . 7.7n58; 9.7n115
Wyman v. James 6.7n91

Y

Yarbrough, Ex parte 7.5n29; 7.6n43
Yarnell; Phoenix, City of v. 9.6n77
Yates v. Warrenton 4.8n123

[References are to text sections]

Yonkers, City of v. Otis Elevator Co. . . . .
6.12n143
York City Sch. Dist.; Dillon v. . . 4.9n132
Young v. American Mini Theaters . . . . .
4.3n31
Young; Illusions on Peachtree Street, Inc. v.
. . . . 3.12n174
Young v. Vill. of Glen Ellyn 5.5n48

Z

Zehenni v. Akron, City of 5.10n98
Zibbon v. Cheektowaga, Town of . . 9.3n25
Ziegler v. Millbrook, City of 6.6n78
Zimring-McKenzie Constr. Co. v. Pinellas
Park, City of 5.9n90
Zoning Bd. of Appeals of Southington; M. & R.
Enters, Inc. v. 4.4n56
Zoning Comm'n of Sachem's Head Ass'n v.
Leninski 4.3n28

INDEX

[References are to Section numbers.]

A

ADMINISTRATIVE AGENCIES
Delegation of local authority to . . . 2.8

ADULT ENTERTAINMENT
Police powers and zoning . . . 3.4

**AGE DISCRIMINATION IN EMPLOY-
MENT ACT**
Liability of local government . . . 9.8

AGENCY
Contracts executed by agent without authority, enforcement of . . . 5.11

ALCOHOL
Regulating sale or use of . . . 3.5

ALTERNATIVE DISPUTE RESOLUTION
Local government's role in . . . 6.10

AMERICANS WITH DISABILITIES ACT
Liability of local government . . . 9.8

ANTITRUST CLAIMS
Liability of local government . . . 9.9

APPEAL
Zoning requirements and decisions . . 4.7

ASSISTANCE AND SERVICES
Delivery of (See SERVICES AND ASSIS-
TANCE)

AUTHORITY OF LOCAL GOVERNMENTS
Generally . . . 2.1
Constitutional requirements . . . 2.7
Contracts, authority to enter into . . . 5.2;
5.11
Delegation of authority to or by local govern-
ments . . . 2.2; 2.8
Home rule authority, delegation of . . 2.2
Implied authority and *Dillon's Rule* . . 2.4
Local governing body and local enactments
. . . 2.6
Officers and administrative agencies, delega-
tion of authority to . . . 2.8
Preemption by state or federal law . . 2.5
State concerns and local concerns . . . 2.3

B

**BIDDING ON LOCAL GOVERNMENT
CONTRACTS** (See COMPETITIVE BID-
DING ON GOVERNMENT CONTRACTS)

BORROWING BY LOCAL GOVERNMENT
Community development, borrowing for
. . . 10.13
Limitations on . . . 10.12
Procedure for . . . 10.14

BOUNDARIES
Changes in . . . 1.7

BUSINESSES
Police power regulation of . . . 3.3

C

CABLE TELEVISION
Local and federal regulation of . . . 3.11

CIGARETTES
Recoupment of public costs from tobacco man-
ufacturers . . . 10.8
Regulating sale or use of . . . 3.5

CIVIL RIGHTS
Generally . . . 9.7
Age Discrimination in Employment Act
. . . 9.8
Americans with Disabilities Act . . . 9.8
Constitutional claims . . . 9.5
Officers and employees of local government,
civil rights protections for . . . 8.5
Protection of rights by local governments
. . . 3.8
Section 1983 actions . . . 9.6
Voting rights (See VOTING RIGHTS)

CIVIL SERVICE
Officers and employees of local government
. . . 8.7

COMMUNITY DEVELOPMENT
Generally . . . 6.11

**COMPETITIVE BIDDING ON GOVERN-
MENT CONTRACTS**
Exceptions to requirement for competitive
bids . . . 5.5
Format requirements . . . 5.6
Judicial challenge to competitive bidding
. . . 5.8
Local action on bids . . . 5.7
Preferences . . . 5.6
Requirement for competitive bids . . . 5.5
Restrictions on . . . 5.6
Specifications for . . . 5.6

[References are to Section numbers.]

CONFLICTS OF INTEREST
Officers and employees of local government
. . . 8.2

CONSTITUTIONAL LAW
Adult uses . . . 3.4
Authority of local governments, federal and
state constitutional requirements as to
. . . 2.7
Liability of local government for constitu-
tional violations . . . 4.5; 9.4; 9.5
Movement of individuals, constitutionality of
restrictions on . . . 3.6
Officers and employees of local government,
constitutional protections for . . . 8.5
Religion in public schools . . . 6.2
Speech, constitutionality of restrictions on
. . . 3.6
Taking of property, liability of local govern-
ment for . . . 4.5; 9.4; 9.5
Taxation by local government, limitations on
. . . 10.3
Voting rights (See VOTING RIGHTS)

CONTRACTS OF LOCAL GOVERNMENT
Generally . . . 5.1
Agent without authority, contracts executed
by . . . 5.11
Authority to contract . . . 5.2; 5.11
Bidding on (See COMPETITIVE BIDDING
ON GOVERNMENT CONTRACTS)
Competitive bidding (See COMPETITIVE
BIDDING ON GOVERNMENT CON-
TRACTS)
Enforcement of contracts
    Agent without authority, contracts exe-
    cuted by . . . 5.11
    Authority to contract, lack of . . 5.11
    Estoppel to deny validity of contract
    . . . 5.13
    Form or procedure, use of unauthorized
    . . . 5.11
    Prohibited contracts . . . 5.12
    Public policy, contracts that are contrary
    to . . . 5.12
    Ratification of contract . . . 5.13
Estoppel to deny validity of contract . . . .
5.13
Fiscal requirements . . . 5.4
Format of contract (See subhead: Procedural
and format requirements)
Procedural and format requirements
    Generally . . . 5.3
    Enforcement of contracts that used un-
    authorized form or procedure . . . .
    5.11
    Ratification or estoppel . . . 5.13

**CONTRACTS OF LOCAL GOVERN-
MENT**—Cont.
Prohibited contracts, enforcement of . . . .
5.12
Public policy, enforcement of contracts that
are contrary to . . . 5.12
Quasi-contracts . . . 5.9; 5.10
Ratification of contract . . . 5.13

CORPORATIONS
Public benefit corporations . . . 6.4

COURTS
Local courts and dispute resolution . . . .
6.10

CREATION OF LOCAL GOVERNMENT
Generally . . . 1.6

CURFEWS
Constitutionality of . . . 3.6

D

**DEBT INCURRED BY LOCAL GOVERN-
MENT** (See BORROWING BY LOCAL
GOVERNMENT)

DEVELOPMENT OF REAL PROPERTY
Generally . . . 4.1
Approval of development of tract of land
. . . 4.6
Conditions on . . . 4.6
Impact fees . . . 4.6
Linkage fees . . . 4.6
Regulatory takings and moratoriums on de-
velopment . . . 4.5
Zoning (See ZONING)

DILLON'S RULE
Implied authority and . . . 2.4

DISABLED PERSONS
Americans with Disabilities Act . . . 9.8

DISASTERS
Local response to . . . 6.9

DISCIPLINARY ACTION
Officers and employees of local government
. . . 8.4

DISCRIMINATION
Liability of local government in actions based
on (See CIVIL RIGHTS)

DISMISSAL
Officers and employees of local government
. . . 8.4

[References are to Section numbers.]

DISPUTE RESOLUTION
Alternative dispute resolution in public disputes . . . 6.10

DISSOLUTION OF LOCAL GOVERNMENT
Generally . . . 1.6

E

ECONOMIC DEVELOPMENT
Generally . . . 6.12

EDUCATION
Generally . . . 6.2
Regulations by local government to promote public welfare . . . 3.7

ELECTIONS
Voting in (See VOTING RIGHTS)

EMPLOYEES OF LOCAL GOVERNMENT
(See OFFICERS AND EMPLOYEES OF LOCAL GOVERNMENT)

EMPLOYMENT DISCRIMINATION
Age Discrimination in Employment Act . . . 9.8
Americans with Disabilities Act . . . 9.8

ENVIRONMENTAL PROTECTION
Regulations by local government . . . 3.7

ESTOPPEL
Contracts of local government, estoppel to deny validity of . . . 5.13

ETHICAL CONSIDERATIONS
Officers and employees of local government . . . 8.2

EXPENDITURES
Expenditure process . . . 10.11
Prohibited expenditures . . . 10.10
Public purpose requirement . . . 10.9
Required expenditures . . . 10.10

F

FEDERAL GOVERNMENT
Cable television, regulation of . . . 3.11
Education . . . 6.2
Financial aid to local governments . . 10.2
Preemption of local authority . . . 2.5
Relationship to . . . 1.3
Telecommunications, regulation of . . 3.11

FEES
Impact fees for development of real property . . . 4.6

FEES—Cont.
Linkage fees for development of real property . . . 4.6
Services and assistance, financing of 10.7

FINANCES
Generally . . . 10.1
Borrowing by local government (See BORROWING BY LOCAL GOVERNMENT)
Expenditures (See EXPENDITURES)
Indebtedness of local government (See BORROWING BY LOCAL GOVERNMENT)
Revenue (See REVENUE)
Taxation by local government (See TAXATION BY LOCAL GOVERNMENT)

FIREARMS
Recoupment of public costs from gun manufacturers . . . 10.8
Regulating sale or use of . . . 3.5

FIRE PROTECTION
Liability of local government . . . 6.6

FISCAL REQUIREMENTS
Contracts of local government . . . 5.4

FORMS OF GOVERNMENT
Generally . . . 1.2; 1.8
History of . . . 1.2
Restructuring of . . . 1.7

FRANCHISES
Generally . . . 3.10
Challenges to grant or denial of . . . 3.12
Telecommunications . . . 3.11

FREEDOM OF INFORMATION LAWS
Public access to information . . . 7.2

G

GAMBLING
Revenue from . . . 10.8

GOVERNMENT CONTRACTS (See CONTRACTS OF LOCAL GOVERNMENT)

GROSS RECEIPTS
Taxation by local government . . . 10.6

GUNS
Recoupment of public costs from gun manufacturers . . . 10.8
Regulating sale or use of . . . 3.5

[References are to Section numbers.]

H

HEALTH, SAFETY AND WELFARE
Protection of (See POLICE POWERS)

HOME RULE AUTHORITY
Delegation of . . . 2.2

HOUSING
Assistance from local government . . . 6.8

HUMAN RIGHTS
Protection of rights by local governments . . . 3.8

I

IMMUNITY FROM TORT LIABILITY
Liability of local government for acts of officers, employees, or independent contractors . . . 9.2
Officers and employees of local government . . . 8.6
Public property liability . . . 4.9; 9.4

IMPACT FEES
Development of real property . . . 4.6

IMPROVEMENTS TO PROPERTY
Special assessments for . . . 10.7

INCOME TAX
Imposition by local government of . . 10.6

INDEBTEDNESS OF LOCAL GOVERN-MENT (See BORROWING BY LOCAL GOVERNMENT)

INDEPENDENT CONTRACTORS
Liability of local government for acts of . . . 9.2

INFORMATION
Public access to (See PUBLIC ACCESS TO INFORMATION)

INITIATIVE AND REFERENDUM
Voting rights . . . 7.8

J

JUDICIAL CHALLENGE
Competitive bidding on government contracts . . . 5.8

L

LAND
Generally (See REAL PROPERTY)

LAND—Cont.
Public land (See PUBLIC LAND)

LAND USE PLANNING
Generally . . . 4.2

LAW ENFORCEMENT
Liability of local government . . . 6.6

LIABILITY OF LOCAL GOVERNMENT
Generally . . . 9.1
Americans with Disabilities Act . . . 9.8
Antitrust claims . . . 9.9
Civil rights actions against government (See CIVIL RIGHTS)
Constitutional claims . . . 4.5; 9.4; 9.5
Discrimination, liability for (See CIVIL RIGHTS)
Fire protection . . . 6.6
Immunity from tort liability . . . 9.2
Independent contractors, liability for acts of . . . 9.2
Law enforcement . . . 6.6
Negligence . . . 9.3
Nuisance . . . 4.9; 9.4
Officers and employees, liability for acts of . . . 9.2
Police protection . . . 6.6
Public property liability . . . 4.9; 9.4
Taking of property without just compensation or without due process . . . 4.5; 9.4; 9.5
Trespass . . . 4.9; 9.4

LICENSE FEES
Revenue from . . . 10.7

LICENSES AND PERMITS
Generally . . . 3.1; 3.9
Challenges to grant or denial of . . . 3.12
Special or conditional use permits . . . 4.4
Telecommunications . . . 3.11

LINKAGE FEES
Development of real property . . . 4.6

LIQUOR
Regulating sale or use of . . . 3.5

LOITERING REGULATIONS
Constitutionality of . . . 3.6

LOTTERIES
Revenue from . . . 10.8

N

NEGLIGENCE
Liability of local government . . . 9.3

[References are to Section numbers.]

NOISE CONTROL
Regulations by local government . . . 3.7

NONCONFORMING USES
Zoning . . . 4.4

NUISANCE
Liability of local government for . . 4.9; 9.4
Police powers used for banning and abatement of . . . 3.2

O

OFFICERS AND EMPLOYEES OF LOCAL GOVERNMENT
Generally . . . 8.1
Age Discrimination in Employment Act . . . 9.8
Americans with Disabilities Act . . . 9.8
Civil rights, protection of . . . 8.5
Civil service . . . 8.7
Constitutional and statutory civil rights protections . . . 8.5
Delegation of authority to . . . 2.8
Dismissal and disciplinary action . . . 8.4
Eligibility and ethical considerations 8.2
Liability of local government for acts of . . . 9.2
Personal liability and qualified immunity . . . 8.6
Regulation of activities and conduct . . 8.3

OPEN MEETINGS
Public access to information . . . 7.3

P

PARKS
Regulations by local government to promote public welfare . . . 3.7

PERSONAL PROPERTY
Taxation of . . . 10.6

POLICE POWERS
Generally . . . 3.1; 3.7
Adult uses . . . 3.4
Alcohol, sale or use of . . . 3.5
Business regulation . . . 3.3
Civil and human rights, protection of . . . 3.8
Firearms . . . 3.5
Human rights, protection of . . . 3.8
Movement of individuals, constitutionality of restrictions on . . . 3.6
Nuisances . . . 3.2

POLICE POWERS—Cont.
Speech, constitutionality of restrictions on . . . 3.6
Telecommunications . . . 3.11
Tobacco . . . 3.5

POLICE PROTECTION
Liability of local government . . . 6.6

POLLUTION
Regulations by local government . . . 3.7

PRAYER IN PUBLIC SCHOOLS
Constitutional limits on . . . 6.2

PREEMPTION
Authority of local governments, state and federal preemption of . . . 2.5

PREFERENCES
Competitive bidding on government contracts . . . 5.6

PRIVACY
Protection against disclosure of information by local governments . . . 7.4

PRIVATIZATION OF SERVICES OR ASSETS
Generally . . . 6.5

PUBLIC ACCESS TO INFORMATION
Generally . . . 7.1
Freedom of information . . . 7.2
Open meetings . . . 7.3
Privacy protection . . . 7.4

PUBLIC ASSISTANCE
Generally . . . 6.7

PUBLIC AUTHORITIES
Public benefit corporations . . . 6.4

PUBLIC HEALTH, SAFETY AND WELFARE
Protection of (See POLICE POWERS)

PUBLIC LAND
Generally . . . 4.1
Acquisition and disposition of local government property . . . 4.8
Liability for public property . . . 4.9; 9.4
Use of public property . . . 4.10

PUBLIC POLICY
Enforcement of contracts that are contrary to . . . 5.12

PUBLIC PURPOSE REQUIREMENT
Expenditures of local governments . . 10.9

[References are to Section numbers.]

Q

QUASI-CONTRACTUAL OBLIGATIONS
Invalid contracts . . . 5.10
No contract . . . 5.9

R

RATIFICATION
Contracts of local government . . . 5.13

REAL PROPERTY
Generally . . . 4.1
Development of (See DEVELOPMENT OF REAL PROPERTY)
Improvements to property, special assessments for . . . 10.7
Nuisance, liability of local government for . . . 4.9; 9.4
Planning . . . 4.2
Public land (See PUBLIC LAND)
Taking of property without just compensation or without due process . . . 4.5; 9.4; 9.5
Taxation of . . . 6.2; 10.4
Trespass, liability of local government for . . . 4.9; 9.4
Zoning (See ZONING)

REAPPORTIONMENT
Local elections and . . . 7.6

RECREATION
Regulations by local government to promote public welfare . . . 3.7

REFERENDUM
Approval or disapproval of local enactments by . . . 7.8

REGIONAL GOVERNMENTS
Generally . . . 1.7

REGULATION BY LOCAL GOVERN-MENTS
Generally . . . 3.1
Franchises (See FRANCHISES)
Licenses and permits (See LICENSES AND PERMITS)
Police powers, exercise of (See POLICE POWERS)

RELATIONSHIP TO OTHER GOVERN-MENTS
Federal government . . . 1.3
Other local governments . . . 1.5
State government . . . 1.4

RELIGIOUS FREEDOM
Schools and . . . 6.2

REVENUE
Education, funding for . . . 6.2
Federal and state aid . . . 10.2
Fees and special assessments . . . 10.7
Gambling revenue . . . 10.8
Gun manufacturers, recoupment of public costs from . . . 10.8
Lotteries . . . 10.8
Taxation by local government (See TAXATION BY LOCAL GOVERNMENT)
Tobacco manufacturers, recoupment of public costs from . . . 10.8

S

SALES AND USE TAXES
Revenue from . . . 10.5

SCHOOL DISTRICTS
Creation and functions of . . . 6.2

SECTION 1983 ACTIONS
Liability of local government . . . 9.6

SERVICES AND ASSISTANCE
Generally . . . 6.1
Changes and disasters, local response to . . . 6.9
Community development . . . 6.11
Courts and dispute resolution . . . 6.10
Disasters, local response to . . . 6.9
Dispute resolution . . . 6.10
Economic development . . . 6.12
Education . . . 6.2
Fees and special assessments . . . 10.7
Fire protection, liability of local government for . . . 6.6
Housing . . . 6.8
Law enforcement, liability of local government for . . . 6.6
Liability of local government for law enforcement and fire protection . . . 6.6
Local courts and dispute resolution 6.10
Privatization of services or assets . . . 6.5
Public assistance . . . 6.7
Public authorities . . . 6.4
School districts . . . 6.2
Special improvement districts . . . 6.3

SOVEREIGN AUTHORITY (See AUTHORITY OF LOCAL GOVERNMENTS)

SOVEREIGN IMMUNITY (See IMMUNITY FROM TORT LIABILITY)

SPECIAL ASSESSMENTS
Flexibility in financing services and improvements . . . 10.7

[References are to Section numbers.]

SPECIAL IMPROVEMENT DISTRICTS
Generally . . . 6.3

**SPECIAL OR CONDITIONAL USE PER-
MITS**
Zoning . . . 4.4

SPECIFICATIONS
Competitive bidding on government contracts
. . . 5.6

SPEECH
Constitutionality of restrictions on . . . 3.6

STATE GOVERNMENT
Education . . . 6.2
Financial aid to local governments . . 10.2
Preemption of local authority . . . 2.5
Relationship of local government to . . 1.4

STATUTORY RESTRICTIONS
Officers and employees of local government,
  statutory civil rights protections for . . .
  8.5
Taxation by local government . . . 10.3

STRUCTURE OF GOVERNMENT (See
FORMS OF GOVERNMENT)

SUBURBAN/URBAN PROBLEM
Changes in government structure as solution
  to . . . 1.7

SUNSHINE LAWS
Public access to information . . . 7.3

T

TAXATION BY LOCAL GOVERNMENT
Generally . . . 10.8
Constitutional and statutory limitations on
  . . . 10.3
Education, funding for . . . 6.2
Gross receipts . . . 10.6
Income tax . . . 10.6
Personal property taxes . . . 10.6
Real property tax . . . 6.2; 10.4
Sales and use taxes . . . 10.5
School districts, taxation by . . . 6.2

TELECOMMUNICATIONS
Regulation of . . . 3.11

TOBACCO
Recoupment of public costs from tobacco man-
  ufacturers . . . 10.8
Regulating sale or use of . . . 3.5

**TORT ACTIONS AGAINST LOCAL GOV-
ERNMENT** (See LIABILITY OF LOCAL
GOVERNMENT)

TRESPASS
Liability of local government for . . 4.9; 9.4

U

URBAN/SUBURBAN PROBLEM
Changes in government structure as solution
  to . . . 1.7

V

VAGRANCY REGULATIONS
Constitutionality of . . . 3.6

VARIANCES
Zoning . . . 4.4

VOTING RIGHTS
Generally . . . 7.1; 9.5
Eligibility to vote . . . 7.5
Equality and the Voting Rights Act . . 7.7
Initiative and referendum . . . 7.8
Reapportionment . . . 7.6

Z

ZONING
Generally . . . 4.3
Adult entertainment . . . 3.4
Appeal from zoning requirements and deci-
  sions . . . 4.7
Applicability . . . 4.4
Enforcement of zoning requirements and de-
  cisions . . . 4.7
Exceptions . . . 4.4
Nonconforming uses . . . 4.4
Regulatory takings and moratoriums on de-
  velopment . . . 4.5
Special or conditional use permits . . . 4.4
Variances . . . 4.4